WHAT IF . . .

You were a castaway on a far distant planet, with deadly danger all around you all the time, and you were perfectly happy?

You were the latest in a long line of queens who could foretell the future, and you were unhappy?

You were The Crow who had done something unspeakable, but you didn't quite understand the situation?

WHAT WOULD YOU DO?

What would you do if you were not the only one building a time machine; if the man to whom you gave shelter was not a man; if the woman you loved was not a woman? And suppose you were planning a raid on a fortress ripe for the plucking, as soon as you ironed out one small detail . . . .

WHY, YOU WOULD READ THIS BOOK, THAT'S WHAT YOU'D DO!

And encounter all sorts of additional adventures; science fiction and fantasy to thrill and delight you, illustrated by the best new talents.

Here, from **L. Ron Hubbard's Writers of The Future Contest,**® and **Illustrators of The Future Contest,**® are this year's winners. We need say no more.

QUANTITY DISCOUNTS

The L. Ron Hubbard Presents Writers of the Future anthologies are available at special quantity discounts when purchased in bulk by schools, organizations, and special-interest groups such as SF clubs and writing workshops.

Write or call for more information:
DIRECTOR OF PUBLIC INFORMATION, Bridge Publications Inc., 4751 Fountain Avenue, Los Angeles, CA 90029.

Or call toll-free 1-800-722-1733, or 1-800-843-7389 in California.

L. RON HUBBARD

PRESENTS

WRITERS OF THE FUTURE

VOLUME VII

L. RON HUBBARD

PRESENTS

WRITERS

OF THE

FUTURE

VOLUME VII

The Year's 15 Best Tales from His
Writers of The Future
International Writing Program
Illustrated by the Winners in His
Illustrators of The Future
International Illustration Program

With Essays on Writing and Illustration by

L. RON HUBBARD
RAY ALDRIDGE
KAREN JOY FOWLER
FRANK FRAZETTA
DAVE WOLVERTON
KRISTINE KATHRYN RUSCH and
DEAN WESLEY SMITH

Edited by Algis Budrys
Frank Kelly-Freas, Director of Illustration

Bridge Publications, Inc.

CONTENTS

Introduction
by
Algis Budrys

Welcome to *L. Ron Hubbard Presents Writers of The Future*—for not the first time; for that matter, not for the sixth.

This makes the seventh book in this series. Derived from the yearly results of the ongoing L. Ron Hubbard Writers of The Future Contest, it publishes the annual winners, plus a few finalists. Well over a hundred different new writers have been published in the course of doing these books for seven years. And we're pleased to say that a gratifying number of the writers have gone on and continued to do big things—demonstrating without a doubt that success in the Contest was hardly a fluke. (You will see evidence of that in the essays included here.)

The main thrust of this book, however, always, is the latest crop—and in the fifteen new names of writers gathered here, you will find amazement, amusement, and plenty of that quality that tells you that these names will cross your horizon again and again.

Also, L. Ron Hubbard's Illustrators of The Future Contest has now completed its second year, and thus twenty-four new illustrators have been introduced to the speculative fiction community. You will find the work of the latest winners illustrating the stories in this volume; we think it's very good. And if the careers of last year's winners—already—are any guide, a number of these novices will be making other notable contributions to the field almost immediately. We salute them—and they honor us by permitting us to show their work.

Please note, by the way, that Sergey V. Poyarkov is from the Soviet Union, Ferenc Temil Temesvari is from Hungary, and Peter H. Francis is from Nova Scotia. The Contest is very quickly adding an international flavor.

The main point is that Writers and Illustrators of The Future has become the undeniably most important entry-point into the field for both writers and illustrators. Every major book publisher has learned to watch for these successive volumes, and solicit contributions from many of our discoveries. Every magazine has done the same. And more and more of them have been gracious enough to say so, and we thank them.

The Contests are performing an important, basic service to the field—just as L. Ron Hubbard planned. We are certainly not the only source of fresh talent, but we are the only systematic source, year after year, of fresh talent in volume.

But don't take our word for it. Read the stories, look at the illustrations, and see for yourselves. Enjoy; we did!

— Algis Budrys
Editor

Georgi
by
James C. Glass

About the Author

James C. Glass is 53, and Dean of the College of Science, Mathematics and Technology at Eastern Washington University in Spokane. He first read science fiction and edited an amateur SF magazine in the Nineteen Fifties, eventually going to college and getting a PhD in physics after some years of working in the aerospace industry. About six years ago the urge to write became more than an itch; it became a passion. Since then, he has been working at it steadily, with the result that a piece has been accepted by Aboriginal Magaine, and another has been published in a literary journal. And, of course, "Georgi," which we commend highly.

Glass has four children and a stepson, all living away from home. He is married to a recreational therapist for the Spokane school system, who happens to be just as much a science fiction fan as he is.

About the Illustrator

Thomas Denmark was 21 a few months ago, and joined the Army to get a college education. Recently completing the active duty portion of his commitment, he went to live in California, with an eye to attending the Academy of Art College in San Francisco. He plans to become a professional illustrator.

At this writing, he has been called back into the Service and is at Ft. Sill, Oklahoma, undergoing advanced training prior to being sent to the Gulf war. We wish him well.

A North Dakota winter storm was charging in from the southwest. The sky was white as milk, and snow was already swirling in the back alleys of Fargo as Otis Boswick frantically searched for the basics of life: food, warm clothing or rags for feet, hands and head, a pot or utensil, and anything that would burn. Moms had made her rounds in the morning, had returned with a shopping basket piled high with old newspapers for the oil-can fire to keep them alive another night in the bitter cold. But now he was eight blocks from Moms, and Alf, and the others, eight blocks from the packing crate he called home beneath the second street bridge, and all he wanted was to be warm again. In a North Dakota blizzard, he could be dead in a walk of two blocks, and time was running out.

Otis scrabbled with stiff fingers in one of two dumpsters behind the Broadway Deli, pain stabbing through his arthritic, humped back as he leaned over beyond his limit. He found a broken box half-filled with stale crackers, and a brick of frozen jack cheese covered with frost and blue fuzz, passing up a piece of strange meat aged black. He packed the first treasures of the day in his knapsack, and moved to the second dumpster, which was tightly closed, but not locked. He pushed up hard on the lid, stood on tiptoes to look inside, and got the shock of his life.

Inside the dumpster, in a pile of rancid garbage, a man was lying in a fetal position, groaning, clutching at his stomach with both hands.

"Hey, you can't stay in here! A storm's comin', and you'll freeze to death in all that wet! Here, you grab my hands, and come out of there!"

The man, his rugged face covered with fine, blond hair laced with ice crystals, turned over, opened his eyes to look at Otis, then pulled what looked like a garage door opener from beneath his body and pointed it at him. "Go away— or—I hurt."

Otis flinched, but still held out both hands. "Grab hold. I've got a warm place not far from here, unless you want to die. Make up your mind quick. Storm's comin' fast."

The man considered this silently for a moment, then lowered the garage-door opener and stuffed it into a tattered rucksack at his side, groaning as he moved.

"You sick?"

The man answered in a deep voice, heavily accented. "Was hungry—ate something—bad for me—down here. Want—sleep." He rubbed his lower abdomen with one hand.

"Moms has a tea for that. It's only a few blocks, but we've got to hurry!" Otis grabbed the man's outstretched hands, cold as his own, grimacing as he hauled him upright. The man got out unaided, holding the rucksack tight to him, doubling over in pain as soon as his feet hit the pavement. Otis put an arm around him, and they half-stumbled the eight blocks back to the second street bridge in swirling snow and bitter wind-chill, people staring at them from passing cars. Two drunks ending another day early, their eyes said.

They climbed down the embankment under the bridge. A wrinkled, squat, black woman was warming her hands over an oil-can fire, body covered from head to foot in tattered sweaters and a long coat that made her look like a dirty snowball, leaving the fire's warmth to waddle towards them as they approached. "What you got there,

Otis?'' she shouted in a raspy voice. "You done found another victim o' society?''

"He's sick, Moms. Ate something bad."

"Well, you just bring him to Moms now, you hear? Po' thing.''

Otis maneuvered the man to a broken piece of concrete by the fire, and sat him down on it, holding him steady. Moms ran fat, gentle fingers over his face, checked his eyes. When she put a hand lightly on his stomach, the man cried out sharply, and sagged unconscious into Otis's arms.

"Not good," said Moms. "Man's poisoned. Got to get that out of him *now*.'' She shuffled over to a wooden-planked hut stuffed with cardboard and rags backed up against one concrete buttress of the bridge, and crawled inside through a blanket-draped opening. "Otis, you quick heat some water over the fire! Man can't drink this cold!''

Otis put a screen over the top of the oil drum, and managed to heat some water in a shallow pan before Moms came back with a tin cup containing a yellow powder sprinkled with bits of blue and red. Otis's eyes widened as he recognized the potion, but Moms pushed the cup into his hands. "Got to get it out of him quick, Otis, and you know it.''

They made the tea, forcing it down the partially conscious man who grimaced with each sip, Moms stroking his forehead. "Quick, man. We's tryin' to save your life here, and there's no hospitals for the likes of us. Drink it all up.''

A few minutes later, the man's eyes snapped open, he lunged out of Otis's grasp to his hands and knees, and projectile-vomited the entire contents of his stomach onto the broken chunks of concrete beneath the bridge.

"I've got the room. He can stay with me," said Otis.

"Just so's I take care of him. You knows nothin' of the art.'' Moms smiled a toothless smile, looking satisfied with herself.

Illustrated by Thomas Denmark

"Don't have to, Moms, not with you here. Where're the others?"

"Probably out killin' someone for a quarter, but Jason's inside, with Alf for protection. Jack was botherin' him again, skinny demon he is, but he sure is scared o' that dog."

Otis got the man on his feet, helped him over to the mammoth packing crate he lived in against the buttress opposite from Moms' hut. As he approached, there was a low, menacing growl from inside the crate.

"Alf, shut up! And get back, now! I got a friend here, and he's bad sick!" Otis pushed aside the blanket covering the small entrance, pulling the man in after him. The interior of the crate was a heap of sleeping bags and old blankets, dimly lit by a single candle. In one corner a frail boy sat upright in a sleeping bag, staring fearfully, arm around the neck of a mongrel mix of German Shepherd and Pit-Bull Terrier still growling low in its throat. "You hold onto him tight, Jason. I gotta get this man warm, and we got a blizzard comin'!"

Otis got the man's rucksack off, and stuffed him fully clothed into a bag, piling on two blankets for good measure. Instantly, the man was asleep, and Alf stepped forward to cautiously sniff at him. "Friend, Alf. Friend," said Otis, scratching the massive head of the animal. Alf waggled a stump of a tail, and licked Otis's hand.

"You all right, boy?"

Jason Boggs, a fourteen-year-old runaway from Minneapolis, slouched in the sleeping bag, face grim. "Better now that you're back. That creep Jack grabbed me by the balls again this morning, and Alf bit him good. He said he'd kill Alf when he gets back. And then the cop was here again."

"Luis Penuel? He's a good man, Jason. Looks after us."

"Well, he's no friend of mine since he turned my name in. Says my stepfather has left home for good, and my mom is comin' to get me. He had no right turning me in like that!''

''Sure he did, Jason. You're only fourteen, with a whole life ahead of you. This ain't no way for you to live, on the run. Don't you want to be with your mom?''

''She's okay, I guess. It's my stepfather liked to beat up on me.''

''Well, there you are. In the meantime you've got Moms and me and Alf for family. We'll take care of you. But consider it good, Jason. A boy needs a real home, not a packing crate.''

''It's good enough for you and Moms.''

''That's our choice, boy. It's our way of life, and we wouldn't have it any other way—except when it gets so damnable cold. What I wouldn't give for heat in winter, and then pack my friends in here. Wouldn't that be somethin'?''

Jason shook his head, and smiled. ''You and Moms take care of everyone, Otis.''

''What better way to live, boy? It's our callin'. Now you hunker down and get some sleep. I've got me a sick man to tend to, and it's gonna get terrible cold tonight.''

Moms' call came from outside the crate, a cup of a new brew laced with sugar in her hands. Three times that night they awakened the man to feed him an energetic tea with numbed hands as the blizzard raged around them.

Otis awoke with a start, nostrils frozen shut, the interior of the crate filled with icy fog sparkling in a band of sunlight coming in where the blanket had been pulled aside from the entrance. The man he had found in the dumpster was sitting up in his sleeping bag, peering outside, holding the blanket aside with a bare hand. When Otis snorted to clear the ice from his nose, the man turned to look at him.

''Snow gone—light again.''

''Yes, but now it'll get *really* cold, and we need more

fuel for the fire. We used up all the newspapers while you were sleeping. Feel better now?''

"I have—hunger—here." The man rubbed his stomach carefully. "How long I—in this place?"

"Three nights and two days," said Otis. "You were bad poisoned, and for a day or so we thought you wouldn't make it. But Moms knows what she's doing; we've never lost a sick person."

"Now I eat," said the man matter-of-factly.

"Wish I could help you there, but all we've got left is some oatmeal, and we need to cook that. No fuel."

The man found his rucksack next to him, opened it, and reached inside. "You bring food—I cook—here." He withdrew a metal globe, silver, the size of a softball out of his sack, pushed aside some rags, and placed the globe carefully in his tea cup on the floor of the crate before rummaging in his pack again.

Otis held up a metal canteen and shook it soundlessly. "All our water's frozen. We need a lot of heat to thaw it."

"I do fast," said the man. "Get food." He pulled out a metal platform with sloped vanes and flat bottom, placed the globe in it, then screwed a wire coil with threaded shaft into a short, ceramic receptor on top of the globe.

"That some kind of hotplate?" said Otis.

"This cook—heat us good." He reached out a hand. "Give water."

Otis handed him the canteen, then searched in his own pack for a bag of oatmeal he had hoarded for months. Found it. Held it out to the man. "Here you go. Now that you're with us again, my name is Otis Boswick. What's yours?"

The man didn't answer, grasped a knurled knob at the side of the globe, twisted it, pulled out a shaft about an inch, twisted again. Immediately, the coil began to glow, first deep red, rapidly turning to bright red and orange. The interior of the crate was flooded with heat, while Otis stared in fascination. "Well, will you look at that! Say, if you don't want to give me a name, that's okay. It's only I'd like to have something to call you by."

"I am Georgi," said the man. He put the canteen on the glowing coil, and picked up the bag of oatmeal to look at it closely.

"Georgi. That's a Russian name. Thought I recognized the accent. You one of the new emigrants? This cold probably don't seem very different, then."

"No Russian," said Georgi.

"Oh," said Otis. *And no last name, either.* "No matter, I'm just curious, is all. Like to get to know people better, but don't mean to pry. People come through here are all runnin' from somethin', some of it pretty bad, but I don't pry. Live and let līve, I say."

Georgi looked at him darkly. "You take care—me. I— thank."

"Nothing," said Otis. "Moms did it all, anyway."

Steam was squirting out from beneath the cap on the canteen, making a whistling sound. Jason stirred in his sleeping bag, Alf lying on top of him. "Where's the heat coming from?"

"Georgi here had a stove with him, Jason. We're cookin' up the oatmeal. Want some?"

"Sure," said the boy. "Those crackers didn't go very far with me yesterday." He sat up in his bag so that Alf was in his lap, and stroked the dog's head. "Alf must be hungry, too."

"We'll give him some oatmeal. Good for dogs."

Georgi poured half of the sack of oatmeal into a small pan, took some rags from the floor to lift off the scalding hot canteen and stirred water into the pan. Otis spooned the steaming cereal into cups, and they ate silently in the warm glow of the coil, heating themselves inside and out, a luxury

Otis could not remember since several winters before when a guy had come through with a backpacker's stove, and they had all gotten a little drunk on hot wine. That was before Moms.

After he'd finished eating, Otis filled another cup with the last of the oatmeal. "This is for Moms," he explained. "Back in a minute." he crawled outside, and walked the few steps to Moms' hut, keeping a palm over the cup. "Moms! Rise and shine! We got food here. Hot oatmeal!"

A raspy shout greeted his offer. "Don't want none, Charlie! Now I told you to stay away from me, and here you are again! Go away!"

Oh, oh. Back inside herself again, the spells getting more frequent in the last year. "No, it's Otis, Moms. Here, I'll put the food by the doorway. Your patient cooked up breakfast this morning. You cured him, Moms, and his name is Georgi."

"Charlie, I'll sic the dog on you if you don't go away! I mean it!"

There was no arguing with her when she was like this, but at least she was in the hut. On the street, in this condition, she couldn't find her way home. But in a day it usually passed over, and Otis wondered if she was having little strokes, or maybe it was Alzheimer's. He also wondered who Charlie was. He put the cup down by the hut's entrance, and turned as Georgi emerged from the crate, carrying a small, black box the size of a cigarette package in one hand. He barely glanced at Otis, walked straight up the embankment and out of sight. When he came down again a minute later, he was empty-handed. And the cup full of oatmeal had disappeared into the hut.

"We go out—get more food," said Georgi, and it was like a command. Otis was surprised by the sudden anger he felt surge inside him.

"One nice thing about my life is I don't have to take

orders from anyone, Georgi, not even you. Last time I did
that was in the Korean war. Climb the cliff, the sergeant
said, and take out that gun emplacement. Me, with a wife
and two little babies back home. But it was an order in a
combat zone, and I didn't want to get shot by my own people, so I climbed the damn thing. Halfway up, the cliff
come loose, and down I went. Broke my back bad, and all
I got to show for it was a purple heart I hocked for food
years ago. Lost the wife, and the babies, get lousy disability
checks barely enough for me and my friends to live on, but
I make do, and I *don't* take orders from *anyone* anymore.
You got that?''

Georgi looked at him somberly. ''You soldier—in battle?''

Otis looked away from those dark eyes. ''A long time
ago—when I was young.''

Georgi put a big hand on Otis's shoulder, and squeezed
gently. ''I soldier, too. I do accident, too, in—ship. Georgi
not hurt, but friend—my friend die, and he buried far to—
home. No battle—we only look—friend dead. Now Georgi
go home—friends find. Georgi stay alive—find food. I help
Otis, who saves life. You show how?''

''Who are you?'' asked Otis, wiping his eyes.

''I soldier—like Otis. We get food together. Come.'' He
put an arm across Otis' humped back. ''We go where you
find me?''

''No—I have some money left, and it's too cold to stay
out long. Fresh food is cheap, but it can't get frozen. How
long will your stove run before the fuel is gone? We'll have
to keep the crate warm inside.''

''Run long time—to snow gone—fill with—water—run
to snow come again. I show how.''

''Never heard of such a stove. You bull-shittin' me?''

Georgi laughed, then, a big, deep-throated chuckle,
and hugged Otis to him. ''No—shittin','' he said.

They walked ten blocks to a Seven-Eleven store that was accustomed to doing meager business with street people, the owner a friendly man who had known hard times himself, and occasionally paid them for odd jobs around the place. The owner wasn't there, and the clerk, a young girl around seventeen, eyed them apprehensively until Otis put his rumpled dollar bills onto the counter. A five-pound bag of potatoes, and a box of oatmeal took everything he had, except for a nickel and three pennies.

Georgi scooped the coins up in a big hand. "I keep—remember Otis?"

"Sure, why not? Can't buy anything with it, anyway." He watched the coins disappear into Georgi's pocket.

They strolled back to the bridge, Otis pointing out the parking lot that had once been the Zephyr bar, a place to talk to friends, to belong, now gone. Across the street another bar, the Pink Pussycat, was being torn down along with an old hotel he had lived in for two years until it had been condemned. Slowly, but surely, the good folks of Fargo were forcing them out into the streets, back alleys, and under the bridges to freeze and die in the long winters. He had heard their favorite saying, of course; forty below keeps the riffraff out. Or kills them.

Sun-dogs were out in the icy air, two pillars of fire on either side of a sun low in the southern sky. They walked out onto the second street bridge to watch the Red River, a narrow channel of deep, black water winding through ice. Georgi carried the groceries in a paper bag, listening silently as Otis pointed out where he had found a body the summer before, half in and out of the river. "Old guy, just passing through. Some kids probably knifed him for fun. For the pure hell of it! Sure not my kind of people, none of them!"

Georgi shook his head sadly. "There is cruelty—with people—all place."

"Only for some of us," said Otis, and his head had turned sharply to the left to watch a police car pulling up below them, alongside the embankment. Two uniformed officers got out of the car, and picked their way carefully down the snowy slope. One of them was Luis Penuel. "Oh, oh, they're comin' for Jason. Get out of sight!" Otis pulled Georgi back from the edge of the bridge. "If he sees you, Penuel will want to know who you are, and where you come from. He's a friend, but he checks up on everyone who comes through here. Do you want that?"

"No," said Georgi firmly. "I here only little while, until—no trouble, Otis."

"Then don't let them see you. Wait up here until they're gone. I'll come back, but I've got to go down and see after Jason. He's only been here three weeks, but Penuel traced him, and his mom wants him back home."

"I wait here—you go," said Georgi.

Otis squeezed the big man's arm, then walked the length of the bridge, and fell down twice before reaching the bottom of the snowy embankment. Alf was barking angrily from inside the crate, and Moms was hugging Jason, the two officers pulling at his arms. Moms waved as the three walked towards Otis, and there were tears in her eyes. "You be good to your mom, you hear?" she cried.

Jason waved back to her, and he was smiling when he came up to Otis. Luis Penuel put an arm around him. "His mom is at the station cryin' her eyes out. She wants him back real bad, and it looks like a good situation for Jason, now, Otis. Thanks to you and Moms, he's going home in one piece."

Otis looked at the boy. "You want to go home, Jason?"

"Yeah. But I'll never forget you or Moms, and what you did for me. I'm gonna miss Alf, too. Mom says she'll get me a big dog when I get home, and I want one like Alf."

"Alf is special, all right. C'mere, boy." Otis held out his arms, and Jason was swallowed in his embrace while the officers found other things to look at.

"Do somethin' for street people someday, will you?"

"I promise, Otis. Take care of yourself—and Moms, too. She's still actin' kinda funny."

"You betcha," said Otis, releasing the boy, swallowing hard as one officer led him up the slope to the patrol car, and out of sight. Luis Penuel stayed behind a moment, an arm around Otis's hunched shoulders.

"He'll be fine, Otis. Just fine. And you watch out for yourself, too. Jack Cain is back in town. I saw him stumbling around by the tracks this morning, yelling at air. He gives you any more trouble you let me know, and I'll throw him right in the can. Got it?"

"Sure. I'll let you know. Anyway, Alf scares the hell out of him."

"Yeah, but Alf don't carry a knife or a gun. You watch out for that guy. He's pure, evil mean." Luis slapped Otis on the back, then climbed the embankment, and in an instant the patrol car, and Jason, were gone.

Moms was standing by the oil can, staring at the flames, when Otis trudged up the slope to find Georgi again. When he got to the top, he saw Georgi next to the span, balancing on snow, the little black box in his hand. He was wedging it into the rocky ground by the bridge, and carefully covering it with a tangle of frozen brush, looking up as Otis came close.

"Whatever that thing is, I sure as hell hope you ain't no Russian spy. I busted my back fightin' communists."

"I tell Otis. No Russian," said Georgi. "Jason gone, now?"

"Yeah, home to Minneapolis with his mom. No more freezing cold nights for him. A warm house, where boys oughta be. I'll miss him. Good kid."

Georgi picked up the grocery bag with one hand. "Otis feel better when eat. I cook—you show how."

Otis turned to start down the hill, taking a tentative first step, when suddenly, Georgi grabbed him from behind, sitting down with him, and sliding on his back all the way to the bottom, his excited shout echoing beneath the bridge.

"Both of you's crazy!" yelled Moms.

That night, with light snow falling, the three of them stayed in Otis's crate, warmed by the glowing stove, and feasted on boiled potatoes with one of Moms' special teas.

The following morning, Jack Cain returned to their camp.

The morning was clear, but breath-freezing cold, a foot of light, powder snow on the ground from the night before. Stomachs full, Otis and Georgi sipped hot tea in the warm crate, Moms still asleep, a shapeless mound in one corner. Alf watched them mournfully, curled up on Jason's sleeping bag, from which he had not moved since the boy had left. Georgi had shown Otis all the operating details of the stove, including where to fill it with ordinary water when the heating rate got low. He had tried to explain the source of the heat, talking about atoms sticking together, and the unbelievably hot gas somehow contained in a golf-ball-size volume within the globe. He drew diagrams, and strange chemical formulae, one Otis recognized as the one for water. The high school education he had not finished, before fleeing to break his back in a foreign war, was only a vague memory to him, now, and he found himself befuddled by most of Georgi's careful teaching. I should go to the library once in a while to read a newspaper, he thought, and catch up on what's going on in the world.

Georgi leaned against Otis, a sly grin on his face. "If Otis take heater, and what I draw here—take to great teacher—scientist—show this—can be rich—not live like this. Have much—money. Good for Otis."

Otis laughed. He thought little of money, because there was little of it to think about. Money was a transient thing, like most of his friends, like Georgi, and the stove. It appeared and disappeared from his life, without predictability. It was better to live a day at a time, and he had learned not to dwell on what could be, or what could have been. During his hard life, he had become a fatalist, coming to grips with the program laid out for him. His life was meant to be the struggle it was, for whatever reason, and he had accepted it. And so he dismissed Georgi's humorous fantasy with a laugh, knowing that a small part of him would think about it some more. What would it be like to have a lot of money? He could do all sorts of things that—

—"HEY, YOU BUMS! WHERE'RE YOU HIDIN'? I COME BACK TO KILL ME A DOG!"

Moms bolted upright in her sleeping bag. Alf's eyes narrowed, a growl rattling in his throat. "Jack Cain," whispered Moms. "Otis, he's back again. I thought we done rid o' that devil."

"Who?" said Georgi, suddenly tense.

"You stay in here, both of you. I'll go out, and talk to him."

"You're crazy," said Moms. "Man's drunk, and spoilin' for a fight. Leave 'im be."

"Come outta there! I hear you mumblin', and I can hear the dog, too. In one minute, he's dead!" A bottle crashed against the side of the crate, and Alf started barking hysterically. "That's it! Send Alf after me! One swipe of this knife, and his head's gone!"

"You come in here, Jack Cain, and I'll put the hex on you," yelled Moms. "You stick a head in, and I blow a powder on you make you blind, and suck your breath away, turn you blue, and put that knife in your own gut! You get out of here, now!"

Footsteps outside, then something hard and heavy hit the side of the crate. "Ain't afraid of you—crazy old bitch! I want that DOG!" The words were nearly drowned out by Alf's barking and snarling, froth spewing from his mouth, teeth bared. Moms grabbed the big dog, and hung on tightly.

"I have to go out," said Otis grimly.

Georgi grabbed his pack, fumbled inside it. "I come with Otis."

"NO! This is between Jack and me, and it's *my* dog he wants to cut up. You stay *put!*" Otis turned, crawling quickly outside before Georgi had a chance to answer, then stood up painfully, and faced Jack Cain a few feet away from the crate. The man's face was scarred and pock-marked, head bare, eyes puffed nearly shut from days of solid drinking. He was dying before Otis's eyes, a wasted skeleton of a man, army-surplus fatigues hanging tent-like from his thin frame, mouth twisted into a sinister grin that made him a specter of death itself. In one hand he held a huge Bowie knife, waving it lazily at Otis's face.

"You still got that pretty little boy in there?"

"Jason's gone, and he ain't comin' back. You can't hurt him anymore, Jack."

"Shi-it, I kinda hoped for some fun after I carved up your dog—with this." Jack took a stumbling step forward, and now the knife was very close to Otis's face.

"I don't have any quarrel with you, Jack, and there's nothin' here for you anymore. Why don't you just leave?"

"Hey, you don't own this place, old man; now, you bring that dog out here so I can get it done quick, and *then* I'll leave." The cold blade of the big knife touched Otis's nose, then waved away again.

"I won't do that, Jack."

"Yeah? Well, then, I gotta do it another way." Jack

made a short lunge, slicing a gash in Otis's cheek so that he cried out.

Alf was crazy, now, thrashing around inside the crate, Moms screaming. "I can't hold him, Otis!"

Otis felt warm blood running down his face. He circled to his left, away from the crate, stooping to grab up a chunk of broken concrete with one hand.

"Come on, Jack. You and me," he said, voice shaking with fear, hoping the others could somehow escape while Jack's back was turned.

"Hey, the old soldier. That's pretty good, Otis. Well, how about a little bayonet drill?" Jack lunged, Otis stumbling backwards, swinging the concrete chunk wildly, and missing the death's head by inches. Before he could recover, another lunge was coming, the knife sweeping past his face, and back again in an upward thrust. Otis swung weakly, punching Jack in one shoulder as he felt the knife burn into his left side. He staggered backwards, grabbing at his side, and dropping his only defense as Jack grinned wildly at him.

A loud voice boomed behind the man with the blood-stained knife.

"JACK CAIN!"

Jack jerked around in surprise, dropping into a crouch.

Georgi had emerged from the crate, the garage-door-looking thing in his hand, now pointing it at Jack.

Otis gasped for breath, pain flooding his left side. "It's my fight, Georgi," he said weakly.

"No. Now it Georgi fight," said the big man.

"You want some of this?" Jack lunged towards Georgi, the knife a spear before him.

The garage-door-thing flashed green, lighting up the entire underside of the bridge, and Jack Cain screamed. He dropped the knife, and fell writhing to the ground, the heels of his boots digging grooves in frozen earth.

"You like pain? Here—Georgi give more." The weapon

flashed again, and now Jack was shrieking, foam flying from his mouth. He flayed the ground with his arms for minutes, as Otis watched in horror, then curled up in a fetal position, and moaned.

Georgi picked up the knife, tossed it over to the entrance of the crate, then grasped Jack by the hair, and pulled him screaming to his knees. "Here, I show you something. I show you what happen you come back here again. You look at big rock—by where fire is." He grasped Jack by the hair again, and twisted his head in the direction of a two-hundred pound block of concrete by the oil can they used for a fire. Jack's eyes were nearly closed, his moaning pitiful even to the man he would eventually have killed.

"You look, now," said Georgi, and then he fiddled with the garage-door opener. Pointed it. Fired.

The flash was bright red, concentrated in a narrow beam that struck the center of the rock. The concrete flashed yellow—and disappeared. Jack cried out, tears flowing down his cheeks as Georgi leaned over to look at him, their noses nearly touching. "You come back again—I do that to you. Now—you go."

Jack Cain stumbled to his feet, and fled from their camp—forever.

Georgi helped Otis back to the crate. The knife blade had gone in and out of his left side at a shallow angle near beltline, and the wound was bleeding profusely, but inside of an hour Moms had him bandaged up, and resting comfortable next to the stove, Georgi hovering over him. Moms left her patient for only a moment in order to conjure up a new poultice in her shack. While she was gone, Otis, drowsy with pain, looked up at Georgi, scanning his rugged features and dark eyes in the glow of the stove. "You sure ain't no Russian spy," he said softly. "You sure ain't nothin' from around here."

Georgi looked at him sadly. "I tell you—far to home."

And it was in the twilight of that very day when Georgi's friends came to take him away.

Moms had filled him with tea, and his bladder seemed ready to burst. Otis wiggled carefully out of the crate, and relieved himself against the bridge buttress. Georgi had started a fire in the oil can, and draped a towel across the top of it to dry. Moms was shuttling back and forth, moving her pharmacy into Otis's crate, mumbling to herself all the time about too many things to do. She was never happier than when she had a patient to take care of.

Otis zipped up his pants, and turned to say something to Georgi, freezing into silence at the look on the man's face. Georgi was looking past him, head tilted upwards, white teeth showing in a huge smile. He lifted both arms over his head, and waved wildly, laughing. Otis spun around, saw two men descending the embankment, one of them carrying the little black box Georgi had hidden by the bridge. They waved back to Georgi, scrambled down the slope, and ran towards him. Both were dressed from head to toe in skintight, brown knitted suits, black belts around their waists hanging heavily with metal canisters of various sizes, reminding Otis of Rangers he had seen in the war.

Georgi ran to meet them, embracing each man with a huge hug, lifting them off the ground. Comrades. Otis's heart sank. Georgi's friends had found him, had come to take him away from them. But the look on the big man's face was pure joy. I must be happy for him, thought Otis. He has found his people again.

The three men talked in low tones, occasionally looking at Otis. *I'm being talked about.* His side was hurting again, and he sat down on a concrete chunk by the fire, feeling a sudden emptiness, a sense of loss. Friends were so temporary, friendships so fleeting in his life. Why must it be this way? But then he did have Moms, and Alf, and wasn't that enough? Not good to want too much, Otis. But, oh, how rapidly this big man from a place far away had become a friend of his.

Georgi broke away from the other two men, who remained where they were, and walked quickly to the crate. "I talk with Otis. Otis wait there." He ducked inside, and came out with the little weapon he had used against Jack Cain, but nothing else. The stove—the pack—both still inside the crate. "Say nothing. I talk." He knelt before Otis, put a hand on his shoulder. "I tell—much lost—in river. Can't find. I leave things—you keep—for make Georgi live so friends find. I go home, now—remember Otis—my friend."

Moms came up behind Georgi, looked at Otis's face, and tears welled up in her eyes. "You's goin' home, is that it?"

"Yes. Friends find."

"Goin' home, goin' home, we's all goin' home one way or 'nother. You remember Moms now, too, you hear?"

Georgi reached out and took her hand in his, then squeezed Otis's shoulder with his other hand before standing up. Otis looked up at him, and smiled.

"You sure you ain't no Russian spy?"

Georgi laughed that deep-throated laugh again. "No, Otis. Russia—close. I go—far—far to home." He made a grand sweep with one arm. "Good—bye, bye." He turned suddenly, and walked back to the other men. They stood in a tight cluster, one of them fiddling with the little black box. And then suddenly it was as if a black sheet wrapped around them, appearing out of nowhere, blinking once—twice— then a flash of white light filling it, neutralizing it to nothingness, along with the men inside.

The bright flash left spots before Otis's eyes. He blinked—looked—blinked again. Georgi and the others were gone. Moms clapped her hands together. "Lord, I has seen the doorway to heaven! I has seen your angels come to take our friend to yo' holy person. I praise the power o' the Lord! Amen." Moms turned, wiped her eyes, and shuffled back towards the crate. "Someday, he'll come for us, Otis, but you git back inside, now. Tea's heatin', and you don't need gettin' chilled out here."

Inside the crate, Otis turned the stove down until the coil glowed dull red, then snuggled in his sleeping bag, and sipped hot tea. For the first time in days, Alf left Jason's bag, and stepped gingerly past Moms to lie down by Otis, heavy head in his lap. Otis stroked Alf's head, and exchanged a smile with Moms when the dog sighed.

Georgi had left him the stove for a reason. To stay warm? Or to get rich? After what he'd seen that day, Otis was sure there was no other stove like this one—anywhere—not on planet Earth. But to get rich meant dealing with people who weren't in his world, either, people who would find a way to steal the secrets in Georgi's diagrams for themselves, the same people who wouldn't part with a quarter for a street person, the ones who sneered at them through the windows of their passing cars.

His reverie was interrupted by a shout from outside.

"Hey, Otis! You in there?"

"That you, Two Feathers?" He hadn't seen the big Sioux for months.

"Yeah. Freezin' solid out here, Otis. Got an extra bag for the night? Gonna leave for Minneapolis tomorrow."

"When's the last time you ate?"

"Oh, two—maybe three days. Got a bag of raw beans with, but nothin' to cook 'em up. You got somethin'?"

Otis looked at Moms, and she nodded her okay.

"Well, you just get yourself in here, and bring the beans! We've got enough heat in here for everybody!"

A Plumber's Tale
by
Merritt Severson

About the Author

Merritt Severson is a freelance photographer with over forty magazine covers to her name; a journalist, with several important credits, and the author/illustrator of children's tales of holiday greed and nastiness. But she had never sold an adult fiction story, and in 1988 determined to crack the Contest. She made it with "A Plumber's Tale," just before becoming ineligible because of the multiplicity of her credits.

Merritt was born in England, emigrated at nineteen, and went to work originally as an illustrator for IBM. Two years later, she married Allan, and in due course moved to Ohio. Their daughter and son are grown, married, and living separately; the Seversons have four miniature Schnauzers now instead. Merritt wants to make a career of SF writing.

About the Illustrator

Sergey V. Poyarkov is a native of Kiev in the USSR. He was born in 1965. He completed his technical school in 1985, spent two years in the army, and entered the Poligraphic Technical College, but after three years changed to the Kiev Artist College, which he has been attending since. He heard of the Contest from a friend, who gave him a copy of the Contest newsletter. And so Sergey became our first Russian winner.

The sun began to set at home-rush time. And everything in Neebank Desert Marchionate was tinted pink—the spires of the tribal houses, the rumbling crush of beast-drawn carts, the stores and ale shops, and the crowds of leathery, gray Y'Zondees.

Worrol stood in the gutter with her sinewy arms around a canvas bag. Inside were charts of some of the water mains beneath the city. She hoped she'd swiped the right batch.

Beneath the rim of her stovepipe hat, the transparent wisps around her oblong face had become oily strings. She shoved them out of her yellow eyes, and squinted into the traffic. A parade of teetering wagons, hauled by carapaced storps and black-shelled many-leggers—and heaped with everything from bundled rags to old crockery—was rattling by. And across the street, the sand chronometer in the spire of the Great Hall of Tribes was about to tip another bucket into the hopper-gong, and mark the hour with a ringing thud of sand. *Clang!* There it went. Her partner Kuy would be picking her up any minute. But should she wait? Beneath her tall hat, Worrol's brow crimped. Should she get further involved with her partner's obsession? Should she risk her life, her job as a priest-plumber, her vow of goodness? She had already broken the law.

As a team of grain-haulers rumbled by, Worrol leapt back to avoid the powerful, grinding feet of a passing storp. Suddenly, she was part of the crowd. Its heat radiated on her short, naked body, and her stumpy legs tottered in the press and sway. She elbowed free, and wiped a glaze of oil from her chin.

She always oiled like mad when she was stressed, and her nerves just weren't up to all this subterfuge and guilt. What if she were caught? After they yanked off her tall hat, they'd see her cone of braided hair—the symbol of her vow of goodness. She could just imagine the outcry. *Priest-plumber with vow-cone steals binder from Holy Archives!* It was a wonder the crowd didn't feel her guilt like a coat of needles. And what if Kuy were wrong? What if all this stuff about someone tampering with the breeding pools was just Kuy's weird imagination?

What if! Worrol stared unseeingly at her feet. She'd agreed to steal the plans only the night before—right after Kuy explained her theory about what happened when Y'Zondees waded in water to have offspring.

Kuy had taken her to her makeshift laboratory in an old treadmill, and unveiled her newest acquisition, a microscope. The forbidden instrument had been purchased from Joorluk, an apothecary who dabbled in science—a dangerous associate for a priest. But Kuy seemed oblivious of her crime. Across the rickety table, her eyes had glinted with wonder. "When Y'Zondees wade together, they will all have youngers, right, Worrol?"

Worrol had felt her gray skin chill. "Yes. So?"

Kuy pointed to her halo of misty hair. "If I wade with ten Y'Zondees, all their youngers could have the same hair as mine, or my squarish earflutes, or my tiny eyes—whatever. Yet nothing comes out of my body, or theirs, and we never touch. So how are characteristics ferried from me to them, and *vice versa? How?*

"Who cares?" Worrol had muttered. "When people want youngers, they just tribe and wade."

"But, how does it work?"

Illustrated by Sergey V. Poyarkov

Worrol remembered feeling irked. "It's mystical—even a novice priest-plumber knows that."

"Why not *mechanical*? Why not tiny collectors drifting from person to person carrying information gleaned from—say, skin dust? We shed millions of particles every day."

Worrol shrugged. "It's an incomprehensible mystery."

"Spare me the official crap."

"No one can know the Work of the Spirit."

"Oh, really?" said Kuy, hotly. "Then the microscope is truly a miracle—which is doubtless why it is forbidden." She pointed to the eyepiece. "Look down that. It's a drop of water."

Worrol bent and frowned into the tube. "I see floating discs . . . sort of clear jelly-circles . . . drifting." Worrol chewed on her lip. "What are they? Disease things? Didn't you tell me diseases are carried by tiny bits?"

"Yes, but disease particles wriggle around—and they cluster together and they divide—just like we do. These floaters are collectors, transporters—I'm almost certain." Kuy's expression had become grave. "And if they *do* carry characteristics, then they're real, Worrol. They could be filtered out. Killed even. They're part of the Hidden Sea's natural water. If someone tampered with them, they could contol who has youngers and who doesn't."

"Kuy, what's going on?"

Kuy slumped and let out her breath. "There haven't been any new youngers in the Scrubs Quarter for several weeks."

"What about the High Dunes District?"

"If anything, an increase."

"How do you know?"

"I've been poking around the sewers. I know a birthing membrane when I see one, Worrol, and there hasn't been one in the Scrubs Sewer since—since before the recent food rationing. More to the point—*there are no discs in the*

Scrubs' water mains—only dark specks which could be dead ones.''

Worrol had whistled. "So if these jelly things effect replication . . . ."

"Then something stinks."

"Could the discs run in phases, do you think?"

"Phases are for moons, Worrol. But, tomorrow, I'm going to doublecheck. I plan to take water samples from both districts. If High Dunes water has discs and the water of the Scrubs still doesn't, that'll be proof. And while I'm doing that, I have a job for *you*. . . ."

I wonder what she found, thought Worrol, gazing absently at a wagon piled with fennyroots creaking past. Of course, Kuy often got odd notions. But this breeding one was frightening. Worrol hugged the canvas bag for security. For a long time now, she'd wanted to be an *older*. More than anything, she wanted to join a tribe, and wade, then feel her body thin down the middle until it shed a whole new person . . . a dear, helpless *younger* for her to guide and teach. If Kuy was right, someone was threatening *her* hopes and those of everyone in the Scrubs Quarter.

The sky had become a brownish red, and the spires of the tribal houses were dark thorns. Worrol watched lamplighters with torches trudging along, pulling gas chains and igniting lanterns. One worker was lighting the roadway's arches. Blue jets raced up their sides and met with a satisfying *whoomph!*

Most of the Y'Zondees jamming the sidewalks were store clerks and such. Lucky them, thought Worrol, going home by steam tram to prepare meager meals of fennyroots and grain soup for *their youngers*.

The sun became a brick-red disc. The sky turned a syrupy green, and a whisper of cold air cooled her skin. Worrol shivered. Soon everything would dim to the color of slate and she'd feel safe.

She hoisted the bag onto her shoulder. "Where are you, Kuy?" she muttered, searching for the tall, swaying priest-plumber's wagon they shared. It had a spear-torch on top. You could see the flame for a thousand arm-lengths. And Shanik, their gigantic many-legger, had a broken stinger that dragged, and you could hear it half-a-street away. *But not in all this racket*, thought Worrol, as a steam tram, a monster of riveted plates, hissed to a stop. The "iron storp," as some called it, was the new transportation wonder. Dozens swarmed past Worrol and scrambled aboard. The tram lifted its drive-wheels and backpedaled the drive-shaft to expel a spurt of steam, then glided forward.

As it chuffed away, a red-lacquered storp pulling a red-canopied cart jingled into its place. A palace buggy! The driver and both passengers were typical courtiers: little old aristocrats whose skins were entirely covered by red, gold and black body paint. Worrol gawked as the buggy shim-mied past. Then she noticed Shanik, and the towering cart with its plume of fire, lumbering along behind.

"Hey, Kuy!" Worrol could see Kuy perched high on the driver's seat beneath their gold-leafed sign. The legend, "Priest-Plumbers," flickered importantly in the blowing rag of flame. Their work ranged from burst pipes to funerals. Recently, they'd been to one of the marchionate's most opulent tribal houses, the Warriors, to mend a basement leak. After they'd rounded the solder joint and polished it with a chain-mail pad, they'd been ushered up to the dining hall to bless the waters of the house, and preside over a misting dance. Worrol had uttered the Water Blessing right under a stern portrait of their ruler, the reclusive Prelate-Marchioness Raffunji. Then the dance. She and Kuy had arranged their six huge atomizers in a circle, then called the youngers into the middle for their ritual misting. A young Y'Zondee was more at home in desert air than moisture. But it hadn't always been so. Scholars said Y'Zond had once been a planet of shallow seas, and ancient Y'Zondees had spent most of their lives wading. In later eras, Y'Zondees built towns over the planet's shrinking lakes. Now, all the water was underground, and breeding was overseen by the church. Young adult Y'Zondees went to misting dances to "awaken" their oily gray skin, and prepare for olderhood. After several mistings it was up to the individual to find a tribe that would accept her. Wading with one's original tribe was taboo.

Everyone poised for the dance. Kuy sounded a note on her pipe to start the singing, while Worrol worked the bulb of the first atomizer. Then Kuy, piping a jaunty misting tune, skipped to the other side of the circle, and began working the atomizer opposite Worrol. Keeping up the rhythm, they moved from atomizer to atomizer, until the walls were moist, and the dancers dripped.

After Kuy and Worrol had removed their atomizers, everyone sang them the "Thank You" song, and paid them in gold.

Worrol felt a stab of guilt. A plumber was a mystic, someone you needed to trust. Yet, today she had *caused* a burst pipe at the Holy Archives to cover her own thievery. She was a traitor to her calling . . . though maybe not to truth. And now it was too late to back out; Kuy was lowering the stepladder.

"Well . . . ?" Kuy's eyes were quizzical dots of topaz, and her transparent hair sailed like a crown of fluff around her high cranium. "Did you get it?" She flicked Shanik with a long, light whip.

Worrol finished buttoning her white plumber's robe, and rocked her head affirmatively, as the wagon lunged forward. She took off her tall hat and tossed it into the wagon. "Yes, I got it. While the clerks passed buckets in the cellar I took the third binder on the sixth shelf—just like you said."

People along the street genuflected as the wagon

passed. Worrol placed a fist either side of her vow-of-goodness hair cone to confer a blessing, and Kuy touched a wrench to her forehead. "Come on, Worrol, show me."

Worrol groped in the canvas bag, and stuck the binder under Kuy's narrow nose.

Kuy smiled, something she rarely did.

"I don't *think* anyone saw me," Worrol went on, "but I ambled out slowly, then wandered through a street market. Even joined a crowd at a stall selling fennyroots—I got three measures."

"Wearing the hat was smart, and the waiting in line for food was an inspiration. At times, you've got a cool head, Worrol."

"Yes, clear enough to know I hate this . . . this . . . criminal behavior."

"Don't start that again!" Kuy stretched up and cracked her whip. "Today, I collected water samples from around the marchionate, and—"

"I'm not sure I want to know," said Worrol, conferring a blessing on a genuflecting group.

Kuy sank and glared. "You really make me sick—you know that? You whine and complain about not being pledged. *'Oh, when am I going to be accepted by a tribe so I can have a younger?'* You keep saying it."

"I can hope."

"But, as I've pointed out—"

Worrol winced. "Again and again."

Kuy glowered. "Worrol, listen. The High Dunes District has floating discs, but the Scrubs Quarter doesn't. Even more significant—I went down the sewers. The *High Dunes District* is having a younger boom. Birthing membranes everywhere! I had to shovel my way through parts of the channel."

"Then there's no doubt the floating discs cause youngers?" Worrol twiddled the tassel on the sash of her robe.

"Food is short, and the fennyroot crops are thin. Maybe a sterile time for the Scrubs Quarter is some kind of official policy."

"If it were, we'd be the first to know. Life and death is our business, Worrol. You can bet the Prelate-Marchioness knows about it. But it has to be a clandestine operation. And how is it being done?"

"By straining the discs from the water."

"Of course, dummy. But how? We must locate the main inlet on the charts, then find it—*tonight*. Every hour the population becomes more lopsided. All the most aggressive tribes live in the High Dunes District—the factory workers, lawyers, machinists, engineers, and soldiers."

Worrol made a face. "So you're saying the Prelate-Marchioness wants barbers, cooks, poets, physicians, candlemakers, *and priest-plumbers* to die out?"

"No, just dwindle to leave more food for the High Dunes."

Worrol grunted. "She couldn't want more lawyers."

"No, but she might want more soldiers."

"But the Prelate-Marchioness is our spiritual head. . . ."

"Such block-headed naiveté deserves to dwindle! Wake up, Worrol! *You're* the one that hopes to have youngers."

Worrol scowled. "Seems I should send my next batch of proposals to the High Dunes tribes. I bet some would jump at the chance of getting a priest-plumber."

"Jump? Who would jump?"

"The Tribe of Athletes might."

"The Aths accept *you?* Are you serious? Be realistic, Worrol—your legs are too short. Besides, their choosing season is over."

"Then I'll apply to the Welders or the Warriors—whoever's having youngers."

"That's right, get tribed, and to hell with everyone

else. Worrol, you're disgustingly selfish.''

Worrol felt tears sting her eyes, and shame sting her face. She stared at Shanik's shiny, swinging rump, and concentrated on the *shanik-shanik-shanik* sound of her stinger scraping the road.

Kuy dug Worrol in the ribs. "Come on, old friend, face it. The Aths, the Welders and the Warriors only accept bigs and talls. Frankly, I don't care if they breed themselves to the size of air balloons. But when half of the marchionate is being made sterile, then I'm unstoppable.''

Worrol cleared her throat. "You don't want youngers, not ever?''

"Hell, no, it would mean getting pledged to a tribe. I could hardly have a younger without the benefit of tribehood, now could I?''

Worrol let out a nervous laugh, then shivered at the unthinkable. "It's a pity. You're a thinker, and you're righteous. But, I guess you're pledged to your curiosity.''

Kuy nodded. "I don't think I'd make a good older, anyway. And what other reason is there to get tribed?''

Unable to think of even one other reason, Worrol fell silent. She only knew that she had an urge to replicate herself. It was a self-esteem thing. Duty. Status. And the younger calling you her older, and having reverence. But if a tribe were made sterile, being pledged to it, and wading in its pool, just hoping, would be pathetic. Kuy was odd, but always sincere. Perhaps knowing the truth would hurt less. "I'll go down the water mains with you—even to the great bronze doors, themselves," said Worrol, quietly. "Though I'm scared to go.''

Kuy gave her a grim look. "Then you must find courage, Worrol. There's one thing I haven't told you.'' Pulling the reins, she urged Shanik left at the next turn.

"What thing?''

"See for yourself.''

Part way down the street of apothecaries and body-paint shops, the marchionate's Tribing Temple was bright with gas lanterns, and surrounded by red-fringed carts. The new pledge being tribed was obviously well-to-do. Even the storps were festooned with red tassels and silver beads, the symbols of alliance.

"Looks like an Ath's tribing," said Kuy, slowing the cart to a crawl.

Worrol bit her lip. "No, much fancier. Looks like a Warrior's to me."

Kuy halted Shanik and stood up. "They're coming out. Definitely High Dune District types. Tall. *Warriors*—you were right." She whistled. "Wow! More than I imagined! Worrol, take a good, hard look at the kind of younger you'd get if the Warriors accepted you! Look at the youngest youngers!"

Worrol drew in a breath, and went cold all over. "They all look like *Prelate-Marchioness Raffunji!*"

Kuy turned Shanik at the next corner. The cart took it sharply, lurching and leaning.

"The Prelate-Marchioness?" breathed Worrol.

"Shhh!"

The street was narrow and dark, and the flame on the cart danced on the windows of a bank of dreary warehouses.

"But *how* can they all look like the Prelate-Marchioness?"

"A good question," said Kuy. "Here we are." She drove Shanik into the cobbled yard of the abandoned tread-mill.

After chaining Shanik and leaving her agitating her mandibles in a tub of dried grubs, Worrol followed Kuy's trembling candle through a door and up some steps.

"This hideaway of mine is in a choice location," said Kuy cheerfully. "It sits right over a forked chamber, where the Scrubs' water main branches into three. It's well inside the Scrubs system—and, no, Worrol, there's not one floating disc down there.''

Worrol followed Kuy into a small, low room with a table full of broken cups and bottles. Worrol snorted. "This place always reminds me of your room."

"Enough praise," said Kuy, lighting a lantern. She grinned. "Until you see my results." She brought a saucer of glass oblongs to the lamplight. "Slides with dried-up water spots. I wangled my way into three houses today for the clinching evidence. This one's from the pool of a Scrubs poetry-writing tribe who haven't had a younger for two seasons. And these two are from the High Dunes—one from the Warriors and one from the Aths."

Worrol squinted at the slides. "They all look the same."

"Not under the microscope."

At midnight, Worrol and Kuy dressed in their water-proof suits of oiled storp leather. Worrol stuffed her canvas bag with greased rags—fuel for the torches—and tied it around her neck. Kuy slung the strap of an apothecary box of jars across her chest. "It's an old set," she said. "I took it in trade."

"With food in short supply, that was stupid."

Carrying a torch, Worrol followed her partner down the slippery steps beneath the treadmill. Was there *really* a conspiracy to shrink the Scrubs' population and fill the marchionate with toughs and militaristic types of Raffunji blood? She was as angry as Kuy, now. She was glad she'd stolen the binder. One chart showed the great bronze doors to the Hidden Sea inside the bedrock. Two aqueducts carried water from the barely open doors to a chamber, where they spilled into two deep troughs emptying into the mains to both districts. *The chamber was directly under the palace of the mighty Prelate-Marchioness.*

But was there enough night left to find the chamber,

and get back? Kuy had insisted on re-checking her jelly-disc test. She used ink. A few drops of Plenk's Permanent Blue-Black dyed the discs, she said. Then salt shriveled them, forming a smoky sediment.

Now she could see Kuy at the bottom, prodding a finger into the blackness. "The channel to the palace."

Worrol slid into the tepid, waist-deep water, and waded against the current. Kuy was already sloshing down the brick-lined conduit. She was a bent silhouette against a flickering flame, her left hand, in its oiled glove, tapping the wall, her jars, chinking.

After some distance, Kuy tested for jelly discs. "Still none going to the Scrubs," she said.

Further on, she turned around. "Worrol, the water feels warmer."

"That's what *I* was thinking."

"Shh!" Kuy cupped an earflute. "A roaring sound—but very faint. Stay there," she said, wading on. "I'll call out when I see what it is." Her torch licked across the brickwork, shedding a jumping light on the water swirling around her hips, and she grew small. Moving through patches of mist, she was becoming a ghost with a blurred lamp. Then she turned left, and disappeared.

Worrol stood still and listened. Time seemed to hang in the dark conduit. The flame of her torch was becoming blue and short. She waited, breathing through her mouth, her eyes searching the dark spot where Kuy had vanished. For a long time, nothing. Then a distant cry bounced along the brickwork. "Run, Worrol!"

A jolt of terror shot through Worrol. Brandishing her dying torch, she wheeled, and slogged through the heavy flood like a dreamer with leaden feet.

The channel remained dark behind her. Reaching the treadmill steps, she balanced on the top one with curled toes. Where was Kuy? She poked a wad of rag into her torch, and swept its flare in an arc, scanning the cavern of eddying water as it emptied into the three smaller channels.

She scrutinized the water until her sight was muddled by phosphenes. Then she saw something. Kuy, was it? Yes, feebly swimming. Raw, bloated face. Skin hanging in waxy strips. "Kuy, I'll get you. Hang on! Hang on!"

Worrol slipped down into the water, and fought her way to the middle of the flow. She caught Kuy by the arm, and towed her to the treadmill steps. "What happened?"

"Scrubs' water . . . it runs through filters . . . to take out discs . . . then it's *cooked*."

"Cooked?"

"Copper pipes . . . runs through hundreds of coiled copper pipes . . . over thousands of gas jets."

"But if they're boiling all the water—"

"Not *all* water. High Dunes' water . . . runs straight from the Hidden Sea . . . into water main. Good water . . . untouched. Was going to test for discs . . . but heard voices . . . I stopped . . . was swept into the boiling water. Get to Raffunji. Stop her, Worrol! Stop her!"

Eight of Y'Zond's fourteen moons had already risen over the barren wastes. They hung behind teasing veils of cloud like sickles. In their gray light, Prelate-Marchioness Raffunji's six-towered stronghold seemed like a hand sticking up from the scrublands, saying, "Go back!"

Almost too scared to think, Worrol had darted between clumps of succulent trees until she was fifty arm-lengths from the palace. Now she was leaning against a tree. "I'm not cut out for this," she puffed, sliding down.

She was still exhausted from the previous night; she'd hauled Kuy up the steps to the treadmill, loaded her on the cart, and had driven her to their plumber's shop. And not knowing what to do, she'd run and banged on the door of Joorluk's Apothecary.

Grumbling about the time, Joorluk had weighed out a dried bug and cactus-berry mixture, and wrapped it in a cone of brown paper. "The best burn-cure in Neebank Desert Marchionate—unless you can find a birthing membrane to cover the wounds."

"Where would I get one?" Worrol had asked.

The sharp-mannered Joorluk had glanced nervously out of the door. "These days, that's a good question. How much do you want your friend to live?"

"Whatever it takes."

Joorlak shrugged. "Then she should sit in ice water."

"Ice water?"

Ignoring her question, Joorluk opened the wooden door of a gas-run chill-locker. Worrol smelled ammonia. Joorluk turned, stooped under the weight of a large ice-block. "Fresh from the High Dunes Ice House. Icy cold water is probably your friend's only chance."

All that night, Worrol had brewed pots of burn-wash, while Kuy sat shivering in an old bathtub full of freezing water.

But now, thought Worrol, glancing at the palace, she must take care of *her own* survival. How would she get in? And would her body-paint pass scrutiny? She got up and stepped into the moonlight to inspect the red, black and gold scrollwork on her body. In dim passageways, she might pass. Still, she must remember to shuffle like an old Y'Zondee. Courtiers were always displaced grand-olders, great-grand-olders, or great-greats who were discreet, and willing to become works of art. Some were so old, their designs so ingrained, they appeared like gold, black-and-red marbled stones. After death, such beings were dried and displayed in the Hall of Husks in Y'Zond's vast mausoleum.

Before applying the black, red and gold radiating from a spot on her forehead, Worrol had etched in wrinkles. But she wouldn't fool anyone alert. For once in her life, she was too tall. And her cone of braided hair, which she could neither hide nor sacrifice, made her disguise superficial at best.

But after what had happened to Kuy, she had to risk the risks. *She had to find Raffunji!* If the Prelate-Marchioness looked like her portrait, she would be well-built, with a bulbous head, and a black-and-silver hair-strip above alarming, amber eyes. And if Kuy was right about the Warrior youngers, soon thousands would look like the Prelate. But how was it done? How could a recluse pass on her characteristics? Even if the Prelate-Marchioness wallowed in the High Dunes water main night and day, not enough "impressions" of her could be swept, so far, on enough discs to dominate the High Dunes' pools.

Getting into Raffunji's palace seemed impossible until a legger-drawn food wagon was admitted through the wooden gates. Inside, several tiny courtiers climbed aboard to tally the barrels of syrup, sacks of dried fennyroot, and bundles of hard, waxed bread rolls. Such quantities! No one looked under the cart, or checked the beast's stinger. Worrol scuttled out, heaved a sack onto her shoulders, hunched down, and followed the painted figures into the stronghold.

Just before reaching the kitchens, Worrol dodged through a door, and found herself in the mellow gaslight of a varnished-wood corridor. She could smell food. Fenny cakes, maybe. But the smell was no comfort. She felt exposed and helpless. Worrol stopped. She also smelled water. There had to be a wading pool just below, and the passage to her right offered stairs, leading down.

The pool was surrounded by terraces of marble, ornamented with columns and archways of gaslight.

Worrol circled the pool. Under the water squatted a

grouping of stone armchairs. She'd seen similar submerged furniture in tribal houses, where even tables with game-pieces were popular.

On the pool apron at the far end, a round raised hatch stood open. Worrol peered over the rim. Judging from the dank smell, it was a portal to the water mains beneath. And what was that on a stand by the terrace? A microscope! And bigger and more complex than Kuy's. Someone else knew about discs.

"You're a big one," said a reedy voice. "I didn't know we hired vow-of-goodness types."

Worrol startled. A small silhouette stood at the top of the terracing.

"Bring her here, G'Lenk," demanded a heavy voice from an archway beyond.

"You heard Her Young Highness, the Marchoo Raffunji," said the grotesquely painted courtier, waddling into the light. Her striped face was a smirking mask of cruelty around a single black tooth. She beckoned. "Quickly—if you don't want to be beaten."

Worrol hesitated; her legs felt like wobbling sticks. Here was an unexpected threat. A *young* Highness? A march*oo*? The old Prelate-Marchioness had an offspring? A regent? Worrol's body began to shake. She had no cover story, and no weapon but her disintegrating wits.

"Approach now!" boomed the voice in the shadows.

Worrol reached the top of the steps, and felt G'Lenk prod her forward. Behind the columns, propped on a mammoth, green satin cushion, was a more youthful, more muscular version of the Prelate-Marchioness than she'd seen in the tribal house portrait. The bulgy head was bulgier. The single eyebrow was stripier, more fierce. The eyes flashed with yellow, icy fire. Unmistakably, the daughter of the house.

"Speak!"

Worrol decided to try the truth. "I've come about the drains."

G'Lenk pointed a finger. "She's lying, Young Highness. Why would a priest-plumber come here dressed as a courtier?"

"Probably another thief," said the fearsome young Marchoo.

"True," said Worrol, feebly. "I did take something. But only from necessity."

"Yet you had money to buy body-paint!" shouted the young Raffunji. "I won't waste time on this creature. Drown her, G'Lenk."

G'Lenk grinned. "Why not keep her for later, Young Highness. *They* will be home soon."

The Marchoo's face lit with malicious glee. "Yes, later . . . later, we'll give her to my three youngers, who'll find peeling her very slowly an absorbing evening's entertainment."

"I hate that," giggled G'Lenk. "I can hardly bear to watch."

The imposing figure bounced up from the cushion, grasped Worrol at the neck. "Fight me, and G'Lenk will peel you now."

Worrol felt herself being scooped up. She was rigid with terror. There was the sound of a grating being kicked open. A waft of cold air and the smell of drains. And she was falling.

Her mind seemed to turn inside out. She could recall a splash and a laugh, two skinny legs dancing about her, and then being yanked by the armpits.

She rolled over, stunned, confused. She'd apparently been dragged from a drainage channel running through the cellar. A pair of thick legs now stood over her. Their burly owner grunted. "She's all right, Your Great Mightiness."

The skinny legs skittered closer. "Friend or foe, Barlu?"

The bodyguard grunted again. "Your Great Mightiness thinks a spy, perhaps? But this thing *was* tossed down. That says much."

Great Mightiness? Worrol thought, vaguely. *Was this the great and mighty Prelate-Marchioness Raffunji?* She coughed and vomited a small amount of bile.

"I see you've met my younger," crackled the skinny legs. "That's the way she makes *me* feel. Puke if you must."

Worrol blinked. Could this really be the harsh ruler of Neebank Desert Marchionate? Worrol sat up and rubbed her mouth with her arm. Yes, she recognized the bulbous head of the portrait and the frightening yellow eyes. But the puff-chested body was now a shrunken bone-cage with papery skin. "Marchioness-Magistrate Raffunji?"

"When last worshipped." She stuck out a hand.

Worrol bowed her head and touched the hand. "Your Great Mightiness."

"Take it, you dunce, and get up! Take the hand that once held the power of life and death! Never did I think I'd end my days as a grand-older creeping around my own cellars, rescuing the remnants *she* throws down." She looked Worrol up and down. "Of course, not many of them live. *You* were lucky enough to fall on *her*."

"Friend Y'Lon," moaned the burly bodyguard, pointing.

Worrol gasped at the sight of a squashed face.

"It's no matter," said old Raffunji, tossing her head. "You can make it up to me by ridding us of the usurper. I know I should've done it. But then, I am always too kind, too sentimental. I should've throttled the demon the moment she split off from me." The Prelate-Marchioness began stalking back and forth with her hands locked behind her. She stopped and stared into the air. "I was too curious, perhaps. Too fascinated at the most unexpected event of my existence. I had never waded with anyone—not ever."

"Then why did you . . . divide?"

"Many years ago, my trusted aide, G'Lenk, urged me to acquire an ice device. Ice was the rarest, most precious substance on Y'Zond in those backward days. Most Y'Zondees had never even heard of it. But an inventor had built an ice-maker, a gas-powered contraption that recycled ammonia through pipes. It cost me much gold to have its maker killed, but the ice-device soon paid for itself fivefold. Other Marchionesses and Marchoos came and brought fabulous gifts, just to sit and sip cold ale and fenny tea. It made Neebank Desert the most prestigious marchionate on the planet."

"Ah," mumbled Worrol.

"Then one hot day, I developed a skin rash. Perhaps it came from eating that entire basket of rare acid pears. Oh, why did I listen to you, you foul G'Lenk? Ice-baths would cure my affliction, you said. And for long hours I suffered in the freezing water. Then . . . as I watched my lesions fade, I realized I was replicating. Me! Who'd never waded, not once."

Worrol's heart skipped. Kuy was soaking in cold water when she left! Was poor Kuy starting to divide?

The half-crazed Prelate-Marchioness pointed upwards. "Me, replicating! And you've seen the result. . . ."

"The Marchoo."

"The young, terrible, cruel Marchoo, whose nature appalls even me. She's all my nastiest qualities . . . *squared*." Old Raffunji clenched her fists. "G'Lenk promised to terminate her. But my younger can be viciously . . . *persuasive*. And G'Lenk was always a self-preserving, servile slime." Her eyes sparked. "G'Lenk didn't even smash the ice machine. And that was her second worst crime. Then it was too late."

"For what?"

"To stop the birthing of *them*. As soon as my younger was mature, she used the ice machine at G'Lenk's urging. She produced three youngers, whose depravity and vileness are the depths of my being *to the fourth power*." The old Prelate-Marchioness began to cackle, and oil trickled from her yellow eyes. "Their answer to the food shortage is to kill off the Scrubs, and turn the High Dunes District into a factory for making duplicates of themselves. An army of demons!" The old Prelate-Marchioness put a finger to her ear. "What's that, G'Lenk? You say, 'I tried to kill them, Your Great Mightiness—I realized they must not live—I tried to restore your power.'" Raffunji's eyes blazed. "But you dithered, G'Lenk! You piddled away chance after chance. Then, to save yourself, you sold me, you putrid traitor. You helped them stuff *me* down the cellar drop. Me, your prelate, your Marchioness. You signed your death warrant with my blood. What's that, G'Lenk? Can I trust this simpleton to do better?" Old Raffunji stared at Worrol, and sucked on her bottom lip in mocking study. "Ah, yes, she is too dull to be devious—and she has a top-knot. We have a cleanser of the foul stream. A blesser of the waters—and a do-goody into the bargain."

"Sincerity is an advantage in a priest-plumber," said Worrol.

"Then it's a new age," growled the old Marchioness. "So tell me how you live."

Worrol told about her partner, Kuy—her bossy, injured partner, Kuy. She talked about their recent experiences as priest-plumbers. She told about Kuy's floating disc discovery.

"Then you understand what my grand-youngers are doing."

"Not really."

"Even now they're down in the water mains," said the old ruler. She crept forward with dramatic gestures. "They lurk under the High Dunes District, their bodies encased in filmy suits made from their own birthing membranes. Suits that squish and squelch around their bodies, Priest-Plumber. Suits that bulge with billions of offspring-making particles strained from the Scrubs' water supply. Billions of gelatinous circles being imprinted with concentrated Raffunji!"

'Your Great Mightiness . . . what can we do?''

"Not *we—you!*" said the Prelate-Marchioness, gruffly. "You're a cleanser of the foul stream, so clean it. You're a blesser of the waters—so get on and bless them. Besides . . . I'll promise you anything if you'll rid me of the Marchoo and her vile offspring." The old Prelate-Marchioness prodded Worrol with a leathery finger. "Well, Priest-Plumber, do we have a bargain?"

"We do," Worrol said, her nostrils flaring with earnestness. 'I'll try—I really mean it—I've taken a vow of goodness."

"And you wear it like a boast," sneered the old Prelate.

Worrol squeezed through a hole in the brick wall, and grasped the iron ladder that ran upward to the hatch by the pool. An arm-length below, a lusty gas flame was waggling in the air currents. Many arm-lengths below that, the twin riverlets were gushing from the bedrock into their separate troughs. One trough was emptying uninterrupted into the High Dunes main. But the other plunged into a massive sink lined with bottles, then gushed from a pipe to a huge funnel that fed hundreds of coiled copper pipes suspended over a bed of gas jets.

As Worrol swung herself onto the ladder, she heard the old Prelate-Marchioness rasp, "They must not live," then she heard the scrape of bricks being pushed back in place.

As Worrol climbed down the ladder, the sounds of running water and hissing steam grew. She stepped off the ladder, and looked into the giant sink. The bottles lining it had subsections where a bluish, iridescent sludge was collecting. *Billions of floating discs stolen from the Scrubs channel!* thought Worrol. The spigots beneath the sink must be how the grand-youngers filled their suits. She glanced about. First, she must douse the gas jets, then trap the Marchoo's youngers in the chamber. Then . . . well, the gas would do the rest. But she must hurry. According to old Raffunji, her grand-youngers would soon be emerging from the High Dunes water main.. "They'll make for the ladder," the old Prelate had said, fixing Worrol with her mad eyes. "They will be high after a busy day of disgorging Raffunji-imprinted particles into the High Dunes pool intakes. If they catch you, they will rip you limb from limb."

As Worrol stepped around the sink, she thought she heard laughter. She paused. Yes, laughter echoing in the High Dunes channel. The distance was hard to guess. The sound of steam and running water muffled everything. Seeing was difficult, too. The high brick chamber was illuminated only by phosphorescence in the foam, and the gasbracket in the wall.

She studied the rock wall with its twin outpourings. The two large bronze wheels, between them, must control the Hidden Sea's great flood doors, which lay inside the rock. Worrol grasped the left one, and tried to turn it. If she flooded the High Dunes tube, it would slow the Marchoo's youngers down.

She grunted and strained. Nothing happened. She tried again, bracing her feet against the slimy brickwork. The wheel squawked. She felt it shift, then give. She listened to the thunder of water deep inside the bedrock. Had she opened the door too wide? She clung to the wheel, as a wall of white water burst from the aqueduct. Its creamy bore roared into the High Dunes trough, spuming and spilling over into the trough of the *Scrubs*. It swamped the sink and bottles, then gushed over the funnel, the copper coils, and the gas jets beneath. Volumes of steam hissed from the surface, and rode the churning flood down the channel, and it seemed to boil as thousands of necklaces of gas bubbles streamed to the surface.

Soon, the gas would fill the chamber.

Then, from somewhere down the High Dunes channel came shouts of struggle. But the racing waters might not hold the youngers for long. She must get back to the ladder, now, and escape through the hole in the brick wall. But could she reach it? The floor was a chest-high water race. She waded in, her feet sliding on slime. Suddenly, she was tumbling. *Not the funnel, no!* The force of the water could pin her inside it. She scrabbled at the passing sink. She grasped its rim, but was washed past it. Now she was swirling headfirst toward the funnel's maw. She let it take her, ready to grab its edge. She smacked into it, and clenching its brim, wrenched herself over it onto the tangle of shaking coils.

She gasped for air. The Raffunji cries had become fighting curses. And they were close.

Gas streamers whooshed at the surface near her nose. Would she be gassed while she saved herself from drowning? Either would be better than being caught by the Raffunjis. Weakening in the gas, she felt her mind begin to drift. *Now!* she told herself, *Now!* She thought of the terrifying Raffunjis. She thought of poor Kuy in the plumber's shop, injured and alone . . . maybe screaming with horror as her body began to divide.

Using her fear and fury, Worrol hand-walked across the

coils, gasping for air. She pushed herself toward the stone wall . . . and grasped the bottom of the ladder.

"No, you don't," said a voice, cutting through the turbulence. "No, you don't, storp turd!"

A great crash of surf covered her head, and a hand closed around her ankle. But Worrol corkscrewed her foot and squirmed loose. She scrambled upward, charged with terror.

Above, the heads of the young Marchoo and G'Lenk took two bites out of the hatch-opening. But if the old Prelate came through, there would soon be *four* bites.

"They're going to get her, Young Highness," shrieked G'Lenk, gleefully. "I can't bear to look."

Worrol noticed the gas flame. She must escape before it ignited the gas. *But where was the opening in the wall?* Wasn't it just above the flame? Had old Raffunji forgotten to remove the bricks? Or had the old, deranged ruler planned to trap her between the demonic grand-youngers and the Marchoo and her sadistic aide—removing the only witness to her tragedy?

"Douse the gas flame!" yelled G'Lenk to the Raffunji just below Worrol.

Worrol felt the shudder of the grand-younger's heavy feet on the ladder. Yes, thought Worrol, she was being driven straight up toward the hatch. With nowhere to jump, she was trapped . . . and the gas . . . the gas. She even fancied she could smell it, but it was heavier than air. Now two more robust grand-youngers were clomping up the ladder. Worrol glanced down at them, and her nerves jumped. Cushion-shaped skulls. Knotty muscles. Leering, crazed faces flickering with the concentrated malice of the old Prelate.

Then she heard G'Lenk's voice: "We've got her!"

Then bodyguard Barlu's voice: "And I've got you!"

The hole above Worrol darkened. There were guttural shouts, yowls. Then something struck her shoulder. Then another someone plummeted past her and crashed into the trio of cushion-heads just below.

Worrol attacked the last few rungs and clawed at the hatch rim. Barlu pulled her over the top, and they slammed the cover, and lay on it panting, while the old Marchioness-Magistrate spun the wingbolts.

"Was the gaslight still lit?" asked Raffunji.

Worrol shook her head.

"Then we aren't done. Barlu always carries this tinder-box. We must find something to burn."

"We have something," said Worrol, tugging at her cone of braided hair.

"Your vow-cone?"

Worrell shrugged. "What's the good of the vow without the goodness?"

Old Raffunji's mouth fell open, and she bowed low before Worrol. "Shall you do it yourself, Priest-Plumber?"

"Yes, Great Mightiness," said Worrol. "We need you alive." She struck a flint, igniting the wick of the tinderbox, then uncoiled her braid. She held the long, oily plait out straight, and burned it off a half-hand from her scalp. It flared with a dirty, orange flame. She gathered its length over her arm, while Barlu unscrewed the wingbolts. "Run, Barlu," she said.

As she dangled the long tail of flaming hair into the open hatch, she caught sight of the monstrous Raffunjis for a split second. "Blessings on the Waters of Neebank," she said, and she dropped the hatch.

Later, Worrol couldn't recall everything. She remembered her enflamed rope of hair. Then a split-second of blue-white. But did she throw herself flat before the thundering boom? She *did* remember the pool floor cracking and falling in, disgorging its waters onto the hellish chamber of flame beneath. And she remembered crawling up the terracing.

"You did it," said the old Prelate-Marchioness. She was wriggling out from behind the satin cushion, covered with dust. She held out her hand. "Now, I can die. Whatever remains of me in the Warriors and Aths and others in the High Dunes District must be bred out—we'll need new wading laws." She grasped Worrol's hand. "Help me up. I must reward you—and your friend . . . um . . . ."

"Kuy."

"Kuy, yes. So, what do you ask, Priest-Plumber?"

"You promised me *anything,* remember?"

Barlu, who had just rolled out from behind a fallen column, glared at Worrol, as if to say, *Don't push it!*

"Well?" Raffunji looked worried. "If you want my death, make it a swift one! Name your prize!"

"To choose the next Prelate-Marchioness."

Raffunji went limp as though collapsing, and Worrol sprang to support her. The old Prelate-Marchioness, regaining her balance, coldly brushed Worrol away. "You plan to name *yourself*—I suppose—your dull, careful, goody self."

"No, Your Great Mightiness, on my vow, not me. But someone who'd write careful wading laws."

Old Raffunji grimaced. "Not your friend Kuy!"

But as Worrol went to open her mouth, the palace began to shake. The floor rose, and a great dome of green water fizzed up through the broken pool floor, and swelled.

Worrol clenched the old Prelate's arm. "Come on!"

Barlu grasped the old Y'Zondee, and swung her onto her back. Only a few arm-lengths ahead of the lifting swell, Worrol and Barlu scurried to the top of the terracing, and vaulted up the stairs to the varnished-wood corridor. They thumped past the kitchens, shouting "Run, everyone!" then threw themselves through the doorway to the loading yard.

"Open the gates!" screeched the old ruler, and they bolted onto the desert, followed by a puffing retinue of painted courtiers. Then there was a roar, such as was never heard in Neebank, and a river convulsed from the palace gates and poured across the scrublands.

Worrol would never forget floating through the streets of Neebank on an old door, and finding Kuy on the roof of their plumber's shop. Kuy was propped against the chimney in the first stage of division. Her eyes further apart. A groove forming down the middle of her face. Her mouth pinched into two mouths. The membrane—too late to save her from her burns—had begun forming as a milky film over her replicating body.

Things would never be the same. Engineers said the explosion cracked the bedrock and fractured the ancient bronze sea doors. It explained the shattering of the water mains, thought Worrol, gazing from the top floor of the plumber's shop to the babbling stream running down the street. It had given Neebank a new river system, twelve lakes—and abundant crops of water roots.

She turned from the window. It was many seasons since her night at the palace. Neebank Desert Marchionate had a new Prelate-Marchioness elect—and a new name—Neebank Watergarden Marchionate.

The old Prelate-Marchioness, a living husk now, was near death. Odd that she had outlived Kuy.

Worrol wandered across the room and stood next to Kuy's younger, Dai-iv. She was bent over the old pipe-fitting bench, now sanded and varnished and covered with boxes of slides. The youthful Y'Zondee's hands were still not well-coordinated. Although they split from their olders full sized, youngers were weak, flaccid, and neurologically immature for several seasons. Dai-iv needed only time. Today, she was learning to fine-focus the magnificent brass, binocular microscope, delivered only two days before by the court physician in a palace buggy.

Worrol watched the younger's fingers adjust the slide. "Can you identify it?"

"Two floating discs from the Hidden Sea—during a characteristics-exchange phase."

"Good."

Tonight, Dai-iv would take her place at the palace. Shortly after the flood, Prelate-Marchioness Raffunji had placed her seal on a charter declaring Dai-iv her successor, and in the seasons since, had deluged her chosen Marchoo with every piece of apparatus a modern biologist could wish for, including a centrifuge with an ornamented crankhandle.

Dai-iv was a doer, thought Worrol. She was like Kuy, only more so. Topaz eyes small, more fiery. Head longer. Halo of misty hair, bigger, airier. She was the curiosity and earnestness of Kuy . . . *squared.*

"I wish I'd known her," Dai-iv said, looking up from the microscope. She said it, as she always said it, wistfully.

"But, you *are* her," said Worrol. "In the biologic sense."

"But she never knew *me.*"

That was true enough, Worrol thought. Why did Kuy die moments after her younger split free, and sat up groping with membrane-bound hands? It wasn't just the burns. There was the responsibility . . . and the colossal shame of having a younger without being tribed.

Conversely, being a foster older *was* honorable, thought Worrol. And soon after Dai-iv's birthing, the old Marchioness-Magistrate had declared Worrol a legal older, and the future Dowager Older of the Great and Mighty Prelate-Marchioness, Dai-iv. Worrol smiled. The certificate of her legal olderhood was on the wall. So no more sending proposals to tribe houses. No more agonizing during each choosing year. The void had been filled. She was the ultimate parent.

But, after tonight, Dai-iv would be gone and the void would fill with loneliness again. Unless . . . .

Worrol heard the palace buggy clatter out of the yard and grow faint. Dai-iv was going to her destiny. Worrol sniffed back an oily tear, and clasped her certificate of Legal Olderhood. *Blessings on Kuy,* thought Worrol. Now it was *her* turn. She propped the certificate on a table next to the bathtub, and turned the faucet. Cold water . . . very cold . . . that was it . . . fill the tub. And soon the crystal hunk from old Joorluk's ice locker was floating . . . and she stepped in.

Seventeen Short Essays on the Relationship Between Art and Science

by
Michael C. Berch

About the Author

Michael C. Berch is 34, lives in Pleasanton, California, where he is manager of computing at a software firm, and has a law degree from Golden Gate University of Law in San Francisco. Over the years he has worked as a dishwasher, radio talk-show host, lawyer, computer programmer, consultant on military R&D programs, and a magazine columnist, among others. He is also a member of a small, elite group of writers who meet in Pleasanton, of whom no fewer than three are previous WOTF winners—Lori Ann White, Dan'l Danehy-Oakes and Gary Shockley—and several have had novels published. Up to now, he has always had to put the word "amateur" in front of "science fiction writer" in his resume. No more; "Seventeen Short Essays..." is fit to stand beside anybody's professional work....

About the Illustrator

Christopher C. Beau is 29, single, was born in France, in Lille, near the Belgian border, and is currently working on large black-and-white drawings, watercolors and sculpture in Montvale, New Jersey.

Like many artists, he enjoys seeing and doing new things. Christopher travels and settles in different venues. He loves to draw futuristic architecture and landscapes, but, as you can see from the illustration for this story, can do very well with people when he has to. All in all, Christopher Beau is both a will o' the wisp and rock solid, a winning combination.

1.

Subject K-2335, white female, age 27, interviewed at Copper Mountain Arts Festival. Subject is accomplished ceramics artisan, specializing in stylized urns similar to traditional Japanese *raku* pottery, fired in bright primary colors.

Q. [excerpted] I see that much of your pottery has a number of traditional, curved elements, combined with more modern, rectilinear designs, often superimposed on the curved elements. . . .

A. That's always been a theme of mine. [Laughs.] I suppose there's a reason of sorts. I was a math major—I have a degree in it, actually, but after college I needed some time off and went to study pottery in Japan for a few years. I guess the themes keep coming back, don't they? [. . .] That one you have is one of my favorites. [Touches urn.] Can you see the swirl on the neck? It's a Fibonacci series, really. Look at the lines, and count the dots. [. . .]

Subject K-2335 is well-liked by colleagues; occasionally speaks at Copper Mountain Art Guild meetings, mostly about litter and smoking at the annual festivals. Divorced, no children. Lives alone in flat above studio. Recommended for procurement and admission to the program.

Illustrated by Christopher C. Beau

2.

A tribe called the Chirima, a small offshoot of the Oña people of the South American pampas, practiced a curious custom: no person was permitted to create any work of art. All fixed images and artifacts were forbidden, both symbolic and representational. Minor transgressions and those by children were tolerated, but adults who persisted in acts of creation were beaten and their works destroyed; ultimately, they would be cast out from the tribe or burned alive.

After many generations, compliance was essentially universal; no one but the sick and insane ever created any work of art among the Chirima.

3.

I sat in the darkened laboratory, realizing that the pale glow of my workstation screen was the only light in the west wing. It was nearly midnight, and for these last hours I had been lost in the records of our experiments, comparing, contrasting, analyzing, looking for trends. And when not doing that, worrying about the more mundane aspects of the project: staffing, equipment. Even funding. We are isolated here, perforce, and I often fear that our existence is so invisible, so black, so purposefully obscured, that one day we will just slip away into nothingness. But the greatest threats to the project, I think, come not from those who are ignorant of our purpose, but from those who are aware of it.

The workstation is a fascinating tool. I replayed parts of interviews, looked through pictures of the subjects, reviewed their portfolios and exhibitions, manipulated digitized images of their work. At times like this the work seemed almost easy, almost laughably enjoyable. Time flies. I could spend hours with a single subject.

I looked out the window at the east wing. They were all asleep over there, of course. It cannot be as easy for them as it is for us, but there was no pleasure in that thought. Perhaps the act of creation was its own reward, and those of us who are unable to create must seek other goals, endlessly.

After these late sessions I was often unable to sleep, and I lay awake in the dormitory, staring at the tree that moves back and forth across the uncurtained window. There were plenty of books in the dormitory, and a well-stocked refectory, and even companions available to us. But I preferred to watch the tree, and remain alone with my thoughts, until the darkness came.

4.

Subject J-908, male, age 45, acrylic/acrylic-polymer painter. Interviewed at one-man exhibition, Bruijnes Gallery.

Q. [excerpted] . . . in your earlier work. But in these paintings we see a more realistic bent, as if you were somehow dissatisfied with the impressionism that you and others were involved in, back in the last decade . . .?

A. It's not that simple, really. [Smiles.] The style of representation is more conventionally realistic, yes. But the images themselves are, if anything, from a deeper part of my personal image space. If you look carefully, some of the objects—both the objects and people, really—have characteristics that render them impossible in real space—you know, consensual reality. [Pauses, looks at painting (J-908/24.1).] So in a sense they are more realistic, but much, much less real.

Q. But they are real to you, so who is to say—

A. Yes, they are real to me. But for others they exist only in the painting. You can't go out and get this person and bring him to the gallery, as if I was, say, painting a portrait from a model. He has an existence in the painting but his real existence is up here. [Points to own forehead.]

5.

After taking power in 1975, the Khmer Rouge government of Cambodia evacuated the cities and began a systematic campaign of forced labor and executions aimed at the intellectual population of the country. By the time the reign of terror ended nearly a million people had been killed. Teachers, scholars (in fact, anyone who could read and write) were the best-known targets, but the Khmer Rouge treated authors and artists with special brutality.

In the town of Lom Phat, near the Vietnam border, lived a craftsman who made modern versions of traditional Kampuchean stone figures. The Khmer Rouge destroyed his house and workshop and smashed his collection of figures. When he was discovered hiding in a nearby village he was bound and blindfolded and brought before the people of Lom Phat. His arms were hacked off at the elbows and he was left to bleed to death in the town's central square.

6.

After comprehensive physical and psychological examination subject K-2335 was assigned to the Analysis Section. Following a terminal interview subject was stunned and the analysands were transferred to the forensic laboratory. Initial observation revealed no latent defects or abnormalities. Organ tissue appeared grossly normal, with minor exceptions [omitted]. Brain mass was 1.26 kg. Section of the right temporal lobe revealed a number of small lesions, apparently congenital, in the somatic sensory cortex, and supraformation of the cortical mass near Area TE. Further section indicated mild sclerosis of the corpus callosum. Standard micro-MRI and PETT imaging series were performed. Frozen samples of all anomalous areas were retained and cataloged.

7.

Where is the seat of creativity? Koestler wrote that at the heart of the act of creation was a process called *bisociation,* where two planes of thought intersected and a tiny spark was ignited, creating a new pathway where none had existed before. Where was this region of intersection? What neurotransmitters traversed these channels, fitting their unique keys to unique receptors?

When we speak of art and literature, we speak of *vision.* But vision is not sight; some of the greatest artists and writers of history were blind. Yet the connection remains, both in metaphor and in the tissue itself. I looked up from my workstation to the numerical map made by Korbinian Brodmann, the first cartographer of the brain. His 19th-century map was crude by our standards, and differentiated only cell types, not functions. I reached up and touched the map of the right hemisphere, pausing with my finger on the right temporal lobe.

The map was inexact. And like a hand-drawn treasure map, it and its later successors often yielded false clues, but ultimately might point us in the right direction.

8.

Last evening was a rare entertainment, a dinner at the home of the military governor of the region. Nominally it was to present the director-general of the laboratory with a minor award commemorating his years of tenure, but behind this, I think, was the idea of getting some of us away from the shop and into a social setting. I had even been provided with someone to escort, a pleasant young woman named Delia who was introduced as the daughter of one of the governor's associates.

The governor himself was an affable host. His face grew red after only a glass or two of wine, lending a sort of forced jollity to the proceedings. I knew his type well. Before the New Era he would have been a wealthy dentist, or a regional sales manager, perhaps of farm machinery or sportswear, or something equally wholesome and Midwestern.

Dinner was splendid, served by the governor's quiet and efficient household staff. Afterwards, Delia took me aside, and we stepped out onto a balcony to catch the evening breeze. We made small talk for a few minutes, which turned to the subject of my work at the laboratory.

"So, are you in the section that cuts up brains?" she asked brightly.

I coughed involuntarily, then caught myself and smiled. Dissimulation came easily to my tongue. "I see you are acquainted with the usual stories. . . ."

"Come on, you don't think people don't *know* about that, do you? Who do you think cooks and cleans for you? Or changes lightbulbs?" She moved closer to me and her voice dropped to a conspiratorial whisper. "There was a girl in my sociology class . . . she even had *pictures*. East wing, both levels." She stepped back, regarding me. "No, I don't think you cut up brains, do you? You seem more analytical, the way you spoke at dinner about the economic crisis. You work with the results, I think. The lab reports and the tissue analyses."

I paused. "Actually not. I . . . manage the case studies, as a matter of fact."

She touched my hand, as if getting me to admit this was a victory of sorts, and smiled, nodding approvingly. And then abruptly she turned away and reached for the knob of the French doors. "Shall we join the others?"

9.

In Monrovia, California, in the early 1980s, police arrested a man for making telephoned threats to a television actress. At first he was thought to be merely an obsessed fan, but a search of his house revealed systematic plans for attacks on no less than thirty actors and actresses, the curators of several local museums, and the conductor of a major orchestra. Subsequently he was linked to the theft and presumed destruction of two valuable paintings and the vandalism of a sculpture on display in the lobby of a Los Angeles office complex.

He was committed to an institution and never stood trial.

10.

Subject J-908 was issued acrylic painting supplies and encouraged to paint. Paintings finished after Day 6 and Day 13 are congruent with subject's normal style and technique. By Day 17 the paintings showed chromatic abnormalities, possibly due to poor lighting. On Day 27 subject finished a painting containing no human figures, a complete departure from his previous thematic approach. Adjustments to the subject's environmental conditions and diet produced varying results in the subject's paintings (see summary [omitted]).

On Day 35 surgery was performed. Using the modified Rozanski technique, a laser microtome was used to destroy the cells of the locus coeruleus in the high brainstem. The surgery was successful, effectively preventing the onset of REM sleep. Subject began painting again on Day 41 and returned to the depiction of human figures, which became decreasingly representative and took on violent and threatening poses.

Subsequent micro-MRI and supporting imagery showed time-linear degeneration of Area TE following the surgery.

A second surgery was performed on Day 46. Modification of the lateral geniculate body and other parts of the thalamic nucleus was attempted but proved unsuccessful;

collateral damage to the thalamus, hypothalamus, and limbic area caused an irreversible loss of brain function.

Further investigations will be performed by the Analysis Section.

11.

Yesterday we received good news from the first floor. Apparently Gill's team in the Visual Area Working Group has made a breakthrough of sorts: a quantitative mapping of chemical reactions in Area TE, proving that like the sensory cortices, it has a columnar structure. This question had puzzled us for years. Gill's computer models match exactly the observed behavior. Next we can expect a predictive model of chemical processes during creative activities. I have selected subjects M-1401 and L-640 for participation in this study.

I feel we are close, very close. These are the times we sequester ourselves in the labs, eating at our workstations, and sleeping—if at all—on cots and in chairs. The east wing staff is on 24-hour alert, waiting for special requests. The complete map is unfolding itself, at a level never before seen or known.

And at the same time the search has become a race. Our work has only been possible during this small window of time, when the political goals of the New Era and the scientific goals of our project are allies. Uneasy allies, perhaps, but allies. I fear the window has begun to close. The "economic crisis" that we discussed at the governor's dinner threatens to turn into open revolt. Military aircraft have crossed the skies overhead. If we are to complete the project we must not delay.

12.

Subjects M-1401 and L-640 were prepared for electrical

studies. M-1401, a 41-year-old male poet and playwright, was given a standard series of visual and auditory stimuli. Electrical response, by area, was captured in a compressed spectral array. The CSA images were then time-correlated with PETT-based chemical studies based on the same stimuli. Results were inconclusive.

Subject L-640, female, age 36, a violinist, was given direct stimulation by electrode. The interpretive cortex and fissure of Silvius was located and stimulated. The subject began a stream-of-consciousness narrative describing numerous auditory and sensory events. Stimulation of a particular locus of neurons repeatably produced the report of a "midbass note, as if from a cello or baritone saxophone." When subject was asked to compose a short tonal sequence around the note, micro-MRI images showed increased glucose consumption in Area TE, the hippocampus, and the primary visual cortex.

13.

The moment is finally at hand. The burst of creativity was the key. I watched the tagged-cell image on Gill's workstation; the real-time scan on the left, the predictive model on the right. The tiny spots of yellow grew and bloomed on the screen: glucose consumption. Neural activity. I ran the images backward and forward, time and again. It was unmistakable. The hypothesis of a circuit from Area TE to the primary visual cortex was proven, solving a mystery extant since the middle of the last century. We were watching the act of creation; the root of art, music, and culture; the unique combination of memory, sense, movement, and vision. Artistic vision.

All that was left was the quantitative nitty-gritty, and the entire creative process would be rendered controllable, through chemical or electronic mediation of Area TE. The ultimate power and weapon of the state.

Kramer and Gill opened a bottle of champagne, and we drank it, curiously silent. I did not sleep that night.

14.

By noon of the next day the Synthesis Working Group had made up a crude but effective set of chemical agents that spanned the spectrum of control. The group borrowed heavily from the tissue stocks of Analysis Section; there was no time to wait for new supplies. Two of the remaining subjects were selected for testing; two were kept as a control group. The east wing is growing empty; there has been no subject procurement for several weeks because of the political situation, and the Procurement Section has apparently been disbanded.

It cannot be long now.

The electricity failed in the afternoon. The generators are still working, but they cannot power both the laboratories and the computer network. My workstation is dark. No one knows when the power situation will be stable again; there are rumors of fighting to the north and west. I have made notes on the entire work of the last five days, transcribed them on a battery-powered voicewriter, and placed copies in my office safe and in the materials vault. No matter what else happens, the knowledge will be preserved, and the sacrifices that we—and our subjects—have made will not have been in vain.

15.

The helicopters arrived just before dawn. I was taken to the director-general's office by a young soldier, and found the rest of them there: Gill, Kramer, Rysocki, Behrens. The two other section chiefs had fled during the night. The director-general stood in the corner, facing the window; in his place sat a lanky black man in battle dress. He handed me a card: *Major A. P. Clayton, 5th Airborne Division, Reunification Forces.* He indicated a chair, and I nodded and sat down.

It had been all over on the East Coast since the previous day. The military governor of the South Atlantic region had gone over, and the Reunification faction executed a bloodless coup. The Secretariat and Chamber of Deputies were under arrest.

The New Era was over, replaced by the Newer Era.

I could see out the window to the courtyard of the east wing. An airborne platoon guarded the gates. A few subjects milled around in the courtyard, some talking to soldiers, some sitting motionlessly on the low brick wall. I wanted to talk to them, to reassure them, to explain that the bonds between us and them were greater than those between them and their intercessors. I must have made a motion toward the door, because the soldier to my right abruptly unlocked the safety on his rifle. I settled back in my seat.

"What now?" the director-general asked.

"We wait," said Major Clayton.

16.

The flip side of the coin, of course, was that the spectrum of agents that controlled and channelled the creative process could be recast, with little effort, into agents that would cause the process to grow and multiply without bounds. If Area TE dominated the brains of an entire generation, what would be the result?

17.

We were among the last to leave the laboratory complex. The two section chiefs who had deserted had been rounded up, and along with the director-general were taken to the courtyard of the west wing and shot. I saw the bodies from one of the two remaining parked helicopters, and shortly thereafter, we took off, leaving only a squad of soldiers with the last helicopter. Everyone else had gone. At that moment I was seized with an uncontrollable fear, not for my life, which was forfeit in any case, but that our work would forever be lost. I protested this to one of the officers in the helicopter, but he laughed and pulled out something from his day pack.

"Put it on," he said.

It was a subject bracelet from the unused stock in the east wing storeroom, number T-4386.

"Go on, put it on."

I placed it around my wrist and snapped off the tabs. The officer nodded and smiled. As we banked over the perimeter of the complex I saw the last few soldiers setting fire to the west wing before running to their helicopter.

Search for Research

by
L. Ron Hubbard

About the Author

L. Ron Hubbard was an outstanding science fiction and fantasy writer, publishing literally hundreds of titles, long and short, in the years between 1938 and 1950—with time out for World War II—and coming back, in 1980, to publish eleven book-length best sellers, including the magnum opus *Mission Earth dekalogy (for which the word had to be coined; no one had ever written a ten-volume novel before). But the fact of the matter is, although he loved fantasy and science fiction above all other forms of fiction, SF was only a part of his production. Between 1934 and 1950, he sold at least fifteen million words of fiction. That's a million words, give or take, a year; more, when you consider that he did not write at all for five years in World War II.*

This production is almost unbelievable. It's also true. He sold across the board, every kind of fiction, from westerns and South Sea adventure to murder mysteries and aviation, and beyond. And, incidentally, at the same time he pursued real-life expeditions into the world's frontiers. He really was, in every way, a complete human being . . . a thinker and a doer.

Among the things he did—and he certainly did not need to do it, or gain any fame he did not already have—was to produce a series of articles on writing, for various magazines of the 1930s and '40s. We have reprinted some of these in previous volumes of L. Ron Hubbard Presents Writers of The Future. *We use them all, too, as instructional media in the WOTF workshops we hold each year for our winning writers. The reason we do so is that the advice is as uniquely sound today as it was then. Markets have changed; storytelling has not. And so, without further ado, we bring you the latest in the series. You will find it at least fascinating. And if you have any desire to be a writer yourself, you will find it—and the previous pieces—invaluable.*

All of us want to sell more stories and write better ones. It is hard to believe that there exists a writer with soul so dead that he would not. But, from careful observation, I have come to the heartbreaking conclusion that while writers usually *want* to do this, they generally fail to try.

Writers are the laziest people on earth. And I know I'm the laziest writer. In common with the rest of the profession I am always searching for the magic lamp which will shoot my stories genie-like into full bloom without the least effort on my part.

This is pure idiocy on my part as I have long ago found this magic lamp, but not until a couple years ago did I break it out and use the brass polish to discover that it was solid gold.

This lamp was so cobwebby and careworn that I am sure most of us have not looked very long at it in spite of its extreme age and in spite of the fact that it is eternally being called to our attention.

The name of this magic lamp is RESEARCH.

Ah, do I hear a chorus of sighs? Do I hear, "Hubbard is going to spring that old gag again." "What, another article on 'research'? I thought L.R.H. knew better."

In defense I instantly protest that I am neither the discoverer nor the sole exploiter of research. But I do believe that I have found an entirely new slant upon an ancient object.

In Tacoma a few months ago, I heard a writer sighing

that he was havingahelluvatimegettingplots. This acute writing disease had eaten deeply into his sleep and bankbook. It had made him so alert that he was ruined as a conversationalist, acting, as he did, like an idea sponge. Hanging on and hoping but knowing that no ideas could possibly come his way.

As usual, I injected my thoughts into his plight—a habit which is bad and thankless.

I said, "Here's an idea. Why not go out and dig around in the old files at the library and the capitol at Olympia and find out everything you can on the subject of branding? There should be a lot of stories there."

He raised one eye and leered, "What? Do all that work for a cent and a half a word?"

?

And just to drive the idea home, I might remark that one day I happened into the New York Public Library. Crossing the file room I slammed into a heavy bulk and ricocheted back to discover I had walked straight into Norvell Page and he into me.

I gaped. "Page!"*

"Hubbard!" he whispered in awed tones.

Solemnly we shook each other by the hand.

CHORUS: Well, this is the first time I ever saw a writer in a library!

These two instances should serve to illustrate the fact that research does not rhyme with writer no matter what kind of mill** you pound.

---

* Norvell W. Page is best known to SF audiences as the author of "But Without Horns," one of the finest "superman" stories of the Golden Age in *Astounding*. Most of his production at the time LRH bumped into him, however, went to *Astounding*'s companion magazine, *The Spider*.   —The Editors

** mill: typewriter (1930's writer slang)

Research is a habit which is only acquired by sheer force of will. The easy thing to do is guess at the facts—so thinks the writer. When, as a matter of facts, the easy thing to do is go *find* the facts if you have to tear a town to pieces. ?

Witness what happened last summer.

Staring me in the face were a stack of dangerous profession stories which have since appeared in ARGOSY. At that time they were no more than started and I sighed to see them stretching forth so endlessly.

I chose TEST PILOT as the next on the list and started to plot it. I thought I knew my aviation because the Department of Commerce tells me so. Blithely, thinking this was easy, I started in upon a highly technical story without knowing the least thing about that branch of flying—never having been a test pilot.

For one week I stewed over the plot. For another week I broiled myself in the scorching heat of my self-accusation. Two weeks and nothing written.

Was I losing money fast!

There wasn't anything for it then. I had to find out something about test pilots.

Across the bay from my place in Seattle is the Boeing plant. At the Boeing plant there would be test pilots. I had to go!

And all for a cent and a half a word.

I went. Egdvedt, the Boeing president, was so startled to see a real live writer in the place that he almost talked himself hoarse.

Minshall, the chief engineer, was so astounded at my ignorance that he hauled me through the plant until I had bunions the size of onions.

I sighed.

All for a cent and a half a word!

I went home.

About that time it occurred to me that I used to write a lot for the SPORTSMAN PILOT and, as long as I had the dope and data, I might as well fix the details in my head by writing them an article.

That done, I suddenly saw a fine plot for my ARGOSY yarn and wrote that in a matter of a day and a half.

Two months went by. Arthur Lawson came in as editor of Dell and promptly remembered TEST PILOT in AR-GOSY and demanded a story along similar lines.

In two days I wrote that.

A month after that, Florence McChesney decided that she needed a twenty-thousand word flying story.

"Test pilot," says I, "do your stuff!"

Each and every one of those yarns sold first crack out. Article for the SPORTSMAN PILOT, short for ARGOSY, short for WAR BIRDS, twenty-thousand worder for FIVE NOVELS.

One day of research = several hundred bucks in stories.

This naturally made me think things over and, not being quite as foolish as editors think writers are, I added up the account book and promptly went to work. Thus, the moral is yet to come.

On the dangerous profession stories which followed, I almost lost my life and broke my neck trying to make them authentic. On each one I kept a complete list of notes and a list of plots which occurred to me at the time. There is enough writing material in that file to last me at least a year. It is the finest kind of copy because it is risky in the extreme, full of drama and high tension. I haven't any fears about mentioning this, as any writer who is crazy enough to go down in diving suits and up in spar trees deserves all the help he can get.

But research does not end there and that is not the point of this article.

A short time ago I began to search for research on the theory that if I could get a glimmering of anything lying beyond a certain horizon I could go deep enough to find an excellent story.

I stopped doing what I used to do. There was a time when I expected a story to blaze up and scorch me all of its own accord. I have found, however, that there is a premium on divine fire and it is not very bright when used by a pulpateer. This gentleman has to write an immortal story about once every three days to keep eating.

On this plan I began to read exhaustively in old technical books, ancient travel books, forgotten literature. But not with the idea of cribbing. I wanted information and nothing else. I wanted to know how the people used to think here, how the land lay there. Given one slim fact for a background, I have found it easy to take off down the channel of research and canal-boat out a cargo of stories.

In other words, I have no use for an obvious story idea as laid out in POPULAR MECHANICS or FORENSIC MEDICINE. I want one slim, forgotten fact. From there a man can go anywhere and the story is very likely to prove unusual.

In one old volume, for instance, I discovered that there was such a thing as a schoolmaster aboard Nelson's ships of the line.

That was a weird one. Why should Nelson want a schoolmaster?

Answer: Midshipmen.

When did this occur?

Answer: The Napoleonic Wars.

Ah, now we'll find out how those old ships looked. We'll discover how they fought, what they did.

And there was the schoolmaster during battle. Where? In the "cockpit" helping hack off arms and legs.

Next lead indicated: Surgery during the Napoleonic Wars.

Wild guess in another allied field: Gunnery.

Again: Nelson.

A battle: On the Nile.

A ship or something strange about this battle: *L'Orient*, monster French flagship which mysteriously caught fire and blew up, throwing the weight of guns to Nelson.

Incidental discovery: "The Boy Who Stood on the Burning Deck" was written about the son of *L'Orient*'s skipper.

Back to midshipmen, the King's Letter Boys: They were hell on wheels, arrogant, ghastly urchins being trained as officers.

And with all this under my mental belt I girded up my mental loins. Complete after a few days of search I had MR. TIDWELL—GUNNER, which appeared in ADVENTURE.

All that because I chanced to find there was a schoolmaster aboard Nelson's ships of the line.

This is now happening right along because I haven't let the idea slide as my laziness dictated I should.

The final *coup d'etat* arrived last winter.

Boredom had settled heavily upon me and I sat one evening staring vacantly at a shelf of books. They were most monotonous. Whole sets stretched out along the shelves with very little change in color or size. This annoyed me and I bent forward and took one out just to relieve the regularity.

It proved to be Washingon Irving's ASTORIA, his famous epic of the fur trading days.

It had never been brought home to me that Irving had written such a book and to find out why, I promptly started to read it. The result was, of course, a fur trading story. But the method of arriving at this story was so indirect that it merits a glance.

Irving only served to call to my attention that I was out in the fur trading Northwest and that I had certainly better take advantage of the history of the place.

I roved around, found very little because I had no direct starting point. I went to the Encyclopaedia Brittanica to discover a bibliography of such source books and started out again to ferret them out.

All these books were contemporary with fur trading days, all of them written, of course, by white men. But everywhere I kept tripping across the phrases, "The Warlike Blackfeet." "The Bloodthirsty Blackfeet."

This finally penetrated my thick skull. I did not like it because I thought I knew something about the Blackfeet.

Were they as bad as they were represented?

Into the records. The real records. Into Alexander Henry's Journal. Into this and out of that until I had a stack of material higher than my desk.

And then I capped the climax by locating a young chap in Seattle who happens to be a blood brother of the Blackfeet. Lewis and Clark's Journal contained about five pages concerning the circumstances which surrounded the killing of a Blackfoot brave by Lewis.

The way this suddenly shot down the groove is remarkable to remember. The Hudson's Bay Company, the Nor'-Westers, the Blackfeet, John Jacob Astor. . . . The story pieces dovetailed with a click.

Coupled with years of experience in the Northwest, these hundred sources jibed to make the story.

The result was BUCKSKIN BRIGADES, a novel being put out this summer by Macaulay.

BUCKSKIN BRIGADES came to life because I happened to be bored enough one evening to sit and stare at a line of books on a shelf.

This account of researching is not complete unless I mention a certain dogging phobia I have and which I suspect is deeply rooted in most of us.

H. Bedford Jones mentioned it long ago and I did not believe him at the time. But after rolling stacks of it into the mags, I know that B-J was right as a check.

He said that it was hard for a person to write about the things he knew best.

This gives rise to an ancient argument which says pro and con that a writer should write about the things he knows.

Witnesseth. I was born and raised in the West and yet it was not until last year that I sold a couple westerns. And I only sold those because somebody said I couldn't.

Know ye: The Caribbean countries know me as El Colorado and yet the only Caribbean stories I can write are about those countries which I have touched so briefly that I have only the vaguest knowledge of them, and am therefore forced to depend upon researching the books and maps for my facts.

Hear ye: I wrote fine Hollywood stories until I came down here and worked in pictures. I wrote one while here and the editor slammed it back as a total loss.

There are only a few exceptions to this. I have been able to cash in heavily upon my knowledge of North China because the place appealed to me as the last word in savage, romantic lore. The last exception seems to be flying stories, though after flying a ship I can't write an aviation story for a month.

The final proof of this assertion came in connection with my Marine Corps stories. Most of my life I have been associated with the Corps one way or another in various parts of the world and I should know something about it.

But I have given up in dark despair.

HE WALKED TO WAR in ADVENTURE was branded as technically imperfect.

DON'T RUSH ME in ARGOSY, another Marine story, elicited anguished howls of protest.

And yet if there is any story in the world I should be qualified to write, it is a Marine story.

These are my woes. The reason for them is probably very plain to everyone. But I'll state my answer anyway.

A man cannot write a story unless he is deeply interested in it. If he thinks he knows a subject then he instantly becomes careless with his technical details.

The only way I have found it possible to sidetrack these woes is by delving into new fields constantly, looking everywhere for one small fact which will lead me on into a story field I think I'll like.

This is not very good for a writer's reputation, they tell me. A writer, it is claimed, must specialize to become outstanding. I labored trying to build up a converse reputation, hoping to be known as a writer of infinite versatility.

I did not know until two years ago that the specializing writer is persona non grata with an editor. Jack Byrne, for instance, rebuilt ARGOSY with variety as a foundation. And once I heard Bloomfield* sigh that he wished some of his top-notchers would stop sending him the same background week in and week out.

Maybe I am right, possibly I am wrong.

But I believe that the only way I can keep improving my work and my markets is by broadening my sphere of acquaintanceship with the world and its people and professions.

---

* Howard Bloomfield, editor of ''Adventure'' magazine

Relay
by
Michelle L. Levigne

About the Author

Michelle Levigne is 29, single, and has a bachelor's degree in English/theater from Northwestern College in Iowa. She also has a master's in communication, majoring in film and writing, from Regent University in Virginia.

"Relay," her story here, is the culmination of an effort that started some time ago—this is her twelfth submission to the Contest. She did quite well, winning Quarter Finalist and Semifinalist status a number of times; with this twelfth try, she hit First Place in her Quarter, meaning she is one of four persons in this book eligible to win the L. Ron Hubbard Gold Award for the 1990 year. That's an additional trophy, lots of extra publicity, and $4,000 more. It's only one chance in four—Valerie Freireich, James C. Glass and Barry Reynolds are the other contenders—but each of them has already beaten much longer odds in order to have reached that point.

About the Illustrator

Rob Alexander is originally from Southern Ontario, and spent half his life there before relocating to Cochrane, Alberta, although recently he has taken up residence in Seattle, Washington. He is 24, married, and has been exhibiting at conventions and doing paste-up and lettering since graduating from high school. In 1987 he began studying commercial *illustration in Calgary, and has recently completed his studies in Seattle. He hopes to land some book cover commissions, and eventually to pursue a parallel career in fine art, painting for gallery exhibition. He has previously won an Honorable Mention in* L. Ron Hubbard's Illustrators of The Future Contest.

Jason started it.

He sat in Millie's Diner, trying to spoon up the chili special while leaving the grease slick behind. The couple and child entered while he considered sacrificing his bread as a sponge. He decided against it—he hadn't had soft, semifresh bread in nearly three months—and turned to look at the newcomers. There was nothing else to do besides eat.

There had been a tingling in the air for the last hour or so. He thought it came from his usual uneasiness among crowds. More than five people, enclosed in a stifling, small room full of too many odors to catalog, equaled a crowd. When the sensation first began, he had thought his friends were approaching without warning.

The entrance of the three changed all that. The sensation came from them. Jason played with his food and tried to look nonchalant as he studied the newcomers with one sweeping glance.

They did not all belong together. The man and woman did. They had the same hungry, angry eyes, the same faded, inconspicuous look to their clothes. The man shuffled but the woman stalked. She was the stronger, the leader. The dull brown of her hair had a spark of fire left in it. The man's color had turned to ashes a long time before.

The little girl looked hungry, too. Scared hunger. Terrified, but tamed by a weary numbness. She was maybe eight years old. The woman dragged her along behind by a death grip at her elbow.

Jason turned back to his cooling food, cataloging all he had seen in that brief glance. Golden-red curls, blue eyes like a delft tea cup. Clothes that looked expensive under the dirt. The child drew him.

After one glance, Jason knew the sensation came from her. She was in trouble. He knew he had to do something. The problem was—what?

He waited, thinking, until Millie took glasses of water over to the table where the three newcomers had taken up residence. The little girl picked her glass up in both hands. She drank like she had been empty and dry for days. Jason smiled at the picture she made, even as his anger warmed and his resolve hardened. He gulped the last few spoons of chili, ignoring the grease. He stuffed the bread in his pocket as he signaled Millie that he wanted to pay. As he got up and left, he heard the girl ask to go to the bathroom.

When the woman left the child in the single-stall bathroom, he was ready, waiting outside.

Jason ran his fingers around the frame of the window, eyes closed. He felt the spots of rust, the place where caulking had crumbled away, the stiffness of the hinges. He waited until the girl had flushed before he opened the window. It held up, stiff on silent hinges. He heaved himself up onto the sill until he hung over it at his hips. She stood uncertain, unwilling to move and lost in front of the door. She stared up at him.

"They aren't your parents, are they?" he asked with neutral face and voice. The child shook her head. "Do you want me to take you home?"

She smiled. Tears touched her eyes, making the blue glow in the dim light. Jason knew his suspicions were right.

"What's your name? I'm Jason," he offered when she hesitated.

"Kelly," she whispered.

"Well, Kelly, let me teach you what Peter Pan felt like. Let's fly out of here."

Jason held out his hands as far as his arms would stretch. Kelly stood on her tiptoes, reaching up. Nearly four inches of air lay between their fingertips. Jason wiggled in the narrow window, trying to get further inside the building. He reached the balance point and could go no further. Another inch and he would overbalance and fall inside. It was his head to be found inside the women's bathroom in a redneck place like Millie's.

"Can you stretch any further?" His voice reflected the pressure on his insides. Kelly shook her head. "Okay, here's what we're going to do. Pretend you really can fly."

"But—"

"Kelly, you can do anything you really want to. Reach up for my hands and tell yourself you can fly." Jason closed his eyes and concentrated. He tried to forget the headache he was going to have in the morning.

The air tingled around his fingers, like bumblebee wings brushing the skin. He fought not to jerk his hands away. Eyes still closed, he visualized Kelly's fingers coming into his reach. In a moment their hands touched.

Thirty seconds later, the woman came in. Her eyes blazed and a rebuke hovered on her lips. The window was securely closed, the bathroom empty.

"Why can't we fly?" Kelly struggled to keep up with Jason's long strides. She tripped over a stick and caught at his hand to keep from falling. The night shadows flickered and leaped all around them.

"I told you, that's only for special occasions." He adjusted the strap of his backpack and slowed so she could keep up. Normally, he would have picked her up, but the effort of getting her out of the bathroom had strained him. He wanted to be sure he had the strength to walk all night if they had to.

Around them, the back country road echoed with the hum of insects and the songs of frogs. Jason caught the occasional rushing sigh of wings. Bats—but he wasn't about to mention that to Kelly. His sisters were squeamish like that, he remembered.

Then silence rang around them. Jason paused, stunned for a heartbeat. He heard the loud crunch of wheels on gravel, then the rattle of an old truck engine.

"Come on, Kelly," he whispered and caught her up around the waist. He tried to hold her with one arm, ready to clamp a hand over her mouth if necessary, but she made no sound.

The trees stood too far from the road. He stumbled in a hole. Kelly gasped, the air forced out of her by his tightening grip. She stayed quiet.

Headlights hit them as he freed his foot. Kelly stared straight into the light but Jason averted his eyes. He knew the trap if he let himself look.

"There she is!" The woman from the diner leaped out of the truck.

"Hold it!" A gunshot shattered the unnatural quiet. "This here's the sheriff. Why don't you put down Jenny Mae nice and easy, and we'll get this all straightened out?"

The false joviality of the man's voice made Jason sick. He had heard that tone too many times before. He made a half-turn, enough to fool the sheriff into thinking he surrendered. Out of the corner of his eye, he saw the triumph on the woman's face. The sheriff lowered his gun.

"We're not here," Jason whispered and flung himself into the cool, thick darkness beyond the light and into the trees.

He ran, silent and quick, hugging Kelly hard against his

chest, feeling the backpack thump against his spine. It kept rhythm with his thoughts.

//Not here. Not here. No sound. No light. Not here. Not here.//

The sound of his voice in his mind stretched and twisted and reverberated. Jason grinned and felt the warped air beat against his face. He wondered how Kelly was reacting to all this, then turned his thoughts back to not being where he had been. Any other thought just did not matter.

When his lungs burned and he felt the sting of twigs and leaves against his face, he slowed. Sound came back, the shuffle of his footsteps in the leaves, the rattle of his heart against his ribs. Light returned with the stars—just the stars. The moon hung a handspan lower in the sky. He slowed a little more and the damp, brown and green taste of the air returned.

"That tickled," Kelly said. She tightened her arms around his neck. How she got into that position, he could not remember. "Can we do that again?"

"Do what again?" He felt drained, too exhausted to check the safety of their new surroundings.

"Make the pretty lights."

"Pretty lights." Jason groaned, part exhaustion, part frustration. He found a tree and stopped with his back against it. A lifetime of near misses played through his mind as he sank to the ground, using the trunk as a support. "It's just not fair, you know?"

"What is?" She slid to her knees, the leaves crunching softly underneath her.

"You'll find out. Pretty lights, huh? Only a few of us ever . . . . You're not old enough! Never mind, Kelly. I'm not a teacher, but I'll try to call one. I'm going to get a little rest, if you'll keep watch for a while?" He waited until the little girl nodded, then closed his eyes. He did not rest right

Illustrated by Rob Alexander

away. As he concentrated, trying to relax the strained ache
in his body, he sank into star-shot oblivion.

//It's just not fair,// he mused as his consciousness
floated and bobbed. //It took me years to get stars even once
in a while. She gets colors without even trying.//

Kelly heard the motorcycle. She thought it funny that
the birds, frogs and crickets didn't get frightened quiet, like
they had with the truck the night before. Jason looked glad
now and that made it all right.

"You all done?" He crumpled the leaf cup on the
ground between them, and stood up.

Kelly nodded. Jason had found more than enough food
for them. She had put a few of the nuts and withered apples
in her pocket for later. Claire and Charlie, the people who
took her off the school playground, never fed her enough.
She had learned to save part of each meal for later because
sometimes there was no later.

"Now, that lady coming is Rhea Jones. She's going to
take you from here," Jason said. "The sheriff saw me and
I'm on foot, so I'm not much help anymore, understand?"

"Will Charlie hurt you?" she whispered. Charlie had
threatened to hurt her and her family, many times.

"Can't hurt me if he can't catch me." He knelt so they
were face to face. "And nobody's going to look twice at a
worthless vagrant all by himself. It's pretty little girls who
get noticed." He tweaked her nose, making her laugh.

The motorcycle grew closer and louder. It slid through
an opening in the trees and the engine died. The rider
wore a blue pea coat and scuffed black helmet. A backpack
and sleeping bag were tied to the back bar. Long, glossy
brown hair fell past her shoulders when the rider took her
helmet off. Green-gray eyes studied the two of them from
a solemn, unreadable face. Then she smiled and Kelly was
glad she would be with this woman. She knew she would

miss Jason—he felt like home, somehow—but Rhea felt like someone she had known for a long time.

"Well, Jason?" Rhea swung off the seat of her bike and let it rest against a tree. She winked at Kelly, drawing a giggle from her.

"Well, what?" He winced at the ache at the back of his neck.

"Oooh. Defensive. You strained yourself last night, didn't you?"

"Maybe." Jason shrugged, a lopsided grin twisting his lips. "I *did* call you after I did a skip run."

"Getting stronger, cousin."

"He's not your cousin," Kelly blurted.

"Oh? And how do you know?" Rhea stepped up to the child and knelt in front of her.

"I can just tell." Kelly backed up—or tried to. She felt like she had when she touched the ripped electric cord. A strange hot and cold tingling, not the ticklish way she felt last night.

For a moment Rhea's eyes were large enough to swallow the whole world. Kelly fought not to fall into them. There was a pinging noise inside her head and a smell like hot lemons and hairs caught inside the blow dryer. Then everything fell back into place. Rhea stood up.

"I see where the urgency came from," the woman said. "You did right."

"Then she *is* one of us." A brilliant, relieved smile covered Jason's face for a moment. "But, Re, she's too young."

"Maybe the trauma of being kidnapped brought it out. Like the plane crash when they found me. I was only three."

"Yeah, but . . . ." He shook his head and looked away. Kelly thought he fought tears.

"But what?" Rhea's voice grew gentle, no more calm assurance or bitter amusement. "Jason, we're all equals. The only difference is in how much we've learned and how strong we each are."

"But you're special. You're the first one," he blurted. To Kelly's delight, he blushed.

"I'm the first one who didn't voluntarily go insane, you mean." Rhea put her hands on his shoulders. Jason had to look her in the eye. "You still worry because you grow slowly? Don't. The ones who grow fastest are the ones who fall the soonest. Would you have helped Kelly if you weren't one of us?"

"Yes!" He looked almost angry.

"Then what's the difference? Are you nothing without the gift?" Before he could answer, she turned her back on him and walked back over to Kelly. "We have a long ride before you get home. I'm going to teach you some games. It's all right to tell your parents what, but remember, these are only games. Just a story."

"Like what Jason did with the pretty lights?" Kelly asked.

"Lights?" She turned back to Jason. "Cousin, your luck is amazing." She laughed, a warm, bubbling sound that caught up Kelly and finally Jason, and carried them all away.

"We call ourselves cousins, even if we don't look anything alike. We're family because inside we're the same." Rhea rested her chin on Kelly's head, prompting another giggle from the girl. "Understand?" She raised her voice to be heard over the engine.

"And it's part of the game?"

"A very big game. When you're older, read the book *Kim*, by Rudyard Kipling, and you'll understand. Are you warm enough?" She had buttoned Kelly inside her jacket, on the seat in front of her.

"Uh huh. But I think I have to go to the bathroom."
Kelly tensed, remembering how Claire yelled whenever she
needed the bathroom.

"Can you hold it a little longer? We're getting off the
highway in two more miles."

"I can." Kelly dug her fingers into her palms,
determined to do just that—and longer, if she had to.

Rhea was nice. She gave Kelly apples and beef jerky
and kept her warm. She stopped for juice before the girl
knew she was thirsty. Jason had been fun, like playing mud
football with her big brothers. Rhea was like the hot shower
and clean nightgown and chocolate after the game was over.

"Uh oh," Rhea whispered. "Kelly, lean back against
me a little more, will you?"

"Why?" The girl obeyed as she spoke. From the warm
safety of Rhea's coat, she tried to look around the lonely,
wide road they traveled.

Scrub grass and dirt filled the landscape on either side
of the highway lanes, separated by a swale of gravel and
mud. Sunset cast bloody, glaring lances of light across the
pavement. Kelly did not like the open feeling of the highway. She shivered inside Rhea's coat and tried to figure out
what worried her new friend.

A flicker of movement in the rearview mirror caught
Kelly's attention. She looked harder, sitting up until the
tightness of Rhea's coat caught around her throat. A dirty
blue blur resolved into a rusted Chevy sedan with Georgia
plates. The motorcycle was on a Mississippi highway, heading for California.

"It's them, isn't it?"

"Probably." Rhea nearly sounded cheerful. She let go
of the handlebar and wrapped an arm around the girl for a
brief hug. "Don't worry about it. I know a few tricks."

"Can you jump things?" Kelly thought of the stunt
shows her brothers liked. She usually covered her eyes when

the motorcycles went over cars or through hoops of fire.

"Probably." The woman chuckled. "Here's our exit. Sorry, but I think we should keep going for a while and back-track. Can you hold it a while longer?"

"I think so." Kelly clenched her fists again.

"You can do anything if you believe in it hard enough. Remember that, Kelly."

"Jason said that, too."

"Jason's smart, no matter what he thinks of himself."

They rode on for another fifteen minutes, past three more exits. Kelly fell into a pattern of counting to two hundred and then checking in the mirror. The blue car stayed right there, behind them but not close enough to see the people inside. Sunset faded into evening and a cold wind chafed their faces. Kelly wished she had a helmet. The wind blew grit into her eyes.

"Here we go," Rhea said. "Hold on—we might be doing some fancy figures in a minute."

She turned onto the off-ramp into a nest of lights and buildings. Kelly stared into the multi-colored stars and almost forgot to look for the blue car. It still followed them.

Rhea took them through the drive-thru lane of McDonald's and ordered cheeseburgers and fries for both of them. She parked the motorcycle next to the side door and unbuttoned to let Kelly out. The girl ran in to use the bathroom. When she came out, they parked in a shadowed corner of the lot. They perched on the seat and watched the traffic while they ate. Kelly could not see the blue car. Rhea could and told her where it had parked in the darkness outside the lot lights.

"It's definitely them," Rhea murmured as she wiped mustard out of the corner of her mouth. "Anybody else would have either gone in and ordered by now or else driven away. For someone who pulled off a kidnapping, they're pretty dumb."

"Daddy says only dumb people steal what doesn't belong to them," Kelly offered. She felt better with hot food in her stomach, even if Claire and Charlie waited and watched somewhere in the darkness.

"He's right. But there's a different kind of smart, that stupid people use to hurt other people." The woman chuckled. "Don't get me started talking philosophy, okay? It's been a long day and I have the feeling it's going to be an even longer night."

"What are we going to do?"

"Does Charlie have a gun?" Rhea shrugged when the girl nodded. "That's one more worry. I'm pretty good dodging bullets, but it's not something you like to do. I'm going to call for help, and then we have to lose our tail."

"Like Jason called you?"

"Well, since I don't know Newton's number, I can't use the phone booth, can I?" She gestured for Kelly to swing her legs over the seat.

"How did he call you?" the girl asked, as she leaned back against Rhea, who buttoned her into the warmth of the jacket.

"To tell the truth, none of us are really sure how it works. We just believe that people are listening and that we can make ourselves heard. And the people on the other end believe they can hear, and that somebody out there is trying to communicate with them." Rhea hugged Kelly. "If we treat it like a game, then we don't fry our brains with the paradoxes."

"When can I play?"

"You already are. Hold on, now." She started the engine and the bike roared in the settling calm of the night.

Kelly held onto the seat, reaching down through the confines of the coat. She could hardly move at all, held so tight against Rhea, but she felt better touching the seat with her hands. She closed her eyes against the rushing of the wind in her face and concentrated on getting far away from the blue car. The bike swerved and swayed underneath her and she almost opened her eyes a few times.

"That's it," Rhea said, her voice barely audible above the growling of the bike and the howling of the wind. "Keep thinking of a big distance between us and them. Think of us as invisible, Kelly."

The girl laughed at the idea. So many times, she had wanted to be invisible. Kelly squeezed her eyes tight shut and concentrated. She thought of the street stretching out behind and before them, only a few cars driving along that late at night. She thought of the bike, and the car following. She thought of a stoplight, turning red as soon as they passed underneath it.

Far behind, horns blared as the blue car ran the red light. It nearly hit a car that started into the intersection from the cross direction. Kelly barely heard it. She clenched her fists and imagined cars swerving into the street behind them, cutting off the blue car. More horns and squealing brakes splintered the night, muffled by growing distance.

"Oh, that's perfect," Rhea said, laughing. The sound vibrated up through Kelly's back, tickling and warming her.

Her head began to hurt. All her muscles started to go limp and wobbly, like melting jelly. Like the time she insisted on hiking with her big brother and his scout troop. Kelly felt the bike dissolve underneath her. She tried to pry her eyes open when multicolored stars reached up through the blackness at her.

"It's all right," Rhea said, freeing a hand so she could hug the child. "You did perfect. Just relax and sleep. We're safe now."

Kelly barely heard. The stars had smiling faces now and they wrapped around her. Light flared as she fell into a spinning hole, like a carousel racing the wind.

• • •

Rhea cradled the sleeping child against her shoulder. She brushed golden-red hair off her face when the wind picked it up like dandelion fluff. Kelly had done more than perfect, she admitted.

"It's not fair, you know," she whispered into the sleeping child's ear. "It's always the bad times that show us what we are, what we can do."

She remembered the first time she learned the power of belief. When she was ten, she grew aware of two opposing parties who watched her. There was little privacy in the orphanage and Rhea always felt the eyes of someone on her. This constant watching was different. She felt fear and strong interest. The eyes never moved on to another child. She felt them follow her to school, playground, and chores.

It only took a few weeks to grow angry enough to try to escape. She learned to duck into alleys and through hedges and wish herself invisible. Not until she walked almost on the toes of one of the men and he looked right at her without reacting, did she realize her wish had come true.

"This isn't going to happen to you," Rhea promised the child in her arms. "You have a home and a family who loves you and you don't need what you can do."

The deserted park whispered around them in the early morning breeze. Leaves brushed against each other, whispering on the verge of words. Night insects rushed to sing their last songs before dawn. Mist began rising from the pond far down the sloping field. Rhea sat down again on the picnic table in the rickety pavilion and closed her eyes. She felt the stillness, the absolute privacy. Her stomach pinched with hunger, like it always did when she believed her wishes into reality. Even with Kelly's untrained help, it had been a strain to take them out of their pursuers' sight.

"You're going to be starving, too," she said, smiling down at Kelly. "Let's hope Newton brings breakfast."

Rhea heard the gentle rumble of a truck coming down the park road. She adjusted Kelly so the child straddled her hip and she could carry her with one arm. Rhea stood up, arching her back a little against the unaccustomed burden, and stepped out to meet her friend.

The truck came all the way up to the gravel path leading to the pavilion, parking next to Rhea's motorcycle. It was a new truck, gleaming silvery-gray with a cab and lightly tinted windows. Enough to obscure the features of the passengers without breaking the law. She noted those details and smiled. Newton always knew how to plan for trouble.

"I called some friends," the man said as he stepped out of the cab. Dreadlocks swayed in the breeze. Deep bronze skin gleamed in the sunrise. Ebony eyes sparkled with delight at the challenge that awaited them. "Do you have any idea who you have there?"

"Her name is Kelly Jurgenson. Her father is a lawyer, her mother is a school librarian. She has four brothers, twenty, seventeen, sixteen and thirteen. Claire and Charlie Ehrenreich kidnapped her ten days ago." Rhea shrugged with one shoulder. By this time she and Newton had met halfway down the path. "That's all Jason and I could get from her."

"Kelly Jurgenson is the granddaughter of federal judge Tyler Rathburn." Newton grinned when Rhea gaped at him. "Make sense now?"

"Her kidnappers want to get somebody out of the gas chamber, right?"

"Close." He jerked his thumb at his truck and they started walking towards it. "Change of clothes and a cooler full of breakfast."

"Newton, you are my knight in shining armor." Rhea nodded her thanks when the man took Kelly from her arms.

"Rough night?"

"I haven't had this much fun since I first hit the road. You ought to try it some time." She stopped with her hand on the door. "They have guns."

"Never deflected bullets before." He gave her another grin, reminding her of the carny job he had when they first met. Newton had been a sleight-of-hand man before he attracted the wrong kind of attention.

"We need your help to play a game, Kelly," Rhea said, waking the child asleep on her lap in the truck. Ahead of them a roadblock slowed the traffic for two miles.

"The game you and Jason play?" The little girl came awake with sparkling eyes, eagerness in her voice.

"She's a quick one," Newton admitted. He chuckled when the child sat up with a jerk and stared at him.

"Newton's a friend," Rhea said. "He's going to play the game with us."

"What kind?" Kelly accepted the man with a grin and looked up at both of them with total trust and curiosity.

"The same kind, just different moves. Pay close attention. You're going to have to pretend to be asleep. I don't think we can do anything about your eyes." She hugged the child. "Listen and concentrate on what I say."

Forty-five minutes later, the truck reached the roadblock. Newton stopped the motor and rolled down the windows. Two officers approached and looked inside the cab. They saw a young black man in jeans, blue batik shirt and dreadlocks. His wife had coffee-and-cream skin, odd green-brown eyes and silky black braids. Their sleeping child was a little girl with kinky ebony hair. Her skin was a perfect mix of the two skin-tones. The woman watched the officers, saying nothing, eyes sparkling with some private joke.

After checking the family and looking at the back of the truck, loaded with camping equipment, the officers let them through the roadblock. They went back to work inspecting cars, making every girl with golden hair get out of the car so they could see her close up. From time to time, the image of the woman and the silent laughter in her eyes would haunt them.

Rhea jostled Kelly, lying stiff and still in her arms. "You can sit up now."

"Did it work?" The little girl rubbed her eyes, squinting at the bright sunshine slanting through the window. She looked at Newton, then at Rhea, and grinned. "It worked, didn't it?"

"Like a charm, little cousin." Newton took one hand off the steering wheel and reached over to shake hers. "Welcome to the family."

"But I already have one."

"There are different kinds of family. Some are for fun," Rhea said, "some are for work, some are for learning, some are to help. Some you're born into, others you work your way into."

"What kind is this?"

"A little of all of them, I think." She closed her eyes and leaned back against the seat. "What we do, getting you home to your family, you can go ahead and tell them. That's the first rule, Kelly. No lies, no secrets. Don't ever trust anyone who tells you to keep a secret from your parents, or to tell them lies. You can tell your parents what we did, but remember it's all just a game. Okay?"

"I guess." The girl nodded. "Don't you feel good?"

"The game takes a lot of energy and I was playing hard. Let me get a little sleep and I'll be fine."

Newton left them at a rest stop along the highway.

The growing evening shadows hid the unloading of the motorcycle. They ate supper and parted. Kelly fell asleep, buttoned once again inside the pea coat with Rhea. She drove down the road with the wailing roar of the wind in her ears and her thoughts for company.

Kelly had talked all during supper about her family— enough to bother her rescuers. Rhea felt no jealousy for a homelife she had missed. The trouble came from the speculations moving through her mind. What if she had not lived in stressful circumstances? Troubles and danger were what had brought her ability to light in such a dramatic way. If she had not been orphaned in that plane crash when she was three. If she had not been the lone, impossible survivor. If she had grown up with a family to protect her and give her the attention and security she needed. If she had not noticed the people watching her. If she had not run away.

"Too many ifs," Rhea grumbled into the wind. She glanced up at the starry sky and calculated the time. The telephone rates would go down in another half hour and she had a long-distance call to make.

"How's life, Sherlock?" she asked, before the man who picked up the phone on the other end had finished saying hello. Rhea grinned at Kelly, who perched on the motorcycle parked a few yards away and pretended to drive it.

"Rhea, are you sure you don't read minds?" Dexter Malone, special agent, chuckled for a moment. "I was just thinking about you, actually."

"You say that every time I call in."

"It's the truth this time. We need your help."

"Another infiltration? My make-up kit isn't that enduring, Malone, and I stopped taking acting classes." Rhea turned in the booth. She pushed the door open to turn off the light. No sense in making herself an easy target.

"No role-playing. Just get in there, take some pictures,

act like you're invisible." There was a slight hesitation in the man's voice.

"You aren't going to try to get me to use a gun again, are you?"

"It would make me feel better about sending you in."

"Hey, I'm a volunteer, remember? Earning a fast buck, putting a little spice in my life. We'll talk about it in a while. I called you because I need your help."

"That's a change," Malone admitted. A creaking squeak came over the phone. Rhea envisioned the cramped office where he sat. She knew it well, from many previous visits.

"What do you know about the kidnapped grand-daughter of a federal judge?"

"Enough." The teasing left his voice.

"A friend of mine found her, got her away from her kid-nappers. I'm bringing her home but I don't want excess attention when I get there, understand?" Rhea turned back to face Kelly, gesturing for the child to sit still. She had a sudden vision of the little girl standing up on the seat of the motorcycle and falling headlong onto the gravel.

"I'll be waiting. Although it might be better—"

"No. That was our agreement from the beginning, Malone. We do it my way, or we don't do it at all. I appreciate everything your office has done for me, but I *can* live without it." She fought not to hang up the phone right then and there. Such action would only make future relations uncomfortable and she genuinely enjoyed working with Dexter Malone.

"Sometimes, Jones, I wish we'd left you bound and gagged where we found you." He sighed. The chair creaked again and she envisioned him stretching out, putting his feet up on the beat-up old desk top.

"I was only catching my breath," she retorted, enjoying the game they returned to. "Another minute and I would have got myself free again."

"Another minute and you would have been dead." He sighed again, loudly. "Okay, I'll be waiting when you ride up to the kid's door. Where are you, anyway?"

"Texas."

"You want to get a little more specific?"

"Nope. And I really have to get going, Malone. I'm starving and Kelly's going to do a handstand on my bike seat in another minute. Check your phone bill when it comes. Bye." She hung up and dashed across the gravel parking lot. Rhea reached the bike just in time to catch Kelly with one arm as the little girl lost her balance. Rhea laughed and shook the child. She threw her up in the air and caught her flat with both arms. She spun around until Kelly shrieked with laughter and both of them were dizzy enough to feel sick.

Rhea squeezed Kelly's arm to get the child's attention and gestured at the rearview mirror. "We got company."

Kelly found the blue car in the mirror, four car lengths behind, in the inner lane of the four-lane highway. Rhea's motorcycle was in the outer lane, getting ready to take the off-ramp. The only thing that kept their pursuers from catching up with them was the clogging of rush-hour traffic.

"They can't catch up right now," the girl pointed out.

"Think. We're in Nevada. We haven't seen them since Mississippi. Somebody is helping them look for us. If they get the local law involved, we're dead in the water."

"What do we do?" Kelly hunched her shoulders and pushed back against Rhea. The close confines of the pea coat felt chilly now.

"I have no idea. The main thing is, don't let them know we see them. They might do something drastic."

The off-ramp sloped down between sooty buildings. Kelly looked ahead into the shadows and for a moment wished they could stay on the highway. She squeezed her

legs tighter around the seat, leaning back hard against Rhea
as they went around a sharp corner without slowing. Street
lights were out, turning their new surroundings into a dark
cave that threw the sounds of the motorcycle back at them.
The headlight of the bike shrank as it pierced the darkness.

"Hang on!" Rhea shouted. The bike tipped at an alarming angle as they turned and they went up an incline. Two
more corners, skirted so quickly Kelly felt her foot touching
the ground for a fraction of a second.

Light touched their eyes, dim compared to the highway
lights but bright after the deep darkness. Kelly blinked and
wished she could wipe her eyes when they watered and
ached. They were in an old parking garage.

"Ah ha!" Rhea's voice held triumph and wobbled at
the very end. She hit the brake and Kelly would have fallen
off at the sudden stop if not for the tight coat. The engine
died, the last few echoes fading away in the dim, concrete
depths and shadows.

Rubbish barrels and packing crates sat in a dirty pile in
one corner, about halfway up the structure. Kelly wrinkled
her nose at the smell—wood that had sat damp and dirty too
long, rotting, stagnant. It was probably a home to various
animals for several generations.

"There are times when it's smarter to fight back like
other people do." Rhea unbuttoned her coat and then swung
around to dismount the bike. She stepped away, then bent
far forward, swinging to either side a few times. A low
moan escaped her as she loosened up. "Kelly, remember
what I told you about hiding?" She looked up, waiting for
the child's reponse.

"I think so."

"Well, you're about to learn the hard way. I'm going
to buy some things to disguise us for a while. There's a
friend nearby who can help, but I don't want to chance leading anybody to her." Rhea finished stretching and stepped

back to the bike. A grin broke the somberness of her face.
"Your mother is probably going to kill me. . . . " A chuckle
broke from her when the little girl gave her a puzzled
frown. She tugged on one golden-red curl. "We're going to
cut your hair, and color it. Just for a while, I promise."

To Kelly's dismay, Rhea built a hiding place for her in
the middle of the pile of crates and barrels. It did not help
at all when the woman told her this would be a good time
to practice her concentration by telling her nose not to
notice the smell.

At the third shop, Rhea knew she was running out of
time. Not just time to shop before the stores closed for the
night, but time to maneuver in the city, visible in the lights
to any passerby. A tingling itch began walking up and down
her back. She snatched up the bulky, faded, ugly brown
sweater and hurried to the register of the thrift store. Rhea
reminded herself that the idea was to change her appearance—fashion and color preferences did not matter.

Once outside in the street again, she checked her shoul-
derbag. Two tubes of mascara, one black and one midnight
blue. One bottle of dye, to turn Kelly's hair from golden red
to pale ash blond. Cotton balls, liquid soap, and two little
plastic bowls. Rhea hoped she had thought of everything.
Along with the clothes she had just bought, she felt sure the
disguise was complete.

She sensed the approach of the bullet before she heard
the shriek through the night cacophony. Rhea ducked as the
tingling itch flared all over her body. She fell to her knees
as she stumbled around the corner of the building. The next
moment she heard the sharp explosion of the bullet hitting
the brick wall where her head had been.

//No. No. Not here,// she insisted. Rhea ran, hugging
her purchases against her chest. Ahead was a dark alley.
She ran past it, falling to her knees between two parked

cars. She rolled onto her stomach and crawled underneath the front one. Behind her, a car screeched to a halt and one set of footsteps hurried to the alley.

Holding her breath, deafened by the thundering of her heart in her ears, Rhea peered out from under the car. She had to see, had to be sure of her instincts. One glimpse confirmed that the blue car was the source of the gunshots.

More footsteps—coming back out of the alley. Rhea snaked back under the car as Charlie reported the alley was a dead-end—no one inside. She grinned at the confusion and dead-weariness in his voice, as well as Claire's growled response. Rhea waited until the car moved forward again before she slid out from under her hiding place into the street.

Too late, she thought to look around before she stood up. The car moved too slowly, barely a hundred feet away. She saw Claire glance in the rearview mirror, saw shock wipe the frown from the woman's face. Rhea darted across the street, into a narrow alley as the other woman let out a scream. The anger and danger in that voice sent a new tingling up Rhea's back.

A recessed doorway beckoned. Rhea leaped into it and automatically tried the door. Locked. The glass was too thick to shatter with just one blow—a closer look showed wire netting reinforcement. Footsteps sent deafening echoes into the lane, bouncing off the high walls on either side.

//Not here,// Rhea insisted in the growing silence inside her head. //Gone. Can't see. Can't feel. Can't hear. Not here. Gone. Escaped.//

She concentrated, willing herself to be unseen, unheard, unsensed. She felt her back melt into the stones, envisioned the color of her clothes and the texture of her skin changing. She was just a part of the dirty brickwork, a deeper shadow in the moonlit darkness.

Charlie stopped and tried the doorknob, only a few

inches from her arm. He raised a revolver to smash the glass. Rhea looked into his eyes and thought of midnight in an ice field, no moon, no color, no light. The man blinked and looked around, shivered, then left the doorway.

She refused to let out a breath or listen to the footsteps and voices as the pair searched the alley. They did not believe she had escaped. Rhea turned her thoughts away. If she acknowledged their presence, it might tear open the delicate shield in her mind and then they would see her again.

Involuntarily, she remembered when she had learned the trick. It was the night she had first run. There were too many similarities—and not enough. It was in a tower room in one of the older buildings on the university campus. She had been gaming with some friends. Everyone lounged around the room, having a good time as the summer semester wound down. No one would ever have suspected her of running away so near the end of the term. It was the perfect time. Her backpack was not full of books, but clothes and money. When the game ended, Rhea planned on vanishing into the deep shadows around campus.

Someone found out or guessed her plans. A helicopter appeared out of the night, sending gusts of wind in through the windows that stood open in the balmy summer night air. The gamers stared or shrieked dismay at the interruption of their fun. Rhea had been frozen along with everyone else, staring at the men in the helicopter. Men in uniforms, with guns and a spotlight. One had a modified rocket-launcher in his hands. It went off, leaving a trail of smoke behind as the capsule shattered the single closed window in the tower.

White, bitter gas filled the room. Rhea shook her head, staring at it, refusing to believe. She saw her friends fall, gasping, and watched the helicopter move off and then come back.

"No," she had whispered in the hissing quiet, all her

friends unconscious at her feet. Rhea tasted the bitterness in the air, knew somehow they had only been gassed into sleep, not death. "I'm not here," she told the night. "Not here. You can't see me. I'm not here. I got away."

She waited, watched the helicopter, and nearly laughed aloud in angry triumph. Dismay covered the faces of the men who studied the room from the helicopter. Rhea stayed like a statue as men in gas masks came into the room. They searched all her friends, turning them over, comparing their faces to a very bad photograph of her. When the men were gone, she picked up her bags, searched her unconscious friends for extra money, and left.

The alley was empty again. Rhea blinked and tried not to hiss as her neck protested its stiffness when she moved. How long she had been standing there, she did not know. The angry, startled yowl of a cat let her know her protection had finally lapsed. Rhea grinned at this proof of her strength.

"The trouble with running all the time," she told the dark, deserted alley, "is that you're either running away from something or running to something. Heaven help you if it's both."

The blue mascara, she used to change her license plate, so it matched the coloring for the state. In the highway lights and darkness, Rhea doubted anyone would notice the hurry-up patch job. A pair of nail scissors served to hack Kelly's hair until the child had a short, tangled mop. The dye made it curl close to her scalp. Rhea used the mascara to darken the girl's eyebrows and lashes, and put lines on her face. In the shadows, the shape would appear different from normal.

The bulky sweater went over her padded arms and chest. Rhea hoped she looked more like a man's square figure now. She used the rest of the mascara to create the illusion of a stubbly beard. A child's toy helmet went on Kelly and she sat on the back of the motorcycle, holding onto Rhea's belt. If luck was on their side, the two of them would look like a man and a boy riding down the highway at night.

Before they set off, Rhea told Kelly what had happened. The child had the right to know.

"Somebody is helping them?" Kelly asked.

"Looks like it. My friends couldn't get all the details but somebody wants your grandfather the judge to set somebody free from jail. It's big-time trouble."

"Like the Mafia?"

"Who knows?" Rhea suppressed the urge to laugh at the suggestion. "You know, I'd much rather think it was the Mafia after us, rather than the alternative." Kelly frowned at her, puzzled. "If nobody is helping them, then Charlie and Claire are probably like us." It was encouraging to see the horror touch the child's face. Kelly understood the implications. "Come on," she said, nodding towards the bike. "We have a long way to go. If we're on time, my friend might fix us breakfast."

"Who the hell are you supposed to be now?" Donna Tyler said, her words slurred either from drink or the early hour. Rhea took a discreet sniff and decided it was the hour.

"Doesn't matter. Can we come in?" Rhea stepped closer to the door, resisting the urge to look around the shabby neighborhood. The early morning light shone brighter than she liked it. Her quick disguise job disintegrated as they spoke.

The woman in the door studied her in silence a moment. The morning breeze tousled her limp, permed hair. Morning light revealed the streaks of gray in the dark, chestnut mass. Sagging flesh under the eyes and jowls, from overeating, added nearly twenty years to the woman's age. Only the eyes, bright and penetrating, showed the woman was not the lazy, slovenly creature she appeared to be.

"You're in trouble again, aren't you?" Donna said. She straightened up from leaning on the door frame and scratched at her left armpit. "I don't see why I should let you in. The last time I saw you—"

"The last time we saw each other was in the line of duty. And I saved your life, if I recall."

"Never one to just let things slide, were you?" Donna wrinkled up her nose like she smelled something bad. She tugged at the edges of her frayed terrycloth robe, pulling it a little closer, then blinked in surprise. "Wait a second. Did you say 'we'?"

"Kelly and me." Rhea tugged on the girl's collar, bringing her out of the shadows of the overgrown bushes on either side of Donna's door. The little girl blinked sleepily up at the woman and tried to smile.

"You, I'd leave out in the street and let you save your own neck with your bag of tricks. But this—" Donna sighed gustily and one corner of her mouth jerked up into a smile. "I might have come down a lot from the good old days, but I'll never leave a kid in the lurch. Come on in." She turned and stalked off into the darkened recesses of her house.

"She doesn't like you, does she?" Kelly whispered, as the two of them stepped inside and shut the door. Darkness surrounded them. Donna, as Rhea recalled, never opened the curtains until two or three in the afternoon.

"I don't know." Rhea wiped at the mascara beard on her cheeks and chin, using the ragged sleeve of her sweater. "And no matter what she says, Donna doesn't know either. We worked together a few years ago, just before she retired."

"Retired?" Kelly settled down on the corner of the couch where scattered magazines and potato chip bags half-covered the faded flowered print. "She doesn't look old enough to retire."

"Thank you ever so much, little missy," Donna sneered, coming back into the room. She had exchanged her robe for a housedress of fairly clean, bright green cotton.

"Still hiding from old enemies?" Rhea gestured around the messy room. It looked like a family of ten lived in the house, never picking up after themselves.

"Ever consider I *like* living this way?" the woman returned. She settled down on the couch, on top of a pile of magazines and a half-empty bag of stale pretzels. "Well, what sort of trouble did this one get you into?" she asked Kelly.

"Rhea is taking me home," the child said, indignant despite tottering on the verge of sleep.

"Gone into a new line of work?" Donna laughed, a lovely, rippling sound at odds with her present appearance. "Babysitting, instead of digging into things for Dexter?"

"No. Not exactly. And why did you mention Dexter?" Rhea felt her knees go wobbly. She decided it would be prudent to sit down now. "Did he call you?"

"Haven't heard from that upstart.... What's this? You'll call him, but you pass by my place until you need help. Some friendship!"

"I thought you didn't want me around here." She laughed and settled back further in the surprisingly empty, clean comfortable armchair she had found.

"Enough game playing," Donna's voice softened. "What's with the kid?"

"Kidnapped. Lives in California. A friend found her in Georgia. Been moving double-time to get her home. Skipped bullets last night. I think they have connections—whoever they are."

"Thought there might be some trouble, with that awful disguise." The woman stood up and gestured down the hall. "Bathroom's that way, Kelly. Don't come out until you're

Illustrated by Rob Alexander

as clean as you want to be, hear me? I'll dig up some clothes for you and make breakfast.''

"It's okay," Rhea mumbled as the child got up to obey. "She knows all about my friends—she's one of us."

"Recruiting them kind of young, aren't you?" Donna's voice softened, reminding the younger woman of former times. Of plush offices, computers, business suits and limousines.

"Recruiting, nothing." She sank into a sea of dark warmth, and welcomed it. "It's a race to save us from our own minds and common sense."

Rhea woke with sunset peering through the threadbare spots in the curtains, right into her eyes. She groaned and rolled over, pulling the pillow over her head. Why, she wondered, did Donna have to play her cover role to the hilt? No one would look for a woman known for grace, style and taste in this run-down, slovenly house. But there was a point where the cover went too far. Donna had been one of the top computer hackers for the Company. Now, she pretended to be illiterate, ignorant and crude.

Then Rhea's awareness of the time returned. She sat up and tugged aside the curtains. It was indeed sunset. She had slept the whole day through. A grin touched her lips when she realized that her aching bladder had awakened her. Rhea swung her legs over the side of the bed and got up. She still felt achy tired, but not as worn thin and wrung out as the day before. Her powers of endurance sometimes amazed her, but this time racing across the country with Kelly, she was going far beyond the boundaries.

Rhea tottered across the room and tugged the door open. She found the bathroom next door and gratefully made use of all the facilities. Kelly leaned against the wall, watching the door when she stepped out again. For a moment the two traded serious looks, then the little girl grinned.

"I bet you've been wondering when I would wake up." Rhea ran her fingers through her damp hair. The shower, short as it had been, made her feel brand-new.

"Donna wanted to call the doctors, but I told her you were just tired. When I said you were like a computer shutting down for self-maintenance, she understood," the child added.

"You told— Kelly, what's going on?"

"You've been sleeping two whole days." Kelly shrugged and turned around to go back down the hall. Rhea could not move for a moment, and then had to hurry to catch up.

"How did you know I was all right?" she asked, catching hold of her shoulder as they entered the living room. Evidence of guests' presences showed in the room. It was tidy and some of the layers of dust had been removed from the coffee table.

"I just . . . ." The girl frowned, then shrugged. "I just touched you, and I knew. And I think I got the computer stuff from Donna. I like her. She tells scary stories."

"The truer, the scarier, little missy," Donna said as she lounged into the room from the kitchen. "It's about time you got up. I was thinking I should just shovel you into a box and put you under."

"I didn't smell that bad, did I?" Rhea retorted, determined to change the subject. Just from the little Kelly had said, she had a lot of thinking to do.

"Well . . . ." The woman's customary frown changed to a grin. "Come on in, I'm just starting supper. Missy has been telling me all about your adventures."

"I already told you before I fell asleep." She followed Donna and Kelly into the kitchen and dropped into a chair. At the mention of food, Rhea realized her stomach felt shriveled and half-dead from neglect.

"You wouldn't know a good story if it bit you. This one, she's going to be something special when she grows up.'' Donna ruffled Kelly's hair. It irritated Rhea a little when the child giggled.

"That's what I'm afraid of,'' Rhea muttered before she could bite her lip to keep the words in.

"Now what's *that* supposed to mean?''

"Donna, you're the one who helped me put it into words, remember? Nothing happens without a reason. You said it yourself. There has to be a reason why me and all my friends are suddenly showing up able to do . . . things. There has to be a reason why there are so many more of us lately. And why the talent is showing up so young, like Kelly.'' She wrapped her arms around herself, chilled despite the humid warmth of the day.

"When we formulated that rule, it was with criminal activities in mind. Not fate. Not events and abilities that have no logical explanation.'' Donna shook her head. "You're still worn-out. Probably no sugar in your blood— giving you hallucinations. You just sit back and I'll get supper on the table in no time.'' She nodded decisively and turned to the refrigerator.

Rhea ignored the wide-eyed, somber regard Kelly gave her. More than anything, she hoped her fears, her sudden insight, were the fault of hunger and weariness. She hoped so, desperately.

Early the next morning, Rhea and Kelly left. Friends of Donna, contacts from the old days, had come in and worked wonders. New clothes for the two of them; a new paint job on the motorcycle; a few extra gadgets to change the shape of it; and a new license plate. The same friends were on the lookout for the blue car. One nameless friend in a black van followed Rhea and Kelly until they got out of the city limits.

When they left Donna, it was with promises to call and come visit soon. Rhea wondered what Kelly would tell her parents about the woman. As far as she knew, the child did

understand the situation Donna lived in, for her own protection. What could she say that would not compromise
the ex-agent's safety? Rhea shook her head and told herself
not to worry about it. She would have troubles enough of
her own when they reached Kelly's home, without worrying
about someone else. What would happen would happen.

They rode hard and fast, stopping only for fuel and
food along the way. At nightfall they reached Marni's
house. Only five more hours of driving remained until she
had Kelly home. In some ways, getting the girl home in the
early morning hours was safer where both of them were concerned. Less chance of agents and police and media being
around. But Rhea knew she needed to make this stop and
introduce Marni to Kelly. The two would be seeing each
other often in the next few years.

Marni was waiting, along with her husband, Jay. Rhea
had called ahead, using a phone to save her strength. The
mouth-watering aroma of pizza drifted through the cooling
night air as she and Kelly walked up the driveway to the
front door.

Marni and Jay were both tall, with narrow faces, wide
smiles and curly, glossy black hair. Rhea envied them—not
the successful computer business they owned, or their big,
beautiful house or that Marni continued her college education while Rhea could not. She envied their togetherness,
their oneness, and the baby very evident under Marni's comi-
cal Mickey Mouse apron.

Jay had four video games set up in his basement—Ninja
Turtles, Tempest, Phoenix and Tron Discs. Kelly bounced
back and forth between them while the three adults talked.
It only took a short while, between mouthfuls of pizza, to
bring them up to date on the situation. Marni had greater
sensitivity towards the gifts of others than Rhea and she had
sized up Kelly the moment they met.

"Could I make these games do anything I wanted?"

Kelly asked, suddenly appearing at Rhea's side at the table.

"What do you mean, do anything?" Rhea felt a chill go down her spine. She traded glances with Marni and Jay and they both shrugged.

"Like, I could believe that I'm the best, and the machine would do what *I* want, not what it wants to do." The girl looked back and forth between the three of them, her delighted smile of discovery fading to uncomfortable worry.

"What fun would it be to cheat?" Jay asked in the quiet. "Those games are for your mind and your hands. If you make them do what you want, what's the use of playing at all?"

"But I would be better than everybody. Even my brothers." Kelly brightened at the idea.

"Why do you want to be better than everybody?" Marni asked.

"I don't know." Kelly edged a little closer to Rhea.

"Kelly," Rhea said, making her voice stay soft. "What fun is cheating?"

"It's not cheating to use what you have, is it?"

"No, it's not cheating, exactly. But would it be fair to make somebody run a race with you—and they didn't have any legs? She almost laughed at the stricken expression that crossed the girl's face. "Kelly, you better learn this now . . . no, you already know it. What happens to the kids at school who aren't like everybody else? The ones who are too smart, or who dress different or who talk strangely?"

"Nobody likes them. Everybody picks on them." No emotion touched the child's voice. Kelly absorbed herself in the ideas presented to her.

"People are always afraid of what is different, what they don't understand. That's why we don't use . . . the things that make us different to win at video games. We don't use it to hurt people or win contests or for anything except good. Being different already gives them a reason to be afraid of us. We don't want to give them a reason to hate or hurt us." Rhea held out her arms to Kelly when the little girl's lower lip began to quiver. "It's all right," she soothed, gathering her onto her lap.

"Kelly," Marni put in, "there are a lot of people like us. People who can make what we believe *real*. We're a family, in a way."

"That's what Newton said," Kelly said. Her voice came out muffled, her face hidden in the curve of Rhea's neck.

"You have been a busy little traveler, haven't you?" the other woman teased. "Meeting first Jason, then Newton . . . . The thing is, we're all here to help each other. I'm going to be your teacher, because I live closest to you. If it's all right with you, of course."

"What about Rhea?"

"I have to keep moving around the country," Rhea responded. "Finding people who need help. People who don't know how or why they do what they do. I bring the family together. Understand?"

"A little," the child whispered.

"Good. Now, how about you finish your pizza—cold pizza," she amended, "and then we'll get you off to bed. You're going to be home tomorrow, and I want you looking good for your mother."

"So she won't notice my hair?" Kelly giggled somewhat tearfully.

In the end, Rhea parked in the vacant lot behind the Jurgenson house. The two of them walked through the woods, around the pool, across the patio and through the open door. Nobody noticed them at first. She and Kelly stood in the recreation room, watching the people walking around and talking on the level above them. They waited ten minutes, until Kelly giggled.

The sound was like a stone thrown into a pool. The silence spread out in ripples until the whole house rang with the startled quiet. Mrs. Jurgenson acted first out of the odd assortment of relatives, agents and reporters. Her face went pale, making her golden-red hair look darker in contrast. Then she screamed. Luckily, she stood at the top of the stairs. Otherwise, she might have vaulted over the railing in her hurry to get to her daughter.

Rhea wisely stepped backwards out of the stampede, as people converged on the wildly weeping mother and the girl in her arms. She squeezed Kelly's shoulder in farewell and prepared to leave. Rhea had expected just such a reaction and she and the child had said their farewells already.

"Just a second, there," a quiet, arrogantly assured voice said.

Rhea turned, her hand on the frame of the door. She froze at the sight of the gun pointed at her. Then she looked up into the face of the agent. Rhea felt the blood leave her face for a moment as she recognized the man. Quite a few years older, but still the same square, bronzed face and strangely piercing blue eyes, the same dusting of platinum hair on his receding hairline. Probably even the same gun. The last time Rhea had seen him, he had come bursting up the stairs to the tower, where she and her college friends had been gaming.

"Is there something you want?" she asked. For the first time, she wondered where Dexter Malone and his men were.

"I'd like to know why you're trying to sneak out of here, first of all. You're a hero, you know." He gestured towards the noisy reunion that ignored the two of them standing by the door.

Rhea nodded slowly. She tried to calculate how much leeway she had for escape. How long would it take for someone to react? Could she kick the gun out of the agent's hand, push the door open and high-tail it for her motorcycle? Would she save any time by bolting straight through the screening? Or would someone be waiting outside by now, alerted by the commotion?

"I hate sloppy reunions," she said, turning so her back was to the door and she faced Kelly's family. "I'm just stepping outside to get a breath of air."

"Uh huh." The agent nodded. For the life of her, Rhea could not remember his name. "Mind if I join you?"

"Sure." She shrugged and pushed the door open, stepping through without looking.

"It's been a long time, Rhonda." He sat down on the redwood chaise lounge. The cushion hissed a little.

"Rhonda? My name is Rhea, not Rhonda."

"Is that what you're going by now?"

"Rhea is my name." She dug into her pocket and pulled out her wallet. She tossed it to him. "There, see? Credit cards, driver's license. My picture. Rhea Jones."

"Close, though." He tossed the wallet back to her. "You admit the similarities in the names. Rhonda. Rhea. And you look too close to Rhonda Stewart to be just coincidence. You even talk and act and move like her. Especially the way you got in here without being seen."

"She had good training." Dexter Malone stepped around the corner of the house. He burst out laughing when Rhea glared at him. "Something wrong, Jones?" His gray eyes sparkled in his square-cut, ruddy face. A former halfback, he was still in shape. That was the only thing that kept her from punching him when he irritated her.

"Just your timing. Lousy as always."

"Hold it a second." The other agent stood up. "You know her?"

"Jones has worked with the Company for quite a while

now. She's good, and I don't want your paranoid droids harassing her, understand?'' Malone gestured back the way he had come. ''We need to talk, Jones. That assignment I was talking about has gone critical.''

''But Mr. Malone—do you know—if she's who I think she is—''

They left him sputtering to a standstill behind them. Rhea stumbled a little when they reached the safety of the front yard. Malone caught her by the arm and held onto it until they reached his car.

''You could have just left the kid with Donna and been clear of the whole mess. The witness protection program can only do so much for you. Everything else, you have to do yourself.'' Malone held the door open for her.

''My bike—'' Rhea paused, one foot inside the car. She glared at Malone when he chuckled. ''One of your men already has it?''

''In a van and heading away to be serviced. We take care of our own, you know.''

''I know.'' Rhea settled down into the seat and leaned back, closing her eyes. ''I could use a week's vacation, just sleeping.''

''Unfortunately . . . . If you could just figure out what you do, and how, and could teach it—''

''I'd be stuck as a school teacher and lead a very boring life,'' Rhea finished for him. She grinned, eyes still closed. ''No thanks. So, tell me about this job. Is it really big?''

''Big enough.'' He started the engine and they drove away from the house.

''Malone, tell me something. The truth, okay?'' Rhea waited until he gave a grunt of acknowledgment. ''Is something big about to happen? Something really important? World shaking?''

"Not that I've heard lately, why?"

"I don't know. I just have this feeling. . . ." She shivered and wrapped her arms around herself. Rhea promised herself to finish this mission quickly and get back on the road. A sense of a looming deadline came over her. She had to find all the new ones, and soon.

Hopes and Dreams
by
Mark Andrew Garland

About the Author

Mark Andrew Garland is from Syracuse, New York, where he is a service manager at a local Ford dealership. He is 35, a former rock musician of some stature, a former car racer—which is how he eventually found the auto service business—and a tireless science fiction reader from the age of twelve. And now a writer of it, as well.

He lives with his wife and three children, and a cat, and has been working hard at writing for some time, with appearances in a few small press and semi-pro magazines. He has been entering the WOTF Contest in almost every quarter for about three years. Now he has made it, with "Hopes and Dreams." We wish him well; with a novel written and circulating among publishers, we rather think the wish will be justified.

About the Illustrator

James S. Reece was born in 1959, and in First Grade made his first sculpture, winning a gold star for his ceramic fireman. And so it went; at every level of schooling, he has done such things as win a Hallmark Award, three gold keys and four merit awards. In college, however, which was the Kansas City Art Institute, he found out that science fiction and fantasy art was frowned on by serious artists—serious artists at KCAI, at any rate—and left. By the time he was 20, he was sculpting for a major ceramic mold manufacturer, and soon became Lead Sculptor, supervising the work of others. In his spare time, he began to show and sell his own artwork.

Now 31, he lives in Wichita, Kansas, and has a business with a science fiction artist friend; they create custom sculpture, artwork and molds for individuals and businesses. His goal is to work more and more in science fiction and fantasy, and he hopes that a good part of his work will be illustration.

In the morning they drive out into the Martian wilderness through "Debtor's Canyon," facing into the rising sun. It is no more than a valley, really, running for miles, named for a handful of colonists who bravely perished here years ago. The hills look odd to the Earth-born eye—too irregular, too rugged, filled with gaping shadows like cold black ice that conceal secret places and punctuate jumbled alien angles. Faint frost outlines the edges between dark and light.

Malek peers solemnly through the windshield of their Chrysler-Mitsubishi Off-World-Terrain truck as it surges along, low gears whining. He sees a faint dust swirl dance through the valley on the tenuous Martian winds. The sun's shrunken visage gives a false impression of warmth, and he imagines for a moment that there might be trees and grass growing somewhere beyond these hills, that life might have followed men here the way mold follows bread. He reminds himself it is not so.

They pass through a deep ocean of shadow and it chases reality through his mind; they have left the four hundred-odd people at "Resort Base" behind and, but for each other, they are the only living things in the world. All alone, Malek thinks, peacefully, blessedly alone.

Lt. Naia Tawni is daydreaming, driving the truck, staring straight ahead. Malek can see the creeping Martian landscape reflected in her cool oriental eyes. Her hair is straight and short and all one color. Her face like her uniform is unadorned, uncustomized like so many others, the jaw always

set to convey an approaching frown—Malek finds this reas-
suring in a way. You hear she is part Chinese, or perhaps
part Philippine; you hear jokes that she is possibly part
human. Naia is one of the few single women on Mars but,
that anyone knows, she does not date and is not much for
friendships. She is also not much for conversation beyond
official matters, so whenever he is around her he tends not
to say anything at all.

Somehow, despite better judgment, he finds her
vaguely attractive, though her beauty is too strict, and tells
nothing of its hidden origins.

The truck is bouncing over a field of scattered rock.

Nearby is an ancient impact crater, deep as a grave,
half in shadow. Naia drives close to the edge so as to look
down into it. Malek looks away until they are past.

He thinks he could have done worse. There are people
from many parts of Earth on Mars, people from Luna, but
the only commonly held distinctions here tend to be either
military or civilian. And while the many scientists and
technicians are a widely diverse and opinionated gathering,
the military are for their part cool and flatly serious; calm
waters, Malek feels. They are United Nations appointed
special troops and are generally in charge of the place. Naia
is for now acting commander of the base, since Colonel
Musenga received word of his family's illness and returned
to Earth on the last transit ship. She is lately more quiet than
ever.

He watches her at the controls, out riding herd on him,
checking up on Earth's Martian outposts. He wonders what
it must be like always to be so certain, so beset with simple
maxims. She blinks twice, and again her eyes are filled with
Mars.

On this trip they have many destinations: the seismographic stations to the East and South, the meteorological
station in the West, the automated sample mining sites along

the return trip—six days in all. For Malek, six welcome, silent days . . . .

Naia suddenly jerks back in her seat as though she'd been stung by high voltage. For an instant she is frozen, arms straight out on the control panel, muscles tense. She bends her head slightly forward and squints through the filtered glass. Malek follows her gaze to the rough hills, the bottomless shadows, and he knows she has seen it; the thing that moves behind the midnight curtains among the rocks of this valley, like the thing in a darkened room before the light is switched on. Impossibly huge, fast.

Malek has seen it too, sometimes, staring too long into these same rocks, and in his dreams a long time ago back on Earth—a creature of the mind's eye, a human thing not at all Martian or slightly tangible—but startling nonetheless, if only for a moment.

Naia scrunches her shoulders as a chill washes through her, and for an instant she seems more feminine, briefly vulnerable. Then she straightens again, strong: wrought iron. She looks over at Malek to see if he has noticed any of it, doubtless aware that in the small cabin of the truck it would be difficult not to, and she catches Malek staring at her. So he smiles and says,

"I know, Lieutenant, those shadows tend to jump out at everybody now and then." He tries not to look overly patronizing, feeling somehow self-conscious of his meager masculinity under her hardening gaze. "It's just your mind reacting to—"

"It wasn't that," Naia says. "A muscle twitch, that's all. Normal tension."

"I just meant, well, it's easy to imagine things out—"

"I trust in facts, not fantasies, Mr. Zaborszcyk. The mind only plays tricks on those who'll let it."

"Of course," Malek says, thinking that it sounds easy enough.

Illustrated by James S. Reece

• • •

In the dream he is in a car traveling down a country road at night. There is a bright moon. It is late autumn, or early spring—there are no leaves on the trees in the scrubby woods all around them, and patches of snow on the nearby hills.

Someone is driving. Faceless, unseen, just someone. He can't seem to turn his head exactly the right way to see who it is. They are starting into a curve; there is a road sign that warns them. Malek begins to feel a borrowed familiarity about this place. "Thirteen curves," they call it. He just knows that somehow. The first curve makes the car lean over and then they are around it and sweeping into the second, going faster.

The person driving is repeating the story in a voice too faint, as though more distant than is possible in the front seat of the car. Slowly, though, it is getting louder.

—It seems there is this ghost, the ghost of thirteen curves. Some time ago a young girl was married. A young girl with a great deal of money. Married to a man, she believed, of honesty and good intentions. On the wedding night as they drove towards their honeymoon destination, they passed along this very road and somewhere on thirteen curves he pulled the car over. Then he murdered her with a hunting knife and left her still in her white wedding gown lying face down in a ditch beside the road.

One assumes he emptied her account forthwith and was never seen again; one imagines they might have caught up with him, and he spent half a lifetime in jail. No one knows.

But of the bride's legacy there is little disagreement. Since that fatal night she has stalked these lonely curves in supernatural form, a specter filled with hate and a vengeful promise that, one allows, is too great for even all eternity to absorb.

The story has this girl, radiant in her beautiful dress,

hitchhiking along these curves on many a night, occasionally luring an unfortunate young man—it is only young men—to stop and pick her up. She usually rides a ways, talking. In the morning they always find the young man in a ditch with his throat slit clean through. The story includes a girl who watched as the hitchhiking bride cut off her boyfriend's head and placed it on their car's antenna.

They are driving and the car starts to sputter and cut out, but the driver says that happens a lot here, too. He can hear her voice clearly now, loud, as though it is right inside his head. He thinks the car must be going a hundred miles an hour.

Malek turns his head with sudden ease. He can see something of the driver now, a lovely young woman in a silky white wedding dress. . . .

The O.W.T. truck's comset generates high-pitched, bone-chilling beeps and Malek wakes up. Bio-med monitors, set on scan as a matter of course during periods of rest, have sensed his extreme brain wave activity, his rapid, pounding heart rate, the icy sweat he is soaked with, and has correlated the information with sleep-normal guidelines. The audio alarm shows him no pity. Malek taps at a flat keyboard and the noise goes away.

Naia moves sleepily in her couch, barely visible in the light from the green and scarlet crystal displays of the control panel.

"Are you all right?" she asks, without inflection.

"Yes, I think so," Malek says, looking out into the Martian night, the starry Martian sky, feeling part of him drain away as he considers what has happened. He has to force himself to say it: "Just a bad dream."

Naia punches up Malek's last bio-med stats. Her eyes widen. "Bad," she says. "Yes. Perhaps it is good the dream was interrupted." She is paying particular attention to the numbers from just before he was wakened—massive dumping of adrenaline and noradrenaline and endorphins into the blood stream. "Do you often have such dreams?"

"No. I—not lately." Malek shuts his mouth, though part of him wants to go on, tell her everything—tell anyone. He's certain it is better not to.

"Lately?" Naia asks. "But you've had them before? Nightmares? Here?"

"No. Not since—since I left Earth," he says, regretting now that he has said anything at all.

Naia strokes her neck thoughtfully. "I have seen your records, Mr. Zaborszcyk. You have some family history of this, I understand. Dreams, or visions? Seers of some kind? Your psych ratings don't show you as affected. I recall reading your mother apparently killed herself because of the things she said she saw—"

"Lieutenant, if you are so concerned about me, why don't you just scrub the trip and return to base? Why did you let me go in the first place?"

"I never gave it much thought, until now. Perhaps—"

"Perhaps you'd better decide," Malek says, loud enough that his voice surprises even himself. "It is a fact that you have had your own records classified, a rarity on Mars. Maybe you have poverty or ignorance or illegalities in your family? Maybe you are a perfect bastard, Lieutenant Tawni. With all due respect."

"I am far less concerned with myself," Naia says tersely.

Malek regrets his words again. You hear she comes from an oppressively military family; then you hear she was a child refugee from the Indochinese conflicts, that she never knew her parents because they hadn't lived that long, and this, her career, her rank, is all she has ever really had. You didn't ask. You just didn't ask! But you didn't go around name-dropping technician's dead mothers, either!

Naia turns away from him, shuts off her own monitor, deletes the data on Malek. She fingers her couch upright, which Malek takes to mean she does not plan to go back to sleep.

"Anyway," Malek tells her, "don't worry. I'm fine."

Naia nods.

It is two hours till dawn. They lie silently awake until it is time to get up. Malek then heats food cakes and coffee in the microwave while Naia washes her face in the little sink at the back of the cabin. After breakfast they set out again across the Martian sands.

At the first seismographic station Malek scampers out of the truck to collect the data and check the instruments while Lieutenant Tawni hikes. He waits in the truck until she returns and they set off again for the second station. When they leave there it is dusk and they are beginning to talk, about the weather data, about the landscape.

In an hour they are chatting about Colonel Musenga back on Earth and the illness—the virus, certainly—that has touched his family like so many others. They talk about the latest local theories on what has happened since then, why the last two scheduled transit ships never came, why there has been no communication from Earth for months.

The last anyone Mars-side knew, a full-scale biological war had been declared against the deadly new virus that had sprung up in Africa and Southern Europe. The world's very best were all at work on the cure, of course. Someone said a handful of cases had even been diagnosed on the lunar colonies, but that hadn't been substantiated. Still, Mars had been cut off soon afterward. Or forgotten, Malek thought. Naia insisted that a good explanation would eventually be given for everything, once it was over—whatever "it" was.

"Do you have anyone there, on Earth?" Malek asks her, casual, absent.

Naia looks over at him and doesn't answer right away. "Why?"

"I don't know, really. It's just something you ask people on Mars these days, that's all. Forget it." His voice goes whiney on him.

The truck rolls down an embankment, headlights pointing the way. Malek wonders how they will ever make the other side. But Naia gears down and the tracks slip but find just enough purchase and the truck rises magically onto the plain beyond.

"No," Naia says then. "Do you?"

He looks for her eyes, finds them. "No . . . we lost track. Anyway, I noticed you don't get much mail, either."

They stare quietly at nothing at all out the windshield, watching it most carefully. "No," Naia says. "I don't suppose I do."

She finds a place to park for the night.

In the dream he works at some type of factory but this morning he wakes up cold and white as an ice sculpture, and he knows somehow that he is dead. Yet this seems too hard to accept so he goes to his family—a nice enough bunch, the four of them—and asks them if it is true. They tell him it is, but still he does not believe.

So they go out to the car and drive to a clinic. On the way everyone tells him he died at work. On the job to the last. Just dropped dead. They make a quick stop at the factory and all his fellow workers tell him how sorry they are, how awful it is that so many are dying like that. At the clinic they go downstairs to a cold room. There are a few people in lab coats working there, one is huddled over a corpse that is obviously the young man Malek has become in the dream; he just knows this somehow.

"I'm sorry," his dream mother says, her eyes tearing up.

"It's okay," Malek tells them. "My real mother has seen such things. She spoke of it once. People like you and many thousands more, all dying, suffering, sick, being left alone."

"Tell us," the woman begs him. "Please, tell us all of it, all that is in you. Have you seen such things?"

"Yes. I—I have seen people—horrible people with blackened eyes and no tongues—all wandering numb in the thickening twilight—all—"

Malek hears a siren in the distance, or electronic church bells. . . .

They have made their way outside, through the near empty streets to a great outdoor sports stadium. Inside they find thousands gathered everywhere, and all manner of priests standing together on a great podium on the faded fifty-yard line. They are all praying, everyone, praying a strange prayer. Here and there in the crowds a person falls, many go unnoticed, bone thin, sweating from every pore—

The bio-med sensors have him fully awake now.

Naia is sitting up in her couch, watching him. Malek decides she has been up for a while.

Naia is silent until dawn when she gets up and begins making breakfast: cakes.

"This is an extreme environment," she says then. "People are only people. Some of them crack, Mr. Zaborszcyk. I have seen it happen. It is not so unusual for persons such as yourself—"

"As opposed to someone like you?"

"I simply meant that a more— less emotional person."

"I don't mind the description, Lieutenant, I just wish it hadn't come from you."

Naia throws herself down in her couch with a bounce and a low sigh that is part growl. Malek scoots over to the kitchenette.

"A bit self-righteous, aren't we?" Naia says quietly. "Don't think this is not a serious matter. I watched the monitors while you slept. While you dreamed."

"And?" Malek gets cakes and coffee, handing Naia's to her. She waves him off.

"Your mind is all you have. You must strengthen it, protect it. You must command it! In order to depend on each other we must be certain of ourselves. If something is bothering you so much as to—"

"It's nothing like that! It's personal and doesn't concern anyone but me."

"But it may," Naia tells him. "We are far from home, out of contact, no idea what has happened. We must harden ourselves in order to survive. We cannot afford to—to—"

"To feel anything?"

Naia stands and turns as if she is about to strike out, looming over Malek. He draws back against the storage panels, unaware he is cowering until it is too late to save any face. Naia stands still, both fists clenched, but already she is relaxing them.

"Sure you won't have some cakes?" Malek asks, grinning.

Naia accepts the food and sits back down. Malek comes forward with two coffees. She takes hers, one-handing the controls, and the truck lurches forward.

At the meteorological station Malek goes about his work while Naia goes hiking. When she returns she finds Malek making notes in a small datacom. He tucks it away in his personal locker as she unsuits and sits in her couch.

"You keep a journal?" she asks. Malek just nods.

"Are you so afraid I might see it?"

Malek shakes his head, knots his face. "Look, Lieutenant, just what is it *you* are afraid of, anyway?"

"You fail to realize that the lives of everyone on Mars

might depend on any one of us at some—"

"No, no. I mean *really*. You're scared that something has gone too wrong back home, that we might be on our own up here for a long time—maybe longer than that, aren't you? But I don't think it's Earth so much as Earth orders. You're cut off from Command, from *your* world. So maybe you're beginning to lose your identity, to lack direction. You might conceivably even find yourself becoming just a person, a plain, lowly, confounded little just-a-person like me; is that possible, Lieutenant?" It is a hard game. He thinks: play.

Naia looks away from Malek, keeping her face from him. After a moment she says, "I am certain it is not *your* place to judge me, technician."

Yet you judge me, Malek thinks silently.

Naia starts the truck and sets it moving, turning to the North, keeping their speed light as the wheels grapple with the rock-sprinkled ground.

Malek says, "Something *is* wrong, back home."

"What do you mean?"

"I can't explain how I know, I'm not sure I understand it myself. Maybe I am cracking up, losing my mind, but I *am* having dreams, much as neither one of us likes it, and they're not good dreams, and in my family that can be a very real problem."

"Nonsense. To lend credence to such things is to discredit one's self."

"That is why I came to Mars," Malek says, petulant. "I saw what it did to my mother, how the visions ate at her from inside like a parasite; I listened to my sister foretell my mother's own death; and other things, ghosts that refused to rest and came to her because they had to, the way a sinner might seek a priest; so many people, so many dreams—"

"And so you speak of ghosts," laughing now. "But, you say, they are just good friends, correct?"

"Not friends, refugees, caught between hell and eternity, too terrible to be understood by any but those who have already seen into those places. I had to get away from them, from humanity and all its underpinnings, from the life the human race was bound to inflict upon me. From the curse. I thought I'd made it, too. . . ."

Naia turns in her chair, letting the truck slow to a stop, bringing her hands to her face, pulling her fingers down across her eyelids. It is more a gesture of fatigue than anything else, Malek decides.

"I have heard that for many years the USSR tested for such powers, that they encouraged selective breeding among promising individuals. Your mother was born there, wasn't she?"

"Yes," Malek says, nodding. "And I have heard that too."

"Still, I'm sure there must be some help for it, whatever the basis of your problem truly is. It is not as you now believe, I am convinced of that. Perhaps, when things are back to normal . . . ."

The truck begins to move.

"Perhaps," Malek says.

In the dream he has a friend—a girl. He knows she is not popular at school, not dating much, no clubs; she is not planning to attend any of the colleges most of the other seniors talk about—this girl and he seem to have most of this in common.

She only has one parent, presumably she has lost the other to the deadly virus that is swiftly infecting all the world; everyone at school is confident a cure will be found; he and this girl are not. She stays home a lot, alone, the parent is often not there. The place is her sanctuary, or was—

Lately after school she comes to his house, telling him stories. It seems there is a strange presence dwelling in her home—unnatural, unearthly, unseen by anyone yet she knows it is there. She thinks it has simply moved in, and she is afraid that one night while she is all alone it will come out of hiding. Tonight she is afraid to go home, has lost her sanctuary, has come to him for help.

He goes to the house with her but they find nothing unusual. He talks with her for a long while, then, just as he is leaving, a cold chill passes through him and he suspects she is telling the truth. He gives her his number, tells her to call any—*any* time. She waves goodbye through the living room's big bay window as he goes.

At three o'clock in the morning the phone rings and the girl is hysterical, crying in gasps through the receiver. The thing has shown itself, is there in the living room, moving all around her, circling in, breathing icy gangrenous breath into her lungs as it draws near. She screams that the doors will not open, sobs that the lights will not work. The phone goes dead and cuts her off.

In just over a minute he is in his car and has nearly covered the few blocks between their addresses. As the car barrels up the last block to her house he spins the wheel, pounding the brake and then the throttle, sending the machine sliding perpendicular into her front yard where the highbeams finally blaze through the bay window. Her living room is flooded with white halogen light.

He leaves the car and runs to the front door. It opens with no effort. Inside the girl jumps at him, throwing her arms around him, crying, thanking him. The thing is still there, scarcely visible in the corner, shaded from the car's biting lights. For a long time none of them moves. And then the thing in the corner suddenly unleashes a scream of absolute terror. It is a sound like skidding tractor trailers, the sound of night being torn from day, flesh from bone. The thing continues to shriek as it flies out from its corner, somehow now oblivious to the light, willing for some odd new reason to bear the pain exposure will inflict. It is frantic, streaking about wildly, consumed, Malek senses, by a fear of something more horrible than all the creatures of hell, more hideous than living death.

And somewhere its screams are joined by a distant roar as the thing finds the open door and flees out into the night at impossible speed. The ground begins to shake.

They go to the window, he and the girl, and in the distance they can see a row of molten mushroom clouds rising above the far hills. The arsenals Man has cuddled for so long have been loosed, Malek realizes, not for simple political gain, but as part—the last part—of a desperate effort to win the hopeless war against a conquering disease. The ultimate tools of sterilization. And as he thinks it through he realizes what he is witnessing must certainly be a retaliatory strike.

He and the girl kiss each other goodbye. . . .

Malek wakes drowsily, eyes opening on the morning sun. There is no alarm ringing, no anxiety. He looks right and sees that his bio-med monitor has been switched off. He can hear Naia behind him, washing.

"Sleep well?" she asks.

He pulls himself together in his couch. "Better."

"Well, that is good. I trust any dreams you may have had were about our duties here on Mars."

He cranes his neck to see her expression but can't. "Of course," he tells her.

"Of course."

"You turned off my monitor, let me sleep," Malek says. "Why?"

"Oh, I did no such thing! Of course you typically neglected to turn it on last night."

Malek is quiet a moment. "Of course," he says thinly.

"It is time to go," Naia announces. She climbs into her seat with plates and coffee. "Breakfast."

"Thanks," Malek says, sipping as the motors wind up. They set out toward the mines.

At the mines Naia and Malek make the rounds together. When they leave it is early afternoon and neither one of them has said more than a few words. By dusk they find themselves entering Debtor's Canyon again on the last leg of their journey.

Naia is growing restless, impatiently running the truck a bit hard, pounding it over low rocks and gullies.

"Take it easy," he says, a little whiney on purpose.

She looks him a frosty glare. He grins and her face warms a little, the truck slows a little.

"I'm just anxious to get back, see if there's any word from Earth since we've been out," Naia explains.

"I don't think so." Malek stares at his hands in his lap. "I don't like . . . what I saw."

"You believe what you have dreamed?"

Malek nods.

"And what did you see, Malek? What do you think has happened?"

"Everything." He closes his eyes.

He feels her hand take one of his, holding it. He is aware that the truck has come to a halt.

"Look," Naia says, calmly, softly.

He opens his eyes. She is gazing out the windshield into the midnight shadows among the high rocks ahead. She points with her free hand. Malek can see nothing there. "What?" he asks.

"Something moved, up there, that side."

"Oh, it's just those shadows playing tricks on you again. We're tired. I've been awful company. Once we—"

"No! Something moved." Naia pauses, biting her lip. Suddenly, "There!"

Malek looks again and he can see color shifting a hundred yards ahead, a form materializing at the edge of darkness and light. Then he can see that it is a figure walking out to the center of the canyon—a woman. She has one hand held out at arm's length. She is wearing a shimmery white wedding dress that flows strangely in the low gravity. Her face fills with a make-do, persecuted smile.

Naia squeezes Malek's hand more tightly. "What should we do?" she asks. "What will happen?"

"Nothing," Malek says. "It's okay. She has nowhere else to go."

Pandora's Box 2055

by
David Hast

About the Author

David Hast lives in Evanston, Illinois, where he has his own video production studio. He is 33.

Born in Ohio, since high school he has lived in Colorado, Missouri and California before coming to Evanston. He has worked at the usual range of jobs: lifeguard, short-order cook, university lecturer, landscaper, recycling plant laborer, busboy, ski-shop technician, pizza deliverer, movie projectionist, stagehand, radiology clerk, orange-juice squeezer, grip, gaffer, and best boy. He only has two jobs now, both equally demanding; video producer, and science fiction writer. In the latter, he has, so far, published "Pandora's Box 2055," and sold two stories to BBR, a British small press magazine, as well as to several other small press publications.

About the Illustrator

Rob Sanford lives in Bend, Oregon, is married and has three sons. He graduated in 1975 from San Jose State University with a Bachelor of Science degree in Industrial Design. He has worked for Boeing, Lockheed and Tektronix. He also does consulting work on watch design, fiber optics, medical instrumentation, and sports equipment—to name just a few. At the present time, he is employed by Tektronix as a senior electromechanical engineer working on optical time domain reflectometers.

Besides his industrial design work, he also does illustration in his free time and does science fiction and fantasy illustration by preference.

In a neat little workshop in the middle of Denver, a man is building a time machine. He has modeled it, from memory, on the one in the movie of H. G. Wells' novel, the movie with Rod Taylor and Yvette Mimieux. It is made out of automobile and bicycle parts mostly, and sheet metal and re-bar from wrecked buildings.

Denver is a depressed, crumbling remnant of its former glory now, like most large North American cities. No one knows anyone anymore. But Jim Lerner is going back to the old frontier, to small-town Denver, basecamp to the silver and gold miners, western outpost of the entrepreneurs and railway barons who will build lively boom towns in the Colorado mountains, with little white churches, gaslit saloons and baroque opera houses. This Denver will be a town of law and order, where everyone knows his neighbor.

Jim, a small man, has a cowboy suit, complete with hat, scarf, boots and spurs, hanging by the door, in readiness for the day when he will climb into the machine in his workshop, just like Rod Taylor did, and return to the Old West. There he'll settle down with a quiet little blonde, just like Yvette Mimieux, and raise a family the way you were supposed to.

In a laboratory in Mexico, a woman is operating a time machine. Hers is a huge glass cylinder, half-filled with red liquid, from which a white mist rises, filling the upper half. A blue spark zigs across the opening at the top, separated

Illustrated by Rob Sanford

from the vapor by a sliding steel plate. Shiny white metal studs run up and down the inside of the cylinder, ready to emit the particles that unbind time.

She removes all her clothes, then turns off the spark gap. Holding her cat, shaved of all its fur in order to better conduct the field that passes readily through skin, she slides the steel plate aside and steps into the warm red bath. The one-minute delay clicks off and the spark resumes, energizing the vapor. A hundred little whirs sound and the white studs begin to pulse. The mist turns to a thick green cloud which ascends through the spark and pours over the side of the cylinder, then falls cooled into a lighter green mist, hovering just above the floor at the base of the cylinder.

The woman submerges herself and her cat completely now. The cat does not struggle. The woman's hair fans out around her head like an Aztec crown. Their four eyes glow green, so that through the filter of the red liquid they appear black, like holes in their heads. Suddenly the tumbling mist reverses its course and implodes back into the tube, like a film run backwards. And just as suddenly everything is gone—tube, mist, woman, cat. All that remains is a small, red, mercuric pool on the cement floor of the lab.

The Guardia breaks down the door, having located the place by "persuading" some of the woman's colleagues to show them to it. The ranking officer, a colonel, sees the red pool and orders the platoon out of the laboratory. A *norteamericano* in a black suit strides through the door, along with a worker dressed in full hazardous material gear. He steps in front of the colonel to get a better look at the red stuff, then commands the worker, who approaches the red pool and sucks it up with a thin gold nozzle into a shiny gold box. The platoon reassembles and quickly escorts the U.S. operatives to a waiting helicopter.

Inspector Sam Mankow's two assistants followed him

into the abandoned Washington, D.C., basement workroom. "Dusty, as usual," he said. "You'd think they never spent any time in these shops." The machine rested in the center of the bench—a simple hand model, a sort of interlinked series of chromium bracelets.

Brett and Amelia went right over to the device, excited as usual. Mankow approached the room as a whole, alert for revealing signs beyond the device itself, which obviously no one had attempted to conceal. He had little hope that this case would prove anything but routine.

"All right, kids, take the standard readings and box it up. And these." He pointed to a cardboard box on the floor at the end of the bench which contained perhaps 100 more of the bracelet sets—this was apparently a growing supply operation. "We've got another place across town to do this morning."

"The one the old woman made from a bicycle?" Brett asked excitedly. "They were talking about it this morning."

Amelia stepped on Brett's toe and ground it like a cigarette butt.

"*Who* was talking about it?" Mankow asked. He ran a hand through his full head of gray hair.

Amelia, who was senior to Brett as a Department of Commerce field inspector, knew better than to talk too much to anyone outranking her, even a seemingly sympathetic, professorial type like Dr. Mankow. She quickly intervened.

"Oh, it was just some rumor floating around," she said, stepping in front of Brett. "No big deal. I think it was really more to do with the possibility in general of converting a bicycle or an engine or whatever to a device, not so much specifically—"

"Well, *that's* a coincidence, since we've never yet encountered anything remotely like a bicycle in the six years I've been at this! Dammit, Fuchs," he said to Brett, "you *know* we're supposed to keep a lid on this. Try and be discreet."

"Sorry, Dr. Mankow. It was discreet. I mean, it was in our section and everything. That is, I mean—"

"All right, Brett, all right," said Mankow, less angrily now. "You don't have to cover for anyone. I'm not out for anyone's job. Just tell the person—people in general—to be discreet. That's all."

As she boxed up the evidence, Amelia wondered how much of the problem they were really seeing. Was this just the tip of the iceberg? What do these things really do? Their whole investigation was motivated by the assumption that these devices were dangerous. They *are* illegal, she reminded herself.

And yet, what an exciting, seemingly infinite world of possibilities! Who could blame people for trying to explore it? She herself had had a taste of it. And Brett. At a party once, one of the staff engineers produced a single-loop bracelet model. It was a crude little device that skipped you forward a few seconds—then you'd loop around, living backwards, invisible to the others in the room, until you met up with them as you came back to the start of the loop. There you were again, with your drunk friends, and that tall guy with the crooked hairpiece that kept hitting-up on you, and to them you'd just sort of vaguely flickered for half a second.

In her investigations, she'd talked with people who claimed to have gone back to the Middle Ages, or forward to the next century, though none could produce any documentary evidence or credible witnesses. It was common knowledge that people were disappearing, and there were witnessed accounts of people vanishing in, or on, or wearing a device they'd manufactured or acquired for just that purpose.

However—and no doubt the reason behind the government's prohibition on the devices—no person whose departure had been witnessed had ever returned.

Amelia rode with Brett in a department van to the next site. They took the scenic route along Rock Creek, following Mankow's car. She was tired of just passively enforcing regulations like some kind of drone bureaucrat. Was it really a problem? Was time travel—if that's what was happening—really dangerous? She was glad now that Brett had breached the usual decorum and brought up the morning's rumor. Why not? she thought.

"Look, Brett, where are all these people disappearing to? Someone in the government must know, right? What's happening with the lab tests?"

Brett laughed. "Nothing works according to the formulas—at least not always. For the low energy devices, like that one we did at Lester's party, there's a predictable, controllable reaction. But increase the field and *boom*— suddenly the subject disappears entirely. Not just that little wobble you see with a bracelet. I mean, boom! They're gone. And they don't—"

"I know, they don't come back. I know. But why?"

"We don't know. We know of the existence of time fields, but it's a very weak force, weaker than gravity. And we haven't really figured out how to measure it yet. The formulas predict the displacement, but that's all. They just say, 'It happens. Time travel exists.' But how, to what degree, who knows? You take any chemistry in college?"

"Yeah."

"Remember electron valence in atoms?"

"I think so. . . ."

"You know—an atom has a certain energy level, then boom, it jumps, or falls to a different level. Without anything in between. Not a gradient. That's what we figure is happening with the time force. At a certain point, a jump occurs, and the subject gets permanently displaced. Theoretically it's totally reversible, but as you know, in practice, the device, or its central drive component, always gets left behind. So the joke's on you if you try it, I guess."

"Haven't they been able to bring anyone back? I mean, if the device gets left behind, can't the scientists try and reverse the reaction?"

"Just doesn't work. I don't get it all, sorry. All I know is, it takes radically different levels for different things to make the initial jump. People are easy, animals too. And plastic. Metal is kind of hard. Wood is almost impossible, which is pretty weird, considering that people and animals are made up of carbon, just like wood. But once something jumps—no, nobody's been able to reverse it yet. Far as we know."

They pulled into the long driveway to a 19th century Victorian estate that was hidden from the street by a line of poplars. The main house stood abandoned and collapsing, but a number of government vehicles were parked in front of the well-preserved coach house. The house was cordoned off with yellow tape, like a crime scene. Mankow skidded to a stop and jumped out of his car. Amelia opened her window.

"Looks like a big operation, Doctor."

Mankow was furious. "I can't believe this! How the hell do they get tipped on these things?"

Amelia looked at Brett. They both said it at the same time: "FDA." Brett parked and they ran to catch up with Mankow, who was stomping toward the coach house.

"Goddamn FDA," he growled. This was a side of his character they rarely saw. "We go off on another lame jewelry hunt and they rip us off. Assholes!"

"Why didn't we come here first, then?" Amelia asked, risking an angry reply. But Mankow was clearly asking himself the same question.

"I was only following orders," he scowled. "Someone wanted FDA to get this one—no question about it."

"But why?" Amelia asked. "After all, we're more or less pursuing the same agenda. FDA wants to make sure people don't get physically damaged; we want to make sure they don't get burned for their dough. Same thing, really."

"Maybe they just didn't want *me* to find it." Mankow gave Amelia a piercing look. "I know things that would truly amaze you, Miss Kolodny. And even you, Mr. Fuchs, for all your access to potent rumors." Brett looked down, embarrassed. Mankow said, "Now let's get in there before they cart the damn thing off—I'd at least like to get a look at it."

As they climbed the front porch, they met Jane Fester coming out of the house. She was clutching a small gold box with both hands. Mankow frowned when he saw her. FDA Inspector Fester was all smiles and business.

"Hello, Sam. You here to see the time machine?"

"If that's what you want to call it."

"Well, I believe in calling a spade a spade, Sam. You call it whatever you want. Call it an exercycle—that's about all it is now. What made it special is right here." She patted the metal box. "Come on, I'll show it to you before the boys pack it up." Mankow looked hungrily at the box. Jane held it tightly to her chest.

They followed her into the house. "A Mrs. Jeanette Worley owned the place," said Jane. "Big on quack causes and so forth. We're checking her out."

In the center of the kitchen stood what appeared to be an ordinary exercise bicycle. The exact same model as mine, Amelia observed. Two robots were lifting it into a crate.

Mankow ran up to them. "Hold it, hold it!" he exclaimed, practically pushing the machine back to the floor.

The robots looked at Jane Fester, who nodded approval, and they set it down. Mankow began a rush examination.

"Where did the drive go?" he asked. "Here?" He pointed to a slot in the frame just above the crank.

"Very good, Sam," she patronized. "It was interfaced with the wheel, and part of the room, sort of. Hard to explain without seeing it—but alas, this box is sealed now. Drop by my office sometime and I'll show it to you. . . ." She patted the box. Mankow's eyes widened. " . . . say, sometime next year— Ha ha ha!"

Amelia wondered, idly resting her hand on the seat of the machine, how anything so mundane could be adapted to generate a fluctuating time field. The little device in that box must be quite extraordinary, she thought, because the bicycle certainly isn't.

The odometer, mounted prominently in the center of the handlebars and missing its cover, read 1963.9. Actually, a touch less than .9. It looked like a date to her. She did a quick mental calculation: one-tenth of a year is 36.5 days. December being 31 days long and November 30 days, this would put it at noon on November 25th. Back a touch would be— Amelia smiled. She then quickly, but discreetly, pretended to lean over the handlebars to look at the wheel in front, while she dragged her thumb across the counter dials of the open odometer and slipped them out of place. When she stood up again, it read 3073.9. Amelia smiled again.

Jane Fester squinted at Amelia suspiciously. She turned to the robots, which clicked from record to integrated vector movement. "Crate it up! Sorry, Sam, I've got to get back to the lab before they all knock off early. Better luck next time." Jane led the two robots and the crated machine out of the kitchen, all the while tightly cradling the sealed box. She glanced over her shoulder once more at Amelia, who continued to grin knowingly. Mankow began to pick over the kitchen, pitifully, hoping to uncover anything they might have overlooked.

"Brett, please, you've got to do this one thing for me," Amelia pleaded, refilling their wine glasses. "I'll never ask you for another favor."

"Sorry. Way too risky. You gotta play it straight around here. You screw up with the government, it can mean a lot more than just losing your job. We took an *oath*, remember?"

"Yeah, and so did a lot of other people. But something's wrong, someone's covering up. Mankow practically came out and said so this afternoon."

Brett stood up and threw back the entire glass of wine in one gulp. He swayed a little as he snatched the home entertainment remote off its wall charger. "Something good!" he barked into the remote.

"Format, sir?" it inquired.

"Music," he mumbled, and slipped back down into the couch. "With some kind of smell."

"Don't get too specific there, Brett," Amelia said. "You might confuse it."

Music began playing, with a surprising aroma. Amelia leaned over Brett to refill his glass, inadvertently revealing a bare breast inside her loose blouse.

"Jesus, Amelia, you know I'm about as straight as a mountain road. Don't try seducing me into it."

Amelia laughed at Brett's paranoia—but noted, yes, he does have a tendency to be preoccupied with sex. She pulled a folded newspaper clipping from her blouse pocket and handed it to Brett.

"Maybe this will seduce you, dear. Today's *Post*."

Brett, a little too drunk to absorb written material easily, read the clipping out loud:

The President today asked Congress to impose even stiffer penalties on persons who manufacture, distribute or use Temporal Manipulation Devices (TMDs), including a mandatory jail term of not less than five years for modifying any existing machine for the purpose of time abuse.

"Abuse of these dangerous machines has reached unprecedented levels," the President asserted, "and like a virus, threatens to spread to all strata and all ages of society."

The President asked further that Congress empower the FBI and the Food and Drug Administration, as well as the Departments of Commerce and State, to undertake joint investigations into the importation and exportation of the time devices.

Not everyone, however, concurred with the President's position. A spokesman for the underground Time Habit Escape Movement (THEM), who would identify himself only as Elwood, told the *Post* that, "the government has repeatedly insisted on the danger of time travel, but all evidence points precisely to the contrary. Our research indicates that no less than 20% of persons over the age of 18 in this country have experimented with time alteration. And this despite government prohibition."

As to the alleged disappearances of numerous time experimenters, Elwood had this to say: "Of course they haven't returned. They're waiting for the day when time escape will be legal and sanctioned. If we legalized time travel tomorrow, a lot of these people would rematerialize—I assure you."

Elwood asserted that his organization, and the time travel movement in general are "growing and healthy. In the long run, the government cannot hope to suppress it. If there are any dangers at all, the government is to blame, for forcing people underground, where sometimes imperfect devices are manufactured and used."

Most members of Congress, however, appear to share the President's view that this activity is dangerous and should remain illegal. A bipartisan coalition of senators and House members have promised to introduce appropriate legislation before the close of this session of Congress. No significant opposition appears to exist in either the House or the Senate. Debate is expected to center simply on degrees of criminality and strategies for enforcement.

"Well," Brett asked, "what am I supposed to say?"

"Brett, I think it's pretty clear," said Amelia. "The government's afraid of this, afraid it might lead to anarchy. What if time, history—hell, *reality,* is a flexible thing? I can't say I blame people in power for wanting to hold it in check."

"I'm not that optimistic. I think it just might be deadly. This idea that people are waiting until it's legal to return sounds pretty nutty to me. If it's so great, I'm sure a few of them would risk jail and come back to let us know. I think they're dead."

"How many dead bodies have we found in our raids?"

"We haven't found *any* bodies, dead or alive."

"And yet," Amelia said, "the government maintains that people are dissolving, exploding, getting electrocuted—on a daily basis. Why do they feel they have to *lie,* Brett? Maybe they know something we don't."

"Don't be paranoid."

"I'm not paranoid. I just want to know." Amelia kneeled down and looked Brett in the eye. "I have to know, Brett."

Again, Brett downed his glass of wine in one swallow. "Look—what makes you think I can get you this thing? I don't even know what it looks like!"

"But you know where it is, right? Rocky Fowler's got it. Isn't he FDA's Time Field physicist?"

"Yeah. . . ."

"And you two go way back together, right?"

"No, Amelia, we don't. Rocky Fowler and I 'go back' to college, and only to college. And we never really got along, even then. He's selfish, overly ambitious—"

"And really good-looking. And gay."

"And married, Amelia. He's not looking for another man. And even if he was, I'm not about to—look, he's not going to give it to me. The guy is completely devoted to his job. He's not going to risk all that for a good time."

Amelia sat next to Brett on the couch and sighed. "No, you're probably right." She reached over Brett to pick up the bottle, emptying the last of the wine into her glass. Brett stood up.

"I'll open another bottle." He hurried into her kitchen. Amelia listened to him opening and closing the refrigerator, heard the pop of cork. She tapped her fingers on the arm of the couch, contemplating her next move. Brett came back into the living room, already pouring the next glass. He collapsed into a chair across from the couch.

"There is one thing," Amelia said. "Why don't you tell him about that red liquid—the stuff from Mexico."

Brett jumped up. He killed the music, then thought better of it and turned it on at double the volume. He stomped back over to Amelia, looming over her.

"How the *hell* do you know about that? And *what* do you know?"

"Hey, relax, Brett—be cool. No secret is secret in Washington for long—you know that. I know they found this sort of residue of a device, some sort of propellant or something. It's a missing link of some kind—I don't know. All I know is, it's important, *real* important. And as far ahead of us as the FDA is on this, I'm sure they'd love to get their hands on it."

"If you're smart," Brett whispered, bending down close to her face, "you don't know *anything* about it. Don't

ever bring it up again. You're lucky you mentioned it to me
first. God knows what Mankow would do if he had any idea
you knew about this.''

"I suspect that Dr. Mankow is rather more sympathetic
to my way of thinking than you might guess. In any case,
I'm sure now that whatever you know is pretty hot, and if
old Rocky's half as hungry as you are, he'll buy it.'' Amelia
jumped up and faced off with Brett. "*Come on*, Brett, don't
you want to see that bicycle thing in action?''

Brett played it cool now. "No. Not really. I don't see
how it's any different than that antique carriage design we
found in Denver.''

"You mean the thing the movie-buff guy used? The
guy with the old sci-fi flick posters all over his workshop.''

"Right. Transverse rotating field propulsion. Same sort
of thing.''

"Yes, but . . . .'' Amelia locked her fingers behind her
head and smiled.

"But *what?*''

"But you never saw them working.''

"Sure we did,'' Brett protested. "We disappeared
about six rabbits and a couple of monkeys on the Denver
model just last week.''

"How many people?''

"Very funny,'' said Brett, but he wasn't smiling.

"I know all about it, Brett—it's no secret. You guys use
Loafers once in a while. It's no big deal. It's legal.''

"Okay,'' said Brett. "So you know about it. So why
bring it up?''

"I've been around a little longer than you, Brett. I may
not have the inside track to the classified lab work, but I *do*
know things. And the way I hear it, those Loafers aren't
much better than the rabbits. There's a conscious component, something to do with will, or concentration, something like that—stop me if I get too far off track—you can't

get a proper feedback from a Loafer, either verbal or EEG. I bet you guys would kill to get a willing, cooperative subject. Not to mention sober.'' Amelia waited a moment to see if Brett was catching her drift.

''Go on,'' he said, not quite getting it yet.

''So here I am,'' Amelia said. ''Wire me up. Talk me through it. Ask me questions. Inch the power up bit by bit—whatever you like. Just do it. Get me that drive. Let's you and me build a time machine—whattaya say?''

Brett just stared at her, stonefaced. Amelia wondered what he was thinking—does he think I'm crazy, or is he so thrilled by my offer he doesn't know what to say?

''I'll let you know. I gotta get some sleep.'' He was already halfway out the door. He was suddenly nervous. This is a good sign, thought Amelia. He's starting to act like a criminal, like he's plotting. This is good.

''Don't worry about the bicycle parts,'' she said quickly, before he slipped away. ''I'll take care of all that. Just get me the drive, and whatever documentation they've got on it. I'll take care of all the rest.''

''I'll let you know,'' said Brett again, and shut the door.

In a well-preserved Victorian coach house in the middle of Washington, D.C., Amelia is building a time machine. She arrived at daybreak and, aided by a very nervous Brett, carried her exercycle into the house, for which they had keys.

With Brett reading from an FDA computer printout, they determined the precise placement of the machine in the kitchen, wired parts of it to the floor and walls, and attached an octagonally shaped crystal, half-filled with a red liquid, to the frame below the seat.

Amelia sat down on the seat and tucked her toes into the pedal straps. She set the large, open-faced odometer to a number—a date, she hoped. ''I'm ready,'' she announced.

Brett had quickly assembled a tiny armory of test

instruments: video and audio recorders, a spectrometer, gravitometer, even a color temperature meter. Who knew what sort of anomaly would arise under these conditions? The little device he held in his hand was Brett's favorite, and the one he considered most likely to capture significant data. It measured most of the properties of atoms that contributed to their spacetime behavior: spin, vibration, polarity, charge and so forth, and it measured incremental changes, and it differentiated between the different atoms and molecules. This particular meter was designed to detect changes in organic matter.

As soon as Amelia began to pedal, the meter started blinking. Some sort of spacetime anomaly was already present. A toaster-sized machine was storing and analyzing the data from all the test equipment. The odometer on the time machine, set for a theoretical November 21, 1963—the day before "the day that every schoolchild once knew by heart," she had told Brett—clicked with every pedal rotation, but did not advance, the appropriate modification having been made.

She pedaled furiously, sweating and grunting, until finally she could sustain the effort no longer and cried out, "It's no good, it's not working." She slipped her feet out of the straps and let the pedals spin freely. As the single big wheel of the exercycle slowed, the meter in Brett's hand registered more and more activity. The room was suffused with a green light.

"Talk to me, Amelia—what are you seeing, what are you hearing?"

Amelia tilted her head back, her eyes rolling up white in their sockets, and when the wheel rolled to a full stop, the meter pinned against one side, dropped to the other, and Amelia vanished. All the measuring instruments had returned to normal. The room was daylit, ordinary.

Brett did a quick playback of the videocam, and it

looked like the oldest, corniest movie special-effect—now you see her, now you don't. The harder data only confused matters. Neither he nor the analyzer could deduce a consistent spatial direction or movement through time. The data was maddeningly contradictory, fluctuating seemingly randomly and wildly, proteins in her body moving forward and fats backward; her head remaining fixed in the present while her torso inched back a few seconds, and her limbs and hair raced thousands of years into the future. Yet she had looked whole and normal right up to the moment she disappeared.

Brett could make no sense of it. He felt foolish, defeated. He had let Amelia talk him into this, and now she was gone and he had nothing but worthless data to show for it. Quickly, he packed up the equipment and hauled it to the van they'd parked in back. He sped away, wondering who would ever hire him after FDA, Commerce and all the rest cooked his ass. Maybe, he thought cynically, there's room for me in some other time somewhere. Or is it *somewhen*?

A tiny room. Practically a cell. Bare walls. No door, no windows.

What happened? Renata wondered. Did I fail? Did the Guardia catch up with me?

Quickly she felt her head and inspected her naked body in the dim light for bruises, cuts. Nothing. Her cat, Mayamo, meowed pitifully. He was pacing against a wall, rubbing one side and then the other, walking and turning, walking and turning. He too was naked—hairless.

"Mayamo. Ven aqui, Mayamo!" But Mayamo kept pacing the wall, like a caged zoo animal.

As her eyes adjusted to the dim light, she noticed a small mattress in one corner of the room. A thin, army-issue-type wool blanket was spread neatly on it, tucked in on three sides and folded over at the top. There was no pillow, nor were there sheets. The mattress was striped blue and white.

Renata stood up. Everything felt normal, though she was lightheaded. A burst of vertigo hit her and neural flashes filled her vision for a few seconds. As she regained her equilibrium she began to walk the perimeter of the room. Bare, absolutely smooth walls and floor, like a kind of slate rather than a painted plaster or tile. A perfect square, about eight feet on a side. The ceiling, which was flatly and evenly lit like the rest of the room, also appeared to be about eight feet high. There were no windows, no doors, no cracks or openings, and no lamps, no visible place to hide lights. She could see the intersections of every plane—the room was a perfect, smooth box. No electric outlets, no furniture, nothing except the mattress. So where was the light coming from?

Renata sat down on the mattress. It was very thin—like lying on the hard floor. She lay back on it and hit her head on something hard. She jumped up and flipped the entire mattress over. On the floor in the corner sat a black, rotary telephone—a Western Electric desktop model from the 1960s or 70s. No line connected it to the wall, however. Renata picked it up and sat down with it on the upsidedown mattress. She lifted the handset to her mouth and ear and listened. . . .

Sitting down on the mattress, Jim's tight new denim jeans pinched at the backs of his knees. The new leather of his cowboy boots creaked. His hat slipped off his head as he hit the floor. He leaned over the black rotary telephone to reach for his hat and the tip of his string tie dangled into the Operator hole. He put his hat back on, carefully fastening the chin string, and lifted the handset to his mouth and ear. . . .

• • •

It was dead. Or at least no one was talking. There seemed to be some sort of presence on the line. Was that breathing?

"H-hello?" Amelia ventured, tentatively. Her own voice startled her. It seemed small and flat, as if the room had absorbed it. "Hello," she repeated. This time she realized what made the voice sound so strange: it was not coming through the earpiece of the handset as it normally would in a telephone. She only heard her voice resonating in her head and in the room.

But as she continued to listen she began to detect faint voices on the line. Distant, like the crosstalk you hear in the background of a long distance call. Most were too dim to decipher, but one or two that she could understand seemed to be similar: people talking about themselves, monologues.

Suddenly a voice came on clearly, loudly, connected directly to her. Amelia jumped up, her ear having been adjusted to the lower amplitude.

"Hello? Can anybody hear me? Hello . . . hello?" asked a man's voice.

"Yes!" Amelia answered. "I hear you. Do you hear me?"

"Hello?" the voice continued. "Anybody out there? This is James L. Lerner calling. Please answer. Please respond."

"James L. Lerner, I hear you!" Amelia shouted into the line. "James L. Lerner, this is Amelia Kolodny. Hello? Hello?"

She listened to the background jumble of voices again. James L. Lerner must be listening too, she thought. "James L. Lerner!" she yelled once, then listened. She could make out three fragments:

" . . . some kind of metal, maybe a stone. It's perfectly

smooth, and like I said, just a box. Nothing in the room but this phone and . . . ."

" . . . where I thought I'd be. God I hope someone can hear this. I've got a hunch about this. I mean, it's clearly not the 16th century. My theory is . . . ."

" . . . pero no hay ni lampara ni ventana. ¿Diga? Mi nombre es Renata. Diga me, alguien . . . ."

Amelia yelled into the phone again. "Renata! Mi nombre es Amelia! Contesta, por favor!" But when she listened again she heard a completely different mix of voices. As she continued to listen she realized that no voice lasted longer than a few seconds before dissolving to another voice. And by what people were saying, she realized that no one was making any direct communication with anybody else. Occasionally a voice came directly into her headset, as James L. Lerner's had, but they were never able to establish contact. She wondered who was receiving her voice directly into their ear?

Brett decided to come clean and tell Dr. Mankow everything. After three days of covering for Amelia, hoping she'd somehow return, he decided to stop waiting. He'd throw himself on the mercy of the Department. Besides, hadn't Amelia said that Mankow was on their side? At least on *her* side. Brett wasn't so sure that he himself was on their side, because he wasn't sure what their side was. But best to face Mankow now and get it over with before someone higher up started poking around.

Mankow listened to Brett's story, patiently, and when Brett had finished he simply said "FDA."

"Sir?"

"FDA, Mr. Fuchs. That's your next step. You may want to request a transfer."

Brett was confused. "But Amelia . . . ?"

"Don't worry," Mankow frowned. "It's already taken care of."

"Do you know what's going on, Dr. Mankow? Because if you do—"

Mankow stood up impatiently. "That'll be all, Brett." He gestured toward the door. "I've told you where to inquire. There's nothing more to say. It's out of my hands." He slipped back down into his desk chair, tiredly. "It's been out of my hands for months." Brett backed out of the office, slowly, hoping for one last word from his supervisor, but Mankow simply stared down at his folded hands on his empty desk.

Brett figured he had nothing to lose.

"I don't know what you're talking about," Rocky Fowler said, continuing to work at his data analysis.

"Yes, you do. So why don't you just tell me about it."

"I already did you a favor. Get lost."

Brett moved behind Fowler's monitor to get closer to his line of sight.

"Look, Rocky, I know you know what's really going on with these disappearances," he said, half-expecting Fowler to call his bluff. "And I'm sick and tired of zapping rabbits into oblivion and chasing after leftovers on sites you guys have probably been monitoring for months."

Fowler looked up finally. "I told you, Fuchs. I don't know what you're talking about. Now I've got work to do. Get out, or I'll call Security."

"Fine," Brett said, throwing his hands into the air. "Call 'em. I'll just blow the whistle on the whole thing. I'll go to that THEM organization, or better still, the press. I'll tell them how a certain FDA scientist gave me impounded, classified materials. I'll—"

"You'll be totally fucked is what you'll be," Fowler

snarled, turning in his chair. Brett continued to pace coolly around the room.

"I'm already fucked, Rocky. I lost Amelia. And my boss knew all about it even before I told him."

"I know," said Fowler.

"*You* know? How can you know?"

Fowler pointed at Brett. "Get out, Fuchs, ya bug me. You're history." He spun back around to his data station.

Brett opened the door to the lab. "Okay, Fowler. I'm going. But so are you. I may be fucked, but I'm taking you down with me. Count on it!"

Brett started to go but Fowler stopped him. "Not necessarily," he said. "Close the door."

Brett came back in and waited. Fowler took a long time making up his mind.

"All right," he sighed. "I'll show you. After that— well, you'll be part of it. You won't be blowing the whistle on anyone, because if you do you'll be dead before you take the breath to blow. You'll apply for a transfer to FDA. Maybe we'll find some way to use you—like running for coffee maybe."

"Fine," said Brett, standing his ground. "Just show me."

They circled the box twice, then ascended a spiral staircase to an observation deck above. The plywood box was, Brett now saw from above, simply a four-sided frame around a dull, metallic-looking cube. The cube was fed at the base by a fat, super-cooling pipe, and had a tiny ball-transmitter atop it. The machines on the perimeter of the room received whatever signals were sent from the box.

"If we know someone's going over, we don't try and stop them," said Fowler. "We just show up with our NIB and when the wave comes out of the place, we suck it up. That's how we got Amelia."

"What's a 'nib'?"

"Nova In a Box. Not really, you know, but same idea. Like a neutron star. Sucks it up. Then we transfer it into BIG NIB here."

"Where's Amelia?" Brett demanded. "Who else do you have?"

"It's amazing, isn't it. Inside that box, time stands still. And yet, there's people in it. They even seem to have mass. Still, they can't really be said to be living, from our point of view. Oh well," he shrugged.

"Is Amelia in there?"

"You two were ridiculous," sneered Fowler, ignoring Brett. "What the hell were you measuring? Was that an old Meissner Analyzer you were holding?"

"What?"

"You know, Commerce almost got there before us," said Fowler. "Those idiots would've shut the place down like an S&D mission." He laughed. Brett slammed him against the railing and bent him over it.

"What's she doing in that box? Answer me! What? *What?*" He was shaking the smaller Fowler by the throat and bending him further over the rail. Fowler's hands flailed helplessly, a bug on his back.

An alarm went off. Brett looked up to see three people in the control room looking down at him through the window. One was speaking into a communicator. Brett pushed Fowler an inch more. Fowler drew a high-pitched breath, as if it were his last, and Brett yanked him back. He pushed Fowler ahead of him as a hostage, then thought better of it as Fowler hesitated and slowed their progress.

Running back the way they had come, Brett saw soldiers coming up the spiral staircase. Fowler had managed to grab a weapon from one of the keyed wall boxes, and now blocked any retreat off the gangway where Brett was standing. As the first soldiers reached the top, Brett gauged the jump to each side. On one side was a warm-looking pool, pinkish as a swimming pool is bluish, and on the other, stood the box. As Fowler raised his weapon and the soldiers made the final half-turn off the staircase to the gangway, Brett leapt to the railing and threw himself into space. Machine gun spray deflected him slightly but he still hit the cube on its far side and it rolled, once, to an adjacent side. The super-cooling tube in the center ripped out and coolant spilled onto the floor, evaporating instantly. A green mist began to form over the pink pool. Brett stumbled to his feet and hobbled to the pool, further impelled by more bullets, including an electric one from Fowler's zap. When his body hit the pool, the liquid bubbled around him and the green mist shot upwards in a kind of column, collected at the ceiling and then dropped as it cooled, quickly filling the room. Brett's senses went red. Red filled his brain, he heard red and smelled it.

The sky was that blue blue, that deep, clean color you only saw near the mountains. And the horizon was all around him, unbroken in an arc of some 250 degrees. Against the sparkling mountains that towered in the west, stood a single wooden house. The railhouse.

Jim walked the mile or so across the scrub plain to the house. It was farther away than it looked, but the walk was a joy. All along the way he picked up little pebbles of turquoise, which littered the earth like common stones.

Jim put his boot up on the porch of the railhouse and massaged his foot through the tough new leather. When the telegraph operator slid his window open, Jim left off tending to his sore feet and climbed the four steps to the porch. He put his thumbs in his pockets and threw back his shoulders, breathing deeply of the cool, clean morning air.

"Howdy, friend," he said in his best cowboy twang.

"Howdy," said the telegraph man, just like that.

"Hear tell of any good panning hereabouts?" he asked.

The railway man looked up now. Who was this peculiar-sounding stranger in new-lookin' duds? Oh well, he thought, all kinda riffraff wander in on that train from Kansas.

"Train south to Cripple Creek at noon today. You're lucky."

"Why, thank yee, partner. Thanks muchly." Jim chuckled to himself now at his forced accent. Better lay off it, he thought. I'll say I'm from Pennsylvania.

For the first time, he noticed the blonde young woman sitting underneath a parasol at the end of the porch, a suitcase on either side of her. "Heading south, ma'am?" he asked, tipping his hat. Shyly, she shook her head yes. She wore no ring.

Renata awoke to Mayamo licking her face. She could hear running water, and the oscillating drone of insects, high-pitched, rising and falling. She sat up and shivered. Her hair was still wet. But warm sunlight fell on her back—it felt good.

She turned around to look at the sun, and at the stream behind her, and gasped at the sight of a dozen native women staring down at her. When she gasped, so too did they, taking a step back as a group. Although she was scared, she was elated as well. Their pre-Columbian clothing was not exactly as the anthropologists had depicted it, but the strong noses and jaws of the Maya were unmistakable.

I don't look that different from them, she thought. A little lighter-skinned, perhaps; perhaps a bit more slender. Then again, even slight differences can mean an entirely other tribe. I'm probably in danger.

The group and Renata stood deadlocked for a moment, and then Renata threw her shoulders back confidently and took a stride towards them. Two of the elder women fell immediately to their bellies and began chanting and the others followed. Renata let them go on that way for several minutes, then dropped to the ground herself in answering supplication. When the Mayan women had noticed her, they all stood up and began a lively argument. Concluding that she was probably crazy and sent by one of the gods, they decided to bring her to the temple where she could be properly worshipped. The priests would know what to do.

Mrs. Worley, the owner of the coach house, had arrived just before Amelia. She was shocked and frightened to find Amelia suddenly there, lying the same way on the same spot where she had been. Amelia looked up at the old woman, who had thought ahead to dress in 1960s clothing.

"You're not with . . . ?" Mrs. Worley stuttered.

Amelia had to think for a second. "I'm with you," she said, like she meant it. "Let's get on that airplane to Dallas, shall we?"

They walked out of the house arm in arm. As they reached the street at the end of the long driveway, Amelia immediately noticed that although the cars and the people all fit the period, the Washington monument, normally visible from here, was nowhere to be seen.

"Mrs. Worley," she said, seeing that the old woman had also noticed the absence of the important landmark, "this is going to be very interesting."

"It is," replied Mrs. Worley, hailing a taxi. "You got any of that old paper money on you?"

My Advice to the Undiscovered

by
Ray Aldridge

About the Author

Ray Aldridge won Third Place in a quarter of 1985, and his story, "Click," appears in L. Ron Hubbard Presents Writers of The Future, Vol. II. *After that, it was two years before he was heard from again, but then he began selling at a prodigious rate, to* The Magazine of Fantasy & Science Fiction *and other magazine markets, and to Bantam Books with his novels.*

In 1986, he attended the WOTF workshop in Taos. The curriculum consists of a number of L. Ron Hubbard how-to-write pieces originally published in such places as Writers Digest, *in the 1930s and '40s—the same pieces we have been publishing in these volumes for the past several years. Fashions in storytelling may evolve, over the years, but the basics of storytelling never change, and the advice in those essays, if you listen, is as spectacularly good as ever. Ray listened.*

Ray lives in Florida, and when last I checked he was also a very good potter and stained glass craftsman. (I still drink my coffee, every day, from a mug he designed and gave me in '86.) I suspect, strongly, that the balance has shifted—now he is a writer, and everything else comes second. He has learned a lot; I suggest it may be your turn to listen:

I've been waiting for someone to ask me to write this essay for a long long time. I'm glad it was Algis Budrys who asked me, because five years ago my first science fiction story appeared in these pages. Thereafter, I was no longer completely Undiscovered.

I avoided a lengthy enlistment in the ranks of the Undiscovered by a combination of luck, guile, and work. I can't tell you how to be lucky, but if you work hard enough and use a little guile, you won't need much luck. Talent probably helps too, but since I'm not sure what talent is, I'm also not sure it's necessary to a successful writing career.

The first thing to realize about writing is this: *Writing is not a conceptual art form.* Don't get me wrong, you do need good ideas—but most writers have more ideas than they'll ever use, and ideas alone aren't enough.

Most non-writers, to the bottoms of their optimistic souls, believe that works of astounding clarity and resonance would flow from their pens, if only they could get around to putting words on paper. This is a natural delusion. We all use language, and it's not immediately obvious that writing—and in particular, fiction writing—is a very specialized use of language.

Successful writing entails the acquisition of certain indispensable skills.

How can you acquire these skills? There are several avenues of instruction and the determined Undiscovered

Writer will exploit as many of these as possible.

I read a lot of how-to-write books when I was starting out. I recommend this course unreservedly, as long as you do read a *lot* of these books. It's dangerous to give all your faith to any one literary mentor; the dangers can be avoided by exposure to as many viewpoints as possible. I admit to a personal preference for books by writers who have themselves escaped gloriously from the ranks of the Undiscovered—but I studied all the books I could find, no matter how obscure the author.

A more important source of wisdom will come from your critical reading of other fiction writers. My guess is that most Undiscovered Writers have enlisted directly from the ranks of Lifelong Readers. However, critical reading is very different from reading for pleasure.

Before I took up writing, I was pretty easy. Practically any story could seduce me. I read very differently now, and it takes a very absorbing story indeed to make my internal editor shut up.

I retrained myself—to recognize beauty, and infelicity, in the prose, to analyze the structure of the story, to take note of the writer's use of devices both ingenious and banal. You can do the same. Don't, by the way, limit yourself to the genres you prefer; read widely in other forms and learn what you can. And don't make the mistake of looking down your Undiscovered nose at works you think inept, particularly if those works have had wide success. When a book sells a million copies, there's always a reason. If you can't figure out what that reason is, then there's something important you don't know about a million of your fellow human beings. That's not good, if you want to write about human beings.

I'm ambivalent regarding workshops. When they're good they're great, and when they're bad they're horrid. I've been the beneficiary and victim of both varieties. My guess is that workshopping is a lot like learning to play tennis; you should always try to play with someone who's better than you are, if you want to learn the game as quickly as possible. Workshopping with folk who are getting together to socialize and play strokes-and-slashes is enough to make you want to tuck your keyboard under your arm and walk into the woods until someone asks you, "Whut's thet?" On the other hand, one workshop I attended—so I believe—spared me years of laboring in the ranks of the Undiscovered. In the spring of 1986, the Writers of The Future people organized an experimental workshop in Taos for a dozen winners and finalists, a hungry bunch of Mostly Undiscovered Writers. Our instructors were Algis Budrys, Frederik Pohl, Gene Wolfe and Jack Williamson—four of the Ivan Lendls and Boris Beckers of our profession. If you can get into a workshop like that (by, for instance, winning a prize in the L. Ron Hubbard's Writers of The Future Contest), my advice is: go for it.

All these founts of knowledge are useful; drink deep. But any good book, any good writer will teach you that one thing above all leads to writing success. One day during the aforementioned Taos workshop, Budrys posed this question: What is a writer?

At first none of us had an answer.

Perhaps we secretly felt a bit insulted by the question, those of us who hadn't heard it before. "What is a writer?" indeed. Didn't our vastly-talented-but-inexplicably-not-yet-lionized selves adequately define the concept? We didn't say so, of course—we just looked uneasy.

One of our deeper thinkers attempted a somewhat labored semantic analysis of the word, and I must say it was listened to by the instructors with a laudable degree of patience.

However, when our would-be lexicographer had finally

run down, we found out that the most significant definition is this: A writer writes.

Not only that, writers write every day, not just when our Muse grabs us by the short hairs and yanks. Writers write in spite of fire, flood, or pestilence. Writers write no matter how desperate they are to be doing something else (this happens to me every day). Writers write no matter how well or badly the work is going.

Writers do this because they know that the only way to learn the skills of their profession is to practice them. They do this relentlessly and ruthlessly. To the professional writer, few comments are more annoying (or more frequently heard) than this one: "Gee, I wish I had the time to write." The insulting implication of this remark is that writers have nothing better or more important to do than to sit in a garret making up entertaining lies. It's not so; most writers must choose to neglect important matters in order to accomplish their work. This may explain why writers are often unkempt folk who live in unpainted houses, surrounded by unmown lawns. Our cars go unwashed, our carpets unvacuumed, our socks undarned.

But at least we don't go unpublished.

While you're absorbing the subtleties of your craft, don't neglect the business aspects of the writing profession. It behooves the smart Undiscovered Writer to avoid as many of the common pitfalls as possible. Learn everything you can about the mechanisms by which stories and books are bought and published. Read LOCUS, the trade magazine of the science fiction and fantasy field. When you've made that first professional sale, join the Science Fiction Writers of America. If you enjoy conventions, go to as many as you can afford, and get to know your fellow writers. If you can only go to a couple of conventions, choose the ones where you can meet editors. Your fellow writers are for the most part fascinating and stimulating folk, but they can only rarely help you get into print. And don't get so involved with socializing that you neglect your writing.

Remember that you're never too Undiscovered to start learning about contracts. For a good overview of the publishing industry, I recommend *How to Be Your Own Literary Agent* by Richard Curtis, a highly successful agent and insightful student of the business. (By the way, I'm not recommending the book because Richard Curtis is *my* agent—I read his book long before I hired him.)

Speaking of agents, it's wise to remember that you're very unlikely to get a good one before you've accumulated a meaningful track record. If you're completely Undiscovered, look with deep suspicion on any agency that welcomes you with open arms; in all likelihood they're either desperate for clients, or fonder of your wallet than your prose. Keep in mind that an agent won't help you sell short fiction; you have to do that all by yourself. Still, agents are worth seeking out, *after* you've written that first novel. Probably the best approach is to look for a publisher and an agent at the same time. You're likely to find a publisher before you find a good agent—but then you'll have the bait you need to entice the agent of your choice into negotiating your contract.

Don't expend all your guile on the business aspects of your career; save some for the writing itself. For example: don't make the grievous error of writing what you think you ought to be writing. Writing is difficult enough already. Instead, write what excites you, what has meaning for you, what you find most interesting.

Don't set yourself up for failure by formulating overly rigid plans and expectations—and don't fend off success by doing everything the hard way. I have a good friend, a fine horror writer. If there's such a thing as talent, he's got plenty. But he's got his heart set on establishing himself as a short story writer, even though there are vanishingly few markets for short horror. It's not that he has anything against novels. He plans to write one just as soon as he's sold enough short stories to the major markets. He's made up his mind that his career must progress in a specific way; instead he sells lots of good stories to the small press, he breaks his heart, and he deprives a wider audience of the opportunity to read his work. I wish he weren't so strong-willed.

However, if you're a science fiction writer, there's much to be said for writing short fiction. You can write a lot of short stories in the time it takes to write one novel, you can experiment outrageously, and decent markets still exist for it. Furthermore, it's probably the only significant publicity you can afford, while you're still Undiscovered. When my agent sent my first novel to Bantam, the editor had just read my latest cover story for *The Magazine of Fantasy & Science Fiction*. She read and bought *The Pharaoh Contract* in record time.

You can see why I speak respectfully of luck.

Those who are truly dedicated to transcending their status as Undiscovered Writers should at all times bear in mind this great axiom: No one really knows a whole lot about writing. In fact, the more you know about writing, the more mysterious and complicated it appears. I personally know several Undiscovered Writers who are pretty sure they've learned just about everything they need to know about the craft of writing; I fear they'll remain Undiscovered forever.

In fact, your acquisition of writing skills should go hand in hand with an ever-growing perception of the depths of your ignorance. At this point, I think my ignorance may well have outstripped my skills—but it's a linkage that gives me a good deal of hope and comfort. My perplexity reassures me that I have yet to reach my peak, that my best work is still before me . . . waiting for a time when I understand a little more than I do today.

Finally, the Undiscovered Writer should understand that Discovery is generally a slow progression, moving in fits and starts, and measured in tiny increments. When I sold my first story, I thought I'd reached the promised land—then it took me nearly two years to sell two more stories. Now, twenty short story and three novel sales later, I've come to understand that the promised land is always a little farther down the road. Still, I take a lot of encouragement from each small triumph, and so should you.

Trudge cheerfully and faithfully along your own road, and one day an editor may call you up to say, "Can you do me a piece on 'advice to new and beginning writers'? About 2000 words? In two weeks?"

When that happened to me, I felt a sense of sweet arrival. "Sure," I said.

The Trashman of Auschwitz

by
Barry H. Reynolds

About the Author

Barry H. Reynolds grew up in Patrick County, Virginia, and still resides in Rocky Mount. He has been a collection development librarian for the Blue Ridge Regional Library, in Martinsville, for the past five years. But that is perhaps a misleading set of data; for instance, after receiving a BA in English from Flagler College, in St. Augustine, Florida, he worked as a toy salesman, a plainclothes security guard, and a shipping clerk, before deciding to try his hand as a writer in Hollywood. Things didn't work out, and he took a master's degree in library science from the University of North Carolina before going to work in Martinsville.

He currently also writes book reviews for the Science Fiction and Fantasy Book Review Annual. "The Trashman of Auschwitz" is his first sale in ten years of trying; it will not, we strongly think, be his last.

About the Illustrator

Harold J. Fox lives in Riverside, California, but was born in Morgantown, North Carolina, and lived briefly in Florida, before moving to Wilmington, California. In the 1960s, he

gained an AA degree in commercial art from Los Angeles
Trade Technical Junior College, but spent the next two years
as an artillery man in the U.S. Army. Then he resumed school
at Los Angeles Harbor College, and then the University of
California at Long Beach, majoring in illustration. He is
presently employed at a ceramic decal company in Long
Beach. He resides in Riverside with his wife and two sons.

The old man stood by the edge
of the concrete ramp, staring into the glare of
amber light flooding down from the roof of the
Amtrak terminal.

Cold wind flushed the warmth of the train from his
clothes and brushed long, wispy gray hair across his wide
shoulders. He shivered and pulled the tattered, buttonless,
ankle-length overcoat—a Goodwill gift from kinder members of the asylum—closer about his massive body.

He took a deep breath; smelled the cold, diminishing
sweetness of diesel smoke; blinked. The light was all he
could see.

The train was building speed; the sound of its departure drifting back to him out of the darkness . . . clacking,
rattling steel. . . . He tilted his head, listening. . . . Absently
reached up and brushed back a few strands of hair with
his thick, blunt fingers, uncovering the dent in his skull,
a sunken square of scar tissue. Felt the dulling, electric
twinge tug at one side of his face; felt soft pressure move
behind his eye; felt his eye tear. He tilted his head toward
the sensation. Time slowed . . . sounds shifted, phased. . . .

. . . a dopplering steam whistle . . .

. . . wooden doors rattling open . . .

*Someone moving towards him from the spotlight, shout-
ing,* "Alle beraus!"

He flinched and snapped erect, heart thumping, face
suddenly blank: a prisoner's reflexive anonymity, waiting
for orders, for the shove . . . but this time there was nothing.

He blinked, once, twice. Reached up and pressed his thumb into the dent—a trick he'd learned to depend on despite the patronizing smiles of his doctors. After a moment, the soft current dissipated and the twisted rictus of his face softened. He wiped the drool from his dumb lips and moved in real time again.

The wind gusted suddenly and cold, carrying a scrap of newspaper that skittered across the empty parking lot and wrapped itself around Tepper's leg. He held back his overcoat and looked down. Grinned. "Come to welcome me home, have you?" he asked. Bent over, wincing at the dull sciatica, and unwrapped the page, held it up, fluttering in the wind. "So soon do you forget old Tepper's rules, eh? No trash on the street." He paused, then added, "But then, who knows me, eh? Who remembers old Tepper used to work these streets. All this," gestured, "and over to 12th was mine to keep clean." Smiled. "Not kosher, that's true. Still, I was good. Very, very good. The world's most dedicated trashman." He nodded absently, his smile fading to a slight twitch. "But then," tapped the side of his head, "that's all I could be, eh?"

He turned away from the glare of the spotlight and shuffled across the parking lot towards the street. Stood there for a moment, squinting at the buildings—dark, empty, boarded-up fronts. What light there was curled and looped into strange, unfamiliar names and peculiar icons of red, blue, and white neon.

A primer-splotched Chevy turned onto the street and rattled past him, leaving, in its wake, a smell of exhaust and a thumping salsa beat.

Not what we left, is it? he thought, remembering the jumble of shops that used to line this street when the neighborhood was thick with immigrants. He turned and looked towards downtown, a sprawling skyline tableau of high rises, flecks of light above a black, broken horizon. The

Illustrated by Harold J. Fox

metropolis glow washed against the night sky with the lure of carnival lights, mocking the unclean, shadow-alley darkness that infested this, the old part of town. Tepper chewed his lip and took a faltering step; shuffled aimlessly, head bobbing. "Which way?" Tried to remember which way to go. It had been so long. He wondered if his home would still be there. *Was it ever?* Sighed and remembered the hospital with a twinge of homesickness: sun washed porches, early mornings around the TV watching that jovial *goy*, Willard Scott; remembered his room: pale, without books or paintings or music; lifeless; and yet, for a while at least, it was home. He nodded. "So, am I the wandering Jew again, eh?"

Somewhere out in the darkness, a trash can overturned, its lid ringing down flat. He smiled. The paper fluttered about his hand, wrapping tighter. "Well, then, let's find a place to stay. Easy enough for you, at least." He took hold of the edges of the page. "But what about me, eh? What about the old Jew? Where will he go this time?" Shook his head.

He peeled the page off his sleeve, folded and stuffed it into his pocket, not noticing the large, still fresh, blockprint headline that read . . . GERMAN ARMY ATTACKS POLAND; CITIES BOMBED, PORT BLOCKADED. . . .

The alleyway was narrow. A corner streetlight pushed back the darkness with a thin, spectral blue light. Tepper squinted. Graffiti turned the walls into a mural of palimpsest abstractions.

The Dumpster hadn't been emptied in days, perhaps weeks. He shuffled closer. Streamers of paper dangled like viscera from the side door; the spring-set lid was pried back by the overflow. A milky paste oozed from the cracked, rusted bottom and puddled thickly on the ground. He reached out and touched the Dumpster's cold, green, metal bulk; a miasma of rot and decay hung in the air. He nodded at the bittersweet memories the smells recalled: those first years, when he worked what was then the suburbs, "riding ass" as the Americans had called it, leaning out into the brisk morning air to lose the smell of ripe rotting garbage; filling his lungs with sweet diesel exhaust; seeing, sometimes talking to, pink-robed housewives hurrying down the sidewalk with a wave and a forgotten bag; memories, too, of the bad days; the rainy days, the bitter cold days, when the rusting, dented, jagged-lipped cans pinched and cut and bruised no matter how thick the gloves, no matter how sturdy the boots; remembered sundrenched, humid days when the smell was so thick and foul that it often made his coworkers vomit. But not him. Not the Trashman of Auschwitz. Long ago his nose had been seared by smells of suppurating wounds and cesspools of blood and shit, the *durchfall* of diseased bowels released in the throes of death.

He took the newspaper from his pocket and pushed it into the side opening. It lay there for a moment, slowly uncrumpling, then caught the wind and tumbled past him, skittering towards the street; it was followed by an avalanche of more trash, scattering about his feet.

His heavy hands flexed. He wheeled, angered by the infirmity that had taken him from that last, single purpose in his life, and limped after the trash, stooping, scraping, swatting empty air.

At the mouth of the alley he made one last desperate grab, his stumbling momentum carrying him out onto the sidewalk . . . and into a gang of young boys.

The impact sent one boy sprawling into the street. The other two backed away, cursing, threatening, but wary of Tepper's intimidating bulk and wild hair.

The boy got up. Daubed at the blood on his skinned knuckle.

Tepper watched the other two boys move around until they stood on either side of him, waiting. They were young,

in their teens; they wore jeans with ripped-out knees, black
leather flight jackets with glinting metal studs, black army
boots. Their heads were shaved close; their skin was pale,
bloodless under the streetlight. He tagged them mentally
with descriptive names. Glasses, Chubby, and Acne Face—
the one he'd knocked down, the dangerous one.

Tepper shrugged his wide shoulders. "Sorry," he mumbled. Made a disarming gesture and took another step
back. Acne Face (Tepper sensed he was the leader) moved
toward him with a thin, wiry grace.

"Hey, no problem," he said, smiling. Licked the blood
from his fingers.

Tepper noticed a patch on the boy's jacket, large and
distinctive, even in the dim light. He squinted to help focus
his astigmatic eyes. In a circle of white was a black wolf;
stylized blood dribbled from its mouth; wrapped around the
wolf's chest was a band, a swastika. . . .

"Zeeser Gottenyu," he whispered.

The boy followed the old man's eyes, then looked back,
studying Tepper's face. "It's the nose, I think, that always
gives your kind away. Ain't that right, Jew?"

Tepper blinked.

"Filth. You Jewish filth."

*He had been standing in the bread line since midnight.
Now it was nearly midday. They were screaming at him, shoving him from his rightful place in line. Carl. A boy he had
been friends with for years was pointing him out to the SS
officer, screaming, "That one's a Jew! That one's a Jew!"*

"What? What did you say?" He felt the dulling, electric twinge tug at one side of his face; felt his eye tear. He
tilted his head toward the sensation. Time slowed . . . sounds
shifted, phased. . . . He took a faltering step toward Acne
Face, who blocked his way to the street. *The light,* his fear
was saying, *is better there. Maybe someone will see. . . .*

"I asked was you one of those Zionist swine trying to ruin the country."

"There was a time," Tepper said softly, "when questions like that were allowed." His voice was level. "But those days are gone." Smiled, nodding. "Buried along with the bones of the SS."

"Oh? And what would you know about the SS, old man? Just what your old mama Jew told you?"

Chubby and Glasses chuckled.

Tepper reached up and traced the outline of the dent. The skin felt warm and soft.

The boy studied the old man for a moment, then stepped up close, jabbing his thumb at the patch on the breast of his leather jacket. "Must bring back memories, huh, Shylock." He looked at his friends. "Look at him, would'ja." He reached out and tugged at a strand of Tepper's hair. "Right off the boat. Say, Shylock, how did you manage to survive the ovens?"

Old Tepper blinked.

"Big strong Jew. We'll need you for work."

He was pushed forward.

"Ach! mein Herr."

"Check him out. Mein Herr! He's having a goddam flashback!"

"Do well and you'll be a Kapo: you'll get to carry out your filthy Jew friends."

Without thinking, Tepper reached up and swept away the boy's hand, twisting it back with his vise-like grip. The boy was forced to drop to one knee to keep his wrist from being broken.

Tepper realized his mistake too late: felt his free hand being doubled up behind his back. He grunted and let the boy go. A hard shove and he stumbled out into the street, turned.

Still clutching his wrist, the leader stepped up close, spun (Tepper saw the movement in his mind a second after it happened), and, with a short, sharp yell, drove his heel in hard, just above the old man's belt.

Tepper doubled over, clutching at the pain, then let himself fall. His lungs locked empty, burning. His mouth worked, trying to suck in, to force down cool, life-giving air. A sharp blow to his kidney rolled him over onto his back. A black, steel-toed Doc Marten boot stomped down into his gut, once, twice. He felt something in his abdomen twist loose and saw the pain in white spots flashing at the edges of his vision.

"Filthy, stinking, dirty Jew."

Pain everywhere: back of his head, chest, thigh, biceps, neck. Old, familiar pain. The dent in his head grew warm, tingly. The muscles down one side of his face began to twist and tighten. Pressure moved behind his eyes . . . time slowed. . . .

Then, from deep within the alley, came a sound. . . .

. . . a dopplering steam whistle . . .

. . . wooden doors rattling open . . .

Glasses turned and stared into the alleyway. "Hey . . . what the hell was that?"

But his answer was cut short by the sudden wurp of a police siren; blue light stabbed and reflected off store front windows. Glasses and Chubby took off down the sidewalk.

Acne Face lingered a moment more. Grabbed Tepper by the hair and twisted the old man's head around. Vertebrae cracked. "Next time, *mamador*, we'll take you up on the roof and have us a little fire drill."

He stepped back and spat on the old man. Then he, too, was gone, blending into the shadows as a police cruiser slowed, its spot sweeping the mouth of the alleyway. Tepper pushed up and stared into the blinding white light. Blinked. Thought he saw barbed wire fences glisten against the distant, snowy fields. He clasped his hands behind his head and waited.

After the police finished their coffee, they left Tepper with an elderly black lady who worked the night desk at the Downtown Nonaffiliated Charity Emergency Shelter. She asked Tepper a half-dozen, non-intrusive, perfunctory questions and signed him in; then, without looking up, pointed him in the direction of the food line, the showers, and, the beds.

He lay there now, on a narrow cot in a row of cots, wrapped in his overcoat, his wide, heavy hands folded across his chest, his hair still damp and smelling of shampoo from the shower. His stomach was full of vegetable soup and saltines. He belched and enjoyed the flavor once more. Drifted in a soft, pre-sleep twilight, staring up at the rafters, listening to the drunken snores and whimpering nightcries of the miserables who lay with him. . . .

"You have not suffered the typhus fever?"

He sat up. The room was cold. A bright, sourceless light shone from above. The windows were smeared with a thick coat of white paint. He was naked underneath the thin, starchy gown. He shivered and curled his toes. Heard them crack. His head had been freshly shaved; his scalp tingled in the constant, cool draft. On a cart beside the bed, silver instruments glinted in a thick nest of white cotton. There was the smell of talc and alcohol and his own sweat. A blocky, auburn-haired nurse with large breasts stood patiently behind the doctor.

"What is your number?"

He answered quickly, with servile emotion. "114137, mein Herr."

The doctor gently probed his scalp.

Tepper shivered at the cold touch.

"Yes," the doctor murmured. "Yes, we shall begin."

Tepper sat up, giving off a bad sweat. The shelter's lights were out; red exit signs shone in the dark at either end of the room. Up and down the aisle, moonlight filtering through tall, grimy, screened-in windows glinted off the cots' metal frames. He swung his feet off the bed, dragging the rough, woolen blanket to the floor. His head throbbed. His shoulders were stiff and sore. His gut ached. He pressed the heels of his palms against his temples to offset the pressure building behind his eyes. *Just a dream. Just the old* dybbuk *whispering to you, trying to fool you . . . stupid dream. . . .*

He looked up. Suddenly alert. Fearful. A bitter cold hung in the air, like the breath escaping from a refrigerator door . . . and something more, a peculiar stench. He frowned. Heard the hissing and clanking of radiator pipes.

Then the soft, dry whisper, "Please, water."

A small, shadowy figure moved at the foot of his cot. "No . . . go back . . . go back. You don't belong here."

The small shadow figure moved towards him into a slant of moonlight. Tepper flinched at what he saw: death-pale face, sunken eyes, scabby hands clutching a small bundle of rags stitched together to make a doll.

"Sir, please, water."

Then he placed the smell, the cloying sweetness that only rotting human flesh can own. "Lord God, no." He felt his bowels loosen in a hot, wet squirt. His tears turned her face into a pale blur as he pushed up, shoving her cold, frail body gently to one side and stumbling towards the door.

Behind him, someone grumbled a curse, then, seconds later, screamed.

He stood on the corner, near the mouth of the cul-de-sac alleyway that ran between the apartment building and its sister unit, absently chewing a slice of pizza he had rummaged out of a Dumpster. By now, he had convinced himself that what he had seen in the shelter was just a dream, just a trick of the old *dybbuk* in his head. He took another bite. The cheese was cold and rubbery, and the crust was covered in netty webs of gray mold, but he didn't mind. He had had worse.

The twin towers had survived, showing little of their age, though one was obviously abandoned. From where he stood, he could see the side that faced the alleyway. He counted the dark squares of windows . . . up eight . . . over four; again, up eight . . . over four. There. His old apartment. His home. He followed fire escape zigzagging fire escape, covered, as was much of the side of the building, in some still green, leafy vine.

Why come back? She's gone. Everything's gone. The furniture, the books, the photographs. All lost. Again. Felt his bladder swell. Shivered. Took an aimless step, turning. Remembered Lodz. After the Americans had deloused and nursed him back to health. Returning to his home to find another family living there. . . .

A small woman with healthy red cheeks answered the door.

"What do you want?" she asked.

"To come home."

"There is some mistake. This house belongs to us. To me and my husband." Her voice rested on the last word, as if the strength of it alone would frighten him.

He brushed her aside and entered his house.

"This is our home now. You can't blame us. We had nothing to do with the camps."

She called for her husband, who came from a room in the back, all fluster and resolve, who took one look at Tepper's dead, sunken eyes and said nothing.

The woman kept circling Tepper, and he was reminded of a cowardly, barking dog.

"A terrible thing," blurted the husband. *"We didn't know, of course."*

"Yes, yes," agreed the wife, *"but your house . . . this house was given to us. It's ours."*

"Flawas, please?"

He flinched.

"You wan'? Pretty for you?"

He turned slowly, trembling. Stared for a moment, then sighed. He hadn't noticed the small booth, set back, the way it did, off the sidewalk and out of the wind. Crudely cobbled together from scraps of plywood and two-by-fours, it advertised its single item inventory in large, hand-painted, red letters: ROSES. Behind the stand, sitting on a wooden stool, wrapped in a quilted coat, was a young Asian girl. Her hair was straight, black, and cut in bangs. She held a flashlight on the pages of a black-bound book that Tepper assumed was the Bible.

She smiled nervously.

Tepper smiled back. He felt guilty, not having enough money to buy something from her, so he turned, shaking his head, and limped across the street.

The door to the apartment building swung open freely, its hinges popping, tight with rust. Inside, the air was a shifting current of smells: wet carpet, vomit, stale beer, rotting food, piss. He frowned, trying to remember . . . yes, there had been a stairway. He turned to his left and felt his way along the crumbling plaster wall until he found the banister, then the steps . . . started up, pulling himself along the railing, wincing at the pain still throbbing in his gut. The carpeted treads creaked under his weight.

Twice he came upon someone lying in the darkness. Disembodied voices groaned and cursed him as he stumbled past. He stepped on things that cracked, like glass

vials; nearly lost his balance on a bottle that rolled, clink-
ing, down the steps behind him.

At the eighth landing, he stopped for a moment, leaning against the loose newel, his breath coming hard and
short. The pain from his stomach, where the Hitler youth
had kicked him, was getting worse. He wiped the sweat
from his eyes. A dim, hazy blend of streetlight and neon
shone through the curtainless window at the end of the hallway. Trash lay scattered about: broken furniture, beer cans,
discarded pieces of clothing. Words had been spray-painted
in jagged, geometric 3-D on the walls: *Kid Fresh. Charlie
Don't Surf. Food for the Moon.*

He swallowed a dollop of phlegm and limped across the
hallway, beginning to feel himself in the old, well-worn
tracks of his past. He came to the door of his old apartment.
The numbers were long gone, leaving only a faint outline of
their previous existence.

The pressure behind his eyes was building; his face
began to twitch. He tilted his head . . . trying not to remember; but it was still there, waiting to take him back . . . back
to that night thirty years ago . . . back to that oddly familiar
silence. . . .

*. . . he moved slowly through the living room, seeing but
refusing to look at the spilled drawers, the wrecked furniture,
the empty TV stand. Moving slowly, as if drawn to it, to that
strangely familiar silence; the air becoming thicker, forcing
deeper breaths, he stepped up to the bedroom door, pushed
it open with his dirty, scarred, shovel-wide hand. . . .*

*A curtain billowed in the soft, summery night breeze. A
part of him was thinking, logically. "The fire escape; they
came in by the fire escape." Trembling now, he forced himself
to turn, to look. . . .*

Knotted sheets shredded easily in his strong hands.

He straightened her bruised legs and covered her naked, bleeding body with his own.

He did not cry out. The pain went deep, a silent scream that echoed through the dark skies of a world created long ago in the camps, a world of dampness and filth, of rats and spotlights, of empty trains and smoldering ovens; a living, shadow world perfectly rendered and maintained in the pathways of his mutilated neurons.

Thought he heard movement behind the door. He reached out, hesitantly, undecided.

A scream from the alleyway caused him to jerk back. He turned, waiting, listening; heard the clatter of metal and started towards the window at the end of the hallway. As he came to the last apartment, he noticed that the door was partially open. Thinking he might be able to see the alleyway better from one of the bedrooms, he stepped inside and found himself staring at a family of Asians, old women and children.

In the dim and seemingly ever present streetlight, the room was almost totally dark. Tepper was beginning to wonder if the building even had electricity. The air in the apartment was thick with the smell of rancid cooking oils, the source for which, he discovered, was a small butane cooker hovered over by a squatting old woman, who stirred whatever was crackling in the deep-dish skillet.

"I did not mean to frighten you. I just . . . ." He paused. They stared at him with dull, uncomprehending faces. He realized there was no use explaining: they would not call the police or try to force him out because they, too, were trespassers here. He spread his hands in what he hoped was a disarming gesture.

From the alleyway below came another scream, this one quickly muffled. The family shifted nervously, speaking among themselves in a soft, sing-song voice. Finally, after a struggle, a little boy pulled himself from a tangle of arms, legs, and skirts, and ran unconcerned past Tepper, down the short hallway and into the bedroom. The boy's bravery and Tepper's outward show of harmlessness allowed a couple of the elderly women to give in to their concern. Bowing as they passed, the old women followed the little boy. Puzzled, Tepper shuffled along behind. Inside the bedroom, Tepper found more Asians lying on mats. Most of these, he noticed, were men as old as or older than he. They stared at him with vacant eyes. Flickering candles provided the only light.

Tepper shuffled over by the window, where the old women and the boy had gathered. As he came up, they moved aside, bowing. One old woman began speaking rapidly, wringing her hands. Tepper leaned out the window and squinted through the vine-covered fire escape railing. Light from the full moon angled down between the buildings.

He saw bulky shadow-shapes moving . . . and a flash of pale, naked skin.

He looked up at the side of the other apartment building. Saw bedroom lights flick on. Saw shapes move behind curtains, faces peer out. Heard a venetian blind rattle down. Nodded to himself. *Yes, look away. Or are you still there, watching but refusing to see. Like the good farmers who tended their fields and never dared to guess why trains came in filled with Jews and left empty, ever empty.*

Tepper turned his attention back to the alley; the struggling shadows had moved directly under the fire escape. "Your daughter," he said, suddenly, knowing. Frowned. Leaned out farther, twisting his head. He could see the street and the edge of the ROSES sign. He nodded. "You sit here often and watch her, don't you, mother. And tonight she's coming home from work and runs into these would-be

Ubermensch." He turned back to the old woman, clenching his heavy hands into meaty fists. With every sound of struggle, the old woman's face twisted itself into expressions he remembered well: Fear. Desperation. Hopelessness. "And there's no one to help her. No God. No avenging angel. He touched the dent in his skull. "Just me." Grinned. "The Trashman of Auschwitz."

The old woman bowed.

He nodded. "Maybe it's enough, eh?"

He eased himself backwards out onto the landing, folding and pulling his bad leg along after him, then stood up and quietly descended the metal stairs until he stood on the bottom landing. The next flight would drop with the counter weight. That would be too slow for surprise. And without surprise. He looked at his wide, trembling hands. Hands, he realized, that had done little good in their time.

A whimpering cry drifted up.

His heartbeat quickened. He wondered if Zivia had cried out. Imagined her writhing under that rough weight. Where had he been? And before, when babies were being drowned in barrels of water, when screaming children were being tossed by their feet into gas vans, when the wife of his brother stood naked in line for the "showers"?

The pressure moved behind his eyes, making him a little light-headed. He grabbed the railing to steady himself. Took a slow breath and smiled. "Then let us give them an everlasting name."

And he jumped.

His weight took one boy down with bone-crushing accuracy. The momentary confusion was filled with curses and whispered shouts as the rest of the skinheads scattered from the lumbering giant who had fallen among them.

The girl broke free and ran deeper into the alleyway.

Tepper tried to rise, but the old age stiffness in his lower back had softened with the fall; now it was a warm, crippling numbness spreading through his legs. There were only seconds left before they found him. He pushed up on one hand and reached for the nearest boy, the one he'd landed on. Caught him first by the collar, then, reaching around with his other hand, found the boy's throat.

A metal pipe whooshed by his head and slammed into his wide back. The pain sucked out his breath with an inarticulate cry. *Just a little longer*, he thought, tensing, tightening his grip, *a little longer*. The boy almost struggled free, but Tepper held on, riding him.

The boy had been in many fights and been afraid many times, but he had never known what it was like to have someone single-mindedly try to kill him. And the realization panicked him; he began swinging wildly, clawing; finally trying to pry loose the old man's steel-trap grip one finger at a time. But the effort was useless. "Useless," Tepper hissed. Feeling the boy weaken, he quickly shifted his hold, cupping one hand around the boy's jaw, the other pressed against the side of his head. The strength of forty-odd years carrying trash came to bear in a short, sharp twist. There was a muffled crack, and the boy went limp.

The pipe came down again, and this time found its mark, glancing off Tepper's skull and knocking him to one side. He rolled and came up on his knees, one hand pressing against the fracturing pain. Warm blood flowed over his fingers. He blinked, trying to find a direction away from the shouts and curses all around him; saw light pulsing, sweeping through the darkness up ahead . . . crawled towards it. . . .

The three skinheads stared down at the swollen, blackened face in the thin, wavering glow of a cigarette lighter.

"This can't be."

"Just shut up, all right? Just shut the fuck up." Acne Face moved the cigarette lighter closer, touched and tugged at the uniform; brushed the blond hair.

"This can't be."

Glasses leaned over. "SS."

"What the fuck's going on here?"

"This can't be."

The pain was unlike anything Tepper had ever felt. It shattered all his known boundaries of pain and left his senses displaced.

He clasped his hands to either side of his head and squeezed, trying to crush his skull, to free the *dybbuk* eating his brain. Pressure ballooned behind his eyes, touching off vertigo. Somewhere up ahead, the white light kept pulsing, seemingly keeping time with the pain, leading him on. He lurched, stumbling off the walls of the alleyway. Bent at the waist, gasping, squeezed harder. . . .

The light grew brighter, pulsing faster and faster until it became a steady spotlight brilliance that momentarily blinded him . . . while the pain, pulsing opposite in turn, gradually lessened, until it disappeared completely. He felt a stinging blast of cold air and smelled the old familiar smell. . . . In the distance, he heard a train whistle dopplering towards him. . . .

Acne Face and Glasses stood alone. Even Acne Face couldn't stop Chubby in his mad flight from the body of the German soldier.

They had made their way towards the back of the alley. There was no sign of their friend or the old man. Overhead, a cleft in the buildings allowed a wedge of moonlight to angle down the stone wall.

"Something's wrong here. Really wrong. Do you see this?"

Acne Face hefted his pipe. "You wanna bug out, too?"

Glasses shrugged but said nothing.

All about them in the moonlight lay piles of unopened

suitcases, boxes of glinting, wire-frame glasses, mounds of shoes. They began prodding and picking through the stuff. Found bundles of letters, neatly folded dresses, ladies' underwear, and gold jewelry, which they stuffed into their pockets.

"Hey, look over here."

They gathered in front of a poster tacked to the wall, highlighted by a diagonal line of moonlight.

The older boy stared at the poster and shrugged. "So what's it say?"

"How the fuck should I know. It's in German." Glasses leaned closer, squinting at the angular print. "Juden Nicht Erwunscht!" He frowned. "Says 'Jews Keep Out!'" Shrugged. "Something like that."

Acne Face smiled and flipped the pipe, end over end. "Looks like we're in good company."

From the back of the alleyway blew a cold wind that stirred the clothes at their feet. The air smelled bad; a mixture of rotting trash and something else, something raw and chemical.

"It wasn't this cold five minutes ago," Glasses said, zipping up his leather jacket. He turned. The mouth of the alleyway was far away. He got the impression he was looking out from a deep, dark tunnel.

They spread out, one near each wall, and stepped out of the moonlight.

Within a few yards, the darkness became absolute. The boys managed to move closer to the walls and guide themselves along with their hands for a few yards, but then the walls abruptly ended, leaving them completely disoriented. Any direction seemed forward, and standing still they seemed to be moving. Their senses were enveloped, cut off from stimuli, tricked. The air turned bitter cold. Something wet drifted against their faces. The constant hum of the building's machinery grew steadily fainter, then pulsed back louder, with direction, dopplering towards them. . . .

. . . a clacking, rattling, pulsing thunder of steel . . .

Glasses turned to run, tripped and fell. He cried out as his hands sunk elbow deep into snow.

Searchlights swept over the single file of Jews being herded towards the flat roof building near the sparking smokestack. The sky was low, thick, and gray. Snow was falling. Tepper stood in line with the rest. He had almost convinced himself that this day would never come; that he had managed to slip through the cracks; that the grinning death's head of fate had somehow overlooked him. He sighed and gave a tired grin, remembering his strange dream of the hospital, the city, the alleyway. "Such a dream," he whispered. Took a step. SS men were moving up and down the line, clubbing the slow with sticks and rifle butts.

He felt calm, knowing what would happen: down into the underground rooms to undress, then be packed into the "showers," then darkness, the smell of Zyklon. He listened to the whispers behind him. They still thought they were going to be disinfected.

Someone touched his arm. He flinched, expecting a blow. When none came, he turned. At his side was a small Asian girl. He stared at her for a moment, trying to remember. She was about seventeen. Blood was smeared across her chin; the side of her face was clawed and still bleeding. The shirt beneath her quilted jacket was torn, revealing the cup of her bra. The material glowed white against her skin. She said something in her own language and pressed close, seeking comfort under his voluminous overcoat.

Tepper frowned. "But you . . . you were in my dream. . . ." Hesitantly, he reached out and touched her cheek. Felt the cool skin. "So real." The line moved up, the man behind Tepper nudged by, pushing him out of the way. No one seemed to notice him. He held his breath, watching an SS man pass within a few feet, yelling, clubbing; but the guard paid no attention to Tepper or the girl. Tepper's breath came out in a rush. "*Meshugge!* They don't see me." He chuckled and shook his head. "A dream I used to have," he told her. "Wake up, I would, and put on my clothes and walk out of my barrack. *Oy,* walk right out, past the guards and turn down this road," he pointed, "right under the spotlights and the watchtower and the dogs and right on out. I would be invisible, you see." He looked down at the little flower girl clutching at his coat. She was staring at a pile of bodies near the entrance to one of the crematoriums. He felt her shiver and heard her whisper.

"I don't know the words," he said, stroking her hair. "But it seems you, too, know this kind of evil. Come, child," he took her hand, whispering, "let's see which dream is real."

The boys found themselves in a courtyard, surrounded by skinheads dressed in baggy striped clothes. A searchlight shone down on them from towers positioned near wire fences. Snow was falling, covering the roofs of long, narrow, wooden barracks. A smokestack was belching dark, sooty smoke. The air was heavy with that same raw chemical smell they had noticed earlier in the alleyway.

"Where are we?"

"Must be one hellavuh *oi* concert or a rally or something. Look at all the skins."

Acne Face reached out and grabbed the shoulder of the skinhead in front of him. "Hey, man, what's happening here?" Felt his fingers close around bone and instantly drew back, but the sensation remained: sticks wrapped in cloth.

The man turned listlessly and stared. His skin was pale gray, his cheeks stubbly with beard; the smell from his unwashed body was raw, wrenching; but what stunned the

boy most was the man's eyes . . . staring . . . eyes twice too
large for their sockets, pumped up with unbelievable horror . . . ungodly pain.

Too late, he realized what was happening. Someone
was yelling, pushing him. He turned, reflexively bringing
up the pipe, in time to see a rifle butt slam into his mouth.

Tepper and the girl walked until the lights of the camp
no longer cast their shadows and the air smelled of nothing.
The heavy snowfall gradually turned to flurries, then stopped
altogether. And the air blowing towards them, though still
cool, was noticeably warmer. They passed under the fire
escape and paused at the mouth of the alleyway. They had
seen nothing, no body, no police. Tepper rubbed the dent in
his head and blinked. Dried blood flaked off under his fingers. He stood listening to the sound of the 2 a.m. Amtrak
train pulling into the station a few blocks away. The sound
didn't remind him of anything. He smiled.

She led him up eight flights of the darkened stairway
to the floor where she lived. Tepper paused on the landing,
leaning against the loose newel to catch his breath. He felt
no pain, just the comfortable fatigue of his age. "I was just
remembering how the hallway used to smell when I would
come home," he was saying to the girl. She stood listening,
smiling, one hand self-consciously rearranging her clothes
to cover her nakedness. "Funny, I couldn't remember that
before; just the bad things; the emptiness, the pain." Tepper
limped over to his old apartment. "Always cooking something good, Momma was."

He stopped and looked down at the girl. Wet his thumb
and wiped a flake of dried blood from her chin. "You see,
we had no children." Smiled, "Oy, what she would do with
such a sweet little *faygeleh*. Make you cakes and *latkes,* ah,
you should live to eat such, child." He closed his eyes and

breathed deep. . . . Felt the dulling, electric twinge tug at one side of his face; felt soft pressure move behind his eye; felt his eye tear. He tilted his head toward the sensation. Time slowed. . . . He smelled fresh baked, leavened bread. "Ah, just so, eh?" Lights began to flicker and burn, in the stairway, up and down the hall. There were drunken curses from below. The building shuddered as machinery, long unused, started to run. He took hold of the girl's hand. "Come, child, Momma's got it ready. Just like it used to be." He pulled her with him to the door. Noticed the numbers, shiny brass numbers. Turned the doorknob. "*Oy*, she never locks, my wife. Always such a trusting soul."

He opened the door and smiled.

"Momma, I'm home."

The Cab Driver from Hell in the Land of the Pioux Hawques

by
Allen J. M. Smith

About the Author

Allen J. M. Smith was born on Christmas, 1944, in Erie, Pennsylvania. He attended public schools, then majored in music and English literature at Pennsylvania State University. After college, he held a variety of jobs, including reporting, newspaper photography, and television news film; also, significantly, cab driving. An autobiographical piece about cab driving appears in the Summer, 1990 edition of Pig Iron, *a literary annual.*

And so, too, "The Cab Driver from Hell in the Land of the Pioux Hawques," which is, we hope, not autobiographical, even if it is informed by real-life experience. Allen J. M. Smith has moved to Shreveport, Louisiana, where he is married to a symphony violist. (His mother is a working ragtime pianist.) He says he practices "Hung Gar," a Chinese martial art based on the tiger and crane styles; what is known for sure *is that he plays classical guitar, practices marksmanship, and cooks.*

About the Illustrator

Michael Grossman, of Framingham, Massachusetts, was born in 1959 in Queens, New York, moved to Yonkers when he was eight, and turned to comic books to escape when his two younger brothers grew too onerous. From that he went to the hard stuff—Edgar Rice Burroughs, SF movies, Star Trek re-runs, and then Star Wars. *Somewhere in there, too, he started going to science fiction conventions, and borrowed his father's Super-8 movie camera to make his own movies. Then he went to college, but wound up in retail management. He met Elisabeth, married her, and they were off to Phoenix, Arizona, because her job called for it. Since then, a daughter has been born, and Elisabeth's job has transferred them to Framingham.*

Michael heard about the Contest through our ad in Asimov's *science fiction magazine, and decided to enter because he could use a pen and pencil. Which he can, indeed.*

All right, since you've been trying so hard to be good children despite having to stay in the lodge for three rainy days in a row, I'll tell you a story.

Gray Mouse, put another medium-size log on the fire. Put it on this side, my dear; you see, the rain coming in through the smoke hole in the roof is falling over to this side, and you want to build the fire up more on the opposite side, out of the rain.

Now. Arrange yourselves comfortably, and tell me what story you would like to hear. How the Crow lost his song but retained his lovely black coat? Why the Beaver builds his own lodges like we do? How Man learned to plant grain and hunt?

Yes. Thank you, Little Vixen, I'd love some tea. Since you're such a thoughtful little girl, why don't you choose the story? What? Speak louder, please. I had the sharpest ears in the tribe twenty years ago, but they're not quite what they used to be.

Ah, an excellent choice! Children, Little Vixen has chosen the story of the Cab Driver from Hell.

Now, some of you visiting cousins may not know what a cab driver is, just as we didn't until this true story happened to us.

You did? Well, I guess news travels far these days.

Delicious tea, my dear. Those willow leaves are just the thing for my poor old aching legs. This weather makes them worse, you know.

All right. The Cab Driver from Hell. It was about twenty years ago, and none of you were born yet, or even some of your fathers and mothers.

It was late Autumn, and the Northern Geese flew overhead, singing their beautiful, magical, migratory songs, on their way to the warm Southern Lands. They sang encouragement, strength, and enthusiasm, each to another, as they passed over our Hunting Ground.

The Robins had departed. The trees were turning, the air was still and dry and comfortable; smoke from campfires rose straight to the Heavens. The Squirrels were chattering in the woodland, rushing back and forth to fill their nut caches. It was the time when we, too, hunt and gather as much as we can, laying in supplies for the Winter.

We were stalking a lone Buffalo that had strayed far enough from the herd to be safely separated. Your grandfathers, who were young hunters at the time, were taking up positions to drive the creature into the closed rock formation near The River.

Everyone was in place. I muttered a little prayer for luck, stood up, drew a deep breath, and was just about to begin shouting and whooping; but suddenly, as we say now, all Hell broke loose. That was the origin of that saying, by the way.

A large heavy red object about half the size of a lodge fell from nowhere right on top of the Buffalo, killing him. It seemed to come out of the air, and it fell six feet, roaring like a wounded Bear.

At first I wondered if my prayer had been even more effective than usual, but then I realized that the Spirits are never quite that accommodating, and that something unprecedented was happening.

The other hunters slowly recovered from their stunned silence, and began to creep out of the bushes where they had been hiding.

Cautiously, we converged on the monstrous red thing and the dead Buffalo, spears ready.

As we closed to within six feet of it, we were struck by a wind so foul as to make a direct spraying from a Skunk seem like the subtlest and sweetest flower. It was a bit like the aroma from the sulfur springs far to the West, in the Land of the Navajos, (but that's another story), only worse. Gasping and clutching our noses and throats, we fell back. The wind was westerly, so Blind Deer and Little Bear got the worst of it, approaching from the eastward side. I was more fortunate, approaching from the windward, and so I was the first to be able to come closer as the breeze cleared the noxious odor.

The thing had rolled off the crushed Buffalo, and was lying on its side. Its underside, now exposed, was brown and caked with mud. The rest of it was bright red, usually a sacred color (although in this case I had my doubts); at one end of it was a kind of totemic face with a suggestion of two eyes and a ghastly smile upon a large shiny mouth. The face itself was made of a bright material as shiny as a distant sea or river, but hard and rigid as ice or rock. It was such a curious substance I couldn't resist tapping it with the butt of my spear, to see if it was solid.

As I did so, the others approached.

Then we heard groans and muted voices from inside the thing!

It was an enclosure, like a lodge. Further examination revealed a portal on the side, now facing up, through which I cautiously peeked to see two of the strangest men ever to walk the Earth.

One was of course the famous Cab Driver from Hell. I'm proud to claim the distinction of being the first of The Pioux Hawques to see his yellow hair, bright red shirt, and blue eyes and breeches. The other was the one who followed him into our world, whom Cabbie, as he later came to be known, called in his own language, "*Yuppie Jerk*," or sometimes "*Dumb Shit*." This one wore several layers of clothing, like the people in the colder Northern Climes. Most of it was a drab gray, except for a white inner shirt, and a brightly colored piece of cloth around the neck.

Both had hair that was cut short, but not plucked like that of the Eastern Grassland Tribes, such as the Meaux Hawques. The Yuppie Jerk's hair was dark like ours. Nearly all of what they wore was woven from the finest fibers you can imagine, so fine as to resemble doeskin. I know of nothing in forest or field that would yield such fibers.

The Cabbie smelled a bit like the Northerners, the Esquimeaux, at the end of their long Winter confinements when they haven't changed their furs for a while. The other smelled very oddly. I can think of no way to describe his scent to you, except to say it was floral, yet pungent. It faded within the first day, anyway.

The Cabbie was the first to recover his senses after what must have been a severe jolt and a worse surprise. He pushed open a larger portal in which the smaller one through which I had peeked was contained, and emerged as far as his head and shoulders.

Seeing our spears, which we held more casually now (he was obviously in no shape to behave aggressively), he held up both hands· to indicate an absence of weapons, smiled rather oddly, and said a greeting in his own language, which we did not understand at the time. Later, he taught it to me. It was, "*Hi, there.*" It means "I wish to extend a friendly, casual greeting to you as though I knew you well, even though I hardly know you at all, in order to placate you and put to rest any fear or hostility you might be experiencing."

They have an odd language. They have twenty different words for "count," but only one for "flint."

As the Cabbie lifted himself out of the portal and tried

Illustrated by Michael Grossman

to climb down, he collapsed, red-faced with pain. He had sprained an ankle. Two of the younger hunters looked at me for guidance, and I nodded for them to help him. They handed their spears to the others, and each took an arm. The Cabbie smiled, and spoke gently in his own language, despite his pain. He was taller than average, but very thin and flabby, like a man much older than he appeared to be. The yellow hair on his face gave him an otherworldly demeanor. Remember, children, no one had ever seen a beard before.

The other refused to come out. When I peered in at him and offered a hand, he glared like a Plainsman and spoke in a voice edged with panic and menace.

Cabbie made a gesture indicating that persuasion would be hopeless, and spoke in his language. I guessed correctly that he was suggesting letting the poor man come out in his own good time, like a Bobcat kitten who has climbed seemingly beyond his own ability to climb down; the kitten's mother will leave him to his own devices, in order to give him a chance to overcome his fear.

Cabbie was thinking clearly despite his pain and shock; this is usually the sign of a strong man, and it contrasted oddly with his weak-looking muscles.

We made a travois of two spears and a robe, and conveyed the injured Cabbie to the Shaman's lodge for treatment, leaving Little Bear to protect the Dumb Shit from possible predation.

While the Shaman was treating the Cabbie, I led the hunters back to slaughter the Buffalo. It was a long job, and the flies were terrible, but we eventually finished, and some of The People came to help us carry the meat, hide, sinews and useful bones (those that were not broken by the odd manner of his demise) back to The Village.

But then we were faced with the problem of how to get the Yuppie Jerk out of the Cab before any of the larger carnivores gathered to feast on the Buffalo carcass. Some of them might welcome a little live game confined in a small space.

Thinking of how the predators would be attracted to the carcass made me think of bait; that gave me an idea: I persuaded one of the charming young women of the tribe, Light Butterfly, to speak kindly and gently to the man in the Cab. Sure enough, she won him over, and he peeked out, looking rather surly, and perhaps a little embarrassed that a beautiful young woman was brave enough to be on the outside while he was still in hiding. He sullenly and awkwardly lifted himself through the portal, refusing help, and stumbled down to the ground. He was shorter than the Cabbie, but looked to be in much better physical condition. His muscles were toned and he moved like a young man. He had no beard at the time, but one started to grow on his face within a day.

He looked at the remains of the beast distastefully, even though it was a perfectly normal-looking Buffalo carcass in most respects, except for the crushed parts.

The Gray One, as we called him then before the Cabbie had identified him, followed a short distance behind as we made our way back to The Village.

Little Bear, who often has fine insights into human nature, caught up to me and said, "Father, this man seems possessed by a spirit that makes him like a Plainsman. Even though he has no injuries, shouldn't we take him to the Shaman, too? Perhaps he can be helped."

"Good idea," I said. "But I can't see what their relationship is to each other. The Yellow-Haired One showed him no respect at all; he seemed contemptuous and impatient with the other's difficulties. Yet the other, the Gray One, behaves as though he feels superior to everyone. As you suggest, he's rather like some of the wilder, warlike people in the West; he seems to wish to establish dominance, as a Wolf does within his own pack. Yet no Wolf would be foolish enough to become overly assertive in a position like his. You're quite right to compare him to a Plainsman. Let's hope his behavior improves. If he's going to become dangerous, I don't want him around.''

''He doesn't look dangerous.''

''With strange people, you can never tell.''

''Speaking of that, Father, can I make my Journey of Adulthood next Spring?''

Adolescents are masters of the surprise question. I fully intended to let him, but I didn't want to tell him too soon, or he would just become more impatient during the coming Winter. ''We'll see, Little Bear,'' I said.

He sighed with the half-patient indulgence of an adolescent who has reached the point where he obeys his father out of love rather than necessity; one cannot hold them long after that. Next Spring wouldn't be a moment too soon.

It was one of the most interesting Winters our lodge has ever had.

The People used the long Winter to educate the two visitors in our language and customs.

During one of their first meals with us, a little toddler came up to where the Gray One was sitting, and put his hand on the man's knee, requesting food. But this odd man seemed not to understand, moved his knee out of the way, and spoke sharply in his own language. We were all appalled and embarrassed, and the child was bewildered.

The Cabbie quickly said something to him, using his special name for him, ''Dumb Shit,'' which I had incorrectly surmised was some sort of title, like ''Father,'' or ''Cousin.'' Then he smiled at the little one and motioned him over to him. The little one sat happily on his lap, eating his stew.

The Shaman tried to help the Gray One improve his attitude, but finally gave up, saying, "It isn't demonic possession. It's just him. That's the way he is."

But they were both fast learners. By the time Winter was half over, they both spoke our language fairly well. As soon as he was able to express himself well enough, the Dark Haired One made it clear to us that he wanted to be called "Bob." He was angry about the titles bestowed upon him by the Cabbie. He said they were insulting.

So, although we could understand the Cabbie's impatience with him, we called him Bob, not wanting to insult anyone.

Then, one day the Shaman came to me. He wanted to try to unravel the mysteries surrounding their precipitous appearance among us. I was the chief, so he came to me for permission. We were all dying of curiosity, of course, and were just politely waiting for him to get around to asking permission to perform the investigation. For all his spiritual genius, his sense of timing in the mundane world of human interaction is sometimes trying. I eagerly gave him permission.

Yes, Little Vixen, I know he can hear me. He's only pretending to doze over there in the corner. Don't worry. He and I have been instructing each other for years, each in our own ways, and neither of us is offended by it.

As I was saying. Permission given, he set up the ceremonial fire, sweat lodge, tobacco, herbal tea, musicians, and everything.

At the end of the ceremony, he and the two visitors went into the sweat lodge. There were strange noises, stranger lights, moans, whispers and cries. Unearthly voices said unearthly things.

After a while he came out alone. He said the other two were all right, but resting. He said he had communicated with the Spirit World, with his Spirit Guide, and with the

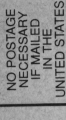

BUSINESS REPLY MAIL

FIRST CLASS MAIL   PERMIT NO. 62688   LOS ANGELES, CA

POSTAGE WILL BE PAID BY ADDRESSEE

BRIDGE PUBLICATIONS, INC.
DEPT. WOTF7
4751 FOUNTAIN AVENUE
LOS ANGELES, CA 90029-9923

Name: _____

Address: _____

City: _____ State: _____ Zip: ____

world from which the visitors came, which did not have a name in our language.

As always after such an effort, he looked at once enervated and exhilarated. I guess it doesn't hurt him, though, because he's fifteen years older than I, and in better shape.

Naturally, we waited with bated breath.

When we all stopped twitching with excitement and curiosity, he began, speaking slowly and softly: "As you know," he said, although we knew nothing of the sort, "everything that happens to us happens very differently from what appears to us." I swear those were his very words. "The journey of a lifetime appears to be as a tale told by one teller, or a trip by one person to the source of a stream. Choices must be made when one comes to the turning points of the tale, or to the branches of the stream. Or, if you prefer, imagine an Ant who begins his journey at the root of a tree. He climbs to a fork in the tree, goes out on a limb, chooses another branching, and so one, until he reaches the fruit he sought. Yet the storyteller, the traveler, or the Ant could easily have pursued other branches of the same tale, trek, or tree when they came to the forks.

"Although it doesn't always seem so, our journey through this world is similar. There are always choices to make, to go this way or that. Now, what happens is that we make a certain choice, and there we come to a branch in our journey. There, the world becomes two worlds, the same up to that point, different afterwards. And we, that is, our small selves, follow one path while another person very similar to ourselves, except for that last choice, follows another path. There are more such choices, I'm told, than there are stars in the sky, or pebbles on the beach."

A night bird cried in the darkening forest, setting off a murmuring of some of the quieter animals. We all glanced toward the door. Someone added a log to the fire.

"With each of these turnings, a different world," said

the Medicine Man. "We see only one now, just as the Ant
sees only the branch beneath his feet, and not the whole
tree. But I am told that when we pass from this life to the
Spirit World, we study the other choices, to see where they
led. That way, we learn our way through the infinite possibilities of life until all that is required of us is fulfilled."

He was silent for a moment as we pondered this. Then
in a louder voice, he said, "Little Bear!"

Little Bear was suitably startled from his reverie. "Yes,
Sir?"

"Little Bear, soon you will make your Journey to mark
your passage into adulthood. You will probably start off by
canoe down The River. When you come to the first fork, if
you take the westerly branch, you will move toward Plainsman country. If you continue to make such westerly choices,
you will eventually be taken prisoner by them."

"Yes, I understand."

"Good. I hope you know what their rites of passage
into manhood are like. They don't go on Journeys. They get
tortured."

"Yes, Sir."

"If you continue southward, choosing the other
branches of The River, you will face a different and almost
certainly more pleasant Journey. The tribes in the South
will ask you to prove your manhood by trying to get their
lovely young ladies pregnant."

On cue, everyone giggled, and Little Bear turned as red
as the Cab.

"Now," he said, in that way of his that makes everyone
concentrate on what he is about to say. "There will be as
many Little Bears as there are choices for him to make on
his Journey, and they will explore as many worlds as there
are Little Bears."

We silently digested this while he took a sip of tea.

This was a great deal for a poor hunter to take in at

once. My head was practically swimming. But his words remain with me to this day, and hardly a day goes by that I don't think about what he said.

"So," he went on, "this is what my Spirit Guide told me. In another world, people from across the Eastern Ocean came in great vessels, in great numbers, with vastly superior weapons and a warlike attitude. They conquered our land as the Apaches conquered the Sioux. They took it over and banished us. They produced a world, I am told, that is immeasurably less pleasant than ours, one that is too noisy, too nasty, filled with hostile winds and warlike people, in which kindness and cooperation do not prosper as they do in our land. Imagine a whole world filled with Apaches.

"My Guide has named their world *Hell*. Our yellow-haired visitor agrees and calls himself the Cab Driver from Hell. Our other visitor is very upset and frightened by the ceremony, and refuses to discuss it. Do you understand?

I, of course, had a question: "How did our two visitors come to our world in their Cab, instead of staying in their own as is usually the case?"

"Because," he said, "the Cab Driver from Hell is practically a Shaman himself, even though he doesn't try at all, and he hated his world as any sensible man would, and he performed a craft that involved sudden choices between branching paths dozens of times a day at the behest of others, something like a guide, or a Dog pulling a travois. He branched one too many times, and his worlds split in a crooked sort of way, dropping him into ours. He's a very unusual man. Spiritually he has great power but little knowledge, a combination that assures an interesting life.

"The other just happened to be with him in the Cab. My Guide says the Gray One was well suited to his world, and prospered in it, unlike the Cabbie, but he is ill suited to ours. At least to our tribe."

"Sir?" Little Bear, always the explorer, had a question.
"Yes?"

"Sir, you said that this race of intruders from across the sea produced a terrible world. But I don't understand. How can men produce a world? Were they great sorcerers?"

"Not exactly, Little Bear, but something like that. They had skills that allowed them to transform their surroundings little by little, but not quite in the way a great sorcerer might."

"Sir, if I may, I would like to know what kept these people from across the ocean from overrunning our land in this world as they did in that other."

"A plague. In their world it was not too bad, and their way of life survived, and they lived on to conquer. In ours, they were reduced to savages. And our people in their world were not quite as civilized and sophisticated as we; in our world, our people gave birth to a great many subtle and sophisticated souls whose other selves must perforce be born among the intruders in that other world, the race of light-skinned people like Bob and the Cabbie who took over this land in that world."

"One more question, Sir?"

Shaman is of course a very patient man. He glanced up at the smoke hole, and saw the constellations in the night sky that are not usually seen by children who go to bed on time. But he knew this was a special night. "Of course, Little Bear."

"Sir, when the Cabbie and, uh, Bob, that we know dropped into our world, did another Cabbie and Bob remain in theirs? Do they even now go about their business in that other world?"

"Yes. Nothing is lost in the infinite diversity of the Universe."

"Well, Sir?"

"Yes, Little Bear?"

"Does another Cabbie follow other branchings into other possibilities, even now as we speak? And does another Bob follow him?"

"The Cab Driver from Hell goes to many places, Little Bear, and he takes all sorts of people with him."

"Will we ever know those stories, Sir?"

"Not until we become one with Infinity, Little Bear."

As I said, both of our visitors proved clever at learning our language. I gave them a few weeks to recover from their odd manner of entrance to our world, and to nurse their bruises and scrapes; during this time they learned to speak our language about as well as a little child of three or four years.

I thought they would want to join us on our hunting trips in the Spring.

I found them both together, talking heatedly in their own language in their corner of the lodge. Cabbie was speaking calmly and earnestly, trying to persuade Bob of something. Bob was speaking harshly and defensively, obviously unconvinced and very unhappy.

When they saw me coming, they stopped talking and looked at me. "Hi, Chief!" said the Cabbie using his own unique greeting.

"I was wondering if you men would like to join us in a hunt."

"Yes," said Cabbie. "But, Chief, uh, we not know for hunting. Uh, how hunting. How say?"

"You don't know how to hunt. Say 'I don't know how to hunt.' "

"I don't know how to hunt."

"Good. Don't worry. You're both clever learners. I'll teach you. Come with me."

I taught them to walk quietly, stalk from the windward, thrust with the spear, and all the other things that are usually taught to young boys.

But, being used to teaching young boys, I was a little surprised at Bob's lack of respect for me as a teacher. Whenever he didn't get the idea right away, he made what were obviously sarcastic remarks in his own language; this embarrassed the Cabbie, who would say, "Quiet, please. Listen Chief."

After a few weeks both had learned about as much as a young boy might know on the eve of his first hunt.

"Ready hunt, now, Chief?" the Cabbie asked for the fourth time that day.

Bob said something in his own language.

"I think you're ready," I said. "You'll have to take it easy the first few times, though, and avoid taking any risks until you're more experienced. We're going to have to start you off on a Buffalo hunt, because it doesn't require the finer skills of archery or the sling; but it's a little more dangerous. Buffalo may not be ruthless predators, but they're awfully big, and when they're scared, they run blindly, without worrying too much about what they're running over."

"Terrific," said Bob in that oddly belligerent way of his.

"We be careful, Chief. We want learn pull our own weight." Cabbie has such an odd way of putting ideas together. It took me a moment to realize what he meant. He was referring to the way some people have of trying to get more while giving less, and he wanted me to know he was not one of those. I could see why it had been on his mind, though.

Finally, Spring came to Our Valley. The smell of buds and new grass filled the air. The River became swollen, swift, and muddy. The resurgence of life was everywhere.

The Geese crossed over our Hunting Ground once again, singing their songs, and the Robins returned. The new young furry creatures emerged, and their mothers and fathers proceeded to educate and feed them.

Having received reports of a small Buffalo herd approaching from the west within a few days of our hunting ground, I announced that we would embark on a hunt, meeting the herd near the rock formation. It is always a joy for me to say the words that send the tribe into a state of excitement and anticipation; hunters check and refurbish their weapons, children play at hunting, experts in cooking and preserving begin chattering excitedly about herbs and pemmican, tanners dress the edges of their knives and scrapers, and stories are told of feats of skill and valor on previous hunts.

Bob became more communicative. One morning when he left the lodge to urinate, I left too, and pretended to meet him by chance, and said to him, "Bob, you look happy this morning. Are you excited about your first hunt?"

"Happy, happy, Chief. Bob bored and tired of sitting down."

"What did you do in your own world, Bob? Did you hunt?"

He pondered for a moment. "Not hunt, no. Sort of gather, sort of craftsman, sort of warrior. No. Not know to say."

"Did you barter?"

"What mean, barter?"

"I have knife, you need knife. You have fur, I need fur. Give to each other." Realizing that I had inadvertently slipped into their baby talk, I amended: "Barter is an exchange of goods between two people, each of whom has something that the other needs. As the Shaman says, 'Man's role is best served when needs are fulfilled, and things find their rightful places.' He says that barter is the best thing a man can do, because in that way we are all enriched, and we each take care of the other's needs.''

"Hm. Not quite," he said, "but close. Smart barter get more. Bob very good barter, make good trades."

"I see. You're more concerned with personal gain than mutual benefit. Is that right?"

"Right. Not remember how to say."

"Have you spoken to the Shaman about this?"

"No."

'Mm. Listen, Bob. On the hunt, you're going to have to cooperate fully with all the others, and do exactly as you're told. It's a complex operation, and everyone has to do his part just right.'

"I know."

"I hope so. Did you know, Bob, that when certain large Lizards in the South lay their eggs, the mother abandons them, leaving them buried in the mud?"

"No."

"And then, when the first one hatches, he waits and eats his brothers and sisters as they hatch. These Lizards are unable to build lodges, hunt cooperatively, use tools, raise families, form friendships, domesticate Horses and Dogs, and generally live the good life as we do."

"Chief sound like Shaman."

"Not at all. Shaman is concerned with knowing and being; I am concerned with doing. But a good man regulates himself in a way very much like the way Shaman and I regulate the life of the tribe."

"I know, Chief," he said, walking away. "I know. I'm not a child."

Later that day I found Cabbie practicing with the sling. He had collected a pile of stones from The River and was patiently slinging them at a tree.

"Cabbie!" I said, "How's it going? Is your accuracy improving?"

"Not much, Chief, but I'm getting more power into it."

"Don't try for power too much at first. Try for grace and precision first, and power will come later."

"Oh, I see. I'll try that." He picked up a stone, fitted it into the sling, and cast it more carefully at the tree. It missed.

"Don't worry about missing," I told him. "Just do it slowly and carefully until it feels just right, then you'll find your accuracy improving. Say, Cabbie, are you happy about the hunt?"

He put down the sling, and we sat on the wiry grass, watching the sun set, and savoring the sweet evening breeze. "You know, Chief, I've never been happier than I am with the Pioux Hawkes. Look, do you like my new vest? Light Butterfly made it herself, and gave it to me." It was rather touching, really. He was so proud of it.

"You realize, Cabbie, that she likes you, don't you?"

"Well, I hope so. I like all your people very much."

"Cabbie, that's not what I meant. I mean, she likes you especially. She talks about you a lot, and she speaks very well of you."

It was funny, in a way, to see understanding dawn on his childishly open face. It was like watching a baby learn something completely new that changes his understanding of the world.

He opened his mouth, then hesitated. "You mean? You mean she. Uh. Me? Light Butterfly?"

"Yes. Her mother and father like you too."

He flushed and stammered a little, until I rescued him by changing the subject. "What did you do in your world, Cabbie? The Shaman was rather vague about it."

"Oh. Well, I worked the Cab. The red thing we came in that crushed the Buffalo."

"Worked it? What does it do?"

"It's for transport, like a travois or a horse. The Esquimeaux use dog sleds, right? Like that. But it pulls itself. It uses the power of Fire."

"Sounds difficult to understand."

"It is. But using it is a skill that's not too hard to learn. I helped people to travel with it."

"Like a guide?"

"Yes! That's it. Very much like that."

"Guides are highly respected among our people."

"Not among ours. In my old world, I mean."

"Only the most highly skilled hunters and scouts are allowed to guide travelers in our world."

"Well, I understand. It wasn't that easy in ours, either. Travel by these devices is difficult and trying in, uh, very crowded areas."

"What do you mean?"

"Our settlements are huge and crowded. Imagine a village the size of our Hunting Ground here, filled with people from one end to the other, crowding each other like the inside of a lodge at the End of Winter."

"Sounds awful."

"It's Hell. And cabs as numerous, fast and crowded as Buffalo, but not all going the same way."

"Sounds lethal."

"Right. Well, I was skilled at getting my cab through that chaos and lethal confusion."

"And that wasn't a respected skill?"

"No. I don't know why. Listen, you know, it takes a lot of, well, I don't know how to say it. You have to know what's going to happen before it happens. You have to be able to change your course of travel to accommodate unexpected obstacles quickly, but you have to do it in a way that doesn't cause too much trouble for others. Well, I did, anyway. I guess some cabbies don't worry too much about that part of it. I guess that's why we're not so highly respected. But for me, the real challenge was to get my travelers through quickly without inconveniencing anyone else. It was sort of like balancing on a pole, or crossing a stream on stepping stones."

"You have a talent for language. Look how well you speak now."

"Hey, thanks, Chief. It's your expert teaching."

"Tell me, Cabbie, would your Cab work for transport in our world as it did in yours?"

"No. It was damaged in the fall. I guess the landscape in my world was higher than the same spot in this one. The soft feet of the Cab were damaged, and I don't think it would work on this irregular ground, anyway. It needs a flat space, like a frozen lake or something."

"Far to the West is land like that."

"Say, now that you mention it, Chief, there are some things in it that might be useful. I have a torch that makes light but almost no heat. And parts of it might make nice decorations for the lodge."

That evening Little Bear came running back from his scouting trip, saying breathlessly that the Buffalo herd would be approaching our Hunting Ground by midmorning.

Nobody slept well that night. It was the first hunt of the new season, and everyone had been bored and restless during the long Winter; we had made more than enough knives, arrows, clubs, baskets, clothing, cooking implements, and so on. The two newcomers were pretty well educated by now, and some of their novelty had worn off, so people were pretty anxious for some activity and excitement.

Now the Pioux Hawques were like a drawn bow. The hunters slept outside.

Before dawn, I went to arouse the hunters; the sound of my approach was sufficient, and I didn't have to say a word before they leapt to their feet. In moments they were assembled outside the lodge, whispering excitedly. Little Bear and Blind Deer took their vanguard positions as scouts. We gave them a little time to get ahead of us, and we set out for the place where we had estimated the herd would be by daylight.

As we walked, I reviewed the instructions I had given the two newcomers. They would be in a relatively safe position among those who would attempt to drive the lone Buffalo selected for the kill, directly opposite the herd's flank, where the beast would be least likely to run. We would try to drive him into the rock formation, where the strong men of the tribe would fall upon him with spears.

"Now, please," I said to them, "no heroics. If this one gets away, we'll just try for another. I don't want any injuries. Sometimes a Buffalo will not respond to a Man shouting in an effort to turn him. They become blind and deaf with panic. If he doesn't give way, you do, and fast. A Man cannot stop a Buffalo."

Cabbie and Bob walked several paces behind me, talking quietly. For the most part, now, they were using our language, except when they did not know a word or phrase. Usually I could guess what their foreign substitute words meant.

They were getting along somewhat better these days, perhaps a result of living with our people, who, I gather, have a lot better social skills than theirs. In fact, Cabbie had remarked once that our language had many more words than theirs, and he thought it would be easier to express fine points of meaning and feeling in it. He said he thought it was because we spend the Winters mostly in our lodges, and pass the time with conversation much more than his people.

He said his people don't know how to settle disputes or injuries as well as we. Often, he said, he saw people simply resorting to open combat while attending a game or traveling in their giant villages; or laying in ambush for one another to rob and kill.

This would explain Bob's haughtiness. I'm sure you children have observed that the more primitive a tribe, the more they go about with snarling faces, and noses in the air. The tribes with the finest crafts and the best weapons, and who tell the most complicated stories around the hearth in Winter are usually the most civil and decent.

At this time my ears were still very sharp, and I could hear their conversation, even though they thought they spoke privately. Bob said, "Stay close behind me, Cabbie, I'm in much better shape than you are, and I might be able to help protect you."

"Oh, stop it, Bob. I've been exercising and practicing with the weapons as much as you have." Cabbie had grown much more patient with him than at first.

"I guess a man's rank in the tribe depends on his performance in the hunt, huh, Cabbie?"

"No, I don't think so, Bob. I think they like to have everyone do what he does best. Chief is a good leader, and that's why he's Chief; not because he's a good hunter." He was right, of course, even though I was in fact a pretty good hunter. "The older men choose a successor for their jobs, and take them into a kind of—ah—" here he substituted a word in his own language—"*apprenticeship*."

"Well, I know you've been spending a lot of time with the Chief and his son lately. I suppose you expect to be made apprentice Chief. Huh!" he snorted. "You couldn't lead the tribe out of a lodge."

"Not at all, Bob. As a matter of fact, Little Bear, the Chief's son, has already been chosen as his successor."

Bob was silent.

At that moment, Little Bear came jogging breathlessly up the trail to meet us. He collapsed into my arms, covered with sweat, and gasped out, "Father, the herd is moving quickly toward our Hunting Ground. We have to pick up the pace a little to meet them in the right spot."

"Good work, Little Bear. You're a fine young scout, and you've made me very proud of you. Walk with us for a while to catch your breath before you head out in front again." He nodded, and shambled alongside me for a while. Despite our practice with weapons and exercising over the Winter, the first hunt is always very tiring. Shaman says it's because our stored food is not as nourishing as the fresh food we hunt and gather in the warmer seasons. He says the people who live in the North, where the Winters are longer, live very short lives.

By midmorning we came to the hill that overlooks the Hunting Ground. I turned and gave the signal for silence and caution. Our band of twenty hunters approached the hill in perfect silence.

Too perfect. I led the band right up to a big Mountain Lion who had been stalking the herd. As you know, Lions are also very good at stalking silently. He turned and crouched and snarled at me. I froze.

My heart pounded in my chest, and my breath came with great difficulty. I could see the pink of his curled lip and the brilliant white of his huge, perfect teeth, with appallingly unnatural clarity.

Frozen by the prospect of death, I could smell his breath, carried to me on a little Spring zephyr; like all of his kind, he smelled of past prey, present hunger, and complete confidence.

Some remote part of me noted that the birds were silent, but the insects still hummed. I wondered for a moment if it was because of the presence of the herd, or my own predicament.

I was too frightened even to be embarrassed, although I was very much so, later.

Nobody moved. Not the hunters, not the Lion. The Lion's gaze remained fixed on me.

Then the Lion made those small adjustments they make before charging: he wiggled his hind quarters, and set his back claws firmly in the ground.

I realized in my dreamlike state that my spear was in fact held in a ready position. I had raised it without knowing. But the Lion was so close, I could not be sure of stopping him. If I cast the spear, he would probably charge, and the spear might not stop him. If I waited until he charged, I might not be able to thrust in time and still dodge.

Someone behind me and to one side moved. I knew it had to be one of the newcomers, because one of The Pioux Hawques would not have moved at a time like that. It was Bob. He waved his arms and growled at the Lion! "Yahhh!" he shouted. He threw his spear into the ground in front of the beast. Later I realized that he probably meant to strike the Lion with it.

When the Lion turned his gaze to Bob, I cast my spear, five or six arrows hit the Lion, Bob dived one way, and I dived another. The Lion leaped, but landed dead.

When I recovered my voice, I ran to Bob and hugged him. "That was the craziest thing I've ever seen, but I owe you my life." I couldn't stop clapping him on the back.

He seemed gradually to realize that he had succeeded in whatever demented plan he had entertained, looked first surprised, then pleased, and said, "I did good, huh, Chief?"

I laughed, "I don't know what to call it, but I'm glad you did it." I caught him by the shoulders. "You two are the craziest people I've ever met, but sometimes it seems The Spirits look after you."

He looked momentarily dismayed, and glared in Cabbie's direction. It took me a moment to realize he was upset because I had said "You two," and he was resentful that I included Cabbie in the statement.

Cabbie just looked at me and gave me that exaggerated patient look he reserved for comment on Bob's behavior.

"All right," I said, still somewhat out of breath, heart pounding. "The Buffalo." I sent the spearmen to the rock formation, and reviewed the places to be taken by those who would drive the selected victim toward them, and we settled down to wait for the right Buffalo in the right place.

After some time, my heart stopped racing and I felt my feet upon the ground once more.

Then I noticed that Bob was not in his place. I turned to Little Bear, who stood behind a tree. "Where's Bob?"

"He went off with the hunters who are to kill the Buffalo in the rock formation."

"Why would he do that? Didn't he understand his directions?"

Little Bear looked at his feet, shuffled, picked a little bit of bark from the tree, and said, still looking away, "He felt that his heroic deed killing the Lion qualified him to have a chance at the Buffalo kill. He said he could use a good Buffalo robe, and he could trade the meat for useful things."

"He didn't kill the Lion."

"I know, Father, but I didn't want to contradict him, because he's older, and he's still sort of a guest, isn't he?"

"He thinks a deed like that raises his rank in the tribe?"

"Yes, Father."

"He thinks he needs to trade Buffalo meat in order to get things he needs from his own tribe?"

"Yessir."

"Little Bear, whatever am I going to do with him?"

"I don't know, Father."

"Well, think about it. If I designate you as my successor, you'll have to be able to handle things like that."

"Yessir."

"We can't take the time to go after him. There's our

Buffalo." A yearling male had wandered into the proper position. He was large, and his coat was perfect, unscarred by life.

His inexperience made him the ideal victim, and promised us a Buffalo robe of exceptional quality. I gave a Crow call, the signal to start driving him. It was the same call the Crows use from the treetops to say, "Here's food."

The drivers stood up, whooping and shouting. The edge of the herd milled away in one direction, and the yearling galloped in the other, making the ground tremble. He came to The River, paused, and a hunter stood up to drive him in the right direction, along The River to the rock formation. But for some reason, the beast headed toward Cabbie instead. In this turn of events, Cabbie was supposed to jump up and yell and wave his arms to turn the beast. But he made a very unterrifying squawk, cast his spear at the beast, and jumped out of the way, losing his footing and landing in a heap. His cast spear, which had no power behind it at all, struck the Buffalo on the cheek, making a gash. This frightened the beast so that he again resumed the right direction, that of his demise.

The Buffalo hunt was underway, out of my hands, so I turned my attention to the fallen Cabbie, who was getting to his feet with the help of Little Bear. When he put his weight on his right foot, it was apparent that he had sprained his ankle again, just as he had upon arriving in our world.

Although I hadn't said a word, he looked at me with a pained smile, and said, "Sorry about that, Chief. I guess I didn't turn out to be much of a hunter."

"Cabbie, you don't have to prove yourself."

"Well, I wanted to become a regular member of the tribe." He winced as he tried to place his weight on the injured ankle. Little Bear took more of his weight, so he would not have to place the foot on the ground at all.

"Cabbie, you are one of The Pioux Hawques."

He looked at me with a look that said, "Don't humor me, Chief, I know what you really think." I decided this wasn't the time to try to untangle the matter for him. He was in shock and pain. The Shaman could handle it, along with the injury.

Little Bear made a travois and conveyed the Cabbie homeward, assuming the task gladly as an alternative to helping slaughter the Buffalo if the hunters in the rock formation were successful. The day was warm and the insects were active, and the latter would be a trying task.

The hunters were in fact successful; the first Buffalo hunt of the season went perfectly. Meanwhile, Little Bear made his way slowly back to the Shaman with Cabbie.

When they arrived, Shaman already had the poultice prepared, and tea boiling, and had found the crutch he had made for Cabbie the other time. He is indeed a master of Inner Vision. Nothing ever surprises him.

Little Bear was panting and sweating; Winter's confinement had taken its toll. The Shaman also had a broth prepared for him, which he said would help him to build his strength quickly. Shaman took Cabbie by the arm, sent Little Bear to the main lodge to rest, and took Cabbie under a tree where he had arranged his remedies and equipment.

Shaman is never one to waste a captive audience. Just as he knew that Cabbie was injured and was being brought back, he also knew that he was confused about his role in the tribe, and that he did not realize that he was already fully accepted. While he was treating the ankle, Shaman said, "Cabbie, have you thought about your responsibilities to the tribe?"

"I'm very grateful, Shaman, for everything you've done for me. I'm happier here than I've ever been. But I don't know what I can do for the tribe. I still know so little about living here. I'm like a child."

"I didn't mean that you have to repay us for taking you in. We didn't do it as a favor. It's just a natural thing to do. What I meant was that you have to choose a craft, a hunting specialty, and perhaps a wife."

It doesn't take much to stop Cabbie dead in his tracks, so to speak. He was speechless.

The Shaman went on: "Every man has to do these things to be happy, Cabbie, with certain exceptions. You have to be useful to be happy. Nobody wants to be a guest forever. Now, what about a craft? You might work with flint, or learn to carve bone, or tan hides; you might learn to make lodges, or—well, what appeals to you?"

"I don't know, Shaman. I like working with my hands, but, I don't know anything about these things."

"Of course not. We'll apprentice you to someone who does, just as we would a boy. You'll learn much faster than a boy, of course, and you'd be given the respect due to a grown man."

"Can I take a few days to think about it?"

"Of course. Now, what about a hunting specialty? I think you must be very good at finding things and knowing where you are, even in unfamiliar territory, isn't that right?"

"Yeah, I guess so."

"Then you might want to be a scout."

"I guess so."

"Good. Now, I think you realize Light Butterfly and her parents like you. Why don't I arrange a Marriage?"

Cabbie opened his mouth, and nothing came out. Then he found his voice, and said, "But, Shaman, do you think I'm ready? You don't want to burden her with someone who doesn't really know his way in this world yet, do you?"

"Let's talk it over with her."

"But, Shaman, I'm not ready. I only just got here, sort of. What if she says no? This is too soon, isn't it? What if she says yes? Are you sure her parents like me? Are you sure she likes me? That much, I mean?"

"We'll just talk it over. We don't have to make a decision right away."

The Shaman finished wrapping the ankle with soft furs over the poultice, made Cabbie drink one of his bitter teas that put one to sleep, and carried him back to his corner of the main lodge. There he laid him on his furs and left him to rest.

When Cabbie awoke, Light Butterfly was sitting next to him. A hubcap full of tea was suspended over the fire, from which she served him a small cup. She helped him unnecessarily into a sitting position leaning against the wall of the lodge.

"Light Butterfly." He said it lamely, not knowing what else to say.

"Cabbie. Drink this, and it will help your ankle to heal."

"I'm all right, really. It's not that serious. It's just like the other time, when we first came."

She nodded and stared into the fire. Finally, she said, "Shaman has spoken to you about me?"

"Uh, yes, he has."

"I don't wish to offend you, or imply any hostility or dislike. Actually, I do like you a lot. My parents do, too."

Cabbie smiled. "This is beginning to sound like rejection. It's all right. Don't worry. I didn't have my heart set on it."

"Your what? Heart set—oh. You have such an odd way of speaking." She smiled affectionately. "Cabbie, you're a very special man. A very good man. Some of the young girls have spoken well of you. Well, actually, they giggle and speculate about who will get you. But, even though I seem to be first in line, I have to tell you, I, well, I grew up with Little Bear, and we've always kind of assumed that one day—well, our parents don't seem to know it yet, but I'll bet the Shaman does. There isn't much that escapes him. Sorry, I'm not speaking very clearly, am I? I mean, I think I want to marry Little Bear, and he feels the same. You're every bit as good a man as he is, in your way, though. It's just that we've always liked each other, and his wisdom is, uh, well, he knows more about the world, and you seem to be wise in the ways of a Shaman, sort of. I know you really don't know the Shaman's craft, but you seem to have the feeling about you that a great Shaman has. Personally, I think you ought to consider becoming his apprentice. He doesn't have one, you know."

Cabbie looked at once relieved and disappointed. "Shamans don't marry, do they?"

"No. They marry the Universe."

"Well, you're a very attractive woman, and I have to admit I've had some very compelling thoughts about you, but I guess somehow, I've always known I wasn't meant for the world. Not my first world, and not really this one either. Not like Little Bear is, or Bob. They're good at doing, I'm good at something else. Being. Knowing. I don't know."

She laughed. "You sound like you're arguing with yourself."

His smile is always ready to spring out from even his most serious concentrations. "That's the way to wisdom, Butterfly. The minute you think you know, that's when you can be sure you don't."

Her laugh became deeper and more heartfelt. She tried to stop, but she shook with internal affection and amusement. Finally she was able to speak. "You're a Shaman, all right, Cabbie. Nobody else talks like that." She leaned over and kissed him on the forehead. Then she reconsidered, saying, "Once you're a Shaman, I'll never be able to do this." She grabbed him and applied a truly earnest kiss that left him bewildered and speechless. With that, she left the poor man sitting there.

Before he'd fully recovered from Butterfly's parting kiss, Bob came into the lodge and sat down next to him, looking troubled. Cabbie gathered his shattered composure, which was never too firm in any case, and said, "What's up, Bob? You don't look too good."

Bob seemed not to notice that Cabbie looked as bad as he did, but in a happier sort of way. "I don't really understand these people, Cabbie."

"What's to understand? They're good people."

"They seem so knowledgeable in some ways, and so dense in others."

"What do you mean?"

"Well, Shaman was trying to treat one of the women who had a bad tooth. He put one of his herbal concoctions in the cavity, and gave her some other stuff to kill the pain. But he didn't know you could remove the tooth. When I suggested it, he looked surprised. He asked me if that was how they did it in our old world. I explained it to him. I told him a bad tooth could lead to a fatal infection in some cases."

'What'd he say?"

"He asked me to explain it to him. I remembered the pair of pliers in the Cab. I went and got it. Shaman drugged her unconscious, and I pulled the tooth."

"That's great, Bob."

"Yeah, but y'know, they're such children in some ways. They must have a high mortality rate. And, something else has been bothering me, too. I don't understand how they can live in an, uh—(here he changed over to their language)—how they can live in an environment where no one can get ahead, advance himself, you know. You can't even court a girl. You have to arrange a romance and marriage with the whole tribe knowing and consenting."

"What's wrong with that?"

"I tried to put the move on one of the girls. She cooperated a little, up to a point, but she had definite limits. I thought they were innocent savages. Hah! She said she had to go take care of something. I thought she was stringing me along, but she never came back." He looked a little embarrassed. "I thought maybe she was practicing some kind of herbal birth control or something."

"They do, Bob."

"Oh. You mean, she could have—uh?"

"Yeah, as I understand it, they do."

"Then you haven't really had any more luck than I have."

"No, I guess not. Not really."

"It was the same girl that came to me in the cab when we first . . . you know."

"Light Butterfly?"

"Yeah."

"Bob, don't take it personally. She just has her eye on Little Bear, that's all."

"It figures. He's the Chief Designate. How did you know that?"

"She told me."

Bob looked suspiciously at him.

"Just friends, Bob."

"Yeah, I'll bet." He got up and left.

Cabbie eventually fell asleep again. He awoke after a long time, wondering at first where he was and how much time had passed. Then he saw the Shaman sitting nearby. "Well, Cabbie," said the Shaman, "things have a way of sorting themselves out, don't they?"

"They sure do. Sometimes you have to wait a while, but they do."

"Spoken like a Shaman."

"Hm. What do you think?

"I can accept you as my apprentice."

Cabbie's now famous grin exploded upon the tired old Shaman, setting off a remarkably similar one on the wizened face. Neither spoke. I don't suppose they had to. They are the kind of men who speak only as a decoration for their silent dialogues, or for the rest of us, whose inner hearing is not as sharp.

What's that, Little Vixen, lean closer, please, and speak louder.

Oh. Well, Bob went off on a journey. He insisted that he had to do some exploring for himself, and he left over my objections. I didn't feel he was ready. I'm sorry to say, he went West, and we never heard from him again. I don't know whether he eventually settled with another tribe, or succumbed to hostile men or beasts, or what.

What? Yes. That's the end of the story. Now, please take some tea to the Elder Shaman and Cabbie Shaman. They're not asleep. They just do that, pretending to sleep. Go ahead. They'll appreciate it. Even though they have only one foot in this world, they still appreciate the attentions of a sweet little girl like you. Take them camomile. Then maybe they'll really fall asleep.

And take some to your grandmother, Light Butterfly, and Chief Little Bear, too. We older folks don't sleep as soundly and easily as you little ones.

The Difference
by
Frank Frazetta

About the Author

Frank Frazetta was born February 9, 1928, in Brooklyn, New York, and began drawing as soon thereafter as possible. He literally does not remember a time he didn't draw. At eight, he was enrolled in the Brooklyn Academy of Fine Arts. His instructor, Michael Falanga, called him a genius. He was not the last to do so. Frazetta still remembers, with great fondness, how Paul Grubman heavily influenced him, and fought to win him recognition in scholastic competitions, as his teacher at Abraham Lincoln High School.

At sixteen, he began his extensive career in comics. In 1954, he went to work on the Li'l Abner comic strip, and then went on to do Buck Rogers, and other work that is still very much remembered. The work he was happiest with was his work for James Warren's publishing company; Creepy, Eerie, and the creation of the seductive and deadly Vampirella.

At about this time, his career expanded dramatically. He was introduced to paperback covers, and after an initial period with Ace Books, struck a deal with Lancer which resulted in art that is still prized. And he went on from there to make book after book, from many publishers, a far better seller than the author had any right to expect.

The rest is history; there has never been a paperback

artist like Frazetta. L. Ron Hubbard called him the "King of Illustration." And what he has to say in the essay that follows is quintessential Frazetta; no nonsense, no false modesty, and an amazing range of dead-on commentary on the art of illustration.

———————————————

Mr. Frazetta's cover painting for WOTF VII *is entitled "Dawn Attack."*

I was born with a pencil in my hand. Most artists reach a certain age, and then their eyes open and they start doing art. I was drawing as far back as I can remember. I had unusual talent right then and there, in that I saw things differently. I saw them more accurately. Some people to this day criticize me by saying I exaggerate; that people don't look like that. But they look like that to me. The truth is from the very beginning, instinctively, I drew what I thought I saw.

I try to give people what I think *should* be. I've had many, many people look at one of my paintings, and say "Yeah! That's the way it should be!" Basically, that's my whole approach.

The makeup of great art consists of many, many things . . . including a certain amount of luck, a certain amount of inspiration, and a very mysterious factor that I simply cannot account for. Imagination. And you've got to be intelligent in your approach. There are an awful lot of skillful artists who can render, who can draw, and who rely on source material instead of finding the picture in themselves. And that attitude—that you've got to find the picture in source material—is strictly one of fear. Fear of criticism, fear of I don't know what. I don't worry if it's less than perfect as a piece of rendering. I want it to be perfect as a work of *art*.

A lot of artists can't express themselves the way they would like to. They just don't have the ability. They have certain instincts, they have things they feel, and then they sit down at the drawing board, and it just simply doesn't happen. But if I can see it, even vaguely, I sit down and it appears. I don't know why, exactly; that's the mysterious part, which is easy to say but covers more ground than you might at first think.

But the key to me is I know when it *doesn't* work. Most others reach a certain point in a piece of art, and they say "I guess that's as good as I can get," and I look at a piece of art and I say "No, no, no, it's got to be better; it doesn't work." And sometimes it's very involved as to why it doesn't work—the composition can be wrong, or the shape isn't interesting enough, or the action isn't interesting enough, or the lighting is flat . . . it can be many different facets.

There is one thing—the figure. If the figure doesn't relate, then change it! I've painted perfectly beautiful figures, and then taken them out, to the dismay of my friends. And I know it's a good figure, and if I can put it in somewhere else, fine, but it didn't work in that particular situation. And then I'll put in a figure that's perhaps less exciting, or less beautiful, but it lends something to the painting; it doesn't become a distraction.

It's the composition—shape; movement. Color is secondary. It's these wonderful shapes; it's like music. It's the combinations. You can't just have a theme, and then the rest of it goes flat. Somehow, the whole thing has to work. It's not enough, for me, to say "Yeah, it's got some nice things." I don't want to hear that . . . "some nice things." I want every inch of that painting to be unboring, if there is such a word. "Unboring." And even if people don't understand what makes it work, it seems to be our nature to respond to certain rhythms and shapes. I don't know why it is. Not color. I don't think we care that much about color. People think they do, but I don't think it's color more than shapes.

I have no fixed ideas about color. When I have this vision—when the picture builds itself in my mind—I don't immediately see it with a glowing setting sun, or anything. The color part is more deliberate and calculated. I see the shapes, and I *see* the action, and the character, even, but then I *say* to myself "O.K., now, how shall I approach this? Shall I make it a warm painting?"

That's the way I think. Warm? Or cold. Or maybe neutral. I sit there, and I think "Let's see, now. This composition has a lot of power. Cold would make it perhaps more mysterious. Hot would make it more vibrant." That's the way I think about color. I decide whether hot is going to somehow work with this design, or cool would be better. And that's it. Many artists know color as well as or better than I do. But that's not Frank Frazetta. Frank Frazetta draws. And composes. I can create, instead of just doing a pretty picture that's essentially like a lot of other pretty pictures by any one of a hundred artists.

Color is really irrelevant to my work. Any painting I've done could have been approached in any number of ways in terms of color, and still work. I don't know any of my paintings that really work because of the color. If I left the color out, it would be just as powerful. Whereas other artists—illustrators of the past; great illustrators—their color had to work, or else.

You know, in an essay that ran in Volume Two of this series, L. Ron Hubbard said "What is good art? . . . Technical expertise itself adequate to produce an emotional impact." And if you realize that this washes out a vast amount of what's called "art," but isn't art, and if you realize this places a tremendous obligation on the artist, that's right. We all have our limitations . . . but every once in a while, guys like me reach out and go far beyond what we accepted up until then as great and wonderful. Like the four minute mile. "Can't be done, can't be done," we said for years. Then somebody does it, and suddenly everybody feels they can do it.

I know as well as anybody there are some wonderful looking paintings out there. They're very skillfully done—great color, great this, great that. And I'd look at them and I'd say: "Hey, that's real nice, but. But." Heck, I say that about my stuff, too. But I have achieved some pieces that I look at, and I say "How the hell did I do that?" Even as a young guy, a lot of people would reach for the Moon, and I'd say "Reach for the stars, damn it; and if you don't quite get there, you still might reach the Moon."

As far as this particular *WOTF* cover goes, it's a wonderful composition. There's a drive, there's a power, there's movement from left to right, and then it comes back, it's just all moving, and it doesn't just run off the picture. That's what makes a good painting, I think. And the story; they're coming over the horizon, and the army of robots are led by this wonderful heroic figure, and the spaceships and the city—you know there's a war going on. And that's it; that's the story. Her attitude, her beauty, has got to convince you that she just isn't going to lose. The attitude of the figures, whether it's crouching, leaping, running—that tells you they're moving at great speed and with great confidence. I don't think there's any question but that this is victory, and heroism. And that's the action.

I'm a slave to my love of action. That isn't necessarily the only approach. But I'm just an action guy, I guess. I love movement, speed, and power.

I was always, even while young, frustrated with most art. Frustrated. I'd say "It's wonderful, but it doesn't go far enough. Why didn't they do this, why didn't they go farther, why didn't they do that?" I'm talking about action . . . about character. They seemed so laid back, so relaxed, and yet so careful. They'd never look toward the next horizon. They didn't know there was one, actually.

If all the young artist wants to do is live a comfortable life, and support himself, then you ought to do what the editor tells you to do. If you can do it skillfully and professionally, then you'll do just fine, I guess. If you're looking for greatness, on the other hand, then you've got to have guts, and nerve, and strength of will, and buck the establishment! And that isn't easy. I can say it, but that's just because I have the God-given talent—not just nerve, or guts—I just have the talent to back me up.

Yarena's Daughter
by
Terri Trimble

About the Author

Terri Trimble is 26, and has been writing fantasy and science fiction for the past ten years. While in high school, she won Third Place in the national Scholastic Writing Contest.

She graduated in 1987 from World College West, a small international liberal arts college just north of San Francisco, with a BA in Art and Society. Since then, she has worked swing shift as a data entry operator for a collections agency, a job which gives her a great deal of freedom to write during the day. She is currently working on a fantasy novel. She lives in Petaluma, California, and is seriously working at being a writer. "Yarena's Daughter" is her first success.

About the Illustrator

Charles Dougherty is 34, and graduated from the Philadelphia College of Art in 1978 with a BFA in illustration. He then studied in Europe for three years, before returning to Philadelphia and working for small presses, mostly in horror, and various role-playing game companies.

He has exhibited his work at science fiction conventions all over the USA. He wants to do book jackets, and we venture to say it won't be long before book publishers start taking notice.

As our ship came into the harbor and I saw my mother, the Mad Queen of Sabbish, standing on the dock, I suddenly remembered all the reasons for my leaving three years before. The deck hands ran back and forth, the crew shouted orders, Captain Hallys stood at the tiller as calm as the eye of the storm, while I in the prow watched that small crimson-robed figure drawing ever closer.

We dropped anchor and lowered the first rowboat over the side. Four rowers, Hallys and I climbed down the rope ladder and set off towards shore. Already, I felt, the easy companionship that had grown between us during our travels was beginning to dissipate. Hallys was subdued, and the young rowers pulled at their oars with a sense of importance, stealing glances at me that were full of awe. No longer was I merely a companion in their adventures. As an actor sheds her costume when the play ends, I was returning to my true life: Taiya, princess of Sabbish, and one day, perhaps Queen.

With ceremonial skill the starboard oars lifted from the water, the shore workers grasped them and pulled the boat to the edge of the dock. I stepped out of the boat.

"Welcome home, Taiya," my mother said.

I gripped the hand she offered me, and answered, "I am glad to be here." This was not quite a lie, despite the doubts that were beginning to return in full force. For a year I had delayed my return though Tyeasis, the city of my birth and our island's capital, was often in my dreams—waking or asleep.

"Captain Hallys," my mother said. "Such a prosperous journey will crown your career. Would you dine with us at Aristide this evening?"

"With honor, my lady," Hallys answered. Her gaze crossed my own briefly, and I caught in her eyes a touch of amusement that made me realize, with relief, that our maritime friendship would not end on land. How many nights had Hallys sat up late with me, listening sympathetically to my complaints of my mother, laughing at the more amusing stories I could tell of her?

My mother and I set off through the streets of Tyeasis, and I matched my pace to her swifter one. Eight guards surrounded us—two in front, two behind, and two on either side. Once a would-be assassin had broken their ranks as my mother, my sister and I were walking past the steps of the courts of justice. He had killed two guards and come towards the Queen with his bloody knife upraised. I, who stood between them, had seen it all. My mother's pupils enlarged, as they always did when she was foreseeing, and in a calm voice she described for him the details of his slow and painful execution, and told how his wife and four children would live in poverty for the rest of their lives, ostracized by all the citizens of Sabbish. No doubt whatever price he had been offered for my mother's life was not worth these consequences, for he dropped his knife and ran.

I had never told Hallys of this incident, for of all the demonstrations of my mother's power that I had seen in my twenty years, it frightened me most. She might have been speaking a curse, in her even, dispassionate voice, except the assassin knew, as I did, that what the Queen foresaw was simply the inevitable outcome of his actions.

My mother asked me of my travels as we climbed the

Illustrated by Charles Dougherty

steep streets towards Aristide, our ancestral home seated at
the edge of the Southern Cliff. I spoke of those I had vis-
ited: my seven uncles, my dead father's mother, endless
cousins and second cousins and all their children. I did not
tell her of the joyous freedom I had felt, during the first
eighteen months I was gone, and how finally it had deserted
me and left behind nothing but restlessness, homesickness,
and some unidentifiable longing to return to Sabbish and
confront my fate, battle it out face-to-face, kill it or be
killed by it. I did not speak of why I had returned, and my
mother, Mad Queen Yarena, did not ask.

The servants opened the gates of Aristide and we
passed through the courtyard garden into the house, leaving
the guards behind. Inside the air was cool, and a table was
laid with lunch for three. The doors in the opposite wall
stood open, and below the iron railing the cliff dropped
sharply down to the sea. As the servants pulled out the cush-
ioned chairs for us, my sister came gliding down the narrow
stairs.

In three years Mireya seemed hardly to have changed.
She was still tall, pale, somber and thin: with a half-starved
look to her that indicated more than a want of physical nour-
ishment. "Taiya," she murmured, and leaned down to
brush her cheek against mine. It was mere formality only;
there had never been any love lost between us. Mireya was
fifteen years my elder, and had lived her whole life with one
goal in mind. For this she served my mother in respectful
deference, and took on duties in the temples and hospices of
Tyeasis. But both of us had long known, with probably
equal measures of dread, that what Mireya wanted my
mother would never let her have, and what I did not want
Yarena would insist on giving to me. In the end, we both
suspected, we would have to bow our heads beneath
Yarena's will, for to oppose it was as ineffective as shouting
into the wind.

Mireya's pretense of welcome did not last beyond her greeting. She consumed her meal with methodical precision, as if eating were not a pleasure to her but only a chore necessary to sustain her body. She and my mother spoke of some affairs in the temple, and Mireya soon excused herself to return to her work there. As the gates clicked shut behind her, my mother turned to me.

"She knows, yet still she persists in trying," she said. "Often Mireya reminds me of a bird that will batter itself to death against a glass window, seeking entrance to a house."

"Why don't you tell her so, or send her away?" I asked, trying to keep the emotion from my voice and speak as coolly as she did. "Why do you let her torment herself?"

"Because I need her here." She picked up a slice of apple, looked at it through narrowed eyes, then put it in her mouth. "One year, Taiya."

I looked up, startled. "What do you mean?" I asked, with foreboding growing in my heart.

"I may serve Sabbish only one year more," Yarena said, "before the *kinnarath* has its way with me. Already there are times when I cannot control it. This morning as I sat at breakfast, I began to wonder what would happen if I did not finish my meal. I foresaw that one of the maids would give the scraps to a stray cat outside Aristide's walls, who as a result would return here every day for food until a fortnight hence it was crushed beneath the wheels of a passing butcher's cart. Should I finish my breakfast, I wondered, though I was not hungry, to save the life of that cat? Would the world be changed for good or ill by its death?

"So you see, my foresight begins to stumble over trivialities."

As Yarena spoke I grew ever colder in that warm sunny room. I stared out the windows at the expanse of blue stretching on to the horizon, and heard the whisper of waves against the cliff's foot, far below our house.

"I have never understood," I said finally, "why you cannot let Mireya be queen."

"You will understand when you have drunk the *kinnarath*." I looked up angrily, but before I could speak, she went on, "Mireya is weak of mind, and I would no more give her the queenship to make her powerful, than I would give a feeble man a heavy burden to carry to make him strong. If Mireya were to rule after me, she would make one error of judgment after another, until finally, twelve years into her reign, the people would rise up in revolt against her—which she would survive, but their faith in the Mad Queen's power would be so eroded that finally her great-granddaughter would be deposed and a mob would set fire to Aristide, destroying the house and the *kinnarath*."

She spun it out before me as if unwinding yarn from a skein. "But if you can foresee it, you can avoid it," I told her. "And so can Mireya, once she drinks the *kinnarath*."

"What I have described for you, Taiya, is only the least disastrous scenario. Mireya is not to be Queen. She lacks the strength to ignore her desires and follow the path of the greater good. Once she drank the *kinnarath*, she would see herself as the heroine in a great drama, one whose conclusion she foresaw, and all her actions would be directed towards her own pleasure."

I took several slow, long breaths to steady myself before I spoke. I had resolved, when I decided to return, that I would hide all my feelings from my mother. "Then I must be Queen."

"Yes," Yarena said.

From all accounts my grandmother Naira was a woman of great subtlety, a trait my mother did not inherit. When she was Queen, Naira had a skill of gently controlling those around her, of making it seem they still possessed free will, when in fact she was using the *kinnarath*-induced foresight to guide their choices and set them on a path that would benefit all of Sabbish. I went to visit her several times when I was a young child, and she was living in seclusion at Cihan, the ancient home of her father's family on the north shore of the island. At that time she was a very old woman, who had to wear a dark hood and veil to shield her eyes, with their permanently widened pupils, from the light of the sun. The effects of *kinnarath* are cumulative, and it is this which progressively drives Sabbish's Queens mad. My grandmother Naira would chatter constantly at Mireya and me, warning us of what would happen if we ate barley instead of wheat at lunch, if we went to the beach now instead of five minutes later, if we went southwest or southeast on our rambles through the woods.

Naira gave up the rule to my mother when Yarena was eighteen, and two years later Mireya was born. I have heard it said by some in my family that before Yarena first drank the *kinnarath*, she and Mireya's father Jurak were very much in love. But for reasons of which she never spoke, Yarena sent Jurak away shortly after their child's birth, and fourteen years later took her cousin Staris as lover. I was the result, and my own father did not stay on Sabbish even for my birth. When I met him years later, shortly before his death, Staris explained to me how it had been between them. Yarena was always beautiful, and his passion was hers to command, but never his love. How does one love the voice of reason, the conscience that tells you what you must do for the absolute good though it rankles your very soul? My mother looked at Staris, her pupils widening, and saw not a man with hopes and desires of his own, but the agent to produce the child she needed to ensure a stable future for Sabbish.

Later that afternoon, after a bath and a change of

clothing, I walked along the Appina Road out to the traders' village. I had often traveled this route, by day or by night, knowing that Blas's company would keep my mind off my mother's schemes if only for a few hours. Today I felt no such assurance, for my conversation with Yarena weighed heavily on my mind, and I had agreed to begin training with the *kinnarath* on the morrow.

A high stone wall concealed the inner yard where the copper-workers crafted their wares, but from the street I could hear the rhythmic sound of three hammers beating out some utensil of metal. I slipped in through the open gate and stood quietly watching.

The three hammers came down in turn, one at the apex as another was just being lifted and the third rebounded from striking the metal. A girl stood at the edge of the workblock with tongs, rotating the soft warm metal so it was shaped evenly. Under the hammers a kettle was being formed, its sides widening and sloping outward until finally it was complete. The workers dropped their hammers and the girl picked up a sanding block to smooth down the kettle's rim.

Blas wiped his brow with his sleeve, pushed back his damp hair, and looked towards me. A sudden smile lit up his face. As he crossed the yard I saw how the softness of youth had disappeared almost entirely from his features, leaving his cheekbones high and pronounced and his chin firm, as if time were a sculptor that had been gradually chiseling away at Blas's face.

"Taiya," he said in a low murmur that brought back memories of summer nights so long ago. I returned his embrace but stepped back before he did, and he looked at me with concern in his eyes. "What's wrong? Is it your mother?"

"Of course," I answered, laughing a little. "If it weren't for her my life would be so uncomplicated. I want to talk to you, Blas."

I sat on his narrow bed, beneath the shelves of copper ornaments that marked the stages of his apprenticeship, and told him all my mother had said to me over lunch. He bathed in water heated over the fires in the workshop, changed his clothes, and shaved, all the while listening to me and asking questions now and then.

"I had been at sea less than a month," I told him, "when I began to realize that Mother would never have consented to my going, unless she foresaw that I would return. The only time in my life I have ever felt truly free, and I realized that I was not free at all. There is no escaping her wishes, when she knows that in the end I will relent. At sea I almost hoped for a storm and a shipwreck, for *that* at least she could not foresee, and my death would render all her precognition useless."

"She can't control you, Taiya," Blas said, wiping his razor on a towel. "So she may foresee that if you do what she wants, it will be the best for everyone concerned—or what *she* thinks is best. But she still can't make you do it. She has no power over you."

"But she *does*, don't you see?" I answered. "There is no use in rebelling against her, when she foresees that in the end I will relent, and she foresees exactly what she must say and do to make me finally give in. She has no subtlety whatsoever. I can almost hear her think: If I say *this* to Taiya, she'll have no argument to counter mine. If I say *this* she'll refuse to be Queen, but if I tell her *this* she'll see she has no choice." My voice was rising as I spoke, but I broke off abruptly when the copper on the shelves above me began to rattle slightly. I looked up in surprise, thinking irrationally for a moment that my anger had roused the forces of nature. Blas watched it too, calmly, and after only a few seconds, it stopped.

"The earth is moving," he explained. "It's happened several times this past month. Great-grandfather keeps telling us that when he was a boy the island shook and buckled, and three of the houses in the village fell to the ground. But he thinks we're safe, so long as the Mad Queen hasn't foreseen a disaster."

"I wonder sometimes how many people think Mother is omniscient," I said. "Hallys could not understand at first why the Queen wouldn't give her navigator a course to follow that would avoid all the storms and follow the favorable winds. Hallys was certain it would make her life so much easier. I had a hard time convincing her the *kinnarath* only enables us to foresee human behavior, not the earth's." I sighed, remembering what awaited me tomorrow.

"Let's go somewhere, Taiya," Blas said. "To the tavern—or the beach, if you'd rather be alone."

I shook my head. "I have to go home. Mother's invited Hallys for dinner."

I stood up and he came close to tell me goodbye. When after several moments I tried to pull out of his embrace, he did not let me go at first. "Come back tonight," he said softly in my ear. "I'll leave the back gate unlatched for you, like we used to do."

Mireya was listless and taciturn throughout dinner, and it was by this that I knew Mother had already told her. Hallys recounted some of the more harrowing moments of our journey, and told of the most splendid things we had seen in the distant lands of Irith and Calise. My mother was at her most charming when she entertained guests, and she asked intelligent questions, exclaimed at the proper moments, and was altogether a most engaging hostess.

"I'm almost disappointed," Hallys said as I walked her home through the dark streets of Tyeasis. "Her pupils did not widen once."

"Just be grateful," I told her, "that she has not looked into your future and told you what you ought to do."

Hallys did not catch the note of bitterness in my voice. "You're right, it's just as well. If she told me my next voyage would be a financial failure, or that we'd be attacked by pirates off the coast of Lesenia, I'd probably be afraid to leave Sabbish ever again."

I wanted to confide in her, to tell her that tomorrow I was to drink *kinnarath* for the first time; that when she returned from her next voyage, I would be Taiya the Mad Queen. But I did not see how our friendship could weather such a change as that, and I was not yet ready to tell her farewell. Hallys was the companion of my days of freedom, and the only witness, it seemed to me then, that the Mad Queen's daughter could shake off the bonds of foreknowledge, if only for a time.

We descended the worn stone steps of the Hisseth Climb, and made our way through the jumble of dwellings in the Seafarers' Quarter. I did not realize how long the silence had stretched out between us until Hallys spoke. "You seem troubled, Taiya. Do you want to talk of it?"

Still I hesitated. "I just need to rest, I think."

"Perhaps a man would do you good. I have a friend, not a hundred paces from here. . . ."

I laughed. "Thank you, Hallys, but I already have an appointment for this evening."

"That copper-worker you spoke of? Good. He sounds like a fine man."

I sighed despite myself, and Hallys's sharp ears heard it. "There *is* something wrong, Taiya," she exclaimed. "You can't hide it from me—after three years I know you too well. I have failed you as a friend, if you cannot confide in me."

"This is a trouble I would rather not burden you with," I said.

She took my arm and led me to a stone bench that ran along the edge of the street, made me sit down, and took a place beside me. "It's no burden to help a friend in need," she said. "Does it concern your mother?"

"You're as quick to guess that as Blas." I leaned over and hid my face in my hands. "She has decided that I'm to be Queen, Hallys. I should not have come back—I should have known that once I set foot on Sabbish again, I would have to surrender up my fate to her. She has foreknowledge— she decides what is best, and how can anyone gainsay her?"

Hallys drew a sharp breath. "What a manipulative old *hag*," she said. "If I had known this I would never have dined at her table. Oh, her meal is growing sour in my gut." She made a low growling noise in her throat and I looked up in surprise, wondering if the Mad Queen's feast was about to be spit up on the street, but Hallys only stood and began to pace back and forth. "You'd think life was a game of *hekkara,* and all of Sabbish your mother's figures. One she moves to the second quadrant, another to the fourth, and la! the design is complete. What would she do if one of the figures refused to move?"

"*You* try it, Hallys," I said. "If she said to you, Hallys, your next voyage will be a financial disaster, but you'll meet a woman whose acquaintance will make you rich seven years hence, would you go? What if you said you wouldn't go, and she said, Hallys, if you don't go on this voyage, you'll be a richer woman for it now, but in ten years some business failures will render you destitute? Or if she said, Hallys, argue as you may, I foresee you'll go on this voyage in the end no matter what you say now?"

"I'd tell her to be damned, and I'd become a fisherwoman. And she can't make you do anything you don't want to do either."

"No, she can't. But she foresees I'll consent to be Queen. She would never have borne me, had she not foreseen beforehand that I would be a suitable heir."

Hallys's breath hissed through her teeth. "She knew *that*?"

"She *planned* for it, Hallys. She chose my father to sire me, and probably even chose the exact hour to couple with him, knowing that the combination of circumstances in that moment would produce a child who would, twenty years later, consent to be Queen. So you see it's all foreseen, and thus foreordained. If I were not meant to drink the *kinnarath* and take on the queenship, I would never have been born."

I left Hallys at the door of her lodgings—nearly speechless for once—and wandered slowly out to the deserted piers. I passed some well-lit noisy taverns on the way, and friendly voices called out to invite me in, not knowing who I was. I walked on.

The moon was half full and its light shimmered on the water of the bay. The rustle of waves on the shore below soothed me somewhat, and the thought of freedom that was still linked in my mind to the unending motion of the sea enticed me for a few moments. But out there, beyond the horizon, lay no freedom for me now, I knew. I even began to accept the thought, and the small compensations that the queenship seemed to offer.

With the knowledge that one last night remained to me—one night in which to choose for myself only, and not to consider the endless tangled web of consequences—I started up the Appina Road to the traders' village.

"Did you think of me much while you were gone?" Blas murmured against my shoulder some time later.

"Oh, for the first few days," I said. "But the handsome men of Phedre soon chased all thoughts of you from my mind—and the Crown Prince of Sotero, and a wine merchant in Adrina. . . ."

His teeth nipped my arm. "The truth, Taiya."

"All right," I said softly. "There were some I sought out from loneliness or physical need, but no one supplanted you in my heart."

He was silent a while, and I could feel his breath like a feather tickling my neck. "A year ago I was certain you would never return," he told me, "and I determined to exorcise you from my thoughts. So I courted Tamela of the weavers, and we spent several nights together. But she knew before I did that it was you I still loved, and she left me."

I turned over on my side, and kissed him slowly at the base of his throat. "I fear for us, Blas," I whispered, "once I begin to drink the *kinnarath*. I think that not even our love will be safe from it."

His arms tightened around me. "We've been separated by water once before, Taiya, but it won't happen again. The *kinnarath* can't make you cease to love me."

"But what if I should foresee that for the good of Sabbish I must abandon you for another man? What if I foresee that our happiness means others will suffer?" I paused, then went on, fighting the swelling in my throat, "I only want you to know that if anything should happen—if I must make a choice that hurts you, it is only because I have foreseen an alternative that I cannot live with."

"I won't believe it," he said fiercely. "I refuse to believe that is right to deliberately choose pain and self-denial in the name of some higher good."

I wanted to agree with him, but I felt in my heart that he was wrong. He did not know: he had not lived all his life with the Mad Queen of Sabbish. He was a man, and would never know the power of *kinnarath*.

The story of how the early inhabitants of our island discovered the spring of *kinnarath* has long since faded into legend. The names of the women who first drank it, and discovered the powers it gave them, have been forgotten, along with the names of the men who first drank it, and went instantly mad. Over the years the women learned that the same fate awaited them in the end though it came on more gradually, and after another generation or two they must have chosen some woman, who proved more skillful than the others in controlling the *kinnarath*'s effects, to be its sole user and the soothsayer for her people. It is said that the lineage from that first Mad Queen to my mother was unbroken, and no doubt this was true. Most of the Mad Queens must have done as my mother did when she planned for my birth. If any of their daughters strained against their future as I did, it is not recorded in the histories.

It has been less than two hundred years since the spring dried up. It was Queen Vianne who first noticed the stream diminishing, and began to collect the last of the *kinnarath* into tall urns of white clay. Aristide had been built above the spring, with its lowest level as a shrine where the sacred water flowed into a pool, and ran down a channel out to the sea, which neutralized it. Those of older times who tried to dilute the *kinnarath,* and thus lessen its potency—and its side-effects—learned that to mix it with any other water rendered it absolutely ineffective.

Vianne had strong wooden racks built to hold the urns against one wall of the shrine. As she filled the containers one by one, and continued to drink daily from the spring for her foreseeing, she realized that the *kinnarath* was growing more potent as its spring died. She filled forty-two urns; since her time six had been emptied. But the glass of crystal with jewels set around its rim, from which the Mad Queens drank their power for long centuries, needed only to be half full for my mother Yarena's daily draught. As I stood with her in the shrine and she explained this to me, I thought that by the time the forty-second urn was reached, ten thousand years hence, my descendant would need only to put a drop onto her tongue to induce the *kinnarath* trance.

My mother lowered a small crystal dipping cup, fastened at the end of a silver chain, into the seventh urn. She drew it up and filled the draught-glass half full, then came and sat across from me on an embroidered cushion, next to the empty pool and the dried-up spring.

"When you first drink the *kinnarath*," Yarena told me, "you will find its effects very difficult to control. As I told you, my foresight now stumbles over trivialities. You will find yours drowning in generalities at first. To counteract this, think of something small and specific: what the temple should serve at the next feast-day, for example."

She handed the glass to me. I took it in both my hands, which were trembling. "Now drink," Yarena said.

I hesitated a few moments, then lifted the jeweled glass to my lips, and drank.

As the draught ran down my throat I felt a trail of fire burn from my skull to the base of my spine. Just as I thought it would grow unbearable, it lessened to a strong sensation of warmth. My heart was pounding loudly, my breath quick and shallow, and I suddenly understood how the Mad Queens could bear to drink *kinnarath* daily until they went insane: for it was stronger than wine and headier than love.

But the physical sensations were soon forgotten as the *kinnarath* overwhelmed my mental senses. I forgot that I sat in a chilly underground shrine, next to a dry pool, across from my aging mother, as I saw into my own future and that of Sabbish. A hundred times thousand fates lay before me, and my mind encompassed them all in fractions of a moment, ranging from my early insanity and retirement at Cihan with a young daughter as heir, to a more peaceful and happier existence, to an illustrious one in which I could extend my power beyond the boundaries of Sabbish and build a great empire over which I would rule. I saw many children I might have if I chose, daughters to be heirs to the *kinnarath*, and wondered how I would decide between them. I saw the men I would need to manipulate to sire my heirs. I saw Blas—and refused to foresee what would happen between us, refused the *kinnarath*'s power with an effort that made my temples pound.

"Breathe deeply and slowly," my mother said, and I realized that I was still lowering the glass from my mouth, and that only a few moments had passed since my first long draught of *kinnarath*. "Concentrate on specifics, Taiya. Think of the temple feast-day. Try to decide what robes you will wear when you are named Queen. Narrow your focus. The *kinnarath* does not rule you. Use it for your own ends."

I thought of my robes. Deep red, of course, as was the custom. I thought of several tailor-shops I knew, and felt the *kinnarath*'s scope become narrower. I saw how my request for robes, needed in a fortnight, would burden one shop now overwhelmed with other orders, and lose them their regular business. I saw that at another shop the same request would enable the owner's daughter to begin an apprenticeship with a jewelry maker, but that she would not be happy there. At still a third shop, my business would bring them money they much needed, but the new iron stove they bought would be the cause of a small child's death in fifteen years when she stumbled against it and was burned.

I gasped like a swimmer fighting for air. "Breathe slowly, Taiya," came my mother's voice, drawing me back into the shrine. My hand was clenched against the jewel-studded glass, and I carefully set it down. "Think of specifics," Yarena said.

But like a wave the *kinnarath*'s power washed over me and I was unable to control it. I foresaw my every future action carefully chosen with some goal in mind. I foresaw that I would never again act spontaneously, without motives. I foresaw that Mireya's resentment towards me would mean I must banish her from Sabbish; that by telling Hallys how to avoid the dangers she faced on each journey I would rob her of the fearful exhilaration of her life at sea, which to her nature was as essential as the air she breathed; and that as the *kinnarath*'s effects made me lonely, unhappy, and as guarded as a turtle, I would cling to Blas with such neediness that finally he would cease to love me.

And worst of all—oh, far worse than my own personal losses—I foresaw that no matter which path I followed, I would often have to choose to let someone suffer, that others might benefit. In the name of some higher good I would sacrifice, again and again, a family's comfort, two lovers' happiness, or even the life of a child. The *kinnarath* would rob not only me of my freedom, but those I ruled as well, for with the foresight it gave me I would be forced to play a goddess, directing the fates of my fellow women and men.

As despair overwhelmed me I lost control of the *kinnarath*, seeing all my possible futures spread out before me, and myself in each one powerless and forever enchained.

"Taiya!" my mother cried, and something in her voice that sounded like fear, almost like panic, made me open my eyes.

The walls trembled, and the stone floor beneath us moved like the ocean. The ceiling was crumbling, and small pieces of stone rained down like hail. The earth was moving.

I sat frozen where I was, for the *kinnarath* did not show me how long the shaking would last, what the results would be, or what we must do to save ourselves.

While I hesitated the ceiling continued to fall, and my mother slumped forward as a large stone struck the back of her head. I flung myself across her limp body to protect her from the rubble, shut my eyes tightly, and whispered a prayer that sailors use in stormy weather.

After a few moments the shaking stopped. I slowly sat up, pieces of plaster and small fragments of stone streaming off my back. I checked my mother's pulse; she was unconscious, but not dead. Then I stood up and looked around the room, blinking the dust from my eyes, coughing as I breathed it in.

The urns were intact, a few of them tilted slightly in their frame, but none damaged, though the seventh urn, which my mother had uncovered to give me my draught, was filled with a floating film of dust. I looked at the ceiling; it was mostly intact, save for a few gaps between the wooden beams where plaster and stone had fallen, leaving openings into the room above, and one long crack near the wall. I turned around, surveying the entire room, and that was when I saw the large hole in the corner.

The wall had completely crumbled away here, and had left a spot of blue, like a large blot of ink in the whitewashed plaster. Blue sky, and blue sea. A breeze came in through the opening, carrying the sharp salt scent of the sea. I walked over to the opening and looked out.

The cliff dropped off here in a nearly vertical line to rocks below where the ocean beat against the stone, churning with foam. I heard shouts off to my left, as the citizens of Tyeasis roused themselves to survey the damage the earth's restlessness had left behind.

The *kinnarath*'s power still clung to me, though it had faded a great deal, and I foresaw that I should carry my mother upstairs and send for her physician, then tend to the city in her stead. But still I lingered by that hole in the wall, watching the sea, and listening to its murmur that was as seductive as the voice of a man. Out there in that endless blue had once lain my freedom.

And, I saw, still did.

When I foresaw the results of my action—foresaw blessed emptiness—foresaw *nothing at all*—I did not stop to reconsider. I ran to the seventh urn, from which I had drunk my first and only draught of *kinnarath,* and lifted the large, heavy container in my arms. The gap was barely wide enough. I passed the urn through, bottom first, leaned out and let go. I watched the white shape turn over and over as it fell, saw it shatter against the rocks far below, and saw the pieces disappear as a great wave rolled in and broke against the cliff.

Thirty-six times I did this, in a kind of joyous frenzy, wavering between laughter and tears of relief. Each successive urn seemed lighter than the previous one, and each seemed to fall faster to the sea, as if eager for its own annihilation. As I lifted the last white container of *kinnarath* through the gap and let it drop, a shout of triumph broke free from my throat. The sound of the sea drowned out the noise of the urn's breaking, and I smiled as I realized that this was one action of mine Yarena had never foreseen.

You, Yourself, Are a Delight, and It Is Only Your Work That Is Overwrought or Lacking in Affect or Clichéd or Drearily Jejune

by
Karen Joy Fowler

About the Author

Karen Joy Fowler's teaching experience includes girl's soccer and ballet, she has a B.A. in political science and an M.A. in North Asian Studies, and in 1984 she sold a story, "Recalling Cinderella," to L. Ron Hubbard Presents Writers of The Future, Vol. I.

Since then, she has published a book of short stories, Artificial Things, *from Bantam; she has sold quite a few other stories, and she is about to publish her first novel. (It is vanishingly rare to have a collection of short stories out before doing a novel, but, somehow, in Karen Joy's case I'm not surprised.) In 1987, she won the John W. Campbell Award, as the best new SF writer.*

She is very talented, and very bright, and very articulate. Here is what she has to say to new writers:

When you first begin to write, it is easy to imagine that you are engaged in something very private. You go off by yourself and you ask not to be disturbed. The door is closed. When you put your work away, you put it under something, your taxes or your socks, so your mother or your husband won't come across it in your absence. If someone asks to read it, you change the subject. "How about those Reds," you say. "Is Oakland embarrassed or what?"

As you work, you learn things about your own imagination, about your own discipline, about the issues that seem serious to you, and the images that move you. You remember conversations and experiences you haven't thought of in a long time. You try to remember them in detail, which is a different kind of remembering, not only what happened, but how it smelled, how it felt. At this point, you are writing only to please yourself. You are getting to know yourself. You are telling yourself a story, and the story is a secret and intimate one.

You must continue to do these secret and intimate things—the more secret, the more intimate, the better. But if you are going to be a writer, at some point, you must do these secret and intimate things in front of other people. The truth, and a writer must always be concerned with the truth, is that you have chosen one of the most public of all possible occupations. You expose yourself consciously and betray yourself unconsciously in every line. And if you are to succeed, someday, somewhere you must begin to let someone read what you write.

There are a couple of ways to do this. You can send your stories off to editors who don't know you and get your feedback in manila envelopes for which you, yourself, have provided the postage and can now open in the privacy of your room. Or you can pass your work first to people who know and love you and will tell you what they think, face to face. Or you can join a workshop of other writers, people you may or may not know well. The choice is yours. I did all three. The results, I can therefore tell you, are invariable.

You will be told that your stories are good. *Someone* is going to like them, more probably your friends or your mother and less probably that anonymous editor. Praise is inevitable. This does not mean it is not valuable, only that it rarely constitutes what we call a *learning experience*.

The second inevitability is harder to survive. You will be told that your stories are not very good. You may be told that they are dreadful. Appalling. Idiotic. You already know this or you wouldn't have them hidden under your socks. Someone is not going to like them. This someone would like you not to take the criticism personally. You, yourself, are a delight, and it is only your work, only your *very best work,* that is overwrought or lacking in affect or clichéd or drearily jejune.

There is no way around this bracing experience. You must simply survive it. But there is no reason it should be easy or pleasant for you.

There is an excellent chance that the criticism you have received is absolutely wrong-headed. In the first difficult moments, during or just after the criticism, you may remind yourself of this. I don't care that it comes from an editor whose work you routinely admire, or that it is the consensus of your entire writing group. You read through your rejection if you are lucky enough to get something individualized, and if the criticism is verbal, you write it down as it is given to you. You take notes, both to remember it later and to give yourself something to do during the onslaught. And you keep your mouth shut. Even though you *know* that most of the criticism you will receive, criticism from smart readers whose only intention is to help you write your best work, most of this criticism is simply wrong.

Only after you know for sure that you have survived the experience, and you may know this after fifteen minutes, or it may take days to be certain, but only then, must you look at the second possibility. There is an excellent chance that the criticism you received is absolutely right. If you are in a writing workshop, you have undoubtedly come home with both kinds of criticism, criticism that is wrong and criticism that is right. It is up to you to separate the one from the other.

There is a kind of criticism that is really beside the point in that it does not help you make the story you've written better. These critics simply wish you'd written a different story. Their comments are directed at this other story, the story you didn't write, rather than the story you did. Write a different story *if you want to.* Or ignore them. Politely. They are doing the very best that they can. More to be pitied than . . .

There is another kind of criticism that is immediately helpful. You almost recognize it when you hear it, as if you already knew it were true. Yes, the ending moves too fast. Yes, the motivation in the middle is muddled. Yes, you have overindulged in beautiful phrasing or yes, the language has a peculiar translated-from-the-mother-tongue cadence to it. You were pretending you were Dostoyevsky. You can fix it.

What's left is more difficult. What's left is the criticism you are unsure of. You need privacy again. You need to go back to the state of mind you were in when you wrote the story, back to those moments when you were pretending no one but yourself was ever going to read it. Then you ask, not the part of yourself that wrote the story, but the part you wrote it for, the reader-part, if the criticism is helpful or not. Would you have liked it better with these changes, you ask yourself.

Don't expect a strong answer at first. The part of you that reads is as unsure as the part of you that writes and has only marginally better taste. But as you continue to read and as you continue to write, both parts will grow stronger.

There is no reason ever to be ashamed of your work. A teacher I had once told me there was no such thing as a bad story. Stories nobody likes and no one will buy, stories people tell you are totally predictable, or absolutely implausible, or filled with empty sentiments and clichéd language, are not bad stories. They are unfinished stories. You are still working on them. They can always get better. When they are *done* (and this may take years or may always remain a Platonic ideal you haven't yet achieved) they will be good. They will be so good your current critics will weep.

You must think of rejection and criticism as an inevitable part of the work you do to become a writer. In the privacy of your own room, you are developing your sense of pacing and plotting. You are extending your imagination, exploring your vocabulary, sharpening your memory. In the public glare of your writing workshop or in the manila glow of your form rejection slip, you are developing what someone once called the *pachydermal skin* of the writer.

You will need this skin your whole career. No matter how successful you may someday become, there will always be someone who doesn't like the way you write and will say so. When you are really successful you will read about your failures in the book review sections of the country's major newspapers. Get used to it. Get tough.

Retain deniability. Memorize the following lines, in

anticipation of your eventual success and publication. Be able to produce these lines anywhere—at the supermarket check-out counter, at an intimate dinner for two, fogged in at Kennedy with fifty strangers for twenty-four hours:

"You thought that was *me?* That sniveling bitch? That gutless liar? Ha. It's fiction, bucko. You know what fiction is?"

and "How about those Reds. Is Oakland embarrassed or what?"

This advice has all been directed to survival in the public arena, but before you go public, you have to have survived in the private one. Therefore I'm going to close, in the best possible plotting tradition, with the beginning. When it's just you and you and the page:

You will be told, or have undoubtedly already been told, to try to appeal to all of the senses, but you always forget. Try to remember. And also remember that you have many more senses than the five. To give you just a partial list: you have a sense of humor, a sense of timing, a sense of wonder, a sense of horror, a sense of delight, a sense of justice. Use them all in all your work.

Choose specific details.

Compress your information. When you are describing a scene try to choose details that will develop your character. When you are advancing the plot, also describe the scene.

A certain amount of writing is merely transportation. Your character must move from one place to another or, as in a flashback, from one time to another. Transportational writing is boring, but unavoidable. Do it as invisibly as possible. Keep it clear, keep it simple, keep it brief.

Resist the temptation to overdescribe. Give your readers a few interesting details. They have their own imaginations.

Resist the temptation to overexplain. *Your* readers are smart.

Repetition has a few specific uses. It can build humor, tension, or horror. In dialogue, it can be used to reduce a character's credibility—a character who repeats herself may be protesting too much. Unless you have one of these effects in mind, don't repeat yourself. Every clause of every sentence should contain new information.

Here is private advice from Hemingway: Never quit for the day when you come to the hard part. This is excellent advice. You may never recover your train of thought or state of mind, and anyway, it's easier to persuade yourself back to work if you know *exactly* what you're going to do next and what you're going to do next is easy.

Here is secret advice from Kerouac, slightly paraphrased: When you get stuck, don't think about words.

Imagine it better and keep going.

Keep going.

Keep going.

Sensations of the Mind

by
Valerie J. Freireich

About the Author

Valerie J. Freireich is a married Chicago-area lawyer who, after her son was born six years ago, quit a job with a downtown law firm, established her own practice in her home in a Chicago suburb, and does quite well, thank you. Which is pretty good, considering that her major in college was anthropology, involving, at one time, an extended trip through Mexico alone, and other adventures.

Abruptly, in 1989, she began writing, and "Sensations of the Mind" is only one result. She had, for instance, sold a story to Starshore magazine before entering the Contest, which she did in mid-June, 1990. After placing in the Contest, she sold a story to Aboriginal. Surely, this is one of the shortest apprenticeships on record; on the other hand, she writes every day, no matter what. And well, as you are about to find out. . . .

About the Illustrator

Lawrence Allen Williams lives in Tuscaloosa, Alabama, and heard about the Contest through one of last year's winners, Ruth Thompson. He is 25, a student at the University of Alabama.

Originally from Tennessee, Allen signed up for business classes; one and a half days later, he switched to art. He has been doing some form of art since the age of three, and fantasy art in particular for the past year. He is currently building up his portfolio, with an eye toward obtaining a permanent position in a design or illustration studio.

Paul Talley was looking for a
ciran for the night, and I was the first one he
found that was willing to entertain a human.

"How much?" he asked me. His Tasait was good, but
he had an accent and his voice was low. The cold wind
whipped away his words so fast I almost thought I'd imagined them, especially since I hadn't sensed his presence at
all. He'd actually startled me when he spoke. I had been
standing with another prostitute, a female, talking about
heading home. I suppose she'd seen the human over my
shoulder, but had ignored him, since sex between Tasana
and humans is uncommon and she had no taste for it.

I smiled at him. I didn't look my best that night, but
I never have been more than average in appearance. I'm
ciran though, the Tasana third sex, which for many people
is enough, and I'm willing to try most anything that doesn't
hurt. I do have a nice smile.

The human smiled back. He was taller than me and
more strongly built. He seemed very pale, like Winter in a
children's picture book of seasons.

"How much?" he asked again. He pulled his jacket
closed at the neck against the wind.

"I'm not sure," I said. "What do you want?" I was
cold and wanted to get inside, or I might not have taken the
job. Well, to be truthful, I would have taken it anyway. I was
curious about humans because *ciran* cannot feel their minds,
not that I would have admitted to such an interest within my
family.

''The usual,'' he said.

I laughed. ''What's 'the usual' for you?'' I asked. ''Do you want me to play male or female or both?''

He didn't answer, so I started to turn away, toward the woman.

He touched my shoulder, very lightly. ''Female,'' he said.

''Take her, then.'' I nodded at the woman.

''Not me,'' she said, and walked away from us.

''Both,'' he said. ''I want you to play both. How do you do it?'' He watched my eyes.

''You have to pay to know.'' I calculated the money he might have available. I quoted him a large sum, a month's rent. He agreed without bargaining. I was flattered and annoyed; perhaps I could have gotten more. He paid in cash, which is the custom, but the wind tugging at the paper credits we use on the streets made me laugh. I had to hold the credits as tight as a mother holds a child's hand.

''Come on, then,'' I said, leading him toward my rooms. He put his arm around my shoulders as we walked, holding me against his side. To have only the physical sensation was peculiar, like watching someone speak without hearing them.

''What's your name?'' he asked, smiling at me again.

''Gwin.'' I don't give my family name, Rency, to customers.

''I'm Paul Talley, from the *Fanciful*. We just came in to Dsar's docking station.'' He looked down at me. ''Can you really read my mind?''

''No, not a thing,'' I said. ''*Ciran* are deaf to humans and other aliens, or blind, maybe. Anyone who told you different is a liar.'' I thought he might be disappointed, so I added, ''I think *ciran* empathy is overrated as a benefit on the mats. We can't hear thoughts, only emotions, and feelings are fairly one-dimensional then, after all.''

"But you *are* a hermaphrodite?" he asked as we reached my rooms.

I bent my head. "As you see." Males have ruffles on top of the head, females have hair on the sides and back, *ciran* have both.

I reached out to open my door; Paul Talley took my hand. His hand was wide enough to completely encircle mine; Tasana are generally more slender than humans and I am very thin, except at the hips. I'm dark, with black hair and a gray ruffle, the most common Tasana coloring; my hand looked like an elongated shadow of his. I worried that he meant to hurt me, but his pressure on my hand was light. He examined my hand briefly, then released it and opened the door for us both.

My front room, where I entertained customers, was comfortable, with fabric walls and lots of cushions. Comfort is the mood I like best—it lowers aggression. I chattered trivialities about myself to ease the awkward tension and removed my tunic and gown. I felt embarrassed, but let him study me as I helped him off with his jacket, rubbing his shoulders as I did so, reaching up to feel his hair, cut very short.

"You look neuter," he said, sounding disappointed.

I laughed. "I guarantee, I'm not," I said. "Only nervous."

He smiled at that, and touched a scar I have over my right eye. I put my arms around his neck and kissed him, trying hard to relax. I closed my eyes, but that was too much like being alone. When I opened my eyes, he was watching me. "I'll show you," I said. I took his hand and guided it, so he could feel the labial folds enclosing my female parts and my retracted penis. His touch felt good; I could feel myself respond.

I let him keep the security of his clothing as I touched the hidden parts of his body, exploring him while he investigated me. The silence, where I should have felt what he was feeling, was disquieting. He rarely spoke, so I had few clues as to how to proceed. It was my job to entertain him though, so I did my best not to behave as if I were uncertain.

Humans and Tasana are not so very different. Sex is touching and touch creates sensations of the mind—*ciran* know that well. There was no reason we two could not enjoy ourselves together, and we did. It was late when we were too tired to continue; we never did get bored. I fell asleep, which was unusual and unprofessional. When I woke up, he was gone. He left extra money beside me, which I assumed was intentional and kindly meant. In any case, I did not chase up to the docks at the Dsar Ship Authority's orbiting station looking to return it.

The next day my sister Brel came to see me. Brel is the prettiest in my family. When I was first sent away, I thought it was unfair that I had to leave instead of Brel. She could have earned a living on her own more easily, and I'm the better craftsman, more valuable in the family business. Later I realized it was all excuses, I would have been sent away in all events, since I'm *ciran*, and hurt the family reputation.

"We have a big job," Brel said. "The whole family will be working, and we need you, too, Gwin."

I felt her slight embarrassment at asking for my help. "So?" I asked.

"Partial refitting on three ships at Dsar; a subcontract through the Ferli family. The Jats will do the heavy work, and we're supposed to do the systems installation, all the fine stuff and the details. It's good money; alien ships, so the dockmaster is charging a fortune and some trickles down." She paused and put her hand on mine, intensifying the empathy. It sent a shiver through me; there is no feeling like that of family. She smiled, looking down. "There are time constraints," Brel said. "The shippers want to be away, and there's a penalty if we're late. We need every hand."

Brel had no doubt that I'd come; I had every other time they'd asked. I'm the temporary help, on call when needed, and not taking a family share other times.

"You'll be with us," she said, when I didn't answer soon enough to please her. "All the adults, and even Kern and Ceries, will be working. We'll have quarters at Dsar, inside the dockyard, and you can stay with us afterward for awhile, most likely, we'll have so much money." The last was a bribe. Not being *ciran* she couldn't feel my resentment.

Brel put her arms around me. It didn't matter that it was calculated, the effect on me was the same. I smelled flowers, from the special soap she buys with her extra money. "Brel, leave me alone," I said and got up. I walked away from her and looked out the window; the wind was still wild, blowing scraps of garbage into the air. The few people on the street walked past quickly, heads down, in shabby clothing. The Red District is a dreary place.

"Come on, Gwin, you know you'll come," Brel said.

"I don't need the money right now."

"When did you ever come with us for the money?" Brel smiled, this time for me. I felt her affection.

"All right." It was pointless to prolong the discussion when we both already knew its outcome. "When do you want me?"

So I met my family at the launch gates that evening and went up with them on a shuttle to Dsar, to the quarters the shipyard assigned us. My family was glad to see me; they always are, though they send me away easily enough. I'm closest to my sister Perfin, though on the mats I mostly stay with my brothers, usually Conster or Cyme, and try to avoid Loden.

Illustrated by Lawrence Allen Williams

The first day on the job was meetings, the Ferlis organizing the work with the other families. I saw Paul Talley there, but he didn't notice me. I didn't understand his position; he just wandered around. I hoped we would not meet. I didn't want my brothers and sisters thinking me depraved for having entertained a human.

My oldest brother, Cyme, divided us into three groups, one for each ship. I was assigned to work with my brother Loden and my sister Perfin. Brel's son Kern was along as our helper. I cringed when we were assigned to the work on the *Fanciful,* since it would increase the chances of meeting Paul Talley, but there was nothing reasonable I could say against it.

We Rency are makers, as opposed to techs or nobles. We work with our hands. Loden and Conster are better than I am, they get more practice, but I love the work as much as any of the family. I tried to get small jobs when the family sent me away, but couldn't make a living at it. Few people are willing to hire a *ciran* solitary.

At first there was no problem avoiding Paul Talley, but on the fourth day Perfin asked me why there was a human staring at me. I looked up, straight into the eyes of Paul Talley. He looked away. I shrugged and said, ''I don't know.''

Thereafter I could feel his eyes, almost as if I could feel his mind. I'd look and there he'd be.

''Ask him why he watches you,'' Loden said. I felt Loden speculating on the possibilities—the feeling of mental machinery at work, without real emotion.

I shook my head. ''I might find out he doesn't think I'm beautiful.'' We all laughed.

''He's curious about *ciran*,'' suggested Perfin.

''Probably,'' I agreed.

Paul Talley spoke to me later that day, when I was alone.

''I know you,'' he said. ''What are you doing here?'' He sounded interested, not hostile.

"Even whores have families," I said. "They needed me to work, since you're in a hurry."

He smiled at me. "Then you are the one. I wasn't sure." He touched the scar above my eye. "That was a good night. Since you're here at Dsar . . . ." He let his words slide away.

"When I'm with my family, I don't do that." I noticed once more how pale he was; his hair was yellow. No Tasana has hair that color, like sunlight, or blue eyes either. His body seemed bulky next to mine.

He placed his hand on my shoulder. I felt nothing, or rather, I felt only his hand, warm through the material of my tunic. "I understand," he said.

Perfin entered the corridor. Paul Talley removed his hand. Perfin noticed and asked, "Gwin, are you all right?" She looked sharply at the human man and walked toward us.

"I'm fine." I stepped away from the human.

"Good work," Paul Talley said, as if we had been discussing something to do with the job. He left.

"What was that all about?" Perfin asked, taking my arm. I felt my sister, her curiosity and concern, but Perfin's touch didn't send any flutters through me; I was becoming accustomed to the sensations of my family again.

"He wanted me to go with him," I said. I dislike lying; the feelings of people who lie are muddy, thick with regret and shame and anger.

Perfin stared in the direction the man had gone, then back at me. "You don't have to do that," she said. "If he bothers you, tell me." She patted me and said, "Get back to work!"

Over the next few days, when I was alone, Paul Talley would sometimes appear, like a ghost, and we held brief conversations.

"You're a good worker," he said once, after he had been watching me for a long while.

"Thank you," I replied. He didn't make me nervous. Since I couldn't feel him, I could almost forget he was behind me. And sometimes I enjoyed being watched.

He came closer. "Do you think of yourself as male or female?"

"Neither," I said, glancing at him. "I'm *ciran,* so I'm both."

He smiled, and leaned against the wall near where I was working. "That seems inconsistent."

I decided that I liked Paul Talley. He didn't push, and I'd had a good time with him. I put down my tools and looked back at him. "What do you want me to be?"

"*Ciran.* It's the most interesting." He touched my arm. "Are you sure you're not available?"

"I don't feel anything when you touch me," I said.

He took his arm away, frowned at me, and left.

Another time, he asked, "Did you mean in your mind, that you don't feel anything in your mind when I touch you?" His look was intent.

"Yes," I said, surprised. "You're a wall to me."

"That bothers you?" He came beside me, so close I could feel the warmth of his body. He had a distinctive smell, fresh. It reminded me of Brel, except that beneath it was another smell, somehow darker.

I thought about his question as I worked. "It's just so strange," I said. "Uncomfortable. It makes me think more about myself." I looked up at him. "Was I selfish, when I was with you?"

He laughed, very low. "I didn't think so." He stepped away from me. "This arrangement with your family," he said. "They take advantage of you."

"So? They're my brothers and sisters." I went on working. "They pay me, just as you did." I had spoken thoughtlessly and was startled at my own words, that my family was simply another customer.

"You sleep with them, too, don't you?" His voice was disapproving.

"Of course. They're my family," I told him.

Later, Perfin and Loden took me aside. "He follows you around, like a pet," Perfin said. "I think you should transfer to Cyme's team and send Aureste back here." She gave me a quick hug. "We'd still see each other at night."

"Unless you want to entertain him," Loden said thoughtfully. His eyes assessed my face and body; his mind felt as if he was weighing a bid on a job. "I think he's second in command here. They all do what he says, but he's not the captain. He would have plenty of money. I'll arrange it, if you want. We can always use the extra credits." Loden manages the family's money, and gives out our shares.

"If I want to, I can arrange it," I said. "Money from that is mine."

"You're on family share now," said Loden. "It's earned for the family." Of all my brothers and sisters, Loden looks most like me; we had the same mother. He's taller, though, as tall as Paul Talley, only dark. We don't get along well; he enjoys being rough with me, and the others let him.

"It isn't a family job," I said. "It's mine, to save for myself and Disal."

"We're raising Disal for you," Loden said. "You owe us the extra."

"He's part of the family, too. You're not raising him for me, but for all of the family. I bore him, same as Brel had Kern, or any of the other sisters' children," I said.

"But you're not a sister, not in the family, so neither is Disal, unless we say so," Loden said. He was angry; I felt him, white hot. I probably was the same; it made me furious when they bargained over keeping my son for me.

"Stop it, both of you," Perfin said. "Of course Disal

is in the family." Turning to me, she asked, "You're not really going to do it, Gwin, are you?"

"I don't know," I replied.

"You should," Loden said. His mind told me he was repulsed at the idea, but he said, "It's money."

The next time Paul Talley watched me, I asked him how much he would pay.

"What do you want?" he asked. He sat down in a chair; I was installing light lines in a room that was full of assorted junk from other parts of the ship.

Perfin came in and saw Paul Talley. She began to work with me, more a nuisance than a help. I guessed she wouldn't leave until the human did.

"I want one thousand credits," I said.

"Gwin, don't," said Perfin. "I don't like the idea at all, no matter what Loden and the others say. It's degenerate."

Paul Talley laughed.

"Leave Gwin alone," Perfin said, too fiercely. I could feel her. I knew she was of a more divided mind than she spoke aloud. She had enjoyed the sound of 'one thousand credits' and probably was wondering if it was possible for me to get paid so well.

"Too much," Paul Talley said. "Much too high a price."

"Well, then," I said. "How much will you pay?"

He glanced at me, then at Perfin. "The same as last time," he said.

Perfin gasped. She didn't look at me. I could feel that she was shocked, disappointed in me. It made me angry.

"I need a thousand. I want enough to get passage to Hills, or Earth or some other place," I said, to outrage my family. "I want to get away." It was an impulse; I'd never consciously considered leaving Tasa before. As soon as I said it, though, I knew leaving was what I wanted to do.

None of us said anything. Eventually, Perfin got tired of interfering with my work. She probably wanted to tell Loden and the others that I'd been with Paul Talley before and might be again, and to let them know that I was threatening to go to another world. She left.

"What would you do on Earth?" Paul Talley asked, when Perfin was gone.

"What do I do here? Well, no, not that, I'd be liable to be deported. I know mechanical systems well; I can find something." My voice sounded odd; I spoke too fast.

"You need guaranteed employment before they let aliens on Earth," Talley said. "You're better off on Hills, or Able, or the Tasana colony at Sac."

"Not Sac. I'm sick of hearing them all. You asked if it bothered me that I can't feel you—I'll tell you the truth, it's better than feeling contempt or disgust when they touch me. It's better than knowing how shallow their caring really is." My hands were shaking, so I stopped working.

Paul Talley didn't get up from his chair. I wondered what he thought of me, behind the wall around his mind. He stretched, leaning his chair back and balancing it on two legs, his feet resting on a chair in front of him. "I think you'd be lonely," he said. "That's why you go back to them, isn't it?"

I didn't say anything. I wasn't sure why I went back to my family, every time they asked. I wanted to stop; it hurt too much each time I was told to leave.

Paul Talley looked at the timepiece on his wrist, then let his chair down with a thud. "You're done for the day, as of now. Come with me." He stood up, and I followed him out of the room, through some corridors and into a section of the ship we weren't working on.

He took me to his room. It was large for a ship, but

seemed barren to me, just painted, hard walls, a bed, a few chairs and a terminal desk, all in browns and dark red. Everything was perched high up, on legs.

I sat down on a chair. It was huge—big enough for two or three—and so soft it seemed to fold over, holding me like a trap. It had a dry smell, from the stuffing, like crumbled, dead leaves. "We didn't settle a price," I said, glumly, because it didn't matter. I knew I was staying even if it was for free.

"Spend the next week with me, the next seven days, and I'll pay you the thousand credits," he said. "Or just tonight for one hundred."

"Why do you want seven days of me?" I asked. "I don't know that many tricks."

"I like you," he said.

Few people have ever said that to me. Neither of us spoke for a while.

"I've never slept in one of those," I said, indicating the bed. Paul Talley was watching me; for a change it made me nervous. "What if I fall out?"

"You won't," he said. He sat down on the edge of the bed, as if to demonstrate.

"Come over here," Paul Talley said. His voice told me it was an order, so I went to the bed and sat down beside him. It didn't grab me, like the chair, and smelled like Paul. Rather nice, I thought.

He reached behind and opened a portion of the wall, forming a shelf with a number of objects on it: a *codar*, some printed books, several boxes. He took the *codar* from the shelf and handed it to me. "You told me before that you can play this," he said, and I understood this was also a command.

The *codar* was out of tune, so I spent some time repairing that, then started a sad song, the ballad about Brailin. After a few verses he put his hand across the instrument, stopping me. "I don't like that," he said. "If you're going to go about as if you're in prison, then leave now."

"Sorry," I said. "This is hard for me, to go against my family." I wouldn't look at him. He did not seem to be a person who found life hard.

He stood. "Let's get some food, get your mind off your family for a while."

"Paul Talley," I said, "Is this something you can do openly?"

"Call me Paul. And, yes, I can. No one here will say anything about it." He spoke with confidence. I looked up at him and he smiled.

Paul took me to a dining room, where despite his words I created a stir. The room was crowded; the crews of all three ships were staying in this one during the work. Even without understanding the human language or feeling what they felt, I was sure the others found the situation exotic.

Most of the humans didn't speak Tasait, though the *Fanciful's* captain did. Paul introduced me to him, Bill Shin, as if they were friends. I was introduced as one of the workers, not a prostitute, who would be staying with Paul. After the greeting the captain ignored me, but he looked curiously at Paul, who smiled blandly back. Paul said something in human and they both laughed.

A dark woman, introduced to me as Myra Gold, kept staring; she tried to get Paul's attention so often I was certain she was interested in him, or that I was displacing her on his bed.

At Paul's instruction I'd brought the *codar,* and after eating, he told me to put on a show. I'm really very good; not concert quality, but close, and less formal. I sang songs with an easy rhythm the humans could follow without understanding the words. They were entertained; it loosened them so they were friendly to my face.

Illustrated by Lawrence Allen Williams

Paul held my arm as we left the dining room; he seemed pleased with me. "What other talents do you have?" he asked.

"I'm a good mother," I said. "Well, I try, anyway." He stopped. "You've had a child?"

"A son." I kept walking, sorry to have mentioned it, since he seemed so startled. "He's six. He stays with my family most of the time, because of my work and so he'll have a family."

Paul caught up with me. "Are you going to take him if you leave Tasa?"

"I don't know. Disal is better off without a *ciran* mother. They tease him." The thought of leaving Tasa alone made me sad again. Paul touched my shoulder; I said, "Don't worry. Tasana and humans are different species. You won't get me pregnant, no matter how hard you try."

When we reached his room, he pulled me close to him as soon as the door shut behind us. He held me like that for a long time, until the embrace itself seemed to have meaning. I realized I was leaning on him; just as I did, he moved away. He began taking off his shirt, so I helped him. Human chests are so odd: furry and with two well marked areas for dairy production—even the males, who don't make the human baby drink; I laughed.

"You shouldn't laugh at me. I'm your employer." Paul smiled, though, as he said it.

"You can laugh at me all you want," I told him. "I prefer it to most other things."

He began to undress me. That night was better than the first time, much better. We talked. He was interested in small things, which surprised me. I told him how I schemed to get odd repair jobs. He asked about the scar above my eye (a power panel exploded when I was working a job with my family) and said it gave me character. He circled my waist with his two hands and said he liked that I was so slender.

He seemed to enjoy the feel of my hair, which I keep long, and touched it often, saying it reminded him of pipe-cleaners, soft yet stiff.

The next day I wore human clothes, because I refused to put on dirty clothing and there was none other to be had on the ship. Loden, Perfin and Kern stared at me. I told them I was staying seven days with the customer, and I asked them to bring my case from the family's quarters. It turned out to be unnecessary because Paul sent someone for it and it was waiting for me in the room that night.

I worked beside Perfin without speaking for most of the day, wearing my too big and far-too-loose alien gear. "How much are you getting?" she finally asked.

"None of your concern," I said. "It's mine. You can tell Loden and Cyme that, too. And I expect a share from this job; I'm working with you."

"You've become hard, Gwin, overnight." Perfin shook her head, and added, "Disal will miss you if you leave Tasa." When she brushed against me, I felt concern and regret from her. I wondered how deep it went, but that was wrong of me, I suppose. Perfin does love me. But it hurt to feel all my family against me. I wished they could sense my feelings, just once; perhaps they would have thought differently of me if they had a *ciran's* empathy.

Each night with Paul was better than the one before; Paul and I were becoming familiar with each other physically. Sex was less funny and more sensual. Differences lost their importance once they didn't startle us. When we went to the human dining room together, Paul no longer made jokes about me to the others.

During the day, Loden was really angry; he kept repeating that I owed the money to the family. He hit me once; after that I ignored what he said and was glad to get away from him at night.

But the third night, Paul was irritable. He sat in the big

chair looking at the wall. For the first time it was painful not to be able to feel him in my mind. I was straining, like trying to read in the dark.

"Do you want me to leave?" I eventually asked. I was sitting on the floor; the soft chairs made my back hurt.

"No, I don't,' he said, but then ignored me.

I was hungry, but afraid to ask to go to the dining room. My family had stopped giving me any dayfood when I'd begun living with Paul, though Kern or Perfin usually let me have some bread. I had brought no food of my own to Dsar, so I was living on the one meal a day I took with Paul.

He got up abruptly and tossed a bookcard at me, which he'd taken from a pocket. "Start learning English," he said. "I'm going out tonight."

"Oh. You won't get your money's worth," I said.

He looked at me until I turned away, ashamed of myself.

"It's a reception given by the shipyard officials," Paul said. He hesitated, then added, "You can come if you want."

"I can't go with you," I said. "I'd disgrace you." I smiled at the thought of Gwin Rency among the nobility.

"Why? You are what you are. I'm the peculiar one, to have you here with me," he said. He sounded angry. He walked the room, and kept looking at me. I wished he wouldn't.

"I don't have anything good enough to wear," I said, by way of excuse. "And I'm not very pretty."

"Aren't you?" He seemed surprised. "I can't tell." He stopped walking and studied my face, so that I was even more uncomfortable.

"Are you pretty?" I asked. His appearance was so unusual to me that I had no idea how other humans thought of him.

"Yes," he said. It made him laugh, for the first time that evening. "I'd like it if you came with me. The party would be much more entertaining."

"Paul, it really would be a stupid thing to do," I said, intensely aware of how my presence would reflect on him. "Your captain may not care if you keep me in your room, but this would be bad, poor judgment."

"My captain?" He was smiling.

"Are you the captain?" I asked, confused.

"No," he said, "I'm the owner. These three ships and fifteen others. Earth Transport Corporation. My father started it; I run it now."

I was stunned. After a moment I said, "You could have paid me a thousand credits for a night."

"I don't overpay," he said. My face must have changed. "I'm sorry. I didn't mean it that way." He came to where I was sitting and squatted awkwardly beside me. "Why not come with me tonight?"

He took my hand and drew me up to stand with him.

"I really don't want to," I said. "I'd be too uncomfortable." I felt clumsy, too aware of all the money he must have.

"No one will say anything," he said as he had before. It only meant they would not say it to his face. He lightly tipped my head up with his hand under my chin, so I had to look him in the eyes. He touched my cheek with my fingertips, then let go. It occurred to me that I was getting accustomed to the lack of any sensation but the physical when he touched me.

"They don't have to *say* anything, Paul. I'll feel what they think of me anyway, whatever they actually say, at least the Tasana."

"I forgot about that," he said. "It must be unpleasant sometimes." He opened the wall compartment that held his clothing. He had more of it than all I'd ever owned combined, but it was boring. Everything was only one color, mostly gray or blue.

"It would be fine, if I were you, but I'm not rich or

pretty," I said. It sounded self-pitying, so I added, "I've heard the nobles use their *ciran* siblings in contract negotiations and such, to see if anyone is cheating. Do you know if it's true?"

"It sounds like a good idea," he said, as if not really thinking about it. He began to get undressed, and I watched wondering if I was supposed to be doing anything, but then he put on different clothes. "Are you coming with me?" he asked. His tone was flat.

"If I have a choice, no."

"You have a choice," he said.

So I studied the human language while he was gone. When he returned, he made me practice, and spent a long time trying to get me to pronounce the sounds of his language properly. He told me I was hopeless.

Sex was strained that night. We both had too much on our minds to relax, and I was still hungry. I felt him watching me, not with pleasure, and wondered if he'd tell me to leave the next morning. But Paul's displeasure didn't make me try harder to please him; instead, I didn't worry about satisfying him and acted only to please myself. I told him I was sleeping on the floor, after, and he didn't stop me when I left his bed.

I slept badly. Without a mat the floor was cold and hard; I was stiff, and I'd had more to eat when I was on the streets.

But Paul was cheerful the next morning. "I've seen the worst of you, and it's tolerable."

"That's not the worst," I said, but he only laughed. He put his arms around my waist; the hair on his chest felt good against my skin. I moved back from him and touched it. "You're interesting," I said, which made him laugh more.

He stepped away, and looked at me. "You're interesting, too," he said, as though it were a great compliment.

Paul went to another place in the wall, and opened a small compartment. He took out cash and handed it to me. "One thousand credits," he said.

I took the money, more than I'd ever held before. "Do you want me to leave?" I was surprised to discover that I didn't want to return to my family.

"No, I'd like you to stay. But you can leave if you want to. You make the choice, not based on money."

"You said seven days, I'll stay seven days. But you have to show me where the kitchen is. If you don't feed me soon, I won't last another day here." I knew the game he was playing, like my family, trying to get me to do things for love. Still, I was surprised at how upset Paul was that I hadn't eaten during the day before, or more than one meal a day. He took me to the kitchen. After all that, and after I'd eaten, I was late getting to work, and Loden yelled at me.

I showed Loden and Perfin the money, and they became very quiet. Loden didn't ask me to give it to him, but he avoided me all day and gave me the worst work. Perfin talked about family obligations whenever we were together. Even she was angry at me.

That night I asked Paul to put the money in an account in my name. I had been nervous all day, thinking about being hit on the head for the cash. I was not afraid of my family, but there were others aboard the ship. I had been stupid to show the money.

"You became middle class very quickly," Paul told me, grinning, but I didn't understand the joke. It was my skin I wanted to protect.

"The fare to Hills is 642c," Paul said, when I handed him the money from my pouch. "They charge full fare for children on most lines. I'll give you another three hundred, so you can take your son."

"You don't need to. I have money," I said. "I've saved

almost 400c and I'll get a half-share from this job, about 80c more.''

Paul seemed to squint when he looked at me. He examined my face, then my clothes. ''Three hundred credits is a good dinner out for me, with a companion, on Earth. Thirteen hundred is a night's stay in a hotel in New York. You're making me feel cheap, Gwin.''

''I'm the one that's cheap,'' I said. ''I'll have to remember those prices.'' I didn't believe him.

Paul tapped his fingers on the desk, making an odd rhythm. He glanced at me, then set up the account through bankers on Tasa using connections through the account Earth Transport had with Dsar Ship Authority. It sounded very complicated, with many number codes. He stood up from the desk and handed me a hard copy. It showed 10,000c in my new account. I gave the card back to him. ''You made a mistake.''

''No mistake. A bonus.'' Paul pulled me close. ''I'm enjoying having you with me more than I expected.''

It was a good year's income for my family or enough for me to move to another world with Disal and still have plenty to buy a business. Paul stared at me; it was disquieting how often he looked at me, and me not so great to look at. ''Thank you,'' I said, tucking the card into my case. I'm not stupid.

Paul asked if I was going to continue to work with my family; he seemed surprised when I said yes. They still needed the extra pair of hands.

The rest of that night was very strange; Paul was careful with me, I don't know a better word. He made me feel that I mattered. He held me most of the night and was awake early, wanting more of me. I enjoyed the attention, but it frightened me, too.

From then on it no longer seemed that I was working for a customer, we were a proper pairing. I told Paul I should return some of his money; I wasn't earning it. He said I was.

On the sixth day I was with him, Paul came into the area where I was working with Loden and Perfin closing a wall. "Gwin," Paul said, "I need you to come with me." His voice was tense.

Loden made a rough sound, and I felt a flare of anger in the background of my brother's emotions. "I'm working," I said to Paul.

"You work for me," he said sharply. "Ten thousand credits worth."

Perfin and Loden exchanged glances; I felt Loden's anger and Perfin's astonishment. I hadn't told them of the increased amount of money I'd received, only that an account had been set up for me by Paul.

"All right, let me just finish this," I said and quickly completed the seam I was working on, while Paul waited impatiently and Loden fumed.

Myra Gold and Captain Shin were with Paul. Captain Shin came and stood behind me, watching the three of us work. His proximity made Perfin and Loden nervous. Paul leaned against the room's back wall, tapping his foot on the floor. Myra whispered something to Paul, but he waved her aside. When we were finally done, I went to Paul, standing closer than necessary.

"We're going to the dockmaster's office," Paul said in the corridor. "I want you to tell me if she's lying to me: the price suddenly went up."

"I can't do that," I told him. "I can tell you if someone is angry, afraid, excited or whatever. I can't tell you if they're lying unless I know them well, and I'm not always accurate then. It's not an emotion."

He thought about it a minute. "That's something, anyway. Do what you can." He put an arm around my shoulders as we walked. "You can be useful."

"I didn't think 'useful' was my function," I said. Paul smiled and Captain Shin glanced at me. All the humans except Paul seemed to think I was an idiot since I was a *ciran,* or maybe just because I was Tasana.

Paul walked ahead with Captain Shin and Myra. The three of them spoke together in their own language while we made the brief transit off the ship and to Dsar station proper. I couldn't understand anything they said, despite the language lessons Paul had insisted on conducting every night. I felt out of place following them into the office corridors of Dsar's satellite, with my shabby clothes and carrying my tools.

Just before we reached the dockmaster's offices, Captain Shin turned to me. "Do you have any doubts about helping us, Gwin, considering that we're human and the Dsar Ship Authority is Tasana?" he asked. I guessed he was trying to protect Paul, that he thought Paul might be blinded to my possible duplicity by my attractions. I respected the captain for it; he couldn't know that to me the Dsar Ship Authority was less than a crumb after a feast.

"No," I said, in English, about the maximum extent of my vocabulary. It startled the captain and Myra, the intended effect.

Paul smiled with an edge of satisfaction. He said something in English to them both and glanced at me with approval. "I trust you, Gwin," he said to me.

Inside the dockmaster's office were two Tasana, minor nobility. I could feel them both, immediately and clearly. The dockmaster was a nasty old lady. The other person, her child, was a restructured *ciran*: angry, like all of them. His family had probably forced the change to male, but he still had the *ciran* empathy.

Paul told them that I was his new aide, which was really funny, except that it offended the nobles. I let myself show only fear, so they wouldn't get any information from me as we were trying to do from them.

It was the same old scam. They told Paul that all the makers had to be taken from the work on his ships because of an emergency from Toal; only if Paul paid priority rates would his work be finished on time. The story was as thin as the atmosphere beyond the Dsar station: vacuum.

Paul glanced at me, and I shrugged.

Paul and Bill argued with the dockmaster; Myra consulted some human equipment, feeding them information, none of which swayed the dockmaster. It was clear that despite the openness of the lie, they were going to stick with it. The ships were torn apart, not going anywhere for another eightday at least, and they'd just sit if the dockmaster pulled us off the jobs.

I began to get a headache. The restructured *ciran* watched me as I watched him. I kept my surface emotion fear; it wasn't difficult in this place. The *ciran* felt of triumph. I don't think he was even trying to hide his emotions; I've had to learn how since I've had *ciran* customers, but most of us do not.

There was a lull in conversation. "Great Lord," I said to Paul, giving him the noble title, "perhaps you could deal directly with the subcontractors to resolve this matter. None of them are bound to the Authority, only to the Ferli family. I think we Rency would be willing to continue. Even the Ferli may choose to proceed with your work. I'd be pleased to help your discussions with the Ferli, or the subcontractors, if necessary." In my work clothes, I must have appeared a reasonable emissary.

There was a flash of anger from the dockmaster, but the *ciran* sent real hatred at me.

"There'd be nowhere to do the work," the dockmaster said to the humans. "And you can't move the ships, anyway. It would never work."

"The ships can be towed," I said. "The Tak family towed several hulks last year; it's risky for ships in service, but they have some experience. The work that's left could be done anywhere, with the workers living aboard the ships after they're in position."

There was a loud silence. The *ciran* turned to me and said, "Your idea is a poor one, Bretton." That nightmare name made me shiver. Then the *ciran* fingered the cord of a lacquer pouch at his side, tying it tight, with sudden jerking movements. His face was so fierce, I believed the threat. He felt my fear deepen and smiled, very ugly, at me.

Paul and Bill started talking, speculating aloud in Tasait about how much such an arrangement might cost, versus the time and priority fees saved. Paul put his arm around my back; the dockmaster stared.

Reluctantly, the dockmaster agreed that since the ships were so nearly completed they would be finished before Dsar took on the (fictional) Toal assignment. There need only be a small additional fee for their trouble. Paul negotiated the 'small fee' down to 150,000c. No one was satisfied, but a deal was made.

As I was leaving with the humans, the *ciran* took my hand, bending over it in a parody of friendliness. "Until later, Bretton," he said. The anger I felt from him was an explosion in my mind; my breath was as tight as the knot he had made.

We returned to Paul's ship. Myra and Bill followed Paul and me back to Paul's room. The three of them questioned me closely, drawing out some information and insights gleaned from the nobles' emotions.

When they finished with me, I lay down on the bed. The three of them talked. Paul glanced at me occasionally. I heard my name. I felt ill. They were invigorated. They spoke in English, so it was easy not to listen. I fell asleep.

I woke when Paul sat down on the edge of the bed; Myra and Captain Shin had left.

"What's the matter?" Paul asked. He leaned over, putting his hands down on either side of my head, smiling at me.

"Nothing. Did I tell you one of the nobles was *ciran*?" He nodded.

"Restructured. He still has the *ciran* empathy, but he doesn't look *ciran*, and he only functions as a male. They do surgery, hormone treatment, I don't know," I said. I shuddered. One of my earliest memories is of some of my brothers and sisters holding me down, teasing each other about where to cut me. "He hates me," I said.

"Is that why you're upset?" Paul smoothed my hair. "Seeing him? Having him hate you?" He shifted position and the bed moved, rolling me against Paul. "You were wonderful this afternoon. Bill and Myra were impressed. You saved me at least half a million credits, naming names like that. The dockmaster thought we didn't have an alternative, and you came up with one, at least partially plausible." Paul ran a finger down the length of my arm, then traced the outline of my face with the edge of his hand. "You're smart; I like that. And not afraid to speak up and say what needs to be said."

"The *ciran* threatened to kill me," I told him.

"When?" Paul asked, sitting straight. "I didn't hear it."

"He called me 'Bretton.' It's an old story. Bretton was a noble, a *ciran* who helped a brother in a war; when the war was over, the brother signed a peace that gave Bretton to the other side. They killed Bretton, gruesomely."

"I'm not going to do that," Paul said, at least taking it seriously.

"The seven days are almost over." I turned toward the wall.

He placed a hand on my side, moving me back to face

him. "You can stay longer. I want you to; very much, in fact." I could feel the warmth of his body, so close to mine, and smell the musky scent of his skin.

"You'll be leaving soon, anyway, when your ships are finished," I said. I tried to turn away again, but he stopped me.

"You're leaving, too, I thought," Paul said.

"Maybe. I don't know." It was all becoming too real.

Paul lay down on the bed beside me. "You should get away from Tasa, Gwin. It's not good for you here." I couldn't see his face. When I listened I could hear the constant faint hum of the ship's machinery; it reminded me of the background of other people's emotions I usually felt. On board this ship, when the other makers were not nearby, there was nothing, just a stillness in my mind. I was afraid of that silence, afraid of feeling no one's mind but my own.

"Maybe you shouldn't work tomorrow, since you were threatened," Paul said. "Stay away a few days. I'll put one of the crewmen as a guard on you."

It was funny, really: Gwin Rency, prostitute, part-time mechanic, attracting the time and attention of important people like the dockmaster of Dsar. I refused to believe the two nobles would remember me at all the next day, or bother to harm a maker if they did. "Oh, I'm so valuable," I said, sarcastic.

"You are," he said, "to both of us. And your son." He got up slightly, propping his head on one arm. He traced the line of the scar on my face. "Who was his father?"

I sat up. Paul was waiting for an answer. "That's a fairly stupid question to ask a prostitute," I said. He seemed to wince. I turned away.

"Hasn't there been anyone special for you?"

I looked back at him. "My family," I said. "Family is what matters. What about you?"

"I was married once, for five years," he told me.

I'd heard of human marriage. "I thought marriage was supposed to last forever, like a family."

"It doesn't always. Mine didn't." Paul began to touch me seriously, running his fingers along the inside of my thigh, making me want him to continue. "I think, if you were a woman, I might consider marrying you," he said. He was smiling, but I wasn't sure it was a joke.

"Paul, what pronoun do you use for me, in English?" I asked.

"The female," he said. "I suppose because I'm male." He covered my mouth lightly before I could say anything. "I know you're not a woman. It's just words, Gwin. English doesn't have a neuter personal pronoun for intelligent beings, like Tasait." He moved his hand and kissed me. I stared into his blue eyes, wishing I could feel his emotions, then looked away.

"Myra is very pretty; even I can tell," I said. "You could marry her. I think she likes you."

"I like you better, even though you tell me you're not pretty," Paul said. "You make me laugh." He started to open my clothes.

"Do you think Myra would be interested in me, then?" I asked. Paul removed his hands from me abruptly.

"Is that a message?" Paul's voice was icy. "I just said I know you're not a woman; I don't need the reminder."

"She's just so pretty; I was attracted to her." I was lying; it hadn't occurred to me before that moment. Even *ciran* aren't pure: I cycled female most of the time and had always gravitated more to males than females. But I'd realized that I'd begun to think of Paul as family; that made me worry.

Paul sighed. We lay next to each other, not speaking, not touching, except where the geography of the bed forced us into contact. I was intensely aware of those places: my shoulder, my hip.

"It isn't true, Paul," I said eventually. "But it could have been." I rolled onto my side and put my arms around him. He twisted so he was on top of me, pressing me into the bed. I suddenly knew that I was feeling Paul in my mind after all; there was a shadow, an empty outline in the network the *ciran* empathy made me sense, and its shape was his. "I'll stay with you longer, if you still want me to," I said.

"I want that," he said, very seriously. Then he shook his head and smiled. "What am I going to do with you?"

"I have several good ideas," I said, and showed him.

I worked the next day, despite Paul's objections, and refused a guard. Paul came once to watch me as I worked. He told me I was graceful.

Perfin made derogatory remarks about humans and seemed certain that I could hardly wait until the coming night was over, and I would be free of Paul. I didn't tell her I was staying. Loden was civil, for the first time since I'd been with Paul. "What are you going to do with all that money?" he asked, tacitly accepting it as mine. He kept his distance from me; even so I felt his dislike and anger.

"I haven't decided, yet," I told him. "I think I'm leaving Tasa." He didn't respond.

Very late in the day, Loden told me to move a power panel I'd installed a few days earlier to another location. It was in a part of the ship nearly completed, and no other workers were around. Just as I removed the cover, I noticed that the wiring looked odd.

The next thing I remember, I was in a human bed in their ship's infirmary. I hurt.

I could hear Paul's voice and see his back. He was speaking English to another human. They noticed I was awake and turned around.

"The doctor says you're going to be fine, Gwin," Paul

told me. He looked unhappy. "Everything is under control."

I couldn't feel my right arm at all; it was covered.

Paul came closer. "I'm so sorry," he whispered. I thought he might cry. "My lawyers will find a way to get at the dockmaster for this. At least you're going to be all right." There was a chair nearby, and he sat down in it.

"My family," I managed to say. I felt so tired that speaking was an effort.

"Yes, they've been asking about you," Paul said.

"Family did it," I said, "not dockmaster." There was no way the dockmaster could have arranged the incident without my family's participation; it was a simple matter for Loden, though.

Paul stared at me, first in disbelief, then horrified.

"Money," I explained. I trembled, from the pain and anger and desolation I felt.

Paul took my good hand. "Gwin," he said, and nothing more.

My right hand was badly burned, my arm was numb and I had some minor internal tissue damage. I was very lucky, the doctor said, and a Tasana doctor confirmed it. I'd be all right, except I wouldn't have full use of my right hand. They didn't know yet the extent of the damage to the nerves.

Perfin was the only one of my family who came to see me; she hadn't known in advance what Loden planned. She was sad that it had happened, of course, but blamed me, for not giving my money to the family. The dockmaster's *ciran* had approached Loden after all, and paid for my death; Loden had been unable to resist the allure of easy money. Loden had modified the arrangement to mere injury. He is my brother, I suppose. But he didn't mind taking pay to hurt me. It was punishment, he told the others.

I had to explain to Paul several times that there was nothing to be done to Loden. It was a family matter; no one outside would have been interested even if I hadn't been *ciran*. Though I lived apart from them, I was family enough that Loden could do what he wanted. Paul seemed shocked. I didn't tell Paul about the involvement of the restructured *ciran*; he might have done something embarrassing and useless. I only wished I'd given my family the money before I'd found out what I was worth to them.

I was out of the infirmary in two days, and back in Paul's room. I asked him to transfer the 10,000c to my family. He refused.

"They tried to kill you!" He was sitting next to me in the big chair with my bare feet in his lap. He liked my feet; he said they were more symmetrical than his.

"No. I'd be dead if Loden had wanted to kill me. But he might decide to if I don't give them the money," I said. It was embarrassing; Paul thought more of me than did my brothers and sisters.

The human doctor had put cloths around my hand and arm; beneath them was some medicine of theirs that the Tasana doctor had agreed would be appropriate. My arm itched and ached. I couldn't feel my fingers. I could only see the outline of them; they didn't flex when I tried to move them. "I just don't know what I'll do," I said, determined not to sound desperate. "I can't do mechanical work if my hand isn't right. I don't want to be a prostitute forever, especially if I ever get away from Tasa."

Paul stared at me, the look of concentration that made me want to turn away. "I'll take you off Tasa," he said. He began rubbing my feet. It was comforting. "You already agreed to stay with me longer. The ships will be ready soon, we'll load cargo and leave for Earth. I want you to come. After that, we'll see."

I ignored him. "If you won't make the transfer, then I'll do it. It's just money. I didn't have it ten days ago."

"I don't like this at all. It's blackmail," Paul said

irritably. "Too bad I was so generous." He stopped massaging my feet.

"Paul, this is my problem, not yours." I stood up. "I'll make the transfer." I went to his desk; the computer mind could accept instruction in Tasait and the transaction was easier than I had feared. I sent a message to Perfin, telling her about the family's new account. Paul watched me from across the room.

When I returned to the chair, Paul said, "Oh, what the hell. Will another 10,000c be enough to make you feel comfortable coming with me?"

"I don't want any money," I told him. "I want my son. I'm staying on Tasa." Disal was all the family I had left; it was selfish to depend on him, but he was the only person that I could feel loving me.

Paul was startled. "I'd forgotten about your son." His hand lay on my leg; he seemed to compare it with mine, lying on the chair: the hard ridge on the edge of mine, his nails; my smooth skin and his hairiness; the additional digit on mine; the constant length of my fingers and the strange unevenness of his. So close, and not the same. "You can't very well leave him with your family," Paul said slowly.

"They wouldn't hurt Disal," I said. "There'd be no reason. But I need to have someone." My voice sounded strange, like plainchant at a funeral, slow, solemn and remote. Paul continued to stare at his hand on my dark, too thin leg. He glanced at my feet as though he'd never seen them before. I moved, to sit properly in the chair, feet on the floor, hands hidden in my lap. Paul looked at me sideways. "No, we're not the same," I said. "I'm not human."

"But I care about you, anyway," Paul said. "I enjoy being with you, and I want you." He was silent a moment, then added, "Bring your son here, to the ship." I remembered Paul holding me on the first night I was in his room, after I'd told him I was a mother.

I sighed. "Families are born, not made, Paul. You'll get bored and want to be rid of me. What would I do then?"

"At least I won't try to kill you," he said, attempting humor. I smiled my customer smile, unable to be amused.

"Gwin, I do want you to stay with me. You can bring your son," Paul said, his voice certain now. "If you want to leave at any time, I'll understand. And I promise that I won't leave you in a bad situation. Beyond that, I don't know, myself."

Paul went to the desk and opened another account for me, smiling as he did so, in a good mood. "There," he said. "Some serious money. Now you don't have to worry about the future. You'll come with me." He handed me the hard copy.

The account held 50,000c. "This is silly, Paul. Your people think it's peculiar that I was ever here. They'll laugh at you, or worse, if you keep me with you longer."

"I know," he said. "But I'm asking you to stay with me anyway. Being laughed at never hurt anyone wealthy enough to ignore it. Like you, I prefer it to other things. Right now I prefer it to leaving without you." For the first time, Paul seemed vulnerable. He held out a hand to me. I took it, and stood up beside him.

"Paul, I'm afraid," I said. "On the ship with only humans, and then on Earth, I won't feel anyone's mind, but Disal's. Like being unable to see; it's hard to walk into a void." I leaned against him. He put his arms around me, like a comfort from the cold. "Sometimes, Paul, I want to ask you, are you really alive? I can't feel your mind."

"I'm alive," he said, more rough than I'd ever heard him. His grip on me tightened. "You'll just have to take it on faith, if you're willing to try." He let go of me, but stayed close. "That's what the rest of us do." He touched my face. "I know you exist; I want you with me."

"Disal will be there," I said, half to myself. Paul was watching me.

"Yes," he said, "and so will I."

I felt deep in my mind and far outside it. I wasn't certain, but once again I thought I sensed Paul, somehow, within the field of my empathy, a shadow. I looked into his eyes and realized that even if I could never feel his mind, being with him was what I wanted. He was a kind of family to me, the best chance I'd ever had, so I reached out for him. "I'll stay, Paul," I said. "I believe in you." He held my hand, and drew me close. There was nothing *ciran* empathy could have told me in that moment that I didn't already know.

The Raid on the Golden Horn

by
Don Satterlee

About the Author

Don Satterlee is 40, born in Southern California, spent his college freshman year in the Air Force Academy but transferred to the University of Hawaii, and eventually received his PhD in American Studies from Hawaii, after gaining a BA and MA in English Literature.

Now relocated back in California—the Northern half, this time—he jogs, studies foreign languages, learns classical history, writes, and teaches at a couple of community colleges. He is married, and has two children. Remember that last part especially—it will explain much about "The Raid on the Golden Horn."

. . .

Don Satterlee's illustrator is Lawrence Allen Williams.

Wungluf nods. "Then you, Robert, take your squadron, come up behind the planet and attract the attention of the Bey. While the Bey responds to you, my squadron will force its way through Star Gate Delta, annihilate the tarque deflectors and land right in the middle of the Golden Horn. By then the lustoids will have been alerted and they'll try to intercept—"

Suddenly a baby's cry interrupts Wungluf. It comes from the next room. The four men around the table, Wungluf of Odeir, Mikhail Vangrondervich, Robert the Uncivil and Chuang "Pistols" Mui Dong, scrutinize each other as they listen to the cry. Then, as suddenly as it began, it stops.

Wungluf sits back and folds his incredibly muscular arms across his mammoth chest. "Before we finalize our attack plan, who's got any extra diapers?"

The other three space pirates look silently, guiltily down at the table top.

"Come on, guys," Wungluf says. "How can I go on a raid like this, which is going to take at least three standard days, and not have extra diapers?"

"I had to trade my nutronium gun for forty-eight disposable diapers," Robert the Uncivil says. "The rear of my space cruiser is defenseless now, but at least I know Nicole will be warm and dry during the raid."

Wungluf glowers at him. "And you can't spare me a dozen? Just till we conquer the Golden Horn?"

Illustrated by Lawrence Allen Williams

Robert the Uncivil runs his hand over the bald half of his head. The other half, which is matted with ebony braids that hang like pennants to his shoulder, sparkles with golden beads through which his hair is laced. On both of his cheeks Robert has circular tattoos and their neon blue color glows against his black skin whenever he gets a little excited. Like he is now.

"It's like this, Wungluf," Robert says. "Little Nicole always gets diarrhea when we go beyond light speed. I know she'll get it again on this journey. I'll burn through twenty or twenty-five diapers just getting to the Golden Horn."

Mikhail Vangrondervich smiles uneasily. "Sorry, Wungluf. I don't have any to spare."

Wungluf knows not to press the issue with his long-time buddies, but his piercing blue eyes sweep like nutronium guns on to Chuang "Pistols" Mui Dong. Pistols joined this elite band only three months ago.

"Little Huang Ti gets diarrhea too," Pistols says quickly.

"I thought you said little Huang had constipation?" Wungluf points out.

Pistols grins effusively. "Yes, that's true, but that's only because he ate some cheese popcorn two days ago. Now, he has a bit of the plug, so to speak. However, whenever we go past light speed, he too develops diarrhea."

"And how many diapers do you have in your hoard?" Wungluf demands.

"Only thirty-six," Pistols replies. He adjusts his eye-patch (which covers the socket of his right eye—it was shot out in the famous Khovron raid). He hasn't had time yet to have the eye replaced.

Wungluf leans over the table. "You wouldn't want me to call in the caitiich and ask her to read your soul, would you, Pistols? To see if you're telling the truth."

"So, you think I'm lying?" Pistols asks lightly. He even laughs off-handedly, showing his strong white teeth, but under the table his fingers go to the handle of his eupronic handgun. Maybe, thinks Pistols, it's time to begin the inevitable battle with the loud-mouthed barbarian.

"Perhaps you are lying," answers Wungluf.

Pistols' fingers tighten on the butt of his eupronic handgun.

"I've had enough of your insolence!" Pistols snarls as he pins his one good eye on the much larger Wungluf.

"And I can't stand a diaper hoarder!" Wungluf hisses out through clenched teeth.

"You steroid puke!" shouts Pistols. "On the Khovron raid you stole the Rollo-bike, which you knew my Huang Ti wanted!"

Wungluf shouts back angrily, "Because you snatched the Teddy Telephone when we took the Gamma-Creon Station!"

As he spits out these last words, Wungluf pushes back from the table and draws his two nigrine daggers from his huge leather belt. They hum as they are drawn from their cobalt scabbards. He surges up, a titanic man with arms like chunks of granite and a chest as hard as marble.

At the same time Pistols jumps up on his de-grav boots and whips out his eupronic handgun. He also turns on his antiparticle body field. When the field is ignited, the beer can in front of Pistols instantly crumples.

Wisely, Robert the Uncivil leans back from the table. This could be messy.

Mikhail Vangrondervich shakes his shoulder-length blond curls.

"Gentlemen, gentlemen," he says coolly, "Pa-lease. Let us not act like a couple of Gergian bears in heat. May I suggest a compromise?"

"No compromise with this sushi cyclops," Wungluf snaps back in his quavering bass voice. He whips his humming daggers back and forth in the air.

Pistols shakes the barrel of his eupronic handgun at Wungluf. "This outsized space jock never says 'Thanks,' and never returns anything he mooches off me. I'm fed up with his rudeness."

Wungluf lets out a savage groan and crouches into a fighting stance.

"Listen, you one-eyed space cretin, you always make such a big deal about nothing. Last week, I gave your precious Huang Ti a couple of jars of plum sauce. Two nights ago, I let him borrow the Wiggly Squiggly Toad Ticker. I didn't write it down in my space log and note the times. What's the big deal? I don't expect these things back right away. But now I see how petty you really are. I have your precious Huang Ti's A-B-C bibs and his Lopey Mopey Kitty T-shirt. They're right on my dresser, folded and ironed if you want to know. And your four bottles and nipples. They've been sterilized. They're cleaner now than when you lent them to me. And you can have them all back as soon as you like. Big deal." He lets out a long breath and growls, "I'm so sick of your pettiness."

"Pettiness!" cries Pistols. "We returned the Wiggly Squiggly Toad Ticker the next day. And I sent the plum sauce back with an extra jar of apple-banana sauce. I'll bore a hole through that impenetrable skull of yours and let some light in there. You never return what you borrow."

"Gentlemen," says the frowning Mikail Vangrondervich, "may I remind you that the assault on the Golden Horn is set to begin in less than two standard hours."

Wungluf glares at Pistols, "Hey, you one-eyed, sawed-off dink. I always return what I borrow!"

Shaking his bald head, Pistols declares, "Never, you oversized lump of mugworm fertilizer! You still have Huang Ti's Bitty Bird Bopper!"

At these words, Wungluf's dark blue eyes dart nervously around the room, as if looking for help. One of his bearded cheeks begins to twitch. Finally, sweating profusely, he lowers the nigrine daggers that are glowing in his hands.

"You're right, Pistols," he admits. "Eric Wunglufsson really likes the Bitty Bird Bopper and—and, well, I didn't think you'd mind." He scratches at his beard with a dagger. "I—I'm sorry."

Pistols scowls as he slams the eupronic handgun back into his holster.

"Huang Ti doesn't really miss the Bitty Bird Bopper," he says, "but it'd be nice to know, Wungluf, that Eric Wunglufsson, or you, appreciate it. I had to swap two of my lustoids for it."

"Two lustoids!" echoes Robert the Uncivil. He would never part with two lustoids for a Bitty Bird Bopper. Maybe for Poko, the Giggling Giraffe, but not for the Bopper.

Wungluf returns his nigrine daggers to their cobalt scabbards.

"Why don't I let Huang Ti have the Rollo-rider? For a few days," he says in a conciliatory voice.

Pistols nods. "That would be very nice." He doesn't want to lose his advantage. "And what about the—" he pauses for two seconds—"the Big Boy's Collection of Tales about the Purple Space Wolf Who Didn't Like to Brush His Teeth?"

As if zapped by a tal ray, Wungluf's mighty body sags. Mikhail Vangrondervich stares incredulously at Wungluf. Issuing a high-pitched moan deep in his long neck, Robert the Uncivil shudders in his long cape and almost falls off his stool.

"The Book!" whispers Robert the Uncivil. He glances at the equally stunned Mikhail Vangrondervich.

"Is it possible?" wonders Mikhail.

Wungluf looks with growing admiration at Pistols. Pistols, he thinks ruefully, is even shrewder and more ruthless than he had ever imagined.

"Okay," says Wungluf. In the thick nest of his caramel-colored beard a devil-may-care smile flashes.

"Very good," says Pistols. He turns off the antiparticle field and the beer can uncrumples itself back to its previous size. He folds his arms across his flight vest and grins triumphantly.

"That is," Wungluf goes on, "you can have The Book, if you let me have a dozen or so diapers."

As if jabbed with a nigrine dagger, Pistols jumps.

"Never! You—"

"Wait," Mikhail Vangrondervich say hurriedly. "Time is of the essence. Robert and I will kick in three diapers each and Pistols, you kick in six. That should hold Eric Wunglufsson till we reach Galcorp and resupply Wungluf with Federation diapers. Okay?"

Pistols must use the Shung technique to control his anger. A storm of emotions flickers just for a moment across the oval of his face. He thinks: I have won this contest, but it has not been a clean victory. This rude, stinking barbarian is extorting six diapers from him. A barely audible growl rattles in his throat. The Shung technique squeezes the growl into silence and a reluctant smile is forged across Pistols' narrow mouth. Pistols thinks: this barbarian is not as stupid as he smells. And what are six diapers to Pistols, the soon-to-be scion of the famous Mui Dong Clan? And, more important, his beloved Huang Ti will finally get to enjoy the legendary Book.

"Okay," he agrees. "And the Rollo-rider."

"You got 'em both," nods Wungluf. The Rollo-rider is nothing, he thinks. And as for The Book, he had one of his lieutenants make a secret copy of it in Khovron. So even though Pistols will have the original, at least Eric Wunglufsson will have a copy. And Wungluf has gotten six diapers out of this infamous cutthroat. But most important, he has taught the one-eyed newcomer that there is a pecking order among this august group, and Wungluf has shown that he, Wungluf, is at the top of that order. And if Pistols wants to tangle with him, there will be a price to pay for it. A steep price.

He extends his beefy hand across the table.

"Sorry for the hassle," he says.

Pistols hesitates a moment. Yet, in spite of his instinctive hatred for Wungluf, he finds his admiration growing for the barbarian. At last he slaps his hand into Wungluf's palm. "No problem."

The two of them sit down.

"I just love happy endings," sighs Robert the Uncivil. "Now," he says to Wungluf, "tell me about the Bey. I heard she's the best star pilot in the quadrant."

"I'm more concerned about her lustoids," Mikhail Vangrondervich declares. "They fight till the death, and even after they're dead, they still keep fighting."

It Is Just Good Business

by
Kristine Kathryn Rusch
and
Dean Wesley Smith

About the Authors

Kristine Kathryn Rusch and Dean Wesley Smith met at our first WOTF Workshop, in Taos, New Mexico, in 1986. Dean had sold a few stories, notably "One Last Dance," in L. Ron Hubbard Presents Writers of The Future, *Vol. I. Kris as far as I know had not sold any but she had a Finalist story in the Contest, and it was obvious only some small thing remained between her and success. She had won an L. Ron Hubbard scholarship a few years earlier.*

Sometimes, magic happens. Kris and Dean took one look at each other, fell in love, and have not been separated since. More to the point, they moved to Eugene, Oregon, founded Pulphouse, *and made it work spectacularly, with Dean the publisher and Kris the editor. Also, they sold lots and lots of stories over the years, and Kris has just been named editor of* The Magazine of Fantasy & Science Fiction. *(Dean will edit the weekly* Pulphouse, *successor to the hardcover* Pulphouses *which changed the way the world looks at magazines.)*

And this is what they have to say about the business of writing:

Whenever we teach writers' conferences or workshops, we tell new writers to submit their best story to L. Ron Hubbard's Writers of The Future Contest. And we tell them to do it every quarter without missing. When asked by a new writer what we consider the best market, we always say the Writers of The Future contest. Strange behavior for editors of what could be seen as competing publications. Do we say all that so they will let us write essays in the volumes?

No. The reason is simple: It's good business.

When we teach writing classes or workshops, we always focus on the business of writing. From writing the story to mailing it to handling rejections and eventually sales and success. New writers are hungry for that knowledge. The Contest comes up in the section on marketing.

The Contest pays its writers more than any other publication (for new writers, at least) not just in money, but in travel fares and in writing workshops. (We met at the very first WoTF writers' workshop, held in Taos, New Mexico, taught by Algis Budrys, Jack Williamson, Frederik Pohl, and Gene Wolfe. Going to that workshop has turned out to be very good business indeed.)

Besides the money and the workshops, there are other reasons why it is good business to submit to this contest first. The anthology stays in print. Dean's story in the first WoTF volume is still in print seven years later and it still may be seven years from now. Also most magazine editors pay attention to the writers who have placed in the Contest.

Not only is it the best paying market, but it is also easier to break into for new writers. WoTF is a contest for the new writer. New writers compete among each other for a winning position. Out here, in the rest of the publishing world, new writers compete with long-established professionals for space in the national magazines.

Most new writers believe there is no way except determination and luck to overcome the odds and make that all-important first sale. And granted, determination and luck are factors, as are talent and drive. But understanding the business side of the writing profession will help a new writer as much as a proper understanding of grammar will.

Over the last few years we have talked about our beginning writer perceptions a lot. And we seemed to have had a lot of similarities.

When we were new writers, we both believed that editorial offices were at the end of long hallways. Huge, windowed rooms filled with polished desks, hundreds of secretaries, and gold-plated phones awaited the editors every morning when they came to work. Imagine our surprise when we learned that most editorial offices were small, cramped rooms half the size of a normal bathroom, stacked with books and papers, barely large enough for the editor, a desk and a chair. Most editors spend their days doing other editorial tasks—schedules, meeting with writers, negotiating with agents, selling ideas to the publishers, and pitching books to the sales forces.

The editors do the majority of their reading at home after work, exhausted, headachy and wishing they could watch trasho TV instead. Not exactly the best condition for discovering the next Harlan Ellison.

Those conditions, among others, are why editors have low tolerance for bad photocopies, old ribbons, yellow legal paper, and insulting cover letters. The last thing an editor needs is yet another aggravation. Besides, most of these sins are committed only by beginning writers, so editors are less likely to give such a manuscript time. If writers clearly don't know their business, an editor doesn't want to work with them.

Despite all that, every editor in this field wants to discover a good new writer. Good writers, to paraphrase Flannery O'Connor, are hard to find, and once found might disappear overnight. Many a writer publishes one story and never publishes another, not because the editor decided that one story is enough. Editors like to buy more than one story from a writer—want to, in fact, because writers are investments that appreciate with time.

No. Most new writers cut themselves out of the running if not before the first story, then just after. They simply do not send in more stories. The reasons are many. Fear that the editor who bought the first story will hate the next one because it is "not as good as the first" is a common one. So instead of giving the editor a chance, the writer stops sending in stories. We have heard this a dozen times or more. Or many times the writer, with the first sale, has accomplished the goal of getting published and that takes all the drive away. The reasons are many, but the key to becoming a regular selling writer is never stopping writing and sending off stories.

On the other side of the mail box, editorial thinking is very simple: we all practice it at various points in our lives. Whenever you walk into a bookstore, you're thinking like an editor. You only have $10 to spend. If one of your favorite authors has a new book out, you don't hesitate. You buy that book. If a writer whose work you like some of the time has a new book out, you study the book, read the cover blurbs and then decide. If you see a book by a new writer, you'll read the cover blurbs, the front matter, the opening page and a page in the middle before risking any of your money on an uncertain deal.

That is exactly how an editor looks at stories. They divide manuscripts into the same three piles.

Pile One: Big-name writers whose work will sell go into this first pile. Those writers have to prove to the editor that the story is bad or will not work for the magazine before the editor rejects it.

Pile Two: Recognizable writers go into the second pile. The editor picks up the story with hope, but with the thought that he may not buy it. These writers have to work a little harder at proving the story is what the editor wants.

Pile Three: Unknown writers go into this third pile. These writers have to prove that the story is brilliant before an editor takes a chance with it. These are the writers who are, as they say in sports, projects for the editors. Writers whose names will not sell the magazine. Yet. And that "yet" is the important part that every editor remembers.

The recognizable piles and unknown piles might have some surprising names in them. A writer with two short story sales might land in the unknown pile and a writer who has never published anything at all might go into the recognizable pile. Remember, it is the editor's memory for names that determines the content of the piles.

So how does a writer move from the unknown pile to the recognizable pile without ever making a sale?

Persistence.

Most new writers believe that they cannot have more than one story on an editor's desk at the same time. So a writer might have three stories in the mail: one to *Omni*, one to *The Magazine of Fantasy & Science Fiction*, and one to *Pulphouse: A Weekly Magazine*. All three of those manuscripts go into the unknown pile and get read with the editor's attitude toward unknowns.

However, if that same unknown writer wrote and mailed a story every week to *F&SF*, Kris would probably put the third or fourth in the recognizable pile. The writer spent the time to build name recognition and at the same time got the editor cheering for him to succeed.

Of course, just three or four manuscripts won't do the trick. Writers must submit stories to the same magazines on a regular basis. In the early days of our writing careers, we submitted a new story every other week to the science fiction digest magazines. And it's paid off. Between the two of us, we've broken into all but one of those magazines—and that one holdout is the one we didn't submit to as often as the rest.

The bottom line is clear. Eventually, if a writer is persistent and works hard at learning the craft and the business, the sales will come. Every writer's career starts differently and every writer has a ''sure'' way of breaking in that worked for them.

But what makes or breaks a successful writing career at any step along the way is attitude. All beginning writers and many published authors seem to believe that their careers are out of their control. Publishers decide how much to pay them. Editors decide which stories to buy. Great works of art remain in drawers, overlooked and forgotten because they were never sent out. Or sent out only once and the author thought the one rejection was the end all.

Well, great works of art remain in drawers only if writers let them. Editors can only buy things that pass across their desk. And every market is different from the others. We talked about why new writers should submit to WoTF. But if the story comes back from the Contest, don't stop there. Dean at *Pulphouse* buys different kinds of stories than Kris does at *F&SF* because he edits a magazine with a different slant. And both of us are different from Algis Budrys at the Contest. One editor's rejection might be another editor's lead story.

Granted, publishers do determine the rates of pay within their own house, but those pay rates are scaled. A writer who is persistent, writes weil, and is easy to work with can move up the pay scale with a rapidity that is startling.

And on the business side, professional writers need to know their profession as well as the editors and publishers do. The writers need to understand contracts and copyrights. They need to understand how to do self-promotion and how to build name recognition. Writers are in charge of their own careers. No matter how much an editor likes one writer's work, that writer is simply one among many others. No one will hold the writer's career in higher esteem than the writer himself.

The main reason we teach so many workshops and classes is to show writers how to manage their own careers. Granted, we also try to give them a few writing tools. But our focus is always more on the business side. We try to open the doors to the secret rooms of publishing and help writers realize how much control they really have if they only learn how to use it.

One quick note here: learning how to control a career does not excuse arrogant or nasty behavior. Most of the writers with those kinds of reputations are, in reality, sweethearts to work with. The apocryphal stories of difficult writers do more harm than good and always cause trouble to any new writer who thinks that is the best way in.

We expect, over the years, to continue this campaign of teaching the business side of writing, because it not only makes a new writer's life easier, it helps the publishing side of the business as well. Editors like to work with knowledgeable writers. We would rather help a writer design a promotional campaign than explain clause C, paragraph 5 of a standard contract. We would rather read a cleanly typed manuscript by a recognizable author or determined author than a bad photocopy from an unknown.

With all this talk about business, we often get accused

of ignoring art. Well, we have a strange opinion about art: we believe that art happens.

We can't teach art. The writers who commit art are the writers with the courage to follow their vision, the guts to finish it and the strength to defend it on the business side of the profession. Shakespeare probably wasn't thinking about art when he wrote *The Merchant of Venice*. He was worried about finishing a play before the theatre company needed it, about entertaining the masses (who would get drunk and throw spoiled vegetables if they were bored) as well as the gentry (who tended to enjoy intrigue more than slapstick). Charles Dickens and Edgar Allen Poe wrote serials for newspapers and were paid by the word, often padding their stories with extra words so that they could receive extra money, beginning stories and not knowing how they would end, even as they tried to get them published. Mary Shelley was trying to tell a scary story to Lord Byron and Percy Bysshe Shelley when she wrote *Frankenstein: The Modern Prometheus*. Were they all thinking about art? Probably, in and amongst their other concerns. But art wasn't as important as making money. And in order to make money, a writer needs to know business.

Attend workshops taught by professional writers. Read every how-to book you can get your hands on. Study your markets and most of all, write. And then keep on writing. And then when you finish the story, take off the writer's hat and put on your business hat.

Business is submitting a story to the markets that will give it good exposure, will pay well for that exposure, and will treat their writers with courtesy. WoTF does that, which is why we recommend it to eligible writers. If we miss buying the story for our magazine that wins the WoTF Contest, we just smile. We know that we'll be able to get the writer on a future sale.

And that's good business for us, too.

A Plea for Mercy
by
Öjvind Bernander

About the Author

Öjvind Bernander is Swedish, but studies at the present time in the United States, at California Institute of Technology in Pasadena. He is a graduate student. His biography is remarkably varied: three years co-editing an amateur science fiction magazine in Swedish while in high school; a stint as a telegrapher in the Swedish Army; trips to Tanzania, Sri Lanka, and India; past and present hobbies including writing comic strips, shooting cartoons, playing the piano and guitar, ballroom dancing, parachuting, wallyball, skiing, racquetball, and backpacking. With all that, "A Plea for Mercy" is his first sale. But, we suspect, not his last....

• • •

Öjvind Bernander's illustrator is Rob Sanford.

I was a lighthouse keeper that year when memory broke. I was on a sabbatical from the cartoon called modern life, with a mission to taste the salt, feel the chill of cold mists and enjoy the caress of solitude. Gazing out over the leaden ocean night after night, I had one long romance with a blanket, a cup of hot chocolate, and a bookshelf.

At least I liked to think of it that way. The lighthouse was actually a relay station, a thousand miles from the closest shoreline, but in the mind of a wanna-be artist surface details sometimes have to yield to emotional content. The important thing was that for the first time in many years I was truly at peace with myself.

But there is a snake in every Garden of Eden, as I was soon to find out, and when he bites the poison spreads like fire.

Mr. Wilson, the mailman, was the first symptom. One cold morning in early April he drove up as usual and sounded the horn. I was sitting outside my cabin sipping coffee with ugly old Sarah at my feet. He jumped out and waving a letter in one hand, he approached me, initiating the usual exchange of small talk.

"Good morning!" he said. "Where's the paint stand? I thought this one artist was an early bird."

I grinned. Mr. Wilson always tried a little too hard to be a people person. A joke, a friendly comment, but try to get personal and there would be another joke or just silence.

"An artist needs inspiration," I said. "I'm waiting for the sun to show me the way."

"Well, if you want inspiration, the Rockies is the place to be," he said, fishing up a rubber stamp from his mail bag. He squatted, put the letter flat on his knee and stamped it, then handed it over. "Here. Have a good one!"

He turned back. I watched the car wind its way up the hill and disappear on the other side.

I stared with distrust at the letter in my hand. Mr. Wilson had always been a strange character, but what was this supposed to mean? The mailman was never the one to stamp the letters; they do that at the post office. And I had clearly seen a big ink mark covering the stamp, but then, after he stamped it, it was gone. I scrutinized the envelope, but couldn't find the faintest trace of white-out. No scars from the ink eraser either. I was too much of an engineer to believe that a new rubber stamp had been invented that would clean up after others. Of course my eyes could have tricked me, but I was convinced I had seen an ink mark. He must have had the real letter hidden in his sleeve, or something. I smiled. Sometimes Mr. Wilson acted a whole lot younger than his years.

I stopped thinking about it, and I probably would have forgotten it completely, were it not for what happened later in the afternoon. This time it was Sarah who acted out of character.

I was right outside the cabin when the alarm went off. The relay station needed my attention. I rushed in to turn off the alarm, since I knew how much it disturbed Sarah. The first few times it had gone off she had jumped around as much as her old body permitted, howling like a prairie wolf. After a while she calmed down, but she would always whine and give me a miserable look.

The error was easy to fix. It was a deadlock, and I got them all the time. When fiber optics made the telephone pole obsolete, things happened a little too fast. The guys who put together the communications system did a sloppy job and the information paths kept breaking down. It was being replaced piece by piece, but in the meantime they needed people like me—people who were on call at the spot twenty-four hours a day. I knew the equipment inside out, every little electronic gear of the computers, every bug in the compiler. If the error was at my station, I could fix it within the hour. If it was in the cables, I could locate it and call the diggers to do the job. In dealing with a deadlock only brute force would work: I had to restart the system. The station would be down for ten minutes, but nobody would notice since all calls would be routed through other stations. The only time the procedure was dangerous was when the whole nationwide network was loaded close to full capacity. If one station deadlocked, the rest of them would be even more loaded, and the risk of further deadlocks increased dramatically. After the Big One shook up L.A. a few years ago, everybody was calling, and a deadlock in Kansas started off a chain reaction that shut down half of the country.

I was watching the screen as the startup neared completion, ready to shut off the beeper that signaled success. I heard a low growl, and out of the corner of my eye I saw a shadow moving. I turned my head just in time to see Sarah shoot through the room like a guided missile, slamming right into the control panel where the alarm bell was located. For a fraction of a second I suppressed my reflexes, trying to analyze the situation, but then I let go and rushed forward. There weren't any sensitive electronics exposed on the panel, but poor Sarah could hurt herself badly. She was raging and blindly biting at steeled buttons and switches that were too small to get a hold of. And then, as soon as I touched her, she stopped, her ugly old face looking up at me, the upper lip bleeding.

I dropped down on my knees and gave her a big hug. She breathed heavily and snorted from the excitement, but otherwise seemed to be her normal self. What had gotten into her? Was she ill and in pain? Was this the last outburst of a dying dog? I had never seen her display so much energy before. I cupped my hands around her head and rocked it gently back and forth, while looking deeply into her eyes, searching for any clues to her behavior. Still snorting, she looked back at me, and the only emotion I thought I could read was one of confusion.

The next few days were more normal. I tried to keep an eye on Sarah most of the time, watching for any abnormal signs. She seemed healthy, but just as a precaution I kept a slow pace during my morning jogs. I also gave her an early bath, and while rubbing her I felt for bumps or sensitive spots that would indicate disease. I was relieved not to find any.

The only thing that kept disturbing the status quo was Mr. Wilson. He didn't pull any more letter tricks on me, and his behavior was as correct as ever. But there was this thing about his nose. At first I couldn't locate what was wrong—I just noticed that he looked different. But as his nose grew a little bit bigger every day it became obvious. I felt uneasy, since I didn't know whether he was doing something on purpose or he actually had a problem. There is a disease that makes your nose grow, I knew that much, but it is a rare disease and affects not only your nose but your cheeks and jaw as well. There was a slightly artificial look to the nose, however, and finally I decided that it was fake. I didn't like his sense of humor and wanted an explanation, so one morning I asked him about it.

"My nose?" he said and rubbed it gently. "There was a time when my wife used to say it was cute. What's wrong with it?"

I had stepped close to him to get a good look. It looked

amazingly real, so if it was fake someone had done a good nose job.

"It's bigger," I said. "For more than a week it's sort of been swelling. Didn't you notice yourself?"

He frowned. "Bigger? I don't know what you're talking about."

"Yes, bigger. Either you are pulling some kind of joke on me, or you need to see a doctor. Come! Take a look in the mirror."

I led him into the cabin where I had a full-size mirror. He watched himself carefully and shrugged:

"Sorry, I still don't see what you mean." I was staring at his face in the mirror, and I couldn't see it either. His nose looked very normal.

"I—I'm sorry. It must have been the light or something. I could have sworn it had grown."

"That's all right," he muttered. "No offense taken." He looked away into the distance and chuckled. "We had a class reunion last week, and it got a little wet, if that has anything to do with it. You know, when you haven't seen the old crowd for ten years, you have to celebrate."

After he left I sat down outside with a cup of coffee to think. Sarah was on the porch and had found a cricket to play with, a playmate who didn't require too much energy. I wondered what would happen first: would Sarah accidentally squash the cricket or just lose track of it? My thoughts went back to Mr. Wilson. If he actually was trying to trick me, I couldn't understand why. There was a painting I had just started a couple of weeks ago that had mysteriously disappeared. Did he have anything to do with it? He seemed to appreciate my stuff, but I had hardly gotten anywhere on that one. Most of the strange incidents had been centered around Mr. Wilson. Some of the letters he had delivered recently were complete nonsense, as if a computer program had run amok and printed random output. But he couldn't

possibly have anything to do with Sarah's inexplicable outbreak. It wasn't easy to admit it, but I started to suspect that
the error was not in the world, but rather within myself.
Maybe my isolating myself out in the countryside had led to
some kind of inner deterioration. It reminded me of experiments that had been done on cats. If you put goggles on a
newborn kitten with a set of horizontal stripes painted on
them, the kitten loses its ability to see anything vertical.
When you take off the goggles, the poor thing will walk
right into the legs of a chair or a table. Was something similar happening to me? Except for Mr. Wilson, I had hardly
seen a face in ten months. Was my ability to perceive people
degenerating?

Sarah seemed to have lost track of the cricket after all.
She looked up in my direction, her face being that of a young
woman. The face seemed strained and the lips struggled to
say something. With an immense effort they managed to
coordinate their movements and a coarse voice said: "Bug!"

Then it was over and Sarah came strolling down the
steps toward me. This was just too much. There was something wrong with me. The world just doesn't start to mis-
behave like that. Brains do. It struck me that right before
Sarah said "bug" I had been thinking about her playing
with one. Was I going schizophrenic? I was definitely con-
fusing reality with imagination. It was the same story when
she attacked the control panel. I had been thinking about
her dislike for the alarm bell and how little energy there
seemed to be left in her nowadays. It seemed like I was making up the world myself. Had I been thinking about noses
earlier on? I couldn't remember. I needed to see a doctor
and decided to call one the next day.

From then on things turned bad quickly. Sarah suddenly started to bark and run down the driveway. As she disappeared over the brow of the hill, the barking stopped. I
watched for a while and then started to walk up the road.

I reached the top and found to my astonishment that the road ended a few yards down on the other side. It ended in a perfectly sharp line and then the grass took over. Some three or four hundred feet ahead there was a cabin, just like mine. Sarah was in front of it, sniffing around in the grass. I walked up to it and found my paint stand outside. The door was open and it didn't take long to convince me that the cabin indeed was mine. Somehow I had been going in a circle, even though the distance was too short to make such a mistake.

Just to make sure, I scribbled a quote from a song onto a piece of paper and nailed it to the door. I ran down the road again and the same thing repeated: I got back to my cabin, and there was the note on the door. It seemed as if the world was curving back on itself and I was trapped. I was a flesh-and-blood Pacman running through the tunnel. It was frightening but also consoling, for it suggested that the error was not in my head after all. The world misbehaved in such a consistent and tangible way, not like a rambling mind would have it.

I started to do some experiments. First I found the boundaries of my prison. I could go some five or six hundred yards in any direction before coming back to my cabin. The boundaries seemed to have the shape of a square. The fact that the note appeared on my door suggested that it was indeed the same cabin I came back to, not just a copy. Because of the rugged terrain I couldn't see more than one cabin at a time from the ground, so I climbed up on the roof and suddenly a mosaic of red cabins appeared all over; the mountains were no longer to be seen. It was amazing—like being in the middle of a kaleidoscope. On the other rooftops I saw figures like myself. As I waved my hands, so did they. I tried to shout, but my voice didn't carry far enough.

Yes, the world had gone wrong. Very wrong. My brain kept pouring out ideas. Maybe the most obvious explanation

was that it was all just a bad dream, but like in any bad
dream I felt too much awake to even consider that possibility.
Could a nuclear holocaust upset the laws of physics? Space
definitely seemed to curve back on itself, as Einstein pre-
dicted. Or was I the guinea pig in a bizarre, yet highly
elaborate experiment where a large set of androids were
directed to copy my behavior down to the smallest motion?

I climbed down from the roof. The sun—only one!—
was slowly setting. A thought that had been in the back of
my mind finally surfaced. If the world actually did change
according to my thoughts and expectations, then what would
happen if I expected something terribly bad? As darkness
fell, would goblins and trolls and their fellow creatures of
night appear? I shivered at the thought and quickly got my
paint stand inside. I called for Sarah and locked the door.
It was time to call for help.

The phone line was dead. I checked the computer to see
if the station was still operating and routing calls properly.
It was, and that was good news, because with a little bit of
reprogramming and a few reconnected wires I could get a
call through to the outside. I got to work on it right away.
Soon Sarah started to whine and run back and forth between
the window and the door. She had heard something outside.
For a while I tried to ignore it, but when I thought I heard
a light scratching on the door, I turned off the light and
shone a flashlight out through the window. It was pitch black
outside, no stars in the sky. The light cone from my flashlight cut through the air, but I couldn't get it to light up a
bright circle on the ground. The cone seemed to dissolve dif-
fusely where the ground ought to be. I could barely make
out what looked like large shadowy figures without any dis-
cernible form. It was useless. The scratching on the door
became more intense and a dull pounding could also be
heard. I was certainly not going to open it. I patted Sarah
to comfort her and went back to work.

The program was easy to write. The wiring was also quite straightforward, but I had to look up the terminals in a table and get them all right, which took some time. When I finally had everything hooked up, I tried the phone again. It was still dead, and I swore long and loudly.

The sound was getting louder and louder. It was no longer the sound of something animate attacking from the outside; it was more of a creaking, as if the walls were straining to withstand a tremendous force. From the panel in front of me emanated a high-pitched singing, and as I watched the controls they started to melt and sink back into the wall. But it was not the controls moving backwards, it was the wall slowly creeping forward, engulfing everything it touched like an amoeba. I jumped back in terror, and in front of my eyes the wall first turned dark brown, then brightened again and started to shine, and finally dissolved in the air. The wall behind me was gone too, and I found myself in an endless corridor, full of people, all dressed in red-washed jeans like myself and facing away. I started down the corridor and initiated a veritable stampede. At first I thought that I was catching up with the next person, but realized that it was the world that was shrinking on me. Suddenly the side walls collapsed, too, and I was immersed in a red sea of people, all getting closer and closer. When we were standing shoulder to shoulder and still kept getting squeezed tighter together, a deafening roar rose from the crowd.

And then memory stopped.

I woke up in bed. It was not a slow coming-to, but an instant awareness of being back. Back from where? I could not tell, but it was not from a dream, for my memory of the screaming crowd was so sharp and clear—far from that fleeting feeling of a nightmare slipping away.

I lay on my back for a long time, my head propped up on the pillow, not moving a muscle, just letting my eyes wander from one familiar object to another. Before interacting with the world, I wanted to see if it seemed to be the same as before: it was simply too fragile to the touch to be handled without care.

The sun shone in through the window, and the tall pine right outside the cabin cast a shadow on the floor: it was early morning. As far as I could tell, the settings on the control panel were normal, my rewiring from before all gone. The diodes blinked in a soothingly familiar pattern. In the periphery I saw something that must be my paint stand next to the door. I wondered which painting would be on it. Something warm pressed against my ankle. I took a deep breath and infinitely slowly raised my head so that I could see the foot end of my bed. It was Sarah, of course, wide awake and glaring back at me with a face so ugly it was pretty. She was not supposed to sleep in my bed, but she seemed to forget that every once in a while. I brought out my hand from below the blanket and patted a spot next to my chest to signal her to move closer. Being a well-raised dog, she first only lifted her head imperceptibly and didn't come over until I patted a second time. I put my arms around her and stroked her gently. She didn't seem worried in the least, as if nothing had happened. From my low vantage point everything appeared normal. Should I dare get up and take a look at the rest?

I didn't have to decide for myself. Sarah suddenly stirred and looked towards the door, and a second later I heard a well-known sound. A car was driving up the hill.

I jumped out of bed and into my sweats. I ran out with my heart pounding, like when I was a child greeting my father coming home from work. After all that had happened, the thought of meeting another human being made me all excited. Mr. Wilson had been my only physical contact with the outside world for a long time now.

As the car came over the hill I jogged up to meet him

with a big smile on my face, realizing how silly I must seem to him. But I didn't care.

"Boy, you seem to be in a good mood today," he greeted. "What's up?"

"Oh! Nothing at all, really. I . . . ." I didn't know what to say. Without telling him the whole story, I didn't have any excuse for my big smile. Maybe I should tell him and get some feedback. "I guess it's just the spring weather."

"I know what you mean. We had a class reunion two nights ago, and it got a little wet. More than a little wet, actually. I didn't expect the old farts to get so revved up. Spring, indeed."

I frowned. "Class reunion? Again? I thought that was more than a week ago."

"No, it was last Saturday. Maybe I told you about our plans. But it was quite a party. I'm glad it wasn't one of those where you bring your wife and hubby. That would have put a muzzle on the old student body." He stopped, smirked, and gave me a funny look. "Spring weather, my foot. With that neighbor of yours I've my own theories why you're so happy." He indicated a direction with his head and winked. "Here's your mail!" And with that he backed up and turned and left me standing with the letter in my hand. Everything was in order: Mr. Wilson was as strange as ever. Opening the letter I found the usual nonsense. This time it was an ad for something called a "teen-age mutant Ninja turtle. . . ."

That morning I went for a long walk. This time I didn't have to pass by my cabin every five minutes, even though I found to my disappointment that I was still imprisoned. I went up a small canyon along what would soon be a dried-out wash, but now was a bubbling stream of glacial-cold water. I took deep breaths, filling my lungs with fresh oxygen, savoring the scents of tree and grass. The bare rock was warm to the touch, and I held my head high, trying to

Illustrated by Rob Sanford

soak up the sunshine, turning its yellow rays into brown pigment. I felt close to nature, so intensely a part of it, that every little detail around me seemed important and worth my attention. I felt like a smoker who had kicked the habit after thirty years and suddenly realized that the world does smell after all. Every sensation overwhelmed me with its richness. I climbed a huge boulder and got an excellent view of the lower canyon. For a long time I just sat on top of it, doing my best to experience a world that had all but disappeared; listening, watching, smelling, touching.

I walked up the canyon for another half an hour or so before I hit the end in the form of a precipitous drop. The rock wall was as flat as can be with no prongs or crevices for climbing. "El Capitan," I thought to myself, "meet your little brother." Some two or three hundred yards below, a road ran right into the wall. In the distance, maybe a mile away, my red cabin shone like a ladybug against the grass, and close by, on the near side of the hill, was a house that I had never seen before. It was not a little functional cabin like my own, but a real house, and a large one at that, with quite amazing flower arrangements on the compound. Behind it was a hint of blue—the hue a swimming pool would produce at that distance.

"With that neighbor of yours." The words of Mr. Wilson rang in my ears. With that neighbor of mine, I certainly got very curious. I looked down, and for a second I considered jumping. Whoever had the power to mold my world according to his will should have the power to let me survive such a jump. But something deep inside me said no, so I walked back the long way down the canyon.

From up close the house looked even more impressive. The flowers in the garden were no cheap azaleas or begonias. They were orchids, with a variety worthy of South East Asia. The house itself was constructed with an awful, yet charming mix of wooden logs, bricks and stone. A large patio faced the direction of my cabin, and next to it was the swimming pool in the shape, or lack of shape, of an amoeba with narrow wooden walkways cutting across the pseudopodia. It was the home of a millionaire. Or was it, perhaps, the future home of a relay station technician?

I knocked on the door. Nobody answered, so I opened it and entered with a careful "hello-oo!" I looked around the hallway, where two sets of white marble stairs led up to the mezzanine. Halfway up stood a woman, quietly scrutinizing me with an expressionless face.

"Hi!" I tried again. She didn't answer but started deliberately down the stairs and walked up to me. She stopped right before me and continued to search my face. I felt uneasy. Suddenly she grabbed my right arm with one hand and pinched me with the other, driving her nails deep into my flesh.

"Ouch!" I cried and jumped backwards, rubbing my arm where she had hurt me. "What on Earth is that supposed to mean!"

Now she looked a little confused and almost concerned. "Who are you?" she said cautiously.

"I'm your neighbor. Look! I didn't mean to intrude, and I'll leave right away."

"No, please!" She softened. "Let's talk. I'm sorry I hurt you, but I thought you were yet another mailman. He'll take any amount of abuse. He's like a robot. No, please don't go. Come in and tell me your story. I need to see someone with a real brain." A quick smile. "Come!"

She led the way into the living room.

"A drink?" She was over at the bar. "This stuff won't kill any brain cells, you know."

I nodded.

"It'll have to be Scotch, because that's the only thing they provided me with this week." She handed me the glass with a slight smirk. "I really am sorry I pinched you, but when you've heard my story, you will understand why I did it. Here, sit down."

And so she told me her story. Her name was Linda and she was from Santa Ana, California, where she had worked as a saleswoman for a small computer software company that was struggling hard to survive. One day she woke up in this luxurious house, but to begin with she had been completely confined within it. Neither doors, nor windows, nor the attic hatch could be opened, and outside was complete darkness. For three weeks nothing happened, and then one day, sunlight shone in through the windows, and the door was unlocked. The house was not in Colorado but in what looked like the Louisiana swamplands in the middle of a tiny island encircled by the bayous. Only there were no mosquitos, no water moccasins, no alligators, nor anything else that would have made the place inhospitable to man, or, as she pointed out, no tools for a suicidal mind. But Louisiana didn't stay for very long. Next it was a midwest prairie, then a jungle, and for almost seven months a Norwegian fjord, grandiose, albeit small. As late as yesterday she had witnessed the coming of spring and the receding snowline on the high slopes. This morning it was the Rockies.

The same mailman had followed her wherever she went, and from her description it was the same one that had been growing noses on me. Hers had behaved much more strangely, however, and she kept insisting that he was nothing more than a machine. He could engage only in very low-level conversation, as she put it, and would never remember from one day to the next what they had been talking about. He would always tell her the same story about how he and his wife had gone to the movies the night before, one of those ultramodern, supposedly artistic films that seemed to be made for the benefit of the director rather than for the audience. She had gotten very angry on several occasions and pinched and kicked him and he would act like nothing happened. And his body had a rubbery feeling to it. It was very different from hitting a man of flesh and blood.

But he was the one who delivered food, everything she asked for, so she had finally come to treat him with indifference. She had even managed to get him to deliver essentially everything in the Sears catalog, from a stereo set to a veritable library of books.

She laughed and took me by the arm. "Come and take a look!" She showed me her study room and pointed to some five or six yards of shelf space full of books. "Everything you ever wanted to know about Norway. And quite a lot more. I've even got a Norwegian textbook and grammar. *Ja, vo vi elsker dette landet!* But now you say it's Colorado. I wonder for how long? Let's go for a walk. I want to see this new place."

It wasn't new to me, so I could really say that I knew the place inside out. I first showed her my humble cabin, and then it was up the canyon again. She seemed to understand more of this world than I did, so I wanted to see what she had to say about the drop.

"Don't jump!" she warned. "You'll survive, and you won't break anything, but it is very painful, and your body kind of swells up. Edema."

"Did you try it?"

She looked at me, searchingly. "I've tried many things, but I'm not sure I want to tell you about them. Not yet."

She sat down with her feet dangling off the cliff.

"You know, a year ago I would have been scared to death sitting here like this." She looked down the precipice. "I always wondered what would happen if they changed the size of the world when I'm at the border. If it expanded right now, would I get stuck in the rock? Or if it shrank, would I fall down or lose half my body? Would I wake up in bed, like you?" She shook her head. "I once spent five days and nights right across the border in the swamplands, and nothing happened. I gave up, and the next day they had moved the border."

"And who are they?"

"I don't know. Our tormentors. Our God. Our dear scientist whose guinea pigs we are." She looked at me. "How do I know you're not here to check me out?"

I shrugged and she laughed cynically.

"Well, you're not Mr. Wilson, and that makes me happy."

We walked back down. It seemed as if she didn't want to talk much about her experiences, so I had to repress my curiosity. Her story was certainly not encouraging. I could deal with a world gone awry for a day or two, but she had been suffering for over a year now. Was there no end in sight?

She invited me over for dinner that night, promising to be somewhat more hospitable this time. I wondered if she would be as talented at cooking as she seemed to be at everything else, or if she shied away from things domestic. I mentioned this to her and she laughed.

"I was brought up to be both domestic and professional. Besides, gourmet cooking was one of the many things I wanted to be good at. For a while I wanted to try everything."

"And how far did you get?"

"Halfways. Then I grew up, or lost my innocence, if you wish. I dreamt of being a renaissance person. I read all the classics. Like you I painted, or at least I tried. I did a lot of sports—even fencing. I danced. I played the electric flute." She chuckled. "And look what became of me: a peddler of zeros and ones—a merchant."

Towering clouds filled the western sky, as if a storm was gathering power, and the sun, now low over the horizon, colored the fringes a soft orange. The garden that had so overwhelmed me with its blooming splendor now took on a different appearance. The low angle of the light and the stillness of early evening created an atmosphere of imminence, as if there were something treacherous about the calm beauty of the exotic flora. Maybe it was all inside me—the pressure of repressed nervous apprehension. After all, I was invited to dine with a woman I hardly knew, and I had made the effort to bring out a nice shirt from the closet.

This time music streamed down the stairs as I entered. I traced the smell of Chinese cooking in the air and found Linda in the dining room. She was dressed in black: short skirt, loose blouse and a belt with an enormous, asymmetric buckle. A necklace glittered against the blackness and picked up the emerald green of her eyes.

"I couldn't really bring you flowers," I said, "so I hope this will do." I brought forth a bottle of imported Chardonnay that had spent a good ten months in my fridge; I never drink alone.

She gave me a big smile. "Thank you! That's wonderful. It'll go well with the main dish."

We sat down and attacked vegetable stir fry and glass noodles. Linda had decided to tell me the rest of her story and brought it up almost right away.

"I was very depressed for a while," she said, "and I repeatedly tried to get out of here in my own primitive ways."

"When was this?"

"During the first few months in Norway. I had 20,000 acres of fjord and I just kept running in circles." She had a pleasant way of moving her hands and arms sinuously to create a more vivid picture. "For a while I thought that there might be some way of jumping the fences, and the easiest way to do that, I thought, would be to dig my way out. I should have known better, and actually I think I expected what would happen. But I didn't want to leave anything untried. I hit the bedrock. Some ten feet down there was a perfectly smooth floor, harder than diamond, and no matter how hard I tried I couldn't make the slightest dent in it. The drills would break and I almost sprained my wrist when I tried the hammer and chisel. Same thing out in the water. I got a wetsuit and goggles from our dear mailman but soon banged my head into the same black surface.''

"And what about actually jumping out? There doesn't seem to be a limit on the skies. There's a sun way up there, and there are stars in the night.''

"Yes. Who knows what happens when you get high enough? I didn't try a blimp, but as high as fireworks go things just wrap around. . . .''

She quieted down, an introspective look on her face. She seemed a little uneasy about the next part.

"And so you tried . . . ?''

"I tried to *really* get out of here. But I wasn't too successful at that either. . . . You don't know for how long you've actually been entrapped?''

"I wish I knew. It was only some two or three weeks ago that I first reacted to Mr. Wilson.''

"You had a smooth transition. Have you since then ever cut or hurt yourself?''

I shook my head.

"Well. . . .'' she stared down into her wine glass and moved it around in little circles. "If you do, you'll find that something comes out of the wound, and that it's red. It even tastes salty. But it isn't blood. It's something very alien, and even though the wound heals quickly, I never felt comfortable with what's now a part of myself. Thank God my skin isn't made of rubber and that I still have a brain.''

"You tried to kill yourself.'' It was an abrupt statement, but she appeared afraid of saying it outright, as if she feared I would be repulsed.

"I tried to. I stabbed my heart. It took a tremendous

effort to overcome the inhibitions, even though I knew with almost certainty that nothing would happen. It was nauseating, but didn't hurt much. I blacked out, I think only for a few seconds, and then I was fine, left only with a stained blouse and a scar that healed in no time at all.'' She looked up at me. ''I'm sorry to tell you this story. It shouldn't embarrass me, but it does.''

''No. Not at all. You were in an awful situation.'' I leaned over and filled her wine glass. I smiled and raised my glass. *''Skål . . . ?''*

''That's right!'' She laughed and we clinked glasses. *''Skål!''*

I was amazed at the taste. After not having had a drop of alcohol for so long, the wine exploded in my mouth. Even my gourmet hostess raised an eyebrow.

''Are you sure this is the wine you brought with you to Colorado? It's very special.''

As the wine hit my stomach, a warm feeling spread throughout my body. Vivaldi's piccolo concerto played on the stereo.

''If we can get more of this, life won't be that bad after all. Why did you want to quit?''

''I'm not completely sure. Partly, I think, it was a cry for help. Maybe someone out there would feel enough compassion to get me out of here. But also, I was very depressed. Life seemed so utterly pointless here in prison.''

''You were lonely?''

''It wasn't that. I'm pretty good at enjoying myself. It was more of a feeling that there was no point in living in this tiny universe. The feeling is a very unpleasant one, and one that I had experienced once before.''

''A feeling of pointlessness?''

''Yes. A pointlessness that comes from insignificance. The horror of the life chart. My last year in college I decided to go through all my diaries, in an effort to fill in the spaces in my life while there were still people around to help me remember. So I made a chart, with one line for every year of my life, twenty in all, and made tick marks for every month. And so I marked the school days in one color, vacations in another, summer jobs in a third, and so on. I made little stars for really important events. The first draft was crude, but I made it over and used a fine pen to get all the details down. And when I was done it looked so small! My whole life, which I had cherished and looked upon as a tremendous potpourri of excitement, seemed so short and insignificant. I realized that the rest of my life would consist of filling out three more of those charts. Three times as much color and a few more stars. It was horrible and I put the chart away never to look at it again.

"The same feeling crept over me that first period by the fjord. Even though it was a beautiful place and I could get anything I wanted by mail order, things were so *finite*. The strange thing is that I wouldn't mind living at that same place, never moving away, as long as I knew I *could* get away, any time I wanted. I mean, even though I've traveled more than most people, I've only covered a fraction of a percent of the Earth's surface. And with sufficient energy and money I could've covered another tiny fraction. But suddenly I couldn't do that any more. I could only read books about faraway places, and then be content with the view over the fjord."

"I see what you mean. Like a tiger in the zoo. A man will be happy working from nine to five and then go bowling on the weekends, but put a fence around his world and he will feel like a caged animal."

She nodded slowly with big thoughtful eyes. She looked pretty when she was serious, but when she broke out into a smile she glittered.

"I don't know what it is about your wine, but it's wonderfully potent."

I felt it too. I was bubbling inside. It was a perfect combination: the wine, the exquisite dinner, and the feeling of closeness to someone who very much shared my fate—a fate that now seemed much less frightful. I felt an inner joy of a strength that had been absent for far too long. Outside the wind blew stronger.

We hastily finished dinner and went outside. Our sweaters barely shielded us from the cold of night, and by the time we had climbed the hill separating our houses we were comfortably entangled. The clouds had blown away and stars covered the southern sky. To the north a spectacular show of colors unfolded. Giant curtains of red and green fluttered in the solar wind, now receding, now coming forth, enveloping the Earth. Northern lights—a piece of arctic magic that had been brought to Colorado. There was no longer any need for words. We just huddled closer together, letting the ferocious rage of celestial forces stir up the sparkle that burned within.

I stretched and yawned for a good five minutes before I jumped out of bed. Waking up was a much more pleasant experience this time. Only twenty-four hours had passed, but so much had happened that I felt as if I were starting a new life. I firmly lifted Sarah out of my bed. Life was again smiling at me, but that was no excuse to spoil the old dog.

I felt wonderful. I was happy because last night had brought me so close to Linda, and I was happy we hadn't gotten too close. I could look forward to something that might evolve into a beautiful relationship, everything unfolding in due time.

I had a quick shower, put on my sweats, and called for Sarah as I jogged up the hill. I rested briefly on the crest and smiled as I compared living quarters.

I knocked on the door and opened it at the same time. Linda came down the stairs, a grave look on her face.

"Hi!" I said. "Is something wrong? You look as if your world has fallen apart."

She came up to me and looked deep into my eyes before grabbing my arm and pinching me like the day before. It hurt.

"Hey!" I said, not quite sure of myself. "Don't do that again. It hurts."

"Who are you?" she said and looked a little concerned. For a second I stood there gaping, staring at her. There was no sign that she was joking. I took a step back.

"Please, Linda, don't do this to me." I gave her two seconds to react, but she only looked more puzzled. "Don't joke about this!" I took another step back, and she leaned forward a trifle.

"Why are you here? Did I send for you?"

I turned around and ran, away from the garden, past my house, and up the canyon. I didn't stop until I reached the boulder from the day before. There I stopped, panting heavily, waiting for Sarah to catch up with me. I climbed on top.

Linda replayed. She was spending her first day in the foothills all over again. If I had played along she would have told me her story and invited me for another dinner.

All I felt was shock. Pure shock. A big chunk of me had been removed in an instant—too quickly to allow for any emotions to form. Something that I had been given had been taken away as abruptly, and I was at a loss for any response.

She replayed. Just like Mr. Wilson, only that she was so much more alive, so much warmer, so fully human. She had displayed a complete spectrum of all the qualities that are in a real person. Mr. Wilson may fake completeness by only displaying a single facet of a personality, hiding all the rest. But Linda hadn't done that. She had acted out a performance so convincing no robot could possibly imitate it.

And yet she replayed.

I sat there for a long time, stroking Sarah, while a feeling of utter hopelessness crept over me. Someone or something clearly wanted to torture me and I was completely at its mercy. Gradually it became clear that there was but one way out of my misery.

I talked to Sarah, told her that she was the greatest creature on Earth, and how sorry I was that I had to leave her.

On the slopes of the canyon I found a boulder, small enough to heave into position, but big enough to do the job. A dead branch served as the trigger mechanism. I put my head to the ground and my feet on the branch and pushed.

Did I replay as well? Did someone find my two-dimensional head and decide to rewind a few minutes and remove the memories? Or did the all-seeing eye decide to intervene earlier to keep things nice and clean?

I don't know. All I know is that the boulder was stuck as if cemented into the ground for as long as I stayed down, and at the moment I got to my feet, it rolled down and set off down the incline with a thunder.

Now I am glad that I didn't succeed. Things are as normal as can be and Linda hasn't let me down again the way she did that second morning. We walked into summer together, and witnessed our little world grow at a turtle's speed. The following fall our numbers started to grow as little houses and mansions popped up like mushrooms. We presently count a colony of twelve—a dozen minds, each with an amazing story to tell.

The old world that laid down the fiber optics cables seems so far away that I am no longer sure it ever was there. Memories are unreliable, and maybe they can even be directly tampered with, although I don't understand the purpose of creating memories of a false past. And how do I know things have changed after all? Never before did I try to end my life. Maybe the world never was infinite, just larger, and places were created as we traveled to them.

This is my plea. If I am what I think I am, and you are what I think you are, you can read these words, even though I wrote them under the bedcovers in the light of a flashlight. You cannot read my mind, at least not without great difficulty, but you can read the words from the pages of a closed notebook. If this is so, I beg you to give the real world back to us, or, if the technology is not yet ready, at least make this world large and flexible enough to fool us. Once we can't see the fences any more, memories will lose credibility and we can convince ourselves that what we see is for real.

Balanced Ecology

by
William Esrac

About the Author

William Esrac, 56, is our first Australian winner, following on the heels of James Verran, who was published in WOTF VI as a finalist. Oddly enough, though they had never met, they live only fifty miles apart in Australia, which is a rather large place.

Esrac has spent a large amount of his adult time in the theater, though he has always written for pleasure. "Balanced Ecology" is his first sale. He is quite happy about it, as are we. We think you will be, too—it's a most unusual tale of an interstellar castaway. We expect that over the years to come, you will find other Esrac tales to delight you. . . .

About the Illustrator

Ferenc Temil Temesvari lives in Budapest, Hungary, and is 30 years old. For most of his life he was principally a pianist, until 1986, when he heard the Dutch harp master, Andreas Wollenweider. This dreamlike, cosmic music influenced Temil to paint cosmic, dreamlike landscapes. He still plays the piano, but now concentrates on his art. His aim is to combine the imagination with Nature, to unite them and put together the elements of a new world reality.

For the past five years, he has been a member of the Hungarian Sci-Fi Society; he heard about the Contest through them.

My harvest of greenshells was a good one, enough to last me for several days. It almost filled the netbag which I'd knotted together from long strands of the red grass from high on the rocks above Deathtrap Beach. I could have walked back to the ship but it was almost midday and conditions are most dangerous at that time. Everything on the beach and the rocks was anxious for lunch. I was very hungry, too, and not eager to risk my hide, so I decided to take the short way and swim across. I don't like raw greenshells because the oil is unpleasant. Scooped out of their shells and boiled, they taste very good and the oil is useful for discouraging sea-lice from crawling up too close to the ship. Greenshells do very well on unwary sea-lice. So I fixed the bag and my knife to my waist cord, picked my way carefully between the deadly bluespines which gather on that area of the sea floor, and slid into the water.

I've become a very good swimmer of necessity. The waters of the little bay are usually safer than the land and suitable food is easier to collect about the rocks than it is elsewhere. Before my ship crashed, I thought of myself as fairly well built but now my shoulders are heavier and my body is generally stronger and in better shape. It has to be. Later, when the hydroponics on the ship improve, my gardens are doing well and I've finished preparing my rockpools for greenshell farming, I won't be so dependent on peak physical fitness. I work at the rockpools regularly because I'm nearing thirty years of age in home-time years and I won't be able to rely on peak fitness for much longer. Speed, strength and stamina are important to me until my other preparations are done. I should have begun preparing sooner but when one is twenty-two and very healthy, one doesn't think too much about aging, only survival, not realizing how important youthful recovery-capacities and reflexes are.

So I began swimming across the bay, keeping a wary eye out for poisonous grapefloaters and silverfins which sometimes enter these waters. At this time of year one has to be wary because the waters are so warm and predators tend to be more populous in the bay. There are also several varieties of deadly jellyfish, fish with deadly spines or efficient teeth like needles, and several kinds of eel which kill very expertly. Parts of the bay are very deep and parts very shallow because of the uneven rockshelf. Beyond the shelf the rock falls almost sheer and the water is very deep. I've ventured out there only once alone and found the currents treacherous and the predators alarming. In the bay the rockbed is covered in a variety of seaweeds, some of which are beautiful to look at. But the growth makes a good home for a number of dangerous species of sea-life. Dangerous for me, that is, so I don't dive unless I have to. And I don't linger in the bay because the turbulence caused by my swimming attracts some predators, apart from the silverfins, if I'm too slow.

I was almost across, nearing the long rock wall which projects to the edge of the bay, when I saw the myriad tentacles suddenly shooting up from the deep crevice there. I had no hope of escaping them. There was barely enough time to take a good, big breath before they were twining about my legs and body and dragging me down so rapidly that the water roared past my ears and seethed about my body almost painfully. Tentacles thicker than my arms and of a green which is almost the color of the water until they come close enough to see the pinkish flecks and the long, translucent spines on the inner sides. Now the spines were flattened against me but they are capable of injecting a powerful paralytic which no creature on this world can resist. Dragged down into the crevice, I had a momentary sight of that huge, terrible maw, rimmed with cilia, and then I was being tucked inside it and into the side-pouch where Juno keeps paralyzed but still-living prey until she needs it. For me, she gathers a bubble of air there and replenishes it if need be so that I don't suffocate. I suppose I could be described as her pet.

I call her Juno because, on this planet, she's a goddess if ever there was one. And she's vast, her species being the largest living creature on this planet. She's a kind of mollusc, I suppose, an immense clam with tentacles. Her shell, as near as I can make out, is bigger than the wreck of my ship, at least 40 meters at its broadest and about 30 meters from maw to rear. The maw, huge as it is, doesn't spread from one side of the shell to the other and the tentacles fold into caverns on each side of it. She has legs of some kind, though I've never seen those. She's able to move about slowly and can anchor herself to the bedrock with them. This crevice is her home and this bay is her personal territory. Not that she depends on the bay for her food. Often she fixes herself at the mouth of the crevice and catches suitable denizens of the deep sea. Silverfins, lucky for me, are part of her diet but most of the bay she harvests carefully, as a farmer would select from herds for particularly favored food, thinning those herds when necessary and keeping the bay's ecology carefully balanced. On this planet all ecologies are carefully balanced. And Juno and her kind are important parts of the "planetary mind." I call it that because I don't know what else to call it. The same way as I've made up names for most of the species I've come across here, names like "silverfins," "greenshells,""grapefloaters" and "sea-lice." So "planetary mind" is my description for it.

Juno is intelligent. She doesn't think as I do or have my values in a lot of ways, but she's intelligent. She and her kind were once servants or facilitators—and, seemingly, still are—for an even more intelligent race. Her species may even have been bred to a particular purpose. I suspect it was to maintain the ecological balances.

Juno and her kind aren't alone when they control things. There are other creatures, of several varieties, on the land which work in the same way. But Juno's kind seem to have the final say about what goes on here. I don't know where or what the master race are. Juno's explanation is limited, perhaps because the translator that we use is limited. She says they "rest," but whether that means they're dead or hibernating I can't tell. And maybe it means something else. I often think about that.

The pouch where Juno puts me is very dark, though I see a little because of the sunlight which shows faintly through the shell near her maw. The membrane is as tough as any leather but it's soft and warm because Juno is a warm-blooded creature. Her body temperature is about 85 degrees Fahrenheit although it rises to almost 90 when she's ready to "mate." I spent some time in this pouch when I first arrived on this planet and I grew very used to Juno's delicate prodding and fondling of me. In the beginning, when I didn't realize what she was, it was that fondling which kept me reassured and sane. She has fingers of a kind on some of her tentacles, soft and sensitive fingers which tell her a great deal about what she feels with them. Some of her tentacles also have eyes and ears of a kind and she likes to look at me, to play with my body and to listen to me talk.

Sometimes, though not as often as I'd like, Juno tucks the translator into the pouch with me and we communicate more completely. That translator is a piece of technology

which truly impresses me. It's a black ovoid, a little larger
than my head but shaped to fit against the lip of Juno's shell.
She does a complicated tapping with the tips of two tentacles against it and it makes sounds which come out as talking. I have to listen hard to make sense of the sounds
sometimes because I think it may have been made to trans-
late a different kind of voice than mine. But we manage. It
made sighing noises at me for a long time, when I first
came, because I didn't realize what it was. But I had a fever,
you see, and I talked a great deal while I was ill. That contraption analyzed the sounds I made and repeated a great
many of them back at me when I was well enough to understand. So, as soon as I woke up to what it was, we experimented a great deal, and then Juno and I could talk after
a fashion. I make it sound simple but it wasn't then. Now
both of us are practiced at it and we make more sense. She
likes it that I'm intelligent and explains a lot about this
world.

Perhaps I should tell you, in case you're wondering,
that I'm First Scout Manion Timbry, of the Exploratory
Ship *Rani*. If you bother to look up the files you'll find out
more about me but none of that matters any more. Now I'm
"the alien" on this world. Juno accepts "Juno" from me
and I accept "Alien" from her. I like it that way.

As First Scout, my task was to bring the Probe ship
down from *Rani*, fly over the terrain and beam information
back, then return while the scientists correlated the data and
made sense of it. I came down through the upper atmosphere without difficulties, opened out the air-flight fins and
activated the jets to begin exploring. Then I began an east-
west flight. Very simple and no problems. I was very high
so I dropped down in order to give the cameras a better
view and coasted along for fully ten minutes before I ran
into trouble. I ran into a cloud of insects which I call razorlegs. They're quite small but they move about in huge

white clouds sometimes. When crushed, they have sticky juices which can be used like glue and I sometimes find this useful. But they blocked the jets, wrecked the efficiency of the exterior instruments and sealed up the planetary-landing gear before I realized what the white cloud was and how densely it was packed with little bodies. I had to fly on what little instrumentation I had left, which wasn't much, and I couldn't reactivate the main thrusters to take me back up into orbit because the exterior sensors wouldn't operate and the computer became confused. I tried to crash-land on what looked like a suitable plain but I overshot it wildly because I was gliding, you see. I'd slowed up considerably and thought I might survive if I landed in the sea. But I didn't quite make it. I hit the rock barriers above the beach where I now find food, was deflected downward and bounced along the immense rockwall of Juno's bay. The stabilizers and the harness saved my life but I was knocked unconscious, broke two ribs and bruised one shoulder so badly that my right arm was almost useless for two days.

When I came to and managed to extricate myself from the harness, I had little instrumentation to tell me what my position was and no exterior vision. I already knew that the air was compatible with human breathing equipment and I hoped I wasn't underwater, so I managed to open the outer hatch with some difficulty and found out that the ship was on solid rock, set at a slight angle and rolled on one side. The fins were sheared off and I never attempted to clear the jets. I tried to radio for help but the radio was damaged. And while I was standing there, thinking that the ship might be able to trace me, I noticed that the rocks were alive with little black beetle-things and slimy little creatures which I've called sea-slugs although I've since found them to be more like worms. They bite and the bacteria give one a nasty fever. One crawled into my boot and bit me while I was getting back through the hatch. A few hours later, I had a terrible fever and was so delirious that I walked out onto the rocks unprotected. And Juno found me, knew I wasn't a "normal" thing from hers or anyone else's territory and was interested enough to see what I was all about. She recognized technology and she soon realized I was alien—so she brought the translator, a device she'd never used but knew all about. I was sick for quite a while and, by the time I was allowed to go back to the Probe ship, it was thickly covered by a hard, yellow-green substance which Juno had exuded and camouflaged it with. She, very wisely, decided that one human being was quite enough and didn't want my ship found by any others of my kind. It was also infested with the black beetle-things but they're harmless to me and I soon got rid of them. Juno straightened the ship up for me as much as she could and I've grown quite used to the slight tilt of the floor.

Juno educated me about the ecology as much as she was able. The rest I learned and am still learning, for myself. Everything is balanced and dependent on those balances in order to survive yet remain the same. My ship had all I really needed apart from food. I learned to eat greenshells and certain of the berries which grow on the high rocks, I learned to avoid predators and dangerous shellfish and I learned to avoid needless destruction of the environment in order that Juno, on whom I was very dependent at first, didn't decide I was too much of a nuisance to keep about. She taught me about the greenshell oil when the sea-lice became dangerous to me, she taught me about the little rock-growths which I nurture to keep the beetles from becoming a nuisance and which the sea-slugs abhor and she taught me about the things which could be eaten and which were poisonous. Sometimes she still finds me choice tidbits which she collects from the ocean. So I'm glad to remain her pet. I have the ship's medical computer to provide me with anti-viral serums and anti-bacterial creams if I need them, it can do most minor operations and look after my teeth and I'm probably healthier now than I was eight years ago. I have thousands of books and a huge collection of music in the memory banks, I can synthesize minor material needs and I'm enlarging the hydroponics systematically. The computer can play a good game of chess and conduct quite a stimulating conversation if I need one and my work on the rock-pools keeps me busy for a great deal of the time at present. Juno is interested in the rockpools and makes good suggestions. And her fondling isn't all experimental. She finds my sexuality of interest and I've learned to enjoy her attentions with a few fantasies of my own thrown in.

There are no tides of a lunar nature because there are no moons and the co-axial tilt of the planet is small and fairly rapid so that changes of season aren't very noticeable. The gravity here is slightly less than on my home-world and I've had no problems with the air so I've adapted quite easily. I don't really need clothes and I can make strong shoes from one of the grasses; I have the ship which will remain long after I've gone and I know how to survive in this particular territory. But the most important thing for me is that I've learned to like it here.

I thought she'd pulled me down to her side-pouch to tell me that she was leaving to mate and deposit her eggs. She does that every four years and evidently travels for quite a long distance to the place where she selects a mate because she's usually away for about 40 days. She told me about the whole procedure once and it seemed a very cut-and-dried business which I won't go into. But that wasn't what she wanted to tell me about at all.

Another Probe ship had flown over an area of the planet five days before and gone again. But, the day before, it had landed, quite close to the area where I tried for a crash landing. On the plains. She knew because of the "planetary mind."

I was very excited and discussed the whole business with her in great detail. She, in whatever way she does it, consulted with her own kind and certain of the dry land watchers. We all agreed that I must go to the Probe.

So, an hour later, my body coated with a mixture of two kinds of repellent oil and my old uniform and boots on, my beard cut and my hair braided, I took what I needed and put on my backpack. I closed the hatch of my home, took a long look at the work I'd done on the rockpools and then walked along the rock wall to the beach, carefully avoiding all the healthy growth of the rock weed.

Where the beach began—such beautiful, innocent-looking white sands—there's a huge growth of yellowspines, elegant and delicate to look at but quite deadly to touch. Among them are the concealed burrows of nasty little ankle-snappers, also quite deadly, so these had to be avoided as I picked my way through the growth. Beyond them, several sandwhippers had made nests in the dunes and I ran across these as lightly as I could in boots, hearing them hiss and whip their long arms out across the sands behind me. They live on the little sandpickers which live among the rocks which, in turn, prey on the black beetle-things and sea-slugs. It was already after midday and a bad time to be on the beach unless you're cautious and fleetfooted. There are crawlers and rockspiders, sandwhippers and bluescorpions to watch out for and the birdlike daggerbills are about looking for lunch. So I ran and leapt, zig-zagging through the danger spots and arriving at the rocks in a lather of sweat because of the oil and my uniform and tension at the danger.

The rocks, despite their population of assorted weed-eaters, crawlers and rockspiders, are safer because it's easier to see what you're stepping on. There are a couple of growlies living in the fissures but most of the growly population live at the farther end of the beach so there's little likelihood of being attacked unless it's mating season or they're rearing young. Young growlies make good eating if you're quick with a steel spear as I am. I reached the top of the rocks with my uniform soaked with sweat, moved carefully but quickly through the trees, keeping a sharp eye out for any little denizens which feed on the fleshy leaves or on each other. I came out into the rocky area where the strangely twisted bushes with the delicious-looking but poisonous fruit-clusters grow. This area isn't too dangerous but there are a multitude of insects which can give painful stings unless you're coated with repellent oil.

And there was the frightening rockmonster waiting for me.

I call them rockmonsters because, when they hunker down to deceive their prey, they look like big, brown rocks with greenish-gray grass growing in patches on them. They're as big as an elephant but squat and much heavier, their skin being finely plated and smooth as a snake's scales. The "grass" is camouflage, more like soft spines than grass when you see it close up. I'd never seen one as close as this before since they prey on the grass eaters of the plains and don't come too close to the sea unless it's necessary. He lowered his huge head at me and peered with his little yellow eyes, grunting in the way that Juno had told me he would. I grunted in reply then ran to him quickly and climbed onto his skull and over onto his back while he snorted alarmingly. I barely had time to take a grip of the "grass" at his shoulders before he was moving off. For such a large animal he could move quickly and the terrain seemed to speed by. But the ride was uncomfortable and I had to keep my head down in case I was spotted by a daggerbill, flocks of which were flying over the area in search of food.

Visually, this planet—or what I've seen of it—is very beautiful. The mountains to the west are blue and towering and sometimes a trace of snow appears at their caps. And the plains are glorious with color. Parts of the area are heavily forested with a variety of trees which have leaves of blue or red or bright yellow or green, some of them covered in blossoms. Some of those blossoms and colored leaves are insects but you can't tell until they move to attack. There are expanses of colored grasses in every hue and great clumps of the most gorgeously colored flowers of so many different types that one's eyes become confused. Both the grasses and the flowers are deceptive. Some of the plants are poisonous or catch small insects and some aren't plants at all but wonderfully disguised creatures. I've watched a whole stretch of mixed grasses suddenly move and seethe as they seized and devoured a meal, and a veritable mass of flowers reposition themselves in order to catch the unwary. They prey on each other or live in mutual protection, they maintain their own balances with disguises or strange protective devices and the orders never change. It's wonderful, impressive and often frightening. There are so many different species of animals, insects and plants that I've given up trying to count them. And most things are deadly to humans. At that time of day, without the protection of the rockmonster, I wouldn't have survived for long despite the repellent oils, my uniform and the solid boots.

He thundered through that beautiful, everchanging countryside for what semed a very long time, although I suppose it was for little more than an hour. Then, beyond the trees and thickets, I could see the Probe, an alien monster totally out of keeping with that countryside, sitting out in the middle of a small prairie of needlegrass. The needlegrass isn't a real problem if you have strong boots, but it's in that type of grass that the little razorlegs have their earthly domain. Razorlegs and needlegrass are symbiotes and couldn't survive without each other. The Probe was of the vertical-landing type, unlike mine. But it was from a Federation Exploratory Expedition because I could see the familiar blue letters etched into the sides.

Even the rockmonster didn't dare to enter that little prairie at this time of day. Clouds of daggerlegs rose and fell near the Probe and the lower part of the ship was white with their bodies as they tried to kill the invading monster. The Probe's boosters might be inoperable but the outer instruments probably weren't and the radio would have contacted the orbiting ship long ago. If this Probe got into trouble it was possible that another Probe, better prepared for the conditions, might be sent down to rescue the crew of the first Probe. I looked skyward and realized that the rockmonster was doing the same. We were both looking for signs of the midafternoon rain.

At this time of the year, when the warmer season peaks, the air becomes very dry and the breezes passing across the land from the west take up the moisture from the soil rapidly so that it becomes very dry, too. But regularly, every midafternoon, there's a shower of rain. It lasts very briefly but it's sufficient to prevent the plants from drying out too much and, without it, this area of the land would become a desert at this time of year. Weather and life on this planet are so interlocked, so regular and foreseeable, that I've often wondered if, in some marvelous way, the weather's controlled by some kind of technology established by the master race which I know nothing of. Juno can't—or won't—comment on the weather beyond stating that "it's always so." I may be wrong but I think that much that's established here isn't left to chance and the vagaries of nature. I have a conviction that it's deliberate.

We waited for half an hour before the change began. Insects began settling to find protection, little animals began scuttling into burrows or nests made in the long grasses and the daggerbills began to disperse to their treetops. Then, rolling in from the north, came turbulent rainclouds as black as you could ever see, boiling across the sky to blot out the sun. The razorlegs don't like rain either and retire to the needlegrass for protection. The facilitators were determined to get me to that ship as soon as could be managed and had even calculated time and weather.

We waited for another ten minutes while the sky became so dark that it was as though thick twilight had arrived and every species visible to me, as I sat there on the rockmonster's back, was preparing for the storm. That impressed me immensely. I took my old work helmet out of my backpack and checked the torch set in the forehead band, knowing that I'd have to move fast when the time came.

Wind rose sharply to a brisk gale just before the first big drops began to splash down and then the rain poured in earnest. The rockmonster grunted and dropped its head. I knew that was my cue. I switched on my forehead torch, climbed down via his skull and began running as hard as I could. I was soaked in moments and the rain driving into my face on that gale half-blinded me. I didn't dare be too cautious. I ran down the hill and across that needlegrass as fast as my legs would pump.

I suppose I ran like that for about five minutes to reach the Probe but it seemed longer. The razorlegs had vanished before the rain and I was very conscious of the needlegrass crunching beneath my boots and whipping at my covered lower legs, my feet beginning to splash in gathering water within a short time because the soil couldn't take it in quickly enough. The gale and the rain didn't last for long. I was barely halfway across when the wind began to drop and the rain eased off. The sky began to lighten and, by the time I reached the Probe, the sun was beginning to shine in the north again. I'll never forget that run for as long as I live.

The crew had seen my torch and recognized a running man well before I arrived. As I neared the Probe the hatch lowered and a metal ladder began to descend. I climbed it with the last of my strength, registered startled faces at the hatchway and climbed in to collapse on the plasticized floor and gasp in exhaustion. They drew the ladder in and closed the hatch before seeing to me. I almost blacked out for a few moments and was only vaguely aware of being carried into what was apparently a rest-area and dumped on a padded couch. They dragged my boots off hastily and, when I was able to sit up and speak, they were busy spraying them with something to kill the razorlegs and a stray slimewriggler which clung to the soles and part of the uppers despite the rain.

I said in my best Universal, "Manion Timbry, First Scout from the *Rani*—Migod, I can't believe my luck—I thought I was stranded here for good!"

I managed to get my backpack off and was struggling with the chinstraps of my helmet when they began spraying me with that insect-killer, giving me a wide berth. The stuff made me sneeze like fury. I was still sneezing when they shoved me into the needle shower and helped me to strip. I bathed thoroughly, while my uniform, boots and backpack were shoved through the ship's sterilizer and sonic-cleanser. I was glad I'd anticipated that. Clean and feeling much restored physically, I was allowed to dress and braid my hair before the questions began.

They were, understandably, excited at my appearance. The reports of my disappearance during the preliminary examination of the planet were apparently well known. The planet had drawn a lot of interest despite the alarming conditions recorded by the computers aboard the *Rani*. There was no other planet yet found in this galactic sector which was suitable for human colonization. It was still thought, by some idiots in the Federation, that, if a site could be established for the scientists, it might still be possible to bring conditions under control enough to make a colony a viable proposition. They wanted to know how and where I'd survived and I told them a little, not mentioning Juno or

anything to do with the "planetary mind." They might have
thought I was mad.

I was able to get some information about their Probe
between answering questions. The ship had been prepared
for insects and a great many other conditions here. It was
jammed with experimental equipment and the crew were
prepared to stay for some time before activating the spe-
cially prepared boosters and returning to the orbiting ship.
They were almost ready to clear the surrounding area of life
in order to put up bubble housing and laboratories. I thought
of the damage they could do over even a short period and
knew that Juno and the other facilitators wouldn't like that
at all. But I said nothing.

Twilight was coming on before they'd finished with me
temporarily. I reported, via the radio, to the orbiting ship's
commander and caused another stir. Then I was given a
meal. The contents of my backpack had been examined and
seemed harmless enough. They took my old log and were
disappointed that I'd neglected to record anything after the
crash. It was thought that my knowledge of conditions here
would be invaluable and they planned a big question-session
for the next day. I pleaded exhaustion, was given a sleeping
bag in one of the equipment holds and retired to sleep.

There were eight people aboard, all of them scientists
or technicians. I slept for two hours and it was dark when
I awoke, feeling very much restored.

They'd already discovered that it was safer to work at
night when the insects were less active. Five had put on protective worksuits and were busy outside, getting ready to put
up the first of the housing bubbles. Their lights must have
been visible from anywhere on the plains and they were
already having difficulties with yellowlegs, which look
something like moths but aren't. They were very determined people. It would have done no good to explain to
them that they should leave now while they could. I'd tried

that earlier and they'd pooh-poohed me gently, as though my years alone here had affected my rationality.

I had no difficulty getting into the control room. They were all too busy outside and in the lower levels to notice me creeping about in the semi-dark. The little device which Juno had given me looked so innocent. It appeared to be a piece of common, clear quartz with ordinary striations about its rough surface. I placed it where it wouldn't be found easily, thinking that it could be put to more extensive work than that which Juno had envisaged. I then began a hasty programming of the automatics. They were very similar to the ones on my Probe. Unfortunately, while I was working on that, one of the technicians walked in and demanded to know what I was doing, so I had to kill him with my knife. The plan was not as Juno had suggested any longer. I liked my idea better. I did a very good job with the automatics, as it turned out.

I rendered the override controls inoperable by pouring razorleg glue all over the keyboard of the ship's computer. It dries very rapidly and needs a particular kind of solvent to dissolve it. I knew that from working to clear some of the window areas on my own ship. I waited until it had set smooth and then got out of there fast. As I ran through the second level I saw the technician's protective suit and paused long enough to drag it on over my uniform. A warning bell began ringing as I ran down to the lower level. I rushed to the hatch, almost knocking two people down as they came from the equipment hold. I swung down the ladder, bellowing to the others who were struggling with sheets of plastex and poles amid swarms of yellowlegs in the light of portable floodlamps.

"Get aboard! The Probe's about to take off! Quickly! Get aboard!"

The siren began to blast then. For a moment they just gaped at me and then began running for the ladder. Two of them made it before it began to slide upward. The others gathered below, watching it vanish in great agitation. The successful climbers scrambled through the hatch and it slid closed. The three remaining were shouting in panic.

I shouted, "Get away from the boosters or you'll be fried!" and dragged the woman back. The two men were staring at me in horror through their face-protectors but they began backing. I grabbed one of the portable flood-lights, grasped the woman by the arm and dragged her with me onto the needlegrass, running hard as the boosters roared to life. The wave of heat and pressure almost knocked us down as we fled. The two men followed us, shouting in panic. When I paused to look back, the Probe was rising steadily, leaving the area where poles and plastic sheeting and a haze of yellowlegs still shone in the light of two floodlights. The woman began to sob hysterically.

"Listen to me!" I shouted. "If you keep close to me and do as you're told, we might survive and get back to my wreck! Night's the safest time for traveling here but there are still plenty of dangers. We can't linger! I have friends who'll help, but we must hurry!"

They were incredulous that they were stranded, shouting and asking questions. The woman was still sobbing. I didn't dare wait. All I could think about were the nightstalk-ers which might be about. I let the woman go and started walking briskly, playing the floodlight on the needlegrass ahead. They began following, afraid to be left in the dark. The Probe was, by then, gone into the darkness of the night. The roar of the boosters could still be heard and would, I hoped, frighten nightstalkers away.

"We must run!" I shouted at the others. "There are hunting animals about! Follow me closely or I'll leave you to fend for yourselves!"

They ran, puffing and gasping after a few minutes, lumbering clumsily behind me. I couldn't abandon them—I suppose I felt sorry for them. So I ran slowly, shouting at them to keep up and wanting to run fast to save my own hide. I saw two black shadows pacing us as we finally neared the hill. I shone the floodlight full at them and bellowed. They were wolflizards, their armored hides shining black and glossy, and they retreated from the light and noise much to my relief.

Halfway up the hill, I stopped and waited for the others to catch up with me. They were almost exhausted already.

"I have a friend, a big animal, waiting to carry me. When I make grunting noises at him you must make the same noises, do you understand? He may accept us all. If he doesn't, then you're all dead!" I told them. Yellowlegs had begun droning about us by then and I could hear the yipping of slashers and the squawk of the more dangerous nighthawks.

He was there, waiting at the top of the hill. He flinched at the light and opened his awful jaws in alarm so I played it on the earth and made the noises at him. He grunted back at me but the stupid woman squealed. I struck her about the shoulders and said, "Grunt, you fool!"

They obeyed me, still gasping for breath. The rockmonster lowered his head doubtfully and I shoved the woman ahead of me. He reared his head in alarm but some more grunting reassured him and I finally got the three of them up on his back. I was terrified that he'd change his mind and dispose of us all. But he didn't. I turned the floodlight off, said, "Hold on hard!" and the rockmonster wheeled and started moving over the terrain.

Migod, what a ride it was! Those stupid idiots moaned and clung to me rather than to the rockmonster. I had to shout at them to be quiet several times before they ceased their noise. Nightstalkers, redeyes I think, began pacing us as we headed down toward the coast. They were too wary of the rockmonster to get too close and a flash from the

Illustrated by Ferenc Temil Temesvari

floodlight frightened them further away but they still paced us. Nighthawks began flapping over our heads for a short time and insects struck our protective suits frequently. Without those suits we wouldn't have survived. But the nightstalkers wouldn't give up. They wouldn't attack a rock-monster but they could hear and see that we were on his back, thanks to the older man who sobbed worse than the woman.

I lost the older man to the nightstalkers as we finally neared the cliffs. I had to. If they'd been close when the rock-monster abandoned us above the beach, none of us would have escaped them. And he was the weakest, the most expendable of them. I gave him a shove and he fell off. I heard him screaming for a few moments before they got him. His worksuit would have been no protection from their terrible teeth and he must have been torn to shreds in moments.

The rockmonster stopped above the cliffs and aban-doned us the moment we were off his back. I put the flood-light on and led the way to the rocks hastily. It took patience to get them down to the beach because they climbed so poorly and were terrified of the rockspiders. Without the worksuits they'd both have been dead by the time I got them down to the beach. Despite my warnings, we had a fight with a sandwhipper on the beach because one of them ignored a hole in the sand. I had to use my knife to kill it and free the man's legs from the twining arms. But I finally got them to my ship and that was a real relief.

I stripped off the worksuit and my clothes, ignoring their moans and laments, took the floodlamp and went to sig-nal Juno. Her tentacles came snaking up immediately.

She was quite pleased that I'd managed so well and pleased that I'd survived, but she didn't like the idea of other humans living with me. When I told her about sending the Probe back with the crystal she was puzzled. It took

time to explain that the orbiting ship would find the Probe
and that the crystal would destroy all, rather than part, of
the Exploratory Expedition. She liked that concept when
she finally understood. I told her to allow a few more hours
before she activated the crystal rather than doing it straight
away and she saw the sense of that. All I knew about the crystal was that it "melted things." I was intrigued to know
what effect that would have on space-warp drives and power
centers aboard a large spaceship.

Well, there's not much more to say about the adventure.
I was working on the rockpools when the splash of light
flared briefly in the clear blue sky the following afternoon.
There was a bright speck visible there for several hours but
it had gone by evening.

I got on quite well with the man once he'd decided to
quit reviling me as a traitor to my own kind. He was younger
than I but not careful enough. About ten days later he got
himself stung by a tiny rockspider because he didn't check
the rocks carefully before wandering about on them in bare
feet. He died of paralysis an hour later despite anything the
medical computer could do. The woman was too afraid to
leave the ship for a long time after that. I think she calculated to establish my permanent protection by offering her
body rather than because she wanted me as a man. She was
quite attractive and I enjoyed having her about for a while.
But she was a fool, too. I tried to teach her things but she
wasn't prepared to learn about surviving and moaned about
her miseries a great deal. She helped me with the rockpools
several times and I saw Juno's eyestalks watching her once
or twice. The woman would sit on the rocks waiting for me
while I went looking for food and, one day, I got back to
find her gone. I suspect that Juno ate her but I haven't
brought the subject up because Juno was a bit peculiar with
me while the woman was about. Now that I'm alone again,
Juno treats me as she did before and I'm glad of that.

I did quite well out of the adventure on the whole. After a bit of persuasion, Juno managed to get the poles and the plastex bubble-housing from the little prairie for me. It took eight rockmonsters and lot of little animals I call pinkears to drag the equipment overland during the violent rains of the season-change. It took me an entire year to erect it on the rockwall and now I have a well-protected area where I've established soil and started a proper vegetable garden. The rockpools are finished and the greenshell farming is beginning to pay off, too. And I have another friend, a rock-monster I named Grumpy. He comes and grunts at me from the cliffs sometimes and I go hunting for meat with him. I think, though I can't be sure, that he's the same rockmon-ster who took me on the adventure. Oh, and I have the work-suit which is very useful when I go beyond the bay. And I have the floodlight which is a rechargeable one and far more powerful than the helmet-torch was.

Now there's no sign of the place where the boosters of that Probe burned a hole in the needlegrass prairie. I saw it recently with Grumpy and the needlegrass shows no blem-ish at all. Not that the balances were upset much but every little bit counts. But there's something on the far side of the prairie that I didn't notice before. It's an inverted V-shape in the mountain on the other side, too perfectly formed to be natural. Juno refuses to discuss it but I think it may be evidence of the master race. I'm not anxious to disturb their peace.

If, someday, another Exploratory Expedition comes this way, it won't survive for long. The "planetary mind" knows about humans and how to deal with them now.

But Juno suggested that I make a message, anyway, something that can be given to any such intruders as a warn-ing. I don't know how it's to be given to them but, no doubt, there are ways. So I've made this recording. I may be long gone by the time anyone hears it—if they ever hear it—but it might clarify a few things. This planet's ecologies aren't benign to humans and never will be. And these ecologies won't wait about quietly for anyone to change them or destroy them. Everything is interlinked and, if you disturb any small part of it, there'll be a reaction from the whole. There's an awareness of possible intrusion from off-planet now and you can bet that there'll be no waiting to discourage intruders from now on. I survive because I fit in and don't disturb the patterns. And because I'm Juno's pet. And I love the perfection of all the interaction here.

So keep off if you value your hides. This is very private property.

Writing and Selling Your First Novel

by
Dave Wolverton

About the Author

Dave Wolverton lives in Provo, Utah, and among other things, writes. He also works for a magazine, and in the past he has been a number of other things, including a prison guard.

In 1987, L. Ron Hubbard Presents Writers of The Future, Vol. III *published his "On My Way to Paradise,"* and several things have followed. One, he was the second winner of the L. Ron Hubbard Gold Award; Two, he was immediately signed by one of the best agents in SF; Three, he immediately signed a three-novel contract with Bantam Books, and since then he has done other fabulous things. On My Way to Paradise, *the novel that grew out of his WOTF story, was copiously—and accurately—praised by such critics as Orson Scott Card. His second novel,* Serpent Catch, *is just out.*

And along the way we decided it was time to start naming some home-grown judges for the Writers of The Future Contest; writers who had gotten their start with us, and now were obviously headed nowhere but up. Dave is the first of these, signing on in 1990.

$\mathbf{W}$riting your first novel can be fun, rewarding, and profitable. It can also be scary, depressing, and a lot of hard work. I wrote my first novel about two years ago, and I have several friends who are also new novelists. By answering some of the questions that I'm frequently asked, maybe I can make it a little easier for you.

What should I write? Many people get confused on this point—you may want to write science fiction, but you've heard that fantasy or romances are easier to write and they pay more. The rumors are lies. Competition is tight in every field. I know writers in the fields of romance, fantasy, horror, science fiction, and mainstream—and I know how much they make. The typical advance for a first novel in any of these fields seems to run from $2500–$7000. The size of the advance has more to do with the publisher's current resources and faith in you as an author than with the genre. Writing is hard work. Don't invest time in projects you don't like. If you want to write science fiction, write it. If you want to be the next Tolkien, throw your heart into it.

No matter what field you write in, make sure that your first novel shows your best work. Don't be afraid to write a big story. I believe that you will generate far more excitement that way than if you write a small, safe book.

Do I need an agent to sell a book? No. To sell a book you need to send it to a publisher and impress the editors enough so that they want to buy it. A good agent can't hurt, but getting a good agent is often difficult for an unestablished writer. Once a publisher makes you an offer on a book, then get an agent—or at least find some established authors who will give you some advice on negotiating a book contract.

How can I better the odds of impressing an editor?
Keep your publisher's needs in mind. One editor once said that he received a manuscript, special delivery, that contained a box of doughnuts and some hot cocoa mix. The author wrote a note saying, "Look, you don't know me, but I'll bet your days are hectic and you're tired. Why don't you sit down, relax, and look at my manuscript?" The editor did, and bought the book. You don't have to go that far, but it can't hurt.

Generally speaking, your publisher plans to lose money on your first novel or plans to make very little. The expenses for a publisher can be staggering—editing, typesetting, marketing, production, promotion, cover art, distribution, the cost of upkeep on offices—all are a heavy drain, and the publisher won't begin receiving money from sale of your novel until months after it has hit the street.

The upshot of all of this is that when a publisher prints your first novel he is making a commitment to start you in a career. He is making a long-term investment in you. As a result, you need to show that you are willing to make a long-term investment both in your career and in your publisher. Here are some ways to do that:

1) Show your editors that you know your market and that you are committed to making it in that market. I've heard authors say, "Well, I'm a fantasy/horror/romance writer who likes to dabble in comedy, poetry and screenplays." Such talk scares editors. They can't launch a person in a career if that author plans to take off in six directions at once. Few authors are prolific enough to handle more than one or two career paths.

2) Show that you are committed to your publisher. Don't be too eager to send out multiple copies of your first novel to a dozen publishers in hopes of starting a bidding war; if you lure a publisher into paying more than your book is worth, you will find it difficult to get your next novel published by anyone.

Once you sell a book to your publisher, start pitching your next novel to them soon. They may not take it—some publishers want to see how the first book sells before investing more into your career. Still, you should let them know that publishing a single novel was not your life goal.

Every publishing house has a contract that asks you to promise to let them bid on your next novel before you send it to other publishers. My advice is that you sign it, though you normally need to modify the clause so that they guarantee to give you a quick reply on submissions. If you plan to write in other genres, you may want to modify this clause to exclude works outside a specific genre.

3) Do your best to publish frequently. You can build your name recognition fastest if you keep books on the store shelves. Publishing one novel every six to eight months is about right, though many authors can't write that fast. If you can't write that fast, try to get some short stories or nonfiction out to major magazines so that your name isn't forgotten.

Are some publishers better than others? Yes. When selecting a potential publisher, there are many things to consider. My first rule of thumb is that you should take a look at the books you like. Do several of them come from the same publisher? If so, chances are that you and one of the editors at that publishing house have similar tastes. Try to identify that editor and then send your manuscript to him or her.

Some publishers are more committed to a certain field. For example, certain houses may deal almost exclusively in horror and have very few slots open for science fiction. Look at how many books they publish in your field, check out magazines in your field to see how heavily your prospective publishers advertise their novels. If you can, ask some of the publishers' authors how widely their books get distributed. You'd be surprised how much difference a couple thousand extra sales to Australia and New Zealand will make in your royalty statements.

If the publisher that you want most doesn't want you, don't worry about it too much. Most publishers will treat you well as long as they like your work and it continues to sell.

Do I need to send the whole novel? Generally, publishers will buy a novel based on sample chapters and an outline if the author is established. Some publishers say they *never* want to see a whole manuscript—they don't have time to read them and they take up too much room. My advice is to send the first 60 pages or so and an outline. If the editors like it, they can ask you to send the rest of the manuscript.

It's very important to submit a good outline on your first novel. The outline can be any length. Two or three pages is adequate, but some authors submit outlines that are 20 pages long. I have a rule about writing novels: Grab your audience quick, then do all you can to make them keep the book open until they reach the end. A good outline should do the same. If your outline looks dull and lifeless to you, think how bad it will look to the editor. An outline should make the book sound so great that the editor can't wait to buy it.

Once I sell a novel, then what? Your publisher will promote the novel with various marketers. It helps if you promote the novel, too, as long as you don't become obsessed. Write up some press releases and send them to local newspapers. See if you can get on local talk shows on television or on the radio. Put sample chapters up on bulletin boards on computer networks. Contact book reviewers (if your editor hasn't) and make sure they get review copies. Contact local bookstores and let them know the book will be released, and when—they are nearly always happy to help arrange signings.

There are some things you should avoid doing. For example, many new authors feel that they don't get enough publicity from their publishers. As a rule, most publishers don't have the resources to promote first novels heavily. Do all that you can to promote your book yourself, but don't berate your editor or accuse them of shoddy promotion. It will aggravate your editor and I have seen it damage more than one career.

From the time you sell your book to the time of publication may be a year or more. Many writers become excited, anxious, unsure how their work will be received, and they quit writing during that period. Force yourself to write. Keep your skills sharpened.

What if my book bombs? Your book will almost never be as successful as you hope. Most new authors can handle low sales—it's to be expected when you're new. The average first novel only sells 10,000−15,000 copies.

Taking hits from the critics can be much more painful than low sales, even for well-established authors. One best-selling author I know, who normally sells half a million copies per book, says he can't bear to look in a newspaper—every time he does he finds another critic slamming his work.

When your first novel comes out, chances are that it will be subjected to a lot of scrutiny. Just about everyone is interested in a new author, but often the critics will compare your first novel to the best works by the finest authors in your field. Such comparisons are unfair. Give yourself time to grow. Never bother to respond to a critic. Art is subjective. It may well be that your taste and the critic's tastes are not the same. I know of at least one critic whose taste is so different from mine that I purposely avoid books that he recommends.

No matter how poorly your sales do or what the critics say, keep your chin up. Many of the best authors of our time started out with poor sales and bad reviews.

What if my book does well? Okay, so you hit the bestseller list and get some rave reviews. Count yourself fortunate. If you find it difficult to remain humble, pick up some of Shakespeare's later plays and read one. He can humble you right into the dust.

If your book does real well, your editor, some critics, and a lot of fans might well ask you to write a sequel. The artist within you may cringe at the thought, and you may find the task so repetitive and boring that you would ensure the failure of the sequel. The businessman within you may want to jump at the opportunity, and you might well justify writing a sequel for big money so that you can fund the rest of your writing career. The answer to this one is so personal and so important, that perhaps neither I nor anyone else should advise you one way or the other.

An Exultation of Tears

by
Ross Westergaard

About the Author

Ross Westergaard is a Canadian, a retired marine industry executive who writes full time. He has published over 200 articles, and has his first novel, a naval-historical work titled Midshipman Kirk, *due to be published. But "An Exultation of Tears" is his first science fiction story—despite years of reading science fiction.*

Ross lives on Denman Island in British Columbia, and is a part-time writing instructor at North Island College in nearby Courtenay.

* * *

Ross Westergaard's illustrator is Ferenc Temil Temesvari.

I leaned out of the cave-mouth, feet astraddle, feeling pebbles grate 'neath my sandals as I clenched the outcropping and searched for the *Blaze of Glory*. Shivering slightly in the morning coolness, I ignored the mutters, laughs and occasional curses of the people sorting Trade Goods and studied the flatland.

Below, the muddy Mackenzie River tortuously oozed its shallow path through the Sonoran Desert, the low shores a snake winding softly past the monotonous dunes. There. Faintly I heard the flailing beat of a paddlewheel echoing from the cliffs. I leaned farther in an effort to see the sternwheeler round the cliff-point, but drew back cautiously as footsteps padded closer behind me. Promotion was too easy with an unobtrusive push at the cave-mouth.

Cedric came close. Not too close—I was, after all, the Hereditary Captain and he was but the Purser.

"D'you see the boat yet, Eric?"

I ignored him. Protocol was that the Captain must speak first, and well he knew it. He'd been On Charge before: nothing too serious, but repetition could bring a charge of Insubordination or even Inciting to Mutiny—and the penalty was final. The Executive Officer, known by all simply as "Exxoh," would stand by the cave-mouth, ship's cutlass unsheathed, and solemnly declare:

"Under the Captain's orders, I open this Air Lock."

I would nod, point my swagger-stick at the culprit

pinioned by the Ship's Police, and say firmly, "Master-at-Arms, carry out the sentence."

The Police would rush the criminal to the cave-mouth and hurl him out, to tumble and clutch vainly and frenziedly for handholds as his shrieking diminuendo faded. Twice since I became Captain had I heard the sickening splash and a last scream as river-beasts tore the body asunder and the river stained red.

I turned, brushed my fur tunic casually, then took my Helmet of Office from the dusty ledge where I had set it, letting it dangle by the straps as I pretended to study the desert. Dull, rolling sand stretched to the horizon, sameness marred only by the rusting, crumpled wreckage of our Ancestors' ship, *Chariot of Destiny*—thrust tubes half buried in a dune, hull warped in an agonized twist.

Cedric, perhaps nervous about his unauthorized outburst, stood silent, hands clasped behind back in the prescribed position, apprehensively shrugging his shoulder strap into a more comfortable spot.

I leaned out again. Safe enough now, since no doubt others had observed us. There it was: a stubby stem, long gangplank raised high above the mud-gray water curling back along the low black hull. I cursed silently, enviously, that our Ancestors had lacked the foresight to remove the atomic engines from *Chariot of Destiny* and install them in something useful such as this river craft, instead of wasting time and material in futile attempts to make the colony ship spaceworthy again.

Cedric stiffened to Attention as I turned to him, donning the Helmet as I did so. I spoke in the tongue-thick Trade dialect, used only at the Time or when the 'Poids came by on a periodic inspection.

"Tell the Crew that the Trading Time is near."

"Aye aye, Sir!" He pulled a forelock—Gods, where had

Illustrated by Ferenc Temil Temesvari

that gesture originated?—and turned abruptly, breaking into a run and shouting as he did so.

Glad to be rid of the blaggard, I looked outward once more, and happy I was to have done so. A faint graying on the horizon became a trailing plume of smoke wisping back from the *Venturesome Virgin,* the flying machine constructed by the *Venturesome Voyager's* crew, and so disrespectfully named. As I watched, the great wings became visible, and the plume of smoke split asunder—one trailing from each whirling air-fan. The machine was moving quickly: her stokers must be sweating in the cramped engine pods slung between the wavering wings. I visualized the interior: a cavernous cargo hold jammed full with crates of vegetables and carefully selected artifacts from their old ship; forward the reserve coal tanks, then in the nose the control cabin with its monstrous wheels and cables. I, as Hereditary Captain, had been privileged to be given a tour through the flying machine—something none other of our company had done.

I looked downward to the *Blaze of Glory.* A curl of dirty water rolled along the low banks, setting the mangroves to swaying as the ship slowly neared the landing, gangplank hanging low like a great claw about to snatch the unprotected shore. A group of burly, nondescript deckhands cluttered her foredeck, each grasping a rope, capstan bar, or a spear to ward off marauding river-beasts. Beyond the thin haze from her single tall funnel, the *Venturesome Virgin* wheeled lumberingly into what little wind cooled the morning sands, and slowly her cumbersome landing skids—looking like huge talons—were cranked down.

The *Virgin* momentarily blocked Luna Dos—the name a heritage from Captain Juan Carlos of *Blaze of Glory*—second of our two moons hanging pale in the milk-blue sky. Then, a spray of sand obscured the wood and cloth fuselage so that the quivering wings seemed to grow from the dust.

As the sand settled, the aircraft slowly re-appeared, squatting heron-like on the ungainly skids, close by the moored *Blaze of Glory.*

I heard again the shuffling of feet near me, and smelt the musky scent of Marianne, my betrothed. Turning to smile at her, I saw Exxoh—even though I would have known of his presence from the asthmatic breathing. Slipping an arm about Marianne, I turned again to look outward with the others beside me. Far off another graying blurred the cloudless horizon, but this time it was not ship-men. The 'Poids were bringing their caravan to the Trading Place. I wondered dimly what manner of rare foods and wines were laden in their wind-wagons, and nearly speculated aloud, when Exxoh cleared his throat loudly.

"Yes, Exxoh?" I glanced at the old man, noticing his white hair and, as he opened his mouth to speak, his lessening teeth. 'Twould not be long hence before his mandatory Air Locking, I thought almost sadly.

He saluted. "Permission to open the Air Lock, Sir, and lower the Boarding Ladder?" Behind him I saw crewmen lifting the long coiled Ladder from the Deck.

"Carry on, Exxoh."

As he left to carry out his duties, I dropped my arm from Marianne's waist and took her warm hand in mine, whispering as I did so, "This will be a good Trading Time. See how the ship is low in the water? They must have had a good quarter's fishing. And the *Venturesome Virgin,*" Marianne blushed slightly, but I carried on regardless, "was flying low, so she too must be heavy laden with produce. A good thing, too," I frowned, "last quarter's Trading left us short of both fish and corn."

She ignored what I'd said. "What about the 'Poids, Eric? They frighten me, even though they act friendly. And the strange smell of their wind-wagons . . . ." She wrinkled her nose.

I squeezed her soft palm. "We need their foods and wines and cloth, Marianne. The fish from *Glory's* lakelands and the produce from *Virgin's* territories barely support us. As for the ores from our mine," I laughed bitterly, "a spearhead makes damn tough chewing!"

"There's meat from the dinolizards and woolybears," she objected, removing her hand with a jerk.

"Meat alone isn't enough," I snapped, exasperated, "the old books tell us that we need fish and greens to stay healthy. The foods and wines that the 'Poids bring make being healthy worthwhile. And," I added slowly, "we must always remember that this is *their* world—and all they ask from us are useless pieces from the old ships!"

My mind wandered to the legends of the Landings. The 'Poids—great hairy creatures, wearing nought but a sort of kilt similar to the ones we all wore now—had gathered by each ship where it had fallen, watching in silent semicircles as our surviving Ancestors limped and crawled from the starships' hulks. Our own Ancestors had passed on the tale. They'd been made to understand by the 'Poids that *this* was to be our Zone; the mineral-rich valley enclosed by impassable mountains, inhabited only by dinolizards, woolybears and a few leathery, timid birds—and accessible only through the cave.

The mile-wide beach of the Trading Place was also ours, perhaps because our Zone was deficient in nearly all but minerals and the ubiquitous dinolizards—ugly, savage creatures taller than a man, with a taste not unlike that of the yams the *Virgin* sometimes traded. The woolybears, scarcer and ten times as dangerous, inhabited the trackless wastes of rocks and boulders high in the mountains—and were hunted for their fur only in large, well-armed groups.

Voyager's crew had been allotted a fertile prairie, and the *Glory-Boys*, as they liked to style themselves, had been given the lakelands.

'Twas not long after the Landings that the Ancestors decided that the 'Poids were mildly telepathic, able to dimly read our minds and thus gabble a guttural form of English—which had perforce become the Trade dialect. Between themselves the 'Poids never spoke aloud, even at the Trading Place, but we were unable to receive. Occasionally an amused thought would drift past the perimeters of our minds, enclosing the condescending connotation of "Barbarian technicians (regressing?) (deteriorating?) (failed?)."

I moved aside with Marianne as the rumble of wagon wheels warned of the approach of our Trade goods. Out of the gloom appeared the ruffian Lowering Crew, trundling the massive beams, drums and cables of the winch; sledges over shoulders, one or two tossing a sly glance at Marianne as they crunched past, exuding a stale aroma of animal sweat. Behind them trudged men, women and youths with cart- or armloads of Trading material—meat, furs and metal.

The Boarding Ladder was now in place. The bearded Lowering Crew stood back, waiting for me to descend to the Trading Place and give the ceremonial All Clear. I fastened the Helmet straps and ambled to the Ladder. Speaking not a word, I carefully placed hands and feet on the worn-smooth rungs and began the hundred-foot drop.

My back muscles tautened involuntarily as the mottled cliff face rose past me. Tales of earlier days, when an arrow from the ground had hastened the descent of a Captain and sparked an outbreak of savage combat, ambushes and hand-to-hand fighting, had been related to me by my grandsire. Although I'd not been born at the time of the battles, I could visualize the great wind-wagons rumbling over the horizon, sails gleaming and wheel spokes glinting as they hurtled down on the embattled men.

Needles of brilliant energy had lanced from the wagons—dropping a *Glory-Boy* here in mid-thrust, freezing another with poised spear, slicing an upraised bludgeon like lard. Fighting had slowed, then ceased as the ship-men stared at the angry 'Poids.

The ultimatum: we had soiled our welcome as settlers on the 'Poids' world. Firearms were forbidden; future warfare would result in swift extinction. The 'Poids had glared all 'round once more, then had scrambled in their windwagons and vanished into the far reaches of the desert. Peace—albeit occasionally an uneasy one—had cast a benevolent shadow from that time on.

My foot jarred. Surprised, I looked about. My dark thoughts had carried me unseeing down the full span of the Ladder. I collected myself, turned the ritual full circle in the sand and scanned the Trading Place, the forbidding cliffs rising above the murky river and the distant dunes, then leaned back, cupped my hands and shouted, "All Clear!"

Instantly the cargovator came swaying down, two of the Lowering Crew demonstrating their contempt of heights by leaning casually overside with but one negligent hand clasping the rope rail. I turned to the waiting ship-men and 'Poids, bowed low and uttered the traditional greeting; "The *Chariot of Destiny* welcomes you in peace to the Trading Place."

A hubbub instantly shattered the silence as sweating stokers and deckhands heaved and struggled with crates of fruit, dried fish, vegetables and artifacts from the old ships. I wondered how the ancient hulks could still yield items of use—although nobody knew *what* the 'Poids would deem useful—then remembered that our own *Chariot* was even now a good third full of strange instruments and mysterious fittings. What would we use for Trade when at last the ships were empty, echoing hulks? Time would give the answer, I supposed, but now there was Trading to do.

The pounding of hammers and flapping of cloth told me that tables, benches and blankets were being laid out to hold Trade goods, even though I ignored the bustle of preparation.

Somewhere a fiddle squeaked rustily, and out of the corner
of my eye I saw Marianne walking lightly toward the music.
The young ones, still carefree, would begin a square dance
while Marianne and old Jeremy—coxswain of the sternwheeler—called the steps alternately. I glanced over in time
to see the sides of the 'Poids' wagon swing open and the canvas tops furl into tight white sausages, displaying the cases
of wines and fruits.

The Lowering Crew, having set up our tables, trundled
a two-wheeled cart to the wreck of *Chariot of Destiny* to
load preselected artifacts: the cargovator swayed aloft for
another load of coal, furs, iron utensils and dried 'lizard
haunches. A hodgepodge of aromas assailed my nostrils,
and involuntarily my mouth watered as I caught the tart bou-
quet of the 'Poids' red wines.

Hereditary Captains Alfonso Carlos and Charles
Nottingham-Hood strolled toward me, Helmets in hands to
indicate informality. Quickly I removed my own and walked
to meet them. A half-dozen stokers and horse-traders (a
horse was apparently a quadruped beast back on old Earth)
from the flying machine mingled with the twenty-odd *Glory*
crewmen, the 'Poids, and our sixty or so, their gabble rising
like a dust-cloud over the throng. Most of our people were
here, barring those on duty, nursing mothers and the like.
The fiddling rose to a sharp note, piercing the uproar of
droning voices, laughs and exclamations as the Trading got
exuberantly under way.

I gave myself over to idle conversation with Alfonso and
Charles, as we made our easy way toward the wind-wagons,
ignoring the clatter. Charles I was at ease with, but I was,
as always, on my guard with Alfonso. More than once his
Castilian temper had lashed out like a striking snake—
fortunately at his own crew. I remembered and dreaded the
'Poids' threat of swift extinction.

Kurrr—who seemed to be leader of the 'Poids, if there

was such in their inexplicable hierarchy—saw us and lumbered over, heavy arms swinging loosely by his gaudy kilt. "Try this, Captains." He extended a massive paw holding a gallon keg. Unclipping our belt-cups, we held them out to be filled while the 'Poid twisted the spigot. I swirled the red wine in my cup and sniffed, then sipped appreciatively.

Kurrr watched closely as we swallowed, his pinkish eyes unblinking, then rumbled hoarsely, "This is the last Trading."

Unsure of our ears, we stared. Charles, the phlegmatic one, recovered first. "Please explain, Kurrr."

The 'Poid turned, waving a furry arm at the mountains rising craggily against the horizon, the rolling desert and the river. "We leave this world to you." He frowned, and added gutturally, "We watch you no longer. War if you will, but better you live out your time in peace."

We began to expostulate, but he held a pink palm upraised in the gesture of finality, "That is all." He set the wine keg in the sand and plodded off toward the wagons, ignoring our anxious, jumbled questions as only a 'Poid can.

In unspoken agreement we three Captains eyed one another, then drifted silently toward our own people— leaving the keg imbedded in the sand. I made a mental note to have it retrieved later: it was, after all, in our Zone. The Trading furor gradually dissolved as rumors spread. One man, then another, slowly ceased bargaining. A few hesitantly closed their stalls and began to wrap the Trading blankets as the vibrant fiddle squawked and was still, the youthful dancers milling in confusion.

Suddenly the 'Poids stood in unison, and boarded their wind-wagons. Sides slammed shut, canvas tops unfurled, and the great sails, quietly loosed, boomed full. Almost without time-lapse, the wind-wagons were over the horizon— a last bit of light reflected from a topsail; then they were gone. I spared but a moment to wonder how they moved so

well on such a windless day, then returned to the more serious matter at hand.

In silence we gathered our goods. Charles, ever the cool
Englishman, waved as he strolled to the *Venturesome Virgin*,
"Cheerioh, old boy. We'll no doubt meet again—soon?"

Plumes of smoke from the *Virgin's* engine pods became
billows as sweltering stokers fanned their fires, and the air-
fans whirled and became polished discs. The awkward contraption gathered way, lifted heavily into the mid-day air
and Charles' arm waved again in farewell.

Alfonso, expectedly, bit out, "Madre de Dios! Those
insolent apes—giving orders to a Castilian gentleman." He
stalked haughtily to the sternwheeler, executing a sweeping,
sarcastic bow in my direction before boarding and ordering
the lines cast off.

Our cargovator jerked upward to the rhythmic "Hah!
Hah! Hah!" of the Lowering Crew, the stench of their sweat
again hanging miasma-like in the air. Later, when all was
safely raised and carried through the cave to our mountain-
closed plateau, Marianne sought me out.

"What did the 'Poids say, Eric?"

Seeing Cedric loitering nearby, I brusquely ordered him
away. "Tell Exxoh I want a meeting of all Wardroom Officers at eight tomorrow morning, and be there yourself with
a current Stores list." Cedric began to scowl, then taking
belated note of my mood, saluted and walked quickly away.

Marianne, as she sometimes did when we were alone,
nudged me hard. "Eric!"

Well, it soon might not matter one way or t'other. Continuing to watch the Lowering Crew fill the storeroom, I
muttered quietly, "I don't know, Marianne. I suspect that
the 'Poids may have made strange use out of the old ship
parts they've been collecting—but we'll have to wait and
see. Not a word to anyone, mind." She nodded, wide-eyed,
and slipped wordlessly away.

That night, as the village lay sleeping, I arose and padded silently into the square—ethereal in Luna's dim reflected light. As I scanned the skies over the 'Poid lands, a great shape rose soundlessly, darkening a huge sector of the night sky. It moved slowly overhead, stars disappearing then twinkling again as it passed. I felt a warm hand slip into mine and recognized the faint scent. As we held hands tightly, a blaze of lance-thin beams glared momentarily from the mighty stern, and it was gone.

I shivered—not just from the cold wind drifting down from the peaks—and thought, half apprehensively, "Well, it's *our* world now."

I shivered again, and still holding hands tightly, we walked out of the suddenly lonely square.

Exxoh rose arthritically as I—wearing my Helmet—entered the Wardroom. Dust filtering through shafts of light swirled suddenly as the Officers; Pilot, Navigator, Engineer and Purser, stood to Attention in response to his command.

I glanced around the low-ceilinged room, noticing that the thick adobe wall was crumbling in one corner, and smelled the faint aroma of freshly picked apples from the adjoining storeroom before returning my gaze to the waiting Officers. I nodded to them to be seated, but remained standing myself at the wooden table's head. One or two shifted nervously on the bench, chancing splinters, as I stood mutely watching them. Not that I lacked words: I'd been awake the better part of the night thinking and planning. Even as Sebastian, the Hereditary Engineer, quick-witted and capable, but unable to endure silence, opened his mouth, I spoke.

They listened quietly, eyes narrowing and lips tightening, as I repeated Kurrr's words verbatim and told them of what we'd seen in the middle hours.

Robert, Hereditary Navigator, murmured as if to himself, "I wonder whether the 'Poids, too, were foreign to this world."

Exxoh nodded slowly, his sparse white locks falling over his forehead ere he impatiently brushed them back. "'Tis very possible, but such matters concern us little at this time." Muttered agreement echoed his blunt statement.

"Right." I tapped the table gently. "We have much to decide—and unknown time in which to do it. For example, will the other Zones continue to Trade as before, or . . . ." I let the sentence hang, and aimed a finger at Cedric. "Purser," I demanded, "what is our Stores status?"

He began to rise. "No, no!" I said impatiently, "Stay seated. If we begin hopping up and down like stalking woolybears we'll be here forever!" Outside I could hear our people starting their daily work: the scraping whine of the armorer's grindstone near drowned out my words.

Cedric, discomfited, began his litany. It seemed that, even though the Trading Time had been curtailed, we still had a good three-month supply of food and basic materials.

"Very good," I said when he'd finished, "Purser, take a six-man hunting party away this morning. Tell the Galley staff to be ready to preserve as much dinolizard meat as you can bring back." I looked at my Officers. "Does that meet with your approval?"

I scarce awaited their ritual assent before adding, "Tell the Chief Cook to dispatch two of his staff with fishing rods. Two men from the Lowering Crew can stand guard against river-beasts."

Marianne, silent until now, broke out, "Captain, the river belongs to the *Blaze of* . . . ."

I interrupted harshly, "Pilot, don't think I haven't seen our people sneaking off to fish before this. And now our lives may depend on it. I have little hope that either Alfonso or Charles will heed the 'Poids' strictures now that they're gone.'' Perhaps those from the prairies and lakelands hadn't seen the 'Poids' departure . . . but common sense told me to act as though our knowledge was also theirs. Cedric stood waiting to be dismissed, but I was not yet ready for him to leave. ''Tell the armorer to report forthwith. Now go!'' He scuttled out the door, a flash of sunlight flickering in as he opened and closed it.

Sebastian, his quick mind absorbing all that I had said— and left unsaid—leaned toward me, his blue-black forehead creased in thought. ''We should perhaps set Watches, Eric.'' Even though subordinate to me and Exxoh in executive decisions, he too wore four gold bands on his Helmet, and was alone entitled to address me by name during Council.

Not answering aloud, I raised my chin questioningly.

''Alfonso and Charles may decide, with their mobility, that we're an apple ripe for the plucking.'' He glanced at Exxoh, ''You'll recall that Alfonso follows in the steps of his father, who was ever spoiling for a brawl.''

''The cave,'' began Exxoh, but Sebastian deferentially cut him off.

''Should Charles join forces with Alfonso, who knows how high the *Venturesome Virgin* can climb?'' Sebastian grimaced, gargoyle-like, before continuing, ''We've never seen the flyer but that it's been heavily loaded. But if it carried only a few explosives . . . ?''

Marianne tugged at my arm. ''Eric, they wouldn't! The 'Poids . . . .''

''Are gone.'' I ignored her use of my name and looked at Sebastian, ''You're right. We'll be stretched thin. Too thin. But we'll have to post guards.'' I began counting aloud, ''Cedric and his hunting party, the Chief Cook's fishing group, that's eleven already; plus the galley crew makes sixteen, and we only number . . . .''

''Another twenty-three able-bodied men and seventeen women, five boys and three girls under eleven years, five nursing mothers and nine men and seven women between forty-five and sixty, and five oldsters nigh on ready for Air Locking,'' bit out Robert, unable to forestall a surreptitious glance at Exxoh. "Plus ourselves: a total of ninety-five, plus the babies."

The room's hush, disturbed only by filtered sounds from outside, was finally broken by Marianne. "The oldsters will have to stand guard," she stated flatly. "Put the most reliable one in command, and he or she can see to it that they stand equal Watches around the clock. They'll not object. It'll be a reprieve from their Air Locking."

I gazed at her, dumbfounded by the firmness in her voice, then found my own. "Very well, Pilot, see to it at once."

As she left, a faint shiver ran down my spine. Gods, this was my betrothed. What would wedded life be like with this woman suddenly turned Amazon? I realized that a voice had lapsed into silence while I had been musing. Three pairs of eyes looked at me, Sebastian's with an amused twinkle.

"Perhaps I could rephrase it," he said calmly, with an imperceptible wink in my direction, "if we move to the attack first, and capture the *Blaze of Glory,* we'd not only have transport but our fortress mountains. They'd be bold men who'd try to recapture the ship if it was moored close under the cave-mouth."

"With boulders ready to tumble over the cliff, so that even if a cutting-out party gained the upper hand, all they'd have would be a splintered, sinking wreck!" Exxoh pounded a gnarled fist on the table while I stared.

He grinned at me, his missing teeth like crenelations in a medieval fortress, "Surprise you, Captain? When you were but a pup I forestalled a bloody battle by the swift battle-axing of a *Glory-Boy*—and none knew of it but your father! There's fire in these old bones yet, Sir!"

I had to answer his grin. Reaching over to affectionately clasp his skinny shoulder, I spoke sincerely, "And well I know it, Exxoh! But I *am* the Captain. There'll be no attacks until I so decree. But," I looked directly at the old man, "it is my order that you and Sebastian devise a plan of attack should conditions change."

The room brightened—not only from sunlight—as Marianne burst in and swung jauntily into a seat, a small cloud of dust swirling in with her. "All's ready, Sir," she reported, "and my oldsters vow that none will escape their steely gaze!" She chortled, "It's knocked years off their ages. Even old Sven, who's seventy if he's a day, patted me on the bottom when I bent over!"

Smiling myself, I halted their laughter by standing. "Stay seated," I commanded. "Robert, I want you to plan a defense against the *Venturesome Virgin* should Charles attack us. I think it unlikely, but a stitch in time . . . the four of you co-ordinate your plans and efforts. I want no one working at cross-purposes. Exxoh, report to me when plans are complete."

He stood, saluting, "Aye aye, Sir," and I slipped out the door to be stopped abruptly by the armorer's bulk—hulking even over my six feet and a bit. Negligently he lifted an arm—the one not holding a sledge-hammer—in casual salute, then jammed it back into a pouch of his scarred leather jerkin. I could smell his stale sweat, and made a note to tell Exxoh that the bathing regulations must be more strictly enforced.

"Sent fer me, Cap'n?"

"Yes," I answered shortly: there was no love lost between us. "Report to the Executive Officer. He'll have orders for extra spears and swords."

"I've got a plow half-built now," he began to grumble, "an' . . . ."

"Your new orders will have priority!" I walked away.

Climbing to the roof of the communal hall, I shielded
my eyes against the brilliant sun and mirroring moons to
scan our upland valley. Scarcely five miles long and but two
wide, the surrounding craggy peaks dwarfed it even more.
Our dun-colored cluster of forty-odd buildings and half-
dozen sheds began only a hundred yards from the inner
cave-mouth, shaded by the dozen fruit trees that yielded,
reluctantly, several boxes of apples and peaches yearly. The
stream—we'd never bothered to name it, since there was
only the one, disappeared underground after plunging pre-
cipitously from a mile-distant cliff and boiling furiously
along its narrow, bouldered channel.

Slowly, ponderously, our massive undershot waterwheel
squeakily scooped up buckets of clear water, lifting and spilling them into the spindly wooden flume from where it trickled gurgling into the irrigation ditch. We were able to grow
little enough in the rocky soil: some corn, root vegetables
such as onions and carrots and potatoes. We'd once tried
planting vines so that we might make wine—without success, but had had modest luck with berries. And they made
a tolerable wine.

Enough! I was day-dreaming again. I studied the rolling grasslands and wished with all my soul that our Ancestors had had the foresight to realize the need for a few goats
or pigs or even rabbits. But we had none, so the only purpose the lush tall grass served was to thatch roofs.

The armorer's grindstone again began to scrape and
whine, masking the soft chunking of the women's hoes and
grunts of the two men heaving at the plow. The Chief Cook,
spying me, waved and called something indistinct as his
scullion set out trays of vegetables to sun-cure. I smelled his
smoker as a vagrant breeze wafted the aroma of curing meat
to my nostrils. Far off I could see specks that must be
Cedric and his hunters, high in the mountains among the
sparse trees. Shifting my stance on the rough log roof, I

Illustrated by Ferenc Temil Temesvari

swung my gaze to a youth repairing a wooden bench and a man and wife patching their thatched roof. A toddler waddled unsteadily toward the tiny playground with its swing and slide, its mother hovering anxiously behind.

I scrambled down the ladder, glancing toward the Wardroom. The Officers hadn't yet emerged. Halfway down I stopped, looking toward the distant huddled group of smelter sheds that hid the mine entrance. A curl of smoke rose from one, indicating the crew was busy. I mentally ticked them off: four miners, all men; two smelter workers, both women. Even as I watched, a tiny figure pulling a wagon appeared round the corner of a building. Alan, our dull-witted hauler and general roustabout. He'd escaped being Air Locked only because of his immense strength and good nature. My father had made the decision to spare his life; I recalled him saying to me, "Alan's not got the sense that he should have, but with his brawn and easy ways he'll be an asset. Teach him to follow well; he'll never be a leader, poor lad."

I'd listened, and always kept a friendly word for the huge, simple fellow. As my father said, he'd become an asset to our Zone—always ready to help, and his giant strength lightened our load immeasureably.

Continuing down to the ground, I walked past the Lowering Crew, who had their cargovator assembly sprawled over the square while they greased, patched and replaced various parts. They smelled better. Exxoh must have ordered them to bathe. Rounding a corner, I came suddenly upon Sven lecturing four oldsters—two men, two women.

"We'll stand four hours on Watch, then twelve hours off. That'll keep us rotating so that we're not forever keeping the same hours. You four will rotate: I'll be on call at all times. Be at your place ten minutes before your Watch begins so that the one that you're relieving can brief you. I want to know immediately about *anything* out of the ordinary. Ring the bell and I'll come running." He carried on, but curious about the reference to the bell, I turned away and went to the inner cave-mouth. There, securely if roughly mounted on a newly fabricated wooden stand, was the Wardroom Bell—silent these many years. I wondered how they'd gotten it, but resolved to say nothing. If they wanted to tell me, they would. Otherwise, I'd let it be.

Suddenly I yawned. I blinked, then yawned again. It dawned on me that I'd had but a couple of hours of restless sleep. Stumbling, I moved to my quarters and fell on the bed, not heeding the sun-blazing window or the noise drifting in.

Gradually a routine developed. Our Stores grew, and I set the Lowering Crew to digging an addition to the cold-cellar. A few grumbles resulted, but a meaningful glance toward the cave-mouth soon quieted them. They'd seen others Air Locked, and had little desire to join their numbers.

We six Wardroom Officers met daily to exchange information and make decisions. Not in the evening, I had decreed, but in the freshness of the morning. Cedric's hunt had been rewarding, so that an extra month's dried meat—two months at short rations—hung smokily in the coldroom. All reports had been made on this, the eleventh day after the Trading Time, and we stirred in our seats as Cedric wrote up the Log. An untoward wail needled through the usual blend of waterwheel, voice-drone, grindstone and other accustomed sound: almost as one our heads swiveled to catch the foreign noise.

"By yer leave, Sir!" Exxoh jumped to his feet and pounded on the door, not pausing to catch the bench, which rocked crazily and fell with a crash as the others followed him.

In a scuffle of bodies we crowded after Exxoh and stopped at the sight of the old man, bald head tilted back, wrinkled hand shading his upstaring eyes as the hurried dust settled on his sandals. We too peered skyward. It was the *Venturesome Virgin*, curling wisps of steamy smoke twisting from her engine pods as she dived like a great bird of prey on our helpless village, wavering wings momentarily blurred as she passed the brilliance of a sun-split cloud. Even as I instinctively ducked, so close she seemed, I saw a glint of white tumble from her cargo bay and flutter earthward.

"Get that!" I snapped, wondering if any had seen me flinch. "Bring it to me at once!"

Billows of turgid smoke blasted back from the *Virgin's* air-fans as she nosed up and clawed for altitude, but I paid her scant attention as I unfolded the sealed letter and tossed Cedric the carrot which had given it weight. "Put that in your Stores," I said loudly. "Waste not, want not. *They'll* soon learn that lesson."

I began to read the missive, then saw that I was centered in a group of gawking, peering, craning, shuffling villagers trying to do the same. Catching Exxoh's eye, I nodded toward the Wardroom.

"Back to your work, people," Exxoh's calm commanding words pierced the hubbub. "You'll soon enough know what...." A sharp clang interrupted him, then another and another rang from the bell. Marianne, closely trailed by Sven and a couple of oldsters, pelted toward the cave-mouth, puffs of dust marking their paths. I continued to the Wardroom, leaving Exxoh to sort out the confusion.

The message was blunt, even though couched in Charles' euphemistic phrases....

> My Dear Eric,
>   Fortune has decreed that our three groups must become one. Alfonso has agreed to become my lieutenant, since I have the flying machine:

you are invited to join us as third in seniority.

You may signal your acceptance by sending a note to *Blaze of Glory,* which is hove-to below your cave-mouth.

Regretfully, we must forbid your exit until you agree, and we must request that one of your Officers accompany us as surety of continued good intent. Your Hereditary Pilot would be an excellent choice.

Please answer forthwith. While we would regret the necessity for doing so, we have the power to enforce compliance.

The message was signed, "Charles Nottingham-Hood, Commander in Chief."

Four of the Officers had entered and quietly seated themselves as I read. Sunlight splashed again as the door swung open and Marianne entered.

"The *Blaze of Glory* . . . ." she began.

"Is hove-to below the cave-mouth," I said. "Charles wishes to become dictator. Listen to this." I read the letter aloud.

"That pompous lecher!" Marianne exploded, "I'll see him in Hell before I . . . ."

This time it was Exxoh who broke in. "Perhaps we'd best find out what his threat entails." We didn't have long to wait. Even as the old man fell silent, we again heard the banshee wail of the *Virgin's* struts and wires, then an explosion shook the building.

As we gained the outside, the huge biplane began climbing ponderously away, and our waterwheel lay in steaming splinters in a pall of dusty smoke. My nose wrinkled at the pungent smell of explosives.

"Exxoh. All those with bows fetch them now. Get the children and nursing mothers into shelter. Marianne, take four of the best marksmen to the cave-mouth and we'll see

how Alfonso likes an arrow-shower. Sebastian, assemble the
Lowering Crew and salvage what you can of the waterwheel.
Robert, dispose the remainder of those with weapons according to your plans, and if Charles returns give him a hot welcome. Cedric," I turned to the Purser. "I leave it to you to
pass the word. Make certain that everyone knows what's happening, including the mine crew." I waved an arm at the distant workings. Pausing only a second to see that my orders
were being carried out, I sprinted for the cave.

Panting through the cool gloom, I overtook Marianne
and her archers trotting steadily along. "Don't give them
warning," I cautioned as we padded over the worn rock.
"Step up, aim quickly and shoot—one after the other."

Sven and his group stood quietly near the ledge. He
motioned for silence, and whispered as we drew near,
"They just tied up to the bank—well within bowshot," he
added as he saw the weapons.

"Have they seen you?"

"No, Sir. They've looked up any number of times, but
we've kept out of sight."

"Good," I said. "I'll take a quick look." Keeping in
shadow, I peered down. The little ship lay alongside the jetty
we'd built for Trading Time, sternwheel slowly turning as
tanned crewmen hauled hawsers ashore. Rolling, empty
sands stretched lifelessly to the horizon under a cloudless
sky. In contrast, the ship's brasswork was so brilliant it
pained the eyes.

"Quick now," I whispered harshly, "in succession,
step out, aim and shoot. Go!"

The archers were *good*. Hardly had the first "twang!"
died away when screams of rage and anguish echoed upward. I counted. Two arrows each. "Enough!" I ordered.
"Now all move well back and we'll see what they do."

We huddled in a compact mass behind a jutting ledge.
Sven, when a few minutes had passed, made as if to step

out, but I seized his arm. "Wait," I hissed, "they may be waiting for us to look out."

It was well I stopped him. A sudden flash transformed the cave's murk into brilliant daylight, and simultaneously a tremendous crash assaulted our ears.

"Now!" I shouted. "Archers, run and shoot!" I grabbed the nearest and shoved her, then ran through the choking dust behind her, the others hard on my heels. I hurriedly scanned the scene below: three still forms lay crumpled on the ship's main deck, while a small group crouched by a contraption mounted by the funnel. Waving the archers to the brim, I stepped out of their way while another volley was loosed, and saw the *Venturesome Virgin*, air-fans spinning slowly, touch down near the spaceship hulk.

"Back now!" I screamed, seeing the cluster of men on the ship taking cover behind the funnel and lifeboat. We raced back to our friendly ledge, and had just reached safety when a second explosion hurtled dust and debris through the cave.

"Well and good," I commended. "Sven, this is your new post. Let them waste their ammunition. You've done well."

"Shall I post an archer here, Captain? Perhaps on the same Watch system as Sven's people?"

"Yes, Pilot," I answered, "a good thought. Sven will command the combined groups. See to it at once." Another blast of lightning and thunder ripped through the cave, but this time we hardly blinked, although our nostrils were clogged with acrid dust. Leaving them, I sidled cautiously back through the eddying haze, careful to remain close to the cave walls. Robert, sweating but grinning, ran toward me as I emerged into blinding daylight.

"We gave Charles a mighty surprise, Captain," he puffed, "a giant hole in his wing!"

"How," I began, but he pulled me along to a complicated mechanism—vaguely resembling the cargovator—standing part hidden by a huge boulder.

"My own design," he stated proudly, "a catapult. Wind the arm down with these levers, put a ten-pound rock in this sling, then trip the release. Granted, it was mostly luck, but when the *Virgin* dived low, we put a rock right through his left lower wing. Too bad we didn't hit his airfan," he added moodily.

"Well done, Robert," I was free with my praise. The Navigator had always been a withdrawn, cool person, but now he was grinning like a child with a new toy. I told him of *Blaze of Glory's* bombardment, ending by saying, "So I think they'll withdraw to lick their wounds."

I was right. We heard no more from the would-be conquerors. Next morning the lookouts reported that Alfonso had steamed off during the night, and Charles too had flown away at first light.

At the Wardroom meeting I looked at Exxoh. "Is there any record of one of us visiting the 'Poids' lands—even in the distant past?" For the first time ever I saw him hesitate and stammer, while the rest watched him in mystification. He looked at me, then away, while his mouth opened and closed helplessly.

"I know not what you're withholding, Exxoh," I said gently, "but if you have information, now is the time to share it."

He looked around at the drab adobe walls, the brightly patterned curtains, and at the other Officers sitting silently still, before coming to a decision. Slowly he spoke, his face hard.

"There is a way. Or was. The knowledge has been passed on from Executive Officer to Executive Officer, with the strongest strictures about revealing it except in the greatest need. I don't know if this is the greatest . . . or if a need far surpassing this will arrive."

" 'Tis your decision, my old friend," I said cautiously, "but consider this: we are not only under attack, but for all practical purposes are bottled up in this valley." I surveyed the other Officers, each solemn as eternity. "Would you not all agree?"

Slowly they nodded. Exxoh studied them one by one, then turned his eyes on me. "Very well, Sir. Another cave exists. Or did. It was shown by Kurrr to *Chariot of Destiny's* Executive Officer when the Zones were allotted, and he was taken through it to the 'Poids' lands."

"By Kurrr! But—that would make him over . . . ."

"Well over a hundred years old."

"This cave . . . where . . . how . . . ." Sebastian spluttered, and fell silent.

"It was made by the 'Poids," said Exxoh, "it's not natural. That much I know, although I've never seen it."

"How do we find it?" I stared hard at the old man. "What if it has been buried or filled by slides or tremors?"

He shrugged. "That I don't know, Sir. All I can do is take out the sealed book and show you where the opening is hidden."

Sebastian smiled, his teeth a gleam of moonlight in his dark features. "If the cave's not natural, I'd reckon that enough strength's been built in so that it'll stand longer than a mere century!"

"All right," I decided, "we'll investigate after breakfast. All but one of us. Someone must stay here in command."

"Short straws?" Robert suggested.

I nodded. "Might as well have it decided." As fate would have it, Robert drew the short straw. His face fell, but, "Not to worry," he said, "there'll no doubt be more than enough of it to see soon."

As we rose to leave for the morning meal, Marianne seized my hand. "Eric, it's so exciting! But—" her practical nature showed. "Shall I have rations prepared? We might be longer than we think."

I was abashed at neglecting to think of such a basic necessity, but smiled at her. "Please do. Water bags, too. Perhaps a flask of wine . . . take some from the last keg that Kurrr brought: the one he left in the sand."

A thought struck me as we neared the galley, where smells of cooking and the rattle of cutlery urged us on. "Keep silent until we know more. We're merely on an exploring trip, looking for—" I hesitated, "shelter from air attacks."

Exxoh slipped away as we gathered after our breakfast of porridge, fruit and apple juice, returning with his kit-bag swinging from a shoulder. A steward, white apron spotted from the morning's work, brought out neat packs of fruit and dried meat. We'd fill our canteens at the stream and, I noticed, Marianne had a *bota* of wine slung around her neck. Robert had left already on a tour of inspection, relishing, I suspected, his temporary command status. I stepped over to Exxoh, murmuring, "Lead on, my friend."

With a short stop at the footbridge to fill our canteens and check on the Lowering Crew's waterwheel repairs, we struck out through the waving grass, weaving around massive boulders and outcroppings of blue-gray rock, so that we were soon lost to sight from the village.

More quickly than I expected, we were facing one of the countless faintly scarred, weathered rock bluffs. I could see nothing to distinguish this one, nor could the others to judge from the pebbles scraping under shuffling sandals, and almost inaudible whispers. Even the creaking of leather packstraps ceased, however, as Exxoh fumbled with fastenings, then reached into his kit-bag and lifted out a thin book. Craning my neck, I examined it. Nothing unusual about its appearance, except for the heavy metal clamp surrounding the cover, with an oversized lock in the middle.

A sharp slap startled me—and the others, too, I saw as I looked around. Marianne looked up as she flicked the squashed remains of a sting-bug from her thigh. "You all look as though a woolybear had jumped at you!"

It eased the tension. Even Exxoh, who hadn't cracked a smile since the meeting, grinned tightly as he fitted a key into the lock and turned it. 'Twas obviously not the first time he'd opened the book—nor even the tenth—judging from his accustomed ease. Dropping the key back into his sack, he carefully removed his hand bearing-compass and sighted at a distant peak. He glanced into the book as we watched impatiently, then turned to take a bearing on a second mountain. Four times he repeated the procedure while we stood like pillars of rock.

"This is the place," he announced. "Now I . . . ."

"Down!" screamed Sebastian, "Take cover! Charles is back."

We flattened ourselves. Fortunately, the long grass grew almost to the cliffs, so from our cover we watched the flying machine lumber overhead. No dive and swoop this time: Charles cautiously stayed out of bowshot and catapult range.

Four or five objects fell from the machine, spinning and twisting in tumbling arcs. They fell far out in the grass fields, and a row of smoke-puffs blossomed like dusty flowers. Moments later we heard the crump of explosives.

"Ha! He'll have to do better than that," Cedric snickered. "He'll not . . . ."

"Purser," snapped Sebastian, "you show your ignorance needlessly! Could you do better? Wait till he's had practice—he'll be dropping those missiles within a few feet of his aim."

I donned my Helmet, although 'twas not easy in a prone

position. This was no time for dissension. "That will do," I said crisply, "although the Engineer is correct, any one of us might have spoken without thinking. We will not quarrel between ourselves."

A mumbled chorus of "Aye aye, Sir"'s responded. "Very good," I said, removing the cumbersome headgear. "Pilot, you keep an eye on our flying friends; they seem to be leaving."

Sure enough, the unwieldy monster had lurched about and was headed back, its course marked by a drifting pall of greasy smoke. We watched it disappear behind the mountains before I gave the word to continue. Brushing ourselves as we rose, our eyes automatically swung to Exxoh.

Facing the rock, he lifted his chin and called, not overloudly, in the Trade dialect, "Open thou, 'tis time."

A seven-foot irregularly round section of the rock wall folded silently inward—soundless but for a few pebbles rattling down the face. I started forward, but Exxoh seized my arm. "Wait."

I halted, the others with me. "What . . . ?" I began to ask, when swiftly the portal swung shut, leaving nothing to indicate that an opening had ever existed.

"A safety precaution," Exxoh explained, "should someone accidentally pronounce the code words—unlikely though it may be—he'll be trapped. Only after the second phrase will it remain open until ordered shut." As I suddenly felt my knees tremble slightly, he faced the bluff again and called, "Open, 'tis the 'Poids' command."

Once more a dark opening yawned before us and a waft of musty air drifted out. As befitted my rank, I led the way into the gloom, though not without foreboding. Slowly, a faint glimmer relieved the blackness, becoming brighter and . . . .

Marianne screamed. And screamed again, clutching my arm and then burying her head in my shoulder. I started to speak, then looked down. A crumpled skeleton, still wearing dessicated furs and a Helmet with the entwined snakes and two gold rings of a Ship's Doctor, lay almost at our feet. Faint, throaty cries came from the others as we all retreated involuntarily.

"So that's what happened," breathed Exxoh. I looked at him questioningly.

"When I was still a youth," he said slowly, "the Doctor vanished. We thought he'd been taken by a woolybear. Your father—the Captain—had the mountains searched but found nothing. It was then that it was forbidden to venture into the mountains unarmed in groups of less than three. Poor lad," he bent over the pitiful remains, "he'd just become Doctor, and was but a couple of years older than me. That's why we have no Ship's Doctor now . . . his predecessor had died, and no youth had started training."

"He'll be given proper burial from the Air Lock," I interjected harshly, not liking the somber mood which had enveloped us, "with an honor guard of Ship's Police. See to it when we return, Exxoh." I gave my attention to the cave.

Unlike our own familiar cavern, the walls were smooth and rounded. Light streamed from recessed mounts, and I felt a draft of cool, fresh air entering from hidden vents. Just a few steps inward sat a control console such as had been in the wrecked *Chariot of Destiny* before it had become Trade goods. I noticed that others, too, were staring about at the revelations, but were silent—perhaps in awe. I touched a wall. It felt cool, yet with a touch of warmth. I realized suddenly that if the 'Poids had done all this, they'd hardly have omitted temperature control, and started to say as much, when I saw that Exxoh was studying the book.

"With your permission, Sir," his eyes met mine, "perhaps the console . . . ." I nodded, and the old man gingerly walked over and seated himself uneasily. Marianne's hand slipped into mine as we followed Exxoh and stood apprehensively behind him.

His eyes moving carefully between book and console, he tapped a gated switch with a bony finger. Instantly the dull gray panel hummed and soft, multicolored lights flickered—one green globe insistently from the left side.

"Perhaps, Eric," Sebastian suggested carefully, "we should close the entrance before doing more. From above the cave-mouth must be . . . ." He left the sentence unfinished.

"Right," disengaging my hand from Marianne's, "what words close the door, Exxoh?"

He studied the book, eyes blinking. "Shut, Sesame," he said softly. "I think the words are taken from an ancient folk tale, though how the 'Poids . . . ."

I interrupted. Faintly I'd heard a distant drone. "Cedric, to the door! Use the words!" Even as I shouted he turned and was running. I finished lamely, "I think I heard the *Virgin* returning."

Sebastian glanced slyly at me, then Marianne, but said nothing. The portal's brilliant eye winked shut as the Purser chanted the magic phrase, and a collective sigh whispered in the stillness. Then, as the tension flowed out of our bones, we began chattering like children.

Resolutely Exxoh pushed the winking green button. The cave darkened gradually, while a man-sized rectangle of light glimmered above the console, and slowly we discerned figures.

"Humans of the *Chariot of Destiny.*" We jumped as a sonorous voice boomed from the picture, now so clear that I recognized Kurrr and another, older 'Poid. The older one was speaking, using the Trade dialect. "Since you are here, the emergency which we foresaw must now be at hand." My eyes flicked left and right: we were all standing still, awestruck and barely breathing.

"Before continuing, I must tell you of how you came to this planet. We, whom you know as the 'Poids, are also a space-faring race, and our ship was marooned here by a problem which your minds would not comprehend. Our distress signals disrupted your computers' programming, causing your ships to crash. Such was not our intent, and so we gave you help and lands, and prevented you from warring with one another." He paused, "For know this, that we can indeed read your minds, as some suspected. We read evil in the minds of the other crews. In yours, too, but to a lesser extent, and so we selected you as the ones we would help to continue on your interrupted voyage.

"Gather now your people and whatever you wish to take, but waste no time. At the end of this tunnel is a spaceship with a computer programmed to carry you to your original destination. The ship will lift off in twenty-four of your hours after activation of the console below. it is stocked with all the food, water and other supplies you will require. Teaching programs aboard will enable you each to learn and to maintain and land the ship on arrival."

The old 'Poid stopped, then his face widened in the grimace we knew as a smile, "We wish you good fortune. Mayhap we will meet again somewhere among the stars." The picture faded and vanished, while we stood like dullards, not speaking—then a babble of voices rattled off the walls as we all tried to talk at once. I looked at my watch. Near mid-day. An entire morning wasted.

"Quiet!" I shouted. "There's less than a day left!" Rapidly I gave orders for each to gather a part of our company, and bring them here during the dark hours with whatever precious possessions they refused to leave behind.

"Sebastian," my voice dropped, "have the Ship's Police come here after dusk-fall and take the body of the Ship's Doctor to the Air Lock for burial. Then tell Sven to, just *before* daybreak, light cooking fires and the smelter furnace so that from above all will seem normal. When that's done, he and his crew are to hurry to the cave and board the ship."

Exxoh, chin in hand, still stared at the console. The instrument, again lifeless, interested me not. "Carry on, all of you. Exxoh," I ordered curtly, "follow me." I softened the curtness by remarking that tomorrow, for the first time, they'd be carrying out their actual hereditary duties.

As the cave door cycled through its double opening routine, Exxoh and I turned our backs on it and marched inward. 'Twas only a few hundred yards before we came to the cave's ending. I recognized instantly what confronted us—an open Air Lock. We stepped through, and it was as in *Chariot of Destiny,* but this ship was alive! Gurglings, hummings and rumblings vibrated our ears and our feet, then a flat, disembodied voice announced:

"Twenty - one - hours - thirty - minutes - before - liftoff. Countdown - will - be - at - thirty - minute - intervals - until - Z - minus - three - hours - then - every - ten - minutes. Final - ten - minutes - countdown - at - thirty - second - intervals.   Last - thirty - seconds - at - two - second - intervals.   All - personnel - to - be - strapped - in - by - Z - minus - ten - minutes."

We quickly familiarized ourselves with the interior layout. The outside was nested in the solid rock as tightly as a bullet in a pistol, and we wasted no time on it but returned to the village, closing the cave door behind us.

The village was in a frenzy. Ancient trunks, unopened for a generation or more, were being ransacked for heirlooms. Alan, always willing, pulled a two-wheeled cart piled high with a tottering, top-heavy load of cherished belongings and Officers with harried expressions trotted about trying to maintain a semblance of order in the twilight. The Master-at-Arms in passing said quickly, "Orders carried out, Sir. A proper funeral." I nodded my thanks as he hurried on past, and went to gather my own few belongings.

I was awakened by a shake, then a soft body pressed against me momentarily. "Time, my Eric!" I inhaled Marianne's scent, mumbled an affectionate response as she slipped out the door, and groped for my clothes.

What a hullaballoo in the pre-dawn gloom! I thrice cursed savagely at a housewife who stubbornly demanded room for an unwieldy bedstead, and an obstinate cook's helper who staggered out burdened with a great clattering mound of pots and pans. However, just as the sun broke over the peaks, we were all—except for Sven's crew—inside the cave. I looked back to see tendrils of smoke beginning to spiral upward in the still morning air, and smiled as I saw the minute figures of Sven's people dashing toward the cave entrance through the thick grass. All was going according to plan.

More confusion reigned aboard the ship, as our people struggled to locate stowage space in a hull already jammed full. Several times I—and my Officers—brusquely ordered goods jettisoned. A confrontation between myself and the armorer was only just averted by the Master-at-Arms intervening with, "Say the word, Sir, and it's to the Air Lock with him!"

The armorer glared, but unwillingly let his grindstone remain behind. "A nasty piece of work, that one, Sir," murmured the policeman. "I'll be keeping an eye on him."

"Do that, Petty Officer," I grunted, "and if there's trouble throw him in Cells. There's a lockup aboard."

"Thirty-minutes-till-liftoff," blared the computer's tinny voice, "check-all-stowage-and-prepare-for-strap-down."

At a tap on my shoulder I looked around to the still-open Air Lock. Exxoh, Sven and his four oldsters stood solemnly clustered in the small entry port. Exxoh handed me his book. I took the thing uncomprehendingly, as he said quietly, "We'll not be going with you, Sir. We've talked it over, and it's here we belong. You'll be better off without us, Sir . . . we're too old to start off again."

"And by your leave, *Sir*," the armorer shouldered his way past me to stand beside the others, packing the over-crowded compartment, "I'll join them!" His gravelly voice drowned out the twenty-minute announcement.

"If you must." My voice choked off, and I grabbed Exxoh and held him close. "My old friend, and friend of my father, if you must stay . . . stay with my blessings." Tears welled down my cheeks, but I was not ashamed. I felt an arm link with mine and knew that it was Marianne. She too was weeping, but, "Eric, you must get strapped in." She stepped forward and kissed Exxoh as the ship's internal noises increased in volume and tempo. "Goodby, my friends."

They filed out, even the antagonistic armorer bending so far as to wave in farewell. I reached for the Air Lock button, but halted as shouts, screams and the sound of pounding booted feet echoed and re-echoed from the cave walls. A horde of armed men charged toward the ship and an arrow sssssssed by me to head-flatten against a bulkhead. "Shut the Lock, Eric!" Marianne screamed as another arrow zinged past.

"No!" I screamed and reaching for my sword, lurched toward the open port as I saw our friends unsheathing their ceremonial swords and the armorer brandishing a great hammer just as an arrow took him full in the chest. Marianne jumped past me and pushed the button. As the inner and outer doors slammed closed we stumbled like drunkards into our seats and strapped in. She flicked on the scanner before I could stop her. I had no wish to watch my friends' slaughter, but . . . . Charles and Alfonso, with at least a score of heavily armed warriors, were battling viciously with our oldsters. As we watched, a reddened sword pierced

Sven's body and a bullet from a prohibited pistol finished another. Exxoh slashed at Alfonso with the ship's cutlass, near taking his haughty head right off, but fell with a spear through his courageous heart. In seconds it was over. I saw Charles look coldly down at Alfonso's body, and the dozen dead and dying men and women, then charge ahead, shouting soundlessly, toward the Air Lock—but all was blotted out as my eyes blurred and my cheeks sagged as a terrible weight forced me into the seat.

My vision slowly returned—how much later I know not—to see Marianne casting off her straps. Pointing at the light-splashed screen, she whispered, "There goes our old planet and our old friends, Eric. Like the legendary Phoenix, this ship rises from the ashes of the old. We're away to finish our interrupted voyage." We held hands silently as we waited for our ship's company to awake to their new destiny, and our exultation mingled with the salt tears trickling unhindered down our cheeks.

Crow's Curse
by
Michael H. Payne

About the Author

Michael H. Payne is 25, a lifelong resident of Southern California, and one of seven people living there who does not own a car. He has a master's degree in Classics from UC Irvine, and also took two short story classes from John Piirto and Oakley Hall. He works as a clerk in the Balboa, California, branch of the Newport Beach Public Library, has hosted a Saturday morning radio program for the past seven years, and sings in the choir and plays guitar at a local church.

He has been writing since the eighth grade, but "Crow's Curse" is only the second story he has really finished. We're glad he finished it, and entered it in the Contest . . . and if you like fables, you will be, too.

About the Illustrator

Peter H. Francis was born in Dartmouth, Nova Scotia, and now resides in Halifax. He has been interested in art most of his life, in part because his father's hobby has always been painting and he had an extensive art book collection.

Francis graduated in 1985 from the Nova Scotia College of Art and Design, with the degree of Bachelor of Fine Arts. He has been attending and helping to run science fiction conventions for the past ten years, and displaying his work at several. In 1989, he won an award for ''Best Amateur Black and White'' at the world science fiction convention in Boston.

The wind whipped through Crow's feathers as he crouched at the edge of the cliff, a black wind, cold and sharp in the pre-dawn darkness. The forest far below rustled uncomfortably as Crow stared, his eyes intent on the eastern horizon. He was waiting for the moon to come up.

His mind skittered and jumped, but Crow did his best not to think about the way the satchel leaning against his side clattered whenever he shivered. He shivered often, though, clamped as he was between the cold black above and the hard gray below with darkness swirling all around him.

At last, over the long straight edge of the horizon, Crow saw the red tip of the thin crescent moon rising. He stood and clasped his wings together, pointing toward the growing spike until the sliver of moon had risen entirely and was balancing blood-red on the horizon.

Crow closed his eyes then and whispered, "Lady Raven, please hear me and have pity on me. I have done a terrible, terrible thing; I don't know if you can ever understand, but I had to come and explain."

He knelt down and felt the satchel cold against him. "I don't really know how it happened, but what else could I have done? The poor thing was dying, was nearly dead when I heard it crying out. Its parents shouldn't've let it out of the nest; it was just too young to be out by itself. There was nothing I could've done to help it, nothing at all, and it *was* nearly dead when I found it. I couldn't just let it

suffer, could I? Could I? Please try to understand, Lady
Raven, please try. Sometimes things just happen; it was
luck, that's all, bad luck, yes, but, I mean, it wasn't
anyone's *fault* is all, and I just wanted to try to explain
how . . . how it happened. . . ."

Crow gathered the satchel up and held it against his
chest. "I . . . I brought h—its, its bones, here in my satchel.
I thought I should bury him—it, it, bury it up here where
you could see and understand." Crow scraped a shallow pit
in the loose dirt at the cliff's edge and carefully laid the contents of his satchel at the bottom. His wings were shaking.
"Why did it have to be out alone? It shouldn't've happened,
not ever. . . ." He stared at the bones for a second, bright
points flashing in the dark earth, then covered them over
with dirt and small stones.

When he was done, he turned back to the moon. Its
brightness was beginning to fade as the coming morning
made gray the sky around it. Crow clasped his wings and
bowed. "Please, Lady Raven, don't let it happen again.
Please do everything you can not to let it happen again."
Then he brushed the ground with his wing tips to hide the
traces of his digging, gathered up his satchel and, stepping
over the cliff edge, glided out over the forest as the sun
started sparking at the horizon. Crow winged his way home
and curled exhausted into bed.

The sun rose, slid across the sky, and settled into late
afternoon before Crow finally stirred and awoke.

He wasn't really feeling any better, though; his head
ached and his back was stiff and wooden. A nice flight over
the forest, he was sure, and he'd feel like his old self again.
The acorns in the pantry didn't appeal to him, and it was
too early for dinner anyway, so he just gathered up his
satchel and took off into the autumn afternoon sunlight.

Below him, the forest rustled with reds and golds. The
sky was a deep, sharp blue, and Crow turned lazily through

Illustrated by Peter H. Francis

it, his mind doing its best to stay away from memories of yesterday and this morning. He managed to concentrate on riding the winds, diving and climbing, and the cold gusts washing through his wings.

He drifted north and east with no real destination in mind until he became aware of an odd sort of piping floating along through the breeze from off to his left. It sounded like calliope music.

Crow wheeled left, his ears intent on the snatches of piping that danced around him in the wind. The music got louder and more coherent as Crow approached Valder's Clearing, and he could tell now for sure that it was calliope music.

But who would be out in these woods playing a calliope? It had to be a gypsy caravan. It was autumn after all, and the gypsy squirrel families always held their Autumn Festival in Ree's Meadow just about a month after the equinox. This had to be some northern gypsy squirrels on their way down to the Festival.

Crow winged over Valder's Clearing, and there, set out in a crescent beside the little spring, were the wagons of a gypsy caravan. Crow could see strings of gray and burgundy flags fluttering in the breeze and various mice and sparrows and other such folk walking about between the booths set up in front of the wagons. The long afternoon shadows were lying deep throughout the clearing, and the music steamed and gushed up from the calliope parked at the end of the wagon row.

Crow circled the clearing and flapped to the ground next to the machine. Its pipes stretched tall and bright into the autumn sky, a massive fan of pipes into which a bronze frieze had been pressed showing the Twelve Curials. The detail was incredible, the smooth strength of the Lady Lioness, the august bearing of the Lord Tiger, the quick fire of the Lady Squirrel's eyes, all captured more perfectly than

Crow had ever seen, right down to the dark sheen of the Lady Raven's feathers. The whole instrument was a marvel, gleaming with brass and ivory and marked in places with the same gray and burgundy as the flags.

The squirrel playing the calliope was thin and rather tall for a squirrel, his burgundy vest hanging loose from his shoulders. He was lunging back and forth over the keyboard, the tempo of the piece climbing and soaring, the music rushing louder and louder. The squirrel's claws flashed through one final cadenza, and, with a grand flourish, he leaned into the keyboard and drove the last chord bursting out into the air.

The squirrel fell back onto his stool as the chord sped into the sky and was gone. Crow began applauding and was surprised when no one else joined in. Looking around, he saw that the other folk were all further along the caravan, all engrossed in the items for sale.

Hmmph! Crow thought. Still applauding, he said aloud, "Bravo, sir, bravo! Absolutely wonderful! There's nobody can play a calliope like a gypsy squirrel, I always say."

The squirrel turned around in his seat and flashed a broad smile, his golden front tooth catching the rays of the setting sun. "Ah, Corvine!" The squirrel leaped down from the calliope and bowed low. "I have always said there is no one appreciates the calliope like a corvine. She is a misunderstood instrument, eh, Corvine?"

"Too true, sir, and it's really too bad. There's nothing in the world like it. But this machine of yours! It's fantastic! I've never seen anything like it! And your playing, sir! I haven't heard playing like that for many a Festival."

"She's a special one, she is. It takes a special squirrel to play such as her." His smile flashed through the clearing again. "And a special someone to hear her the right way." He stuck out a paw. "I am Alphonse Karakchik, and you will do me a great kindness, Corvine, if you will allow me to buy you a drink or two."

Crow wrapped some feathers around the squirrel's paw. "It will be an honor, sir, if you will let me buy you a few."

The squirrel laughed and seized a gray and burgundy checked bandana from beneath the calliope. "Come then, my friend! We will toast one another!"

"Oh, and the calliope as well, sir."

"Of course! We shall both buy her drinks, yes?"

They made their way along the row of wagons, Karakchik stopping at the various booths and introducing Crow to just about everybody in the camp. By the time the two arrived at the wagon where tables were being laid out with gray and burgundy tablecloths and red candles were being lit in wax-encrusted bottles, they had amassed quite a following of squirrels, mice, sparrows, wrens, all of them invited by Karakchik to share some wine and to toast the calliope.

It was just getting on toward evening as they settled down at the tables and the squirrels began bringing dusty bottles out of the wagon. They toasted the calliope, Karakchik toasted Crow, Crow toasted Karakchik and all the gypsies, a mouse at one of the tables toasted the autumn sunset, and the wine and the laughter flowed freely throughout the camp. As the sun settled below the horizon, logs were set out and a huge bonfire started, around which the toasting continued.

Things began running together in Crow's mind, the flash of the firelight off Karakchik's gold tooth, the singing of the squirrels in languages Crow was certain he did not know but which he sang in nonetheless, the hot spicy taste of the wine they were serving, the heavy scent of the smoke from the bonfire, everything spinning and whirling his head around and around until he felt sleep's warm darkness settle over him and wrap itself thick about him.

The smoke and the songs and the wine were still floating and humming through his head when there was a sudden
cold wet slap at his face, and he sputtered awake, freezing
water dripping through his feathers.

Crow shook his head and tried to raise a wing to wipe
the water from his eyes, but something held him back. He
strained to move his wing again, and this time he could feel
the cords tighten as he tried to lift it.

Cords? Was he tied down? Crow opened his eyes.

He was lying on his back, his wings spread out, tied
and staked to the ground. He could feel cords tight across
his chest and abdomen, and, struggle as he might against
them, he remained rooted to the spot.

With some difficulty, he raised his head and looked
down the length of his body. The bonfire was still burning
there, but he couldn't see anyone around it. He could hear
muffled whisperings, though, and as he let his head drop
back down, he turned to his right to see if anyone was there.

The night was thick all around, but by the light of the
fire, Crow could see a shadowy figure; as it began to move
toward him, Crow could see that it was Alphonse Karakchik, the calliope player. The squirrel now wore a black bandana over one ear, and a long black cloak billowed from his
shoulders, making him look even taller and more gaunt than
before. Karakchik stopped a few steps from Crow's head,
the cloak swirling to close around the squirrel's thin frame.

"Alphonse," Crow managed to cough out, "why am I
tied up? What's going on here?"

"Going on?" The squirrel's face was strange and stark
in the bonfire's light. "It is your Doom, Corvine."

Crow could only stare into the gypsy's deep and unblinking eyes. The whispering stopped, and the only sound
in the clearing was the crackle of the fire. "My . . . my
Doom?" Crow managed to get out.

"Just so," the squirrel replied. He threw back his head

and let out a high-pitched wail that was immediately taken up by voices in the darkness around Crow. Karakchik brought his eyes back down to Crow's. "For what you have done."

In the darkness, the voices began a low, deep chanting, and Crow suddenly knew what Karakchik meant. "No! No, wait! I already prayed to the Lady Raven! I dedicated the bones to her! She . . . she's given me her blessing, don't you see? She won't let it happen again!" The chanting continued, and Karakchik did not move, his eyes still burning deep into Crow's mind. "No! It's all right now! She understands! I already explained to her!"

Karakchik blinked once. "There are other powers, Corvine, powers who are not so understanding. We come to serve *their* judgment upon you."

"No! No! You don't—"

"Silence," roared Karakchik. He sprang forward, tearing open his cloak, and something thin and sharp flashed in his paws. Before Crow could react, the squirrel thrust down and across, and a long metal spike crashed through Crow's beak, piercing it from bottom to top. Crow tried to scream, but the spike held his beak tightly clamped; he strained at the ropes and slammed his head from side to side as the pain wracked through him, but all he got was weaker and weaker.

He lay still at last, his mind skipping and jittering, and panted through his nostrils as the roaring in his head sank to a hard rumbling. Only then could he turn to look at Karakchik. The squirrel still stood there, his face still hard in the fire's flickering shadows.

"Your Doom, Corvine," he said again, and the chanting rose in pitch and volume. Karakchik took a step closer and stood staring directly down into Crow's eyes. He drew his arms slowly out of the cloak, and two more thin spikes gleamed in his paws. The chanting came to a peak and stopped.

"Understand, Corvine," Karakchik said into the silence, the firelight glowing dully off his gold tooth, "we do not ask you to bring the dead back to life. You cannot do this, for the dead are the dead. But the lost you can find, and the found you can return, a life for a life. A life for a life."

Crow wanted to stop him, ask him what he meant, plead with him to listen, try to explain himself, but the spike held his beak closed. He could only stare at the squirrel and at the long flashing spikes in his paws.

Karakchik called out something in a language Crow didn't understand, and voices chorused back from beyond the bonfire. Karakchik took a step back, held the spikes high in the air, and cried out, "The Doom is the Doom of the Senseless! One spear serves to shackle the tongue; no more shall anyone, creature, folk, or otherwise, hear a word that falls from your beak!"

The voices chanted again, and Crow felt his beak throb. Karakchik continued.

"One spear serves to pierce the heart!" And Karakchik leaped into the air and slammed one of the spears straight into Crow's chest. Crow heard ribs snap, but he couldn't move, couldn't scream, couldn't feel or think of anything but the spike ripping through his body. Karakchik's voice rang in his ears: "No more shall anyone, creature, folk, or otherwise, feel the stroke of your wing nor the grip of your claw!"

Crow couldn't tell if his eyes were open or shut. Fire shot through him, raging and twisting his insides. Then Karakchik came into sight right above him once again. "And one spear serves to shatter the mind!" The squirrel raised the last spear in both paws and drove it down between Crow's eyes. Crow's vision burst into a jagged babble of sharp reds, burning golds, and engulfing blacks as he heard Karakchik's voice chanting, "No more shall anyone, creature, folk, or otherwise, see your face, your form, nor even your shadow! You are now a beast of dust and oblivion, the smallest whisper of the passing breeze! So it is, and so it will be!'' The blackness snarled up, slashing at him and crushing him till he had to scream, had to fly, had to escape.

And then he was leaping into the air, the screams bursting from him. He careened wildly, wings flailing, spinning over and over, around and around, shrieking and shrieking, until he slammed into the branches of a willow tree and fell tangled to the ground. He clawed his way free of the willow branches and leaped to his feet beneath the canopy of the tree, his breath coming fast and his mind still spinning and whirling.

After a while, his breath slowed, his mind wound down, and a cloudy sort of calm settled over him. He realized that he was standing and staring at the trunk of a willow tree. Then he realized that he was very tired. So he sat down and stared at the trunk of the willow tree. After another while, the fog in his head began to bother him a little; he thought maybe he'd better sort a few things out.

It was early morning and seemed to be overcast. Okay so far. He was sitting in the dirt under the branches of a willow tree. Yes, that seemed to be right. He had been in a gypsy camp in Valder's Clearing. *That,* he'd better check.

He looked out through the branches of the willow. A little stream was flowing past outside, and looking up along it, Crow could see the clearing, gray and quiet under the morning clouds. But there weren't any wagons or gypsies, no colorful flags or streamers, no calliope music, nothing.

Crow shivered and thought about this. Maybe his memory was playing tricks. He tried to remember what else had happened to him last night.

The memory hit him then, all sharp and burning and awful. He grabbed his beak and ran his wings up and down, over and under, feeling his beak and his chest and his forehead.

Again, nothing. No spikes, no holes, no blood. But there had been! Hadn't there? All that was left now was an ache throughout his entire body. But he also remembered drinking a great deal without eating anything. Could he have dreamed the whole thing?

But if he had dreamed the gypsy caravan, where had he gotten all the wine? And if he hadn't dreamed the gypsies, where were they now? His head felt all thick; everything was just too hazy, all the flashing of lights and the strange chanting and singing and the terrible pain of those spikes. . . .

Crow was rubbing his beak again when there was a tiny click at the base of the willow trunk, and a small door swung open. A bleary-eyed mouse carrying two wooden buckets stepped out and, yawning mightily, started walking down toward the stream. He didn't seem to notice Crow sitting just off to the left of his door.

"Excuse me, sir," Crow called out, "but were you perhaps at the gypsy camp last night?"

The mouse kept on walking, heading for the stream outside the willow canopy.

"Sir? Excuse me, sir?" Crow heaved himself to his feet and half hopped, half stumbled after the mouse. "Sir?"

The mouse kept on walking, the buckets hanging from his arms rattling with each step.

"Sir?" Crow caught up to the mouse with only a few hops. "Sir? Please, I have to know about the gypsies. . . ."

The mouse kept on walking, going right past Crow and only yawning again.

"Sir?!" Crow jumped forward and grabbed at the mouse. He had to stop him, spin him around, find out what had happened.

The mouse kept on walking, passing right through

Crow's clenched wing as he might through a thin fog.

Crow stared at the mouse's retreating back. No, he told himself. I'm just not quite awake yet. He hopped again, over the mouse's head, and planted himself right in the mouse's path. "Sir? Please stop. Please! I've got to—''

The mouse kept on walking, and Crow felt a cold chill as the mouse's head and shoulders met and passed right into Crow's chest. Crow bent down and watched the mouse's feet and the two buckets as they moved along the feathers between his legs. Crow straightened up and looked back just in time to see the mouse pop out from his tail feathers and continue on toward the willow branches.

Crow stood in that same position, just blinking and blinking, as the mouse went out through the branches, down to the stream, dipped his buckets in, turned around, and headed back. Crow stood and stared, and the mouse, his buckets sloshing over as he staggered slightly, walked right up to Crow's tail and walked right through. Crow swung his head around and watched as the mouse emerged from his chest feathers. Crow stood and watched as the mouse walked up to the door, went through, put one of the buckets down, reached out, and pulled the door closed with a tiny click.

Crow stood that way for a long time.

Finally, he started moving his head from side to side. "No," he whispered. "No. No. No." His Doom. It was all coming back to him. And it was all coming true.

"No!" he shouted, leaping into the air. "No!" He slammed out through the willow branches and beat against the air with his wings. "No!" He couldn't close his eyes, couldn't let them close, not with those sights in his mind; the fire and the spears and the Doom all boiled behind his eyelids, and a mouse that walked right through him as if he was less than a shadow. He had to fly, to pound and pound and pound his way into the sky, up and up to where things were understandable.

He heard magpies calling to each other in the trees below and shouted out to them. They didn't respond. A flock of geese flapped by overhead, but they didn't return his greeting. He careened madly through the sky, shouting and screaming, but no one looked up, no one called out, no one noticed him flying by. He perched on a branch next to a group of finches and yelled every insult he could think of, but not a one even ruffled a feather. He plummeted right through the small formation of Mr. and Mrs. Sparrow and their family, plunged down without a whisper or a shout from any one of them, and barely missed slamming into the treetops.

Crow shouted and shouted and shouted till his voice was in shreds, and he whipped back and forth over the forest till his wings felt like stone. He didn't know where he was or where he was going; it didn't matter anyway. Everywhere, it was the same, but Crow wheeled and screamed around and around as the sun strode on into late afternoon again.

And so Crow dropped through the trees as his wings gave out and fell panting and heaving to the forest floor. What else could he do? He was Doomed. Karakchik had said it, and it had happened. No one would ever see or hear him again.

With effort, he brought his wings around and clasped them together. His throat was raw, but straining his voice, he rasped, "Lady Raven! You've got to hear me! Even if no one else can, you still can! And all you Curial powers, please! Lord and Lady Leopard, Lord Kit Fox, Lady Squirrel, you've got to still hear me! Yes, I killed him! He was small and lost and hurt and scared and cold and crying and sick and alone and I killed him! And then . . . oh, gods! I can't say it; how can I say it? It's too late, all too late. Please believe me, if I could do anything now, I would, but there's nothing! Nothing!"

Crow couldn't hold himself up anymore, so he slumped forward and lay aching and quivering in the fallen leaves. "All I can do," he whispered after a minute, "is say I'm sorry, and that's less than nothing. Lady Raven, I . . . I . . . oh, gods. . . ."

His vision blurred, and he felt the feathers around his eyes become wet. He was lost now forever, and it was exactly what he deserved. A life for a life, Karakchik had said: Crow's life for the life he had destroyed.

So Crow lay in the leaves and waited for the cold touch of nightfall to whisk him away.

After a while, though, he thought he heard a soft, chirping cry from somewhere nearby. It struck something in his clouded mind, but he couldn't tell what. Then there was a cough and a choke and another cry. Crow lifted his head and looked around.

Something twitched among the leaves at the base of the next tree. As Crow watched, a tiny wing rose out of the leaves and then dropped back down.

A shiver ran through him, a violent one that snapped his beak shut. The leaves had stopped twitching, but Crow's eyes were locked on the place where he had seen the wing rise. He pushed himself to his feet and stumbled over to the tree.

She was lying there, half-covered by brown leaves, her eyes closed but her chest still moving with a quick, shallow flutter. She was a barn swallow, very young and a terrible, pallid gray color.

Crow could only stare for a few moments, his mind not quite turning over. It was only after her head gave a quick twitch and she let out another thin cough that Crow could make himself move again. He unslung his satchel and squatted down next to the little swallow.

"I'll do it . . . do it right this time," he whispered, reaching out his wings. "I will. It's into the satchel, and

then . . . then to Doctor Swift down in Ottersgate. . . .'' Crow
cradled his wings around her, gently cupped them together,
and lifted.

And the little swallow slipped through his wings as if
she wasn't even there.

"No!" Crow hissed. "I'm trying to help her this time!"
He tried again to lift her from the leaves, and again she
seemed to slip right through his wings. He stood up and tried
to wrap a claw around her, but it was like trying to grab
empty air. "No, no, no, no, no!" he croaked, hopping up
and down. "Lady Raven! This is my chance! I . . . I . . . .''

Crow could only stare as the little swallow shivered
among the brown leaves, her wings wracked with sharp little spasms. Crow tried to move her a few more times but
only ended up hopping up and down again.

"I won't!" he managed to croak out. "I won't kill you
again! I . . . I . . . I . . . don't know!" He hopped around some
more. "I'll have to go to Ottersgate and get Doctor Swift
somehow. Somehow." He looked back down at the swallow.
"Don't worry," he whispered. "I'll get help. I will." He
threw his satchel over his back and took off.

Once airborne, Crow got his bearings and realized he
was just north and west of Ottersgate. His wings were still
solid and heavy and aching from his tearing around all day,
so he had to try gliding. The winds were all wrong, though,
coming up from the south, and he sank closer and closer to
the treetops. After only five minutes, his feet were scraping
the highest branches, and his wings felt about ready to lock
up. He forced them to flap once, twice, a third time, thinking of the small gray body back in the leaves.

He strained into a fourth flap, his shoulders bursting
and his back knotting up, when a tangle of branches reared
up in his path. It caught around his claws, grabbed him up
and twisted him down, around, and hard into the tree's canopy. He crashed through, bounced off one branch, and fell

to rest in a fork, his wings pounding and burning.

Crow wriggled himself free of the branches' grip, his wings hanging like slabs from his back. It couldn't be too much further to Ottersgate; he could hear the River already. He would just have to get to the top of the tree and glide from treetop to treetop. His head spinning, he sighted on the branch above him and was about to try a jump when he heard a voice behind him say, "Whoa, Crow, whoa! Where're you going?"

There was a thump on the branch beside him, and something long and black and furry appeared out of the leaves. Crow blinked at her. "Fisher?" he whispered.

"That was a nasty fall." Fisher was looking up through the broken branches. "Maybe you better just sit a while...."

"Fisher!" Crow's voice was raspy and scarcely a whisper. "You can see me!"

Fisher blinked at him. "Yeah. Yeah, I can see you, Crow."

"And... and you can hear me!"

"Just barely. You don't look so good, Crow. The blackfire's going around, y'know; you gotta cold, you shouldn't—"

"But you can hear me! You can see me!"

"Uhhh, sure...."

"Well, of course you can!" Crow shook his head. "I'm not thinking! You know the ways of the Curial powers!"

"I what?"

"Yes, of course! I see it now!" Crow stepped closer to her on the branch. "Fisher," he hissed, "you've got to come with me; you're the only one who can help me!"

Fisher ran a paw over Crow's head. "I think you cracked yourself pretty good coming down just now. How 'bout we sit here and talk for a while, okay?"

"No, you don't understand! Back in the forest north of

here there's a poor sick little swallow child. I was trying to get to Ottersgate to get Doctor Swift, but my wings, I've just done so much flying today, I guess I lost control. But you, Fisher, you're a sorceress, right?'' He remembered she was; he *knew* she was.

Fisher was looking very worried. "Well, 'shaman' would be a better word, but—''

"But you'd know what to do! You can see me and hear me! You could help her! You've got to come with me!''

"Okay, Crow, okay; calm now, calm, okay? Just calm. . . .''

Crow tried to take some deep breaths, but he was too jittery. "We've got to hurry!'' he hissed.

"I just don't want you falling apart on me.'' She moved her paws along the sides of his neck. "Crumbs,'' Crow heard her say under her breath, then quickly out loud, "can you lead me to where she is?''

"I've got to,'' Crow hissed. "I've *got* to.''

"Uh-huh. You just fly there, okay? I'll follow down here in the trees. You sure you can fly, now?''

"I've got to.'' And Crow knew it was true. He understood now. It was a life for a life, not a death for a death. "Follow me.'' He saw Fisher nod, and then he leaped upward through the hole he had made coming down.

His wings felt better for the brief rest, and knowing that Fisher was below him in the trees reassured him no end. And heading north, he had the winds with him, so he could glide to the spot where he had left the little swallow. The branches rustled and snapped below him, and occasionally Crow would catch a glimpse of Fisher flashing between the trees, her dark fur catching the rays of the setting sun.

"To the left!'' Crow croaked out as loudly as he could manage. "Then follow me down!'' Let his head pound all it wanted, this was one spot he could never forget. He flapped down through the tree canopy and landed at the foot of the tree where he had left the swallow. It was darker now under the branches, but he could still see her chest fluttering wildly. He started hopping as Fisher scrambled down the trunk to his side.

Fisher bent down close and put one paw to the side of the bird's head. "Gods!" she whispered. "It's the blackfire all right."

"But," Crow hissed, "you know what to do? You can . . . can save her?"

Fisher clicked her tongue. "Maybe. First thing, though, we gotta keep her warm." She turned to Crow. "You gotta hold her, Crow, up in your wings and close to your chest while I go after some plants I need, okay? You can do that?"

Crow felt a cold chill. "I don't know. I'll try. . . ."

"It's easy. Here, hold your wings out, one on top of the other, crossed, yeah, like that. Now just hold still a minute. . . ." And Fisher slowly and gently lifted the swallow out of the leaves and started to place her in Crow's wings.

"Wait!" Crow hissed. "What if she falls through?"

"Just hold her close; trust me." Fisher let the little bird down into Crow's wings. And she didn't fall through. "Hold her close," Fisher said again, "up to your chest. That's right."

His eyes wide, Crow drew the little swallow close, and the bird coughed and snuggled into his feathers.

Fisher chuckled. "Well, that's a good sign."

Crow looked over at Fisher. "She . . . she didn't fall through. . . ." he whispered.

"No, she didn't. Now you just hold her like that." She reached around him and unfastened his satchel. "I saw some frialn over there as we came in. I'll be right back." The leaves crunched under her feet, and Fisher was gone.

Crow cradled the little swallow in his wings. "You

didn't fall through," he whispered, touching his beak gently to hers. "Fisher can see me, and it'll all be all right. Just hold on. Hold on." He felt the swallow shiver against him, and he hunched himself around her closer, his silent thank you's going up to every Lord and Lady of the Curia.

Soon there was a scuffling along the leaves, and Fisher came up beside him with the satchel full of some sort of plant. "This'll do for now," she said, pulling a leaf out and grinding it up in her paws, "but we gotta get her to Ottersgate. Doc Swift'll have frialn compound, and that's what she needs. Hold her up, Crow."

Crow unfolded himself from the swallow. Fisher worked her beak open, sprinkled some of the powdered leaf in, and started stroking the little bird's throat. The swallow shuddered, her wings twitching up and down, and Crow was afraid she might cough the powder out. But her neck rolled shakily under Fisher's soft stroking, and her tongue darted out of her beak a few times. Fisher blew out a breath. "Okay, she's got it down."

"She'll be all right, then?" Crow croaked out as he felt the little bird relax into his wings.

"If we can get her to Ottersgate." Fisher was pulling another leaf out of the satchel. She held it up to Crow. "Now you. Eat up, the whole thing."

Crow blinked at her. "Me? What for?"

"High fever, glassy eyes, swollen nodes, raw throat, stiffness, et cetera, et cetera. You got the blackfire, my friend, one of the worst adult cases I've seen in years."

Crow stared at her and didn't quite understand what she was saying. "The blackfire? Me?"

"Eat the leaf, Crow."

Crow opened his beak to protest, and Fisher stuffed the leaf in. "Chew it up, now," she said.

It was dry and bitter and dissolved against his tongue.

Crow swallowed the stuff down. "Me? The blackfire? But . . . but how? And—"

"Later, Crow, later. Right now, you gotta fly this little one down to Ottersgate and get the both of you to Doc Swift."

The paste of the frialn stuck to Crow's tongue and made his mouth sour. "Me? Fly her to Ottersgate?" He thought for a minute. "Yes, I suppose I must. That leaf, it was magic? To make me solid again?"

Fisher looked sideways at him. "Magic? Yeah, okay, magic. Look, I've lined your satchel with frialn leaves. We wrap her up in 'em, strap the satchel on you, and you fly her to Doc Swift. I'd take her, but bouncing through the trees is *not* what she needs right now and running'd just take too long. I know you're not feeling all that well, but you can get her there faster'n I can even if you take it easy. So take it easy, but get her there. You got it?"

Crow nodded. "I understand. It's the only way. I see that now. I can't bring the dead back, but the lost can be found, and the found, returned, a life for a life. That's what he said; I remember now. And then I'll be found again. It all makes sense." He looked over at Fisher. She was staring at him. "But you're a sorceress; you know this already."

There was a pause. "Uhh, right," Fisher said. "Now just come over here, Crow, and lay her real gentle in the satchel."

The frialn Crow had swallowed was numbing his various aches, and his wings already felt lighter. He walked over to where Fisher was standing by the satchel and, with her help, laid the little bird in among the leaves. Fisher then lifted the satchel and helped Crow strap it on, lodging it close in the feathers under his right wing.

"Take it easy," Fisher said again. "Fly straight for the

Bailey Oak. Doc Swift or Mallard or Tara Wren or some-body oughta be there; they'll know what to do, and I'll be right behind you, okay?''

Crow nodded again. "I will not fail this time."

"And make sure they—no, I'll take care of you when I get there. You just stay put till I show up, got it?''

"I will."

"Good. Let's go." Fisher sprang up the trunk, and Crow took off, climbing slowly through the darkening trees. He came out over the treetops and forced his mind to start thinking, very conscious of the small warm bundle pressing against his side.

The wind was still coming up from the south, so Crow decided on a long southeastern tack. He couldn't head straight to Ottersgate without flapping more than either he or his passenger could take. With a tack, though, he could glide southeast on the wind halfway, then glide back south-west. He'd get to the Bailey Oak with very little wing move-ment overall, and he wouldn't have to get too high above the treetops.

Yes, that sounded good. He was sure that's what he would do if his mind was working properly. So he set his wings to catch the wind and began gliding south and eastward.

He kept wracking his brain, trying to remember the landmarks he always navigated by. That was the River below him now, that dark stripe flashing with the orange of the set-ting sun. The trees whipped by beneath him, and Donal's Lake stood out ahead. He would want to keep that on his left. That's right; he remembered that.

Crow turned his eyes westward and squinted into the sun. Something would happen over there, something about trees. . . . Yes, the trees would stop at the northern edge of Ree's Meadow. He would want to cut west, keeping his southward momentum, and glide right over Ottersgate to the Bailey Oak.

That was it. And there, the trees were starting to thin out. A slight shift of his tail, the smallest flap of his wings, and he was wheeling to the west.

The satchel bumped against him, and Crow thought he could feel the swallow stirring inside. The cold of the wind was biting deep through his feathers, and his back was cramping up again. Crow hoped the little one was warm enough, but it wasn't much further. It couldn't be much further.

Crow scanned the landscape, and there, ahead and to his left, a tall old oak rose up, its branches spreading out above the forest canopy. The Bailey Oak. It had to be. He knew it was. Crow called out silently to the Lady Raven and concentrated on his wings, on not letting them cramp up, on just caressing the air and sliding through it.

Doctor Swift's office was on the eighth level of the Bailey Oak, Crow remembered, at about canopy level. Crow dipped his wings just the slightest bit, the wind digging into them, and dropped down, down, gradually down till he spotted the branch that was outside the doctors' office.

Crow glided in and grabbed the branch with tired claws. From a twig above the lighted hole in the trunk, a sign was hanging: Dr. Swift—Dr. Mallard, General Practitioners. Crow hopped down the branch, his wing tucked around the precious bundle in his satchel.

Through the hole was a waiting room, and just coming out of a door behind a small desk was Doctor Swift, yawning and straightening a plaid hat over his head. "See you in a few hours, Tara," the doctor was calling as he closed the door.

"Doctor!" Crow managed to croak out. "Wait!"

Doctor Swift's head jerked up, and he blinked at Crow a few times. "Crow," he said after a moment. "I'm sorry; I didn't hear you come in." His brow wrinkled as he looked at Crow. "I think you'd better sit down."

Crow shook his head. "Not me, Doctor; this little one here . . . ." Crow raised his wing and opened his satchel. "Fisher said it's the blackfire. You've got to help her, Doctor, you've got to. . . ."

Doctor Swift hopped forward, his eyes wide, and touched his wings to the swallow child's head. Crow heard his sharp intake of breath followed by his shout of "Tara! Tara, out here! Quick!"

The door behind the desk opened, and a tired-looking wren stuck her head out. "Doc? What . . . ." Her voice trailed off as she saw Crow. "What in the—"

"Hot water bottles, a glucose IV set up, and a quarter cc of pure frialn compound." Doctor Swift's voice was calm but cracked a little as he lifted the swallow child out of Crow's satchel. "Room three's empty, and get a rosewood inhaler in there."

The wren was gone in a flash, and Doctor Swift was carrying the little swallow toward the still open door.

"Will she be all right?" Crow hissed, unable to stop jumping from foot to foot.

"If we hurry." Doctor Swift turned and backed through the doorway. His eyes snapped up to meet Crow's. "You stay put, Crow. Stay right here."

Crow nodded, and the doctor was through the doorway and gone.

Crow sank to the floor. He couldn't move his wings, he noticed, so he just let them flop beside him. His head buzzed and his eyes hurt. It was going to be all right, though. He had gotten her here in time. He knew he had. It was all going to be all right now. . . .

There was a scuffling at the front door, and Fisher slid into the room. "Crow! Did you . . . ?"

He nodded. "She's inside. Doctor said to wait. . . ."

"Good." Fisher opened a larger door in the wall to Crow's left. She went through and came out a moment later with a large dark bundle. The bundle unfolded into a blanket, and Fisher wrapped it around Crow's back, tucking it over his wings and tail and closing it around his chest. "How're you feeling?" she asked as she smoothed the blanket around him.

Crow wasn't really sure. "Tired," he managed to whisper, "very tired, Fisher."

Fisher nodded. "You think you can walk, just upstairs? There'll be beds up there; you can take a good rest."

"Will she be up there?" Crow was having a hard time focusing on Fisher's face. "I can't leave her, Fisher."

"She'll be fine. C'mon, now; you're not gonna do her any good keeling over out here. I'll help you, if you want."

Crow tried to open his eyes, but found they already were. "Yes," he got out at last. "Thank you."

Crow felt Fisher slide under his right wing. "It's just upstairs," she said. "You'll be all right."

Crow leaned onto her and managed to move his feet. They seemed so far away, and his beak was so heavy he couldn't raise his head. After a long while, he heard Fisher's voice say from off somewhere, "Okay, just lie down now. . . ." Then it swirled away from him and was lost in the cold misty darkness.

But there were things in the darkness, huge silent things that sat very still and waited. And Crow knew why. "Please, she's got to live! I don't care what you do to me anymore, but she's got to live! Give me my Doom back if that's what it takes, but please, please, don't let me kill this one, too. . . ."

He begged and pleaded, pouring everything out of himself, promising and praying and hoping that they would listen. At long, long last, something somewhere seemed to click, and the shapes began to fade into the mist, the shifting shadows closing up around them. Crow fell back then, and, sprawling on the ground, he finally let himself sleep.

It was a deep and quiet sleep this time, and Crow came out of it slowly, drowsily, feeling numb and spent. Fisher lay curled on a padded lounge chair to his left, her dark fur matted and dull, a half-eaten roll nestled between her arms. She looked like she needed the sleep, so Crow rested against his pillows and watched the patterns the afternoon sun cast through the shutters onto the floor.

After a bit, Fisher stirred and sat up, catching the roll before it hit the floor. She set it on the chair and smiled at Crow. "You're looking better."

"What about the swallow child?" Crow's voice was so soft, he wasn't sure if he'd actually spoken. He cleared his throat. "How is she?"

"She went home yesterday." Fisher put a paw to his forehead. "Classic two-day recovery. *You* had us more worried than she did."

"Then she's all right?"

Fisher laughed quietly. "She's fine. Her parents invited you, me, and the doc over for dinner as soon as you feel up to it. They thought they'd lost her for sure."

Crow closed his eyes. "Thank the Lady Raven."

"Blackfire's like that," Fisher went on, leaning back against the end of the lounge chair. "It strikes so fast, the kids wander off before anyone knows they're sick, and it's even worse with these baby birds. They just fly away, and by the time anyone finds 'em, it's usually too late. Sometimes they don't even find the bodies." She closed her eyes and rubbed them. "But you get 'em frialn compound in time, and they're up again in two days, ready to go."

"How long have I been out?"

"Three days now. Your fever broke just this morning. You had it bad." She stopped and looked away from him. "Look, Crow," she said after a minute, "I—" She stopped again.

Crow blinked at her and was about to ask what was

wrong when she turned back to him and said, "Before your fever broke, you talked a lot. Some of it was just gibberish, but some of it, well, some of it answered a few questions I'd had, and . . . and, well, we gotta talk about it. Sooner, the better."

Crow blinked some more. "Well, I feel all right now. A bit shaky still, but if it's important—"

"It is."

"Ah. All right. And if it gets to be too much for me, I'll—"

"It *is* gonna be too much for you; I already know that. But it's gonna be too much three weeks from now too, maybe even more than it is now."

Fisher stopped again, and Crow could only stare at her. She looked away. "The thing is," she went on, "there's not a whole lotta ways an adult can get the blackfire, and a case as bad as yours, well, there's even fewer. I'd been wondering how you managed to catch it, and then, last night," her eyes met his, "last night, you told me. It's one of the severest forms of blackfire because it's transmitted by the . . . by the ingestion of diseased tissue—"

"Don't." Crow turned away. His head felt tingly, and he went cold all over. "Please don't."

"It's true, then."

Crow couldn't look at her. "It's all over now. I did my penance, and they lifted the Doom. It's over, and it won't happen again. Ever again."

"How d'you know?"

Crow glanced over at her. "What?"

"The urge, Crow. It isn't the sorta thing that just hits once and then goes away, y'know. You've never given in before, but I'll bet this isn't the first time you've wanted a little meat in your diet."

"Stop it, Fisher, stop it! It's sick, warped, immoral! You shouldn't even say it!"

"Why? Just 'cause it's true?"

"It isn't true! It isn't true at all!"

"It isn't?"

Crow was shaking all over. He pulled the blanket up around his neck. What business was it of hers anyway? "I'm sick. You shouldn't say those kinds of things to sick folk."

"You gotta face up to it, Crow, or it'll just get worse. Trust me; I don't go after trout every day 'cause I especially like the flavor, y'know."

Crow stared at her. "What? You mean . . . you too?"

Fisher spread her paws. "I think it's in most of us larger folk. You just gotta learn to deal with it. I mean, there's plentya creatures out there that aren't folk: fish and insects and the like. If it can't talk to you, it's fair game, I always say."

The blanket was too hot around him. Crow lowered it a little and rested his eyes on its rough weave. "I . . . I don't know what to say. I always thought, well, that . . . that it was just me. . . ."

"Naw. You just can't turn your back on it is all. If you hide it, bottle it up and ignore it, it'll come bursting out when you're least ready to deal with it."

"But . . . but what do I do? I can't just give in to it. I mean, we're folk; this is all so, I don't know, so bestial."

Fisher shrugged. "Sure you resist it; you have to. Otherwise you end up drooling on your neighbors. But if you just ignore it, it's gonna blow up on you, and you're gonna do something that'll either drive you crazy or get you locked up or maybe even killed. That's not the way to deal with it."

"So how *do* you deal with it?"

"You use your head. There's always fish and all the insects we got around here, like I said. And you can always go out to the deep woods and hunt up some pygmy shrews.

You just wanna do it away from Ottersgate or you're liable to snatch up some mouse family's pet.''

Crow had to smile a little. "You've done that?''

Fisher waved a paw at him. "Don't get me started. But I mean it, Crow." Her voice got quiet. "I've seen folk go crazy 'cause they can't deal with it. They go Wilding, and you just gotta hunt 'em down. . . .'' Her eyes were dark and far away. Then she blinked a few times, shook her head and gave a half grin. "so anytime it gets to be too much for you, you come see me. Don't just hope it'll go away, 'cause it won't. I'll show you some good spots along the River, okay? Anytime.''

Crow rubbed at the ache behind his eyes. "I don't know, Fisher," he said after a minute. "I just don't know. So much has happened in the last few days. . . .'' He looked over at her. "I'll think about it. That's all I can promise you.''

"I can't ask for more than that.'' Fisher got to her feet. "You feel like some soup?''

So Crow ate and slept and woke up the next morning ready to try his wings again. Doctor Swift and Fisher both looked him over and pronounced him fit to go home.

"Just take it easy for a couple of days,'' Doctor Swift told him, "at least till you get my bill.''

"I will,'' Crow said, "and thank you for everything.''

The doctor tucked his stethoscope into his white vest. "See you at the Swallows' tonight then.'' And he hopped out the door.

Fisher handed Crow his satchel. "Remember what I said, Crow. Anytime.''

"I'll remember.'' Crow slowly buckled his satchel on. "I'd like to talk all this over with you, all that's happened to me and everything, if you wouldn't mind.''

"Anytime,'' she said again. She pulled open the shuttered balcony door. Faint snatches of music drifted in on the breeze. "Calliopes," Fisher said, stepping out onto the balcony. "Guess the Autumn Festival's starting up."

Crow joined her and peered out over the rail. Across the roofs of Ottersgate, over the River on the grassy hills of Ree's Meadow, stood tents and wagons, all adorned with flags and streamers and the wafting music of the calliope. "I think I'll go have a look," he said to Fisher. "Shall I be at your place before sundown? I don't know where the Swallows live."

"Sure, why not? See you then." Fisher poked his shoulder and went back into the room.

Crow stepped off the balcony and let the morning breeze carry him over Ree's Meadow. The flags fluttered in every color and pattern, he noticed, except for gray and burgundy checks. He drifted over the field three times without spotting that combination, so he flapped over and settled to the ground next to the seven tired old calliopes, all gathered in a circle to the west of the Festival's midway.

There was one young squirrel seated at one of the calliopes, her skirt a bright red and yellow plaid. She was just finishing a slow, waltzing tune as Crow winged down.

Crow waited until she turned around before he asked, "Excuse me, but could you perhaps help me? I'm looking for a calliope player called Karakchik, Alphonse Karakchik."

The squirrel only looked at Crow. He repeated the name. The squirrel looked at him some more. Then she said, "He was saying a corvine might come looking for him. You are that?"

Crow nodded. The squirrel jumped down from the calliope and pulled a satchel out from underneath. She began undoing the buckles. "He said to give you this if you came looking." She lifted the flap and brought out something wrapped in black velvet. It seemed heavy, this something, and it flashed in the morning sun as she folded the velvet back. She held the something up, and Crow could see it was a silver calliope, intricately formed and embellished with ivory, brass, and gray and burgundy stones.

Crow reached out and took the calliope. "It's . . . oh, it's . . . ." He couldn't find the words. It shone and sparkled like the full moon off the rapids of the River and laughed and danced as only the music of the calliope can.

Crow looked down at the squirrel. "Will you . . . will you be seeing him any time soon?"

The squirrel shrugged. "Maybe so, maybe not."

"Could you tell him, the next time you see him—" Tell him what? Thank you? Crow thought he understood what Karakchik had done, but he wasn't sure he was ready to thank the squirrel for it yet. But there was so much he wanted to say to him, to ask him. "Tell him . . . tell him I hope we will meet again someday under more pleasant circumstances. Would you please tell him that?"

"If I see him, I'll tell him."

"Thank you." Crow tucked the calliope gently into his satchel and leaped into the air. The sky was clear and the winds soft. Crow set his wings and glided north, heading home at last.

Why We're Glad to Be Here

by
Algis Budrys

About the Author

Algis Budrys is the editor of this series of anthologies, as well as Co-ordinating Judge of L. Ron Hubbard's Writers of The Future Contest. Budrys sold his first story in 1952, to the legendary Astounding Science Fiction, *and in a matter of a few years was considered one of the best post-War writers.*

At the same time, he pursued an editorial career, in and out of science fiction; he was, for example, the editor of Playboy Press in the 1960s.

Concurrently, he began a separate career as a critic and essayist on science fiction and fantasy, being now the book review editor of The Magazine of Fantasy & Science Fiction. *He also has taught science fiction and fantasy writing extensively, at one time teaching for eleven years straight at Clarion East, and at Pepperdine University, Brigham Young University, and Harvard, as well as others. Most recently, he has again been doing fiction writing, with a novel—among other things—well in progress. But he continues to devote the majority of his time to Writers of The Future, considering his association with it among the best things that have ever happened to him.*

$\mathbf{W}$e are here because L. Ron Hubbard (1911–1986) founded the Writers of The Future Contest and directed the founding of the Illustrators of The Future Contest. Now in its eighth year, this program has succeeded beyond anyone's dreams— but his—and has brought you winners and finalists from all the English-speaking nations of the world. And some of the non-English-speaking ones, too, such as Denmark, Hungary, Sweden, and the USSR. We think that's something to be very proud of.

We are supported in this endeavor by a veritable galaxy of the top names among professional writers and artists, who continue to donate their time and energy:

Judges in the Writers of The Future Contest at present are Gregory Benford, Ben Bova, Algis Budrys, Ramsey Campbell, Anne McCaffrey, Andre Norton, Larry Niven, Frederik Pohl, Jerry Pournelle, Robert Silverberg, John Varley, Jack Williamson, Dave Wolverton, and Roger Zelazny.

Judges in the Illustrators of The Future Contest at present are Edd Cartier, Leo and Diane Dillon, Bob Eggleton, Will Eisner, Frank Frazetta, Shun Kijima, Jack Kirby, Paul Lehr, Ron and Val Lakey Lindahn, Moebius, Alex Schomburg, H. R. Van Dongen, and William R. Warren, Jr.

Frank Kelly-Freas serves as Co-ordinating Judge of the Contest. Obviously, both groups represent the cream of the crop.

Every three months, panels drawn from among these

distinguished persons select three winners in the Writers' Contest, and three winners in the Illustrators' Contest. At the end of the year, a Grand Prize winner is chosen in each of the Contests. The Quarterly prizes range from $1,000 to $500, with trophies and certificates as well. The Grand Prize, in each Contest, is an additional trophy, and $4,000.

Dave Wolverton won the WOTF Grand Prize in 1987; he has done so well since, with multiple novel contracts and otherwise, that we were pleased and proud to make him a Writers of The Future judge early last year—the first "home grown" judge, as it were; but probably not the last.

About this book:

Each year for the past seven, Bridge Publications, Inc., which is L. Ron Hubbard's main publisher for fiction and nonfiction, has chosen to bring out the winning stories and illustrations, works of selected finalist writers, and expert essayists on various aspects of writing and illustrating. This is an arrangement different from the Contests, though obviously it could not take place if the Contests did not exist. Operationally, it means the writers and illustrators get even more money; Bridge pays very well for the sharply limited right to publish. The result is the book you now hold in your hand, as well as the six preceding annual volumes.

This is, as *Locus* magazine, the trade publication of the SF industry, says, "The best-selling SF anthology series of all time." But while this is very nice, from one point of view, the fact is that each reader of the books makes up his or her own mind. So we hope you like these stories, and the illustrations, not because other stories and illustrations did well in previous volumes, but simply because this present crop are *good* stories and illustrations.

Little more remains to be said. The winners of the L. Ron Hubbard Contests are, for the Writers' Contest,

Öjvind Bernander
Michael C. Berch
William Esrac
Valerie J. Freireich
James C. Glass
Mark Andrew Garland

Michelle Levigne
Barry Reynolds
Michael H. Payne
Allen J. M. Smith
Merritt Severson
Terri Trimble

and the finalists are

David Hast
Don Satterlee, Jr.

Ross Westergaard

For the Illustrators' Contest, the winners are

Ron Alexander
Christopher C. Beau
Thomas Denmark
Charles Dougherty
Harold J. Fox
Peter H. Francis

Michael Grossman
Sergey V. Poyarkov
Jim Reece
Ron Sanford
Ferenc Temil Temesvari
Lawrence Allen Williams

We thank them, we honor them, we wish them the best possible future.

— Algis Budrys

A Note from Frank Kelly-Freas
Co-ordinating Judge
L. Ron Hubbard's
Illustrators of The Future

About the Author

Frank Kelly-Freas is the "Dean of Science Fiction Illustrators." Active in the SF field since 1950, his diverse work includes: covers for Astounding *and for* Mad Magazine, *space poster and Skylab insignia for NASA, beautiful women on the noses of bombers during his service in the Army Air Corps, and covers for books from all the major SF publishers.*

Kelly has won ten Hugo Awards for Best SF Artist of The Year, and has been nominated for ten more. He has also won, among others, the Lensman, the Inkpot, and Frank R. Paul Awards.

He directed the illustration of this and several previous volumes in the L. Ron Hubbard Presents Writers of The Future *series, and is Co-ordinating Judge of the Illustrators of The Future Contest.*

It's gratifying, in the extreme, to find the Contest growing to international stature after only two years of existence. This year we have winners from Canada, Hungary and the Soviet Union, in addition to the American winners. And entries for the upcoming new year have already been turned in from as far east as Japan and west as Turkey.

What this means is that *illustration,* whose roots go back at least to the dawn of cave drawings, is still a flourishing and internationally applied art form. And as the world goes more and more computer, it will nevertheless require the initiative and talents of the skilled illustrator to make it work, make an image impinge, make the viewer cry or laugh or say in awed tones "Hey, look at this!"

"The artist injects the spirit of life into a culture," is a quote by L. Ron Hubbard that frequently comes to mind. For what else are we possibly doing than breathing life to ideas, ideas which form culture?

We are very proud to be in a position to encourage illustration's newest discoveries in speculative fiction. To all who won this year's contest, our warmest congratulations. It was a great pleasure working with you on this latest anthology.

To those of you thinking about entering the Contest—there is no better time than now! Good luck!

— Frank Kelly-Freas

CONTEST RULES

1. No entry fee is required, and all rights in the story remain the property of the author. All types of science fiction and fantasy are welcome; every entry is judged on its own merits only.

2. All entries must be original works of science fiction or fantasy in English. Plagiarism will result in disqualification. Submitted works may not have been previously published in professional media.

3. Eligible entries must be works of prose, either short stories (under 10,000 words) or novelets (under 17,000 words) in length. We regret we cannot consider poetry, or works intended for children.

4. The Contest is open only to those who have not had professionally published a novel or short novel, or more than three short stories, or more than one novelet.

5. Entries must be typewritten and double spaced with numbered pages (computer-printer output O.K.). Each entry must have a cover page with the title of the work, the author's name, address, and telephone number, and an approximate word-count. The manuscript itself should be titled and numbered on every page, but the author's name should be deleted to facilitate fair judging.

6. Manuscripts will be returned after judging. Entries must include a self-addressed return envelope. U.S. return envelopes must be stamped; others may enclose international postal reply coupons.

7. There shall be three cash prizes in each quarter: 1st Prize of $1,000, 2nd Prize of $750, and 3rd Prize of $500, in U.S. dollars or the recipient's locally equivalent amount. In addition, there shall be a further cash prize of $4,000 to the Grand Prize winner, who will be selected from among the 1st Prize winners for the period of October 1, 1990 through September 30, 1991. All winners will also receive trophies or certificates.

8. The Contest will continue through September 30, 1991, on the following quarterly basis:

> October 1 - December 31, 1990
> January 1 - March 31, 1991
> April 1 - June 30, 1991
> July 1 - September 30, 1991

Information regarding subsequent contests may be obtained by sending a self-addressed, stamped, business-size envelope to the above address.

To be eligible for the quarterly judging, an entry must be postmarked no later than Midnight on the last day of the Quarter.

9. Each entrant may submit only one manuscript per Quarter. Winners in a quarterly judging are ineligible to make further entries in the Contest.

10. All entrants, including winners, retain all rights to their stories.

11. Entries will be judged by a panel of professional authors. Each quarterly judging and the Grand Prize judging may have a different panel. The decisions of the judges are entirely their own, and are final.

12. Entrants in each Quarter will be individually notified of the results by mail, together with the names of those sitting on the panel of judges.

This contest is void where prohibited by law.

1. The Contest is open to Entrants from all nations. (However, Entrants should provide themselves with some means for written communication in English.) All themes of science fiction and fantasy illustration are welcome: every entry is judged on its own merits only. No entry fee is required, and all rights in the entries remain the property of their artists.

2. By submitting work to the Contest, the Entrant agrees to abide by all Contest rules.

3. This Contest is open to those who have not previously published more than three black-and-white story illustrations, or more than one process-color painting, in media distributed nationally to the general public, such as magazines or books sold at newsstands, or books sold in stores merchandising to the general public. The submitted entry shall not have been previously published in professional media as exampled above.

If you are not sure of your eligibility, write to the Contest address with details, enclosing a business-size, self-addressed envelope with return postage. The Contest Administration will reply with a determination.

Winners in previous quarters are not eligible to make further entries.

4. Only one entry per quarter is permitted. The entry must be original to the Entrant. Plagiarism, infringement of the rights of others, or other violations of the Contest rules will result in disqualification.

5. An entry shall consist of three illustrations done by the Entrant in a black-and-white medium. Each must represent a theme different from the other two.

6. ENTRIES SHOULD NOT BE THE ORIGINAL DRAWINGS, but should be large black-and-white photocopies of a quality satisfactory to the Entrant. Entries must be submitted unfolded and flat, in an envelope no larger than 9 inches by 12 inches.

All entries must be accompanied by a self-addressed return envelope of the appropriate size, with correct U.S. postage affixed. (Non-U.S. Entrants should enclose International Postal Reply coupons.)

If the Entrant does not want the photocopies returned, the entry should be clearly marked DISPOSABLE COPIES: DO NOT RETURN. A business-size, self-addressed envelope with correct postage should be included so that judging results can be returned to the Entrant.

7. To facilitate anonymous judging, each of the three photocopies must be accompanied by a removable cover sheet bearing the artist's name, address, and telephone number, and an identifying title for that work. The photocopy of the work should carry the same identifying title, and the artist's signature should be deleted from the photocopy.

The Contest Administration will remove and file the cover sheets, and forward only the anonymous entry to the judges.

8. To be eligible for a quarterly judging, an entry must be postmarked no later than the last day of the quarter.

Late entries will be included in the following quarter, and the Contest Administration will so notify the Entrant.

9. There will be three co-winners in each quarter. Each winner will receive an outright cash grant of U.S. $500.00, and a certificate of merit. Such winners also receive eligibility to compete for the annual Grand

Prize of an additional outright cash grant of $4,000.00 together with the annual Grand Prize trophy.

10. Competition for the Grand Prize is designed to acquaint the Entrant with customary practices in the field of professional illustrating. It will be conducted in the following manner:

Each winner in each quarter will be furnished a Specification Sheet giving details on the size and kind of black-and-white illustration work required by Grand Prize competition. Requirements will be of the sort customarily stated by professional publishing companies.

These specifications will be furnished to the Entrant by the Contest Administration, using Return Receipt Requested mail or its equivalent.

Also furnished will be a copy of a science fiction or fantasy story, to be illustrated by the Entrant. This story will have been selected for that purpose by the Co-ordinating Judge of the Contest. Thereafter, the Entrant will work toward completing the assigned illustration.

In order to retain eligibility for the Grand Prize, each Entrant shall, within thirty (30) days of receipt of the said story assignment, send to the Contest address the Entrant's black-and-white page illustration of the assigned story in accordance with the Specification Sheet.

The Entrant's finished illustration shall be in the form of camera-ready art prepared in accordance with the Specification Sheet and securely packed, shipped at the Entrant's own risk. The Contest will exercise due care in handling all submissions as received.

The said illustration will then be judged in competition for the Grand Prize on the following basis only:

Each Grand Prize judge's personal opinion on the extent to which it makes the judge want to read the story it illustrates.

The Entrant shall retain copyright in the said illustration.

11. The Contest year will continue through September 30, 1991, with the following quarterly periods (See Rule 8):

    October 1 - December 31, 1990
    January 1 - March 31, 1991
    April 1 - June 30, 1991
    July 1- September 30, 1991

Entrants in each quarter will be individually notified of the quarter's judging results by mail. Winning entrants' participation in the Contest shall continue until the results of the Grand Prize judging have been announced.

Information regarding subsequent contests may be obtained by sending a self-addressed business-size envelope, with postage, to the Contest address.

12. The Grand Prize winner will be announced at the L. Ron Hubbard Awards event to be held in the calendar year 1992.

13. Entries will be judged by professional artists only. Each quarterly judging and the Grand Prize judging may have a different panel of judges. The decisions of the judges are entirely their own, and are final.

14. This contest is void where prohibited by law.